Margaret Snyder writes:

> Can economic growth and human well-being be maximised without the women who run more than half of the informal sector businesses? Without those women who provide half or more of family incomes?

Long-time development professional Margaret Snyder makes a compelling argument that farm and business women are an economic and social force that a nation cannot afford to overlook. By boosting women's entrepreneurship with positive policies and actions, policy makers and international investors can counter poverty while giving the world an economic justice and growth model—a new, non-western model for grassroots, democratic development. *Women in African Economies* shows the way.

... invaluable for development planners and field workers who have so far operated in doubt about the extent to which women in small-scale businesses contribute to economic development and family well-being.

... indispensable for teachers in need of case materials and for women entrepreneurs looking for role models. The cases demonstrate how women have turned meagre resources into viable enterprises and income-generating businesses, ... against the odds.

Hilda Mary Tadria, Regional Adviser
on Economic Empowerment of Women, UNECA

About the Author

Margaret Snyder lived and worked in Kenya, Tanzania, Ethiopia and Uganda for a total of 15 years. In 1995–96 she was a Fulbright scholar at the Department of Women Studies of Makerere University in Uganda. In 1992–93 she was a visiting fellow at the Woodrow Wilson School at Princeton University. She is the founding director of the United Nations Development Fund for Women (UNIFEM). She was also a co-founder of the African Centre for Women at the UN Economic Commission for Africa (ECA) and was a member of the committee to organise Women's World Banking (WWB). Snyder co-authored with Mary Tadesse *African Women and Development: A History*, and wrote the history of UNIFEM, *Transforming Development: Women, Poverty and Politics,* both published in 1995.

Women in African Economies

From Burning Sun to Boardroom

Margaret Snyder

Fountain Publishers

Fountain Publishers Ltd
P.O. Box 488
Kampala, Uganda
(256) (41) 259-163 (tel), 251-160 (fax),
fountain@starcom.co.ug (e-mail)

First published by Fountain Publishers 2000

Distribution in Europe, North America and Australia by African Books Collective (ABC), The Jam Factory, 27 Park End St., Oxford OX1 1HU, United Kingdom +44(0) 1865-72686 (tel), 1865-793298 (fax)

ISBN 9970 - 02 - 187 - 7

Text typeset in Monotype Garamond 10.5/12.6
Display typeset in Hewlett-Packard CG Omega
Printed in Kenya

05 04 03 02 01 00 5 4 3 2 1

Cataloguing in publication data

Snyder, Margaret.
Women in African economies: from burning sun to boardroom / Margaret Snyder.—Kampala: Fountain Publishers, 2000.
360 p. 15 x 22 x 1.8 cm.

Includes bibliographical references and index.
ISBN 9970 02 187 7

1. Informal sector (Economics)—Uganda 2. Business women—Uganda
1. Title.

338.61

Dedication

To Uganda's women farmers, merchants and entrepreneurs, who create wealth and well-being for their families and their nation.

Contents

2 The Urban Informal Economy: Marketplace, Roadside, Home and Backyard Farm 37

3 Capitalising Micro Enterprise: Informal Savings Groups 83

4 Women Farmers and Traders 123

Acknowledgements

The first persons to whom I am deeply indebted are the 74 women farmers, merchants and entrepreneurs and the leaders of groups concerned with micro and small enterprise who shared their knowledge and experience with readers of this book. My special thanks go to Dean Joy Kwesiga, then head of the Department of Women Studies at Makerere University, for allowing me time for research in addition to teaching, during my enriching two academic years as a Fulbright scholar. Joy, MP Winnie Byanyima, and Ida Wanendeya provided the history of Ugandan women's entrepreneurship. My colleagues and M.A. candidate students at women studies were very supportive—a special thanks to Grace Bantebya and Mary Mugyenyi and those whose research appears here.

Professor Marion Doro, Fulbright scholar at Makerere, put a roof over my head during my return to Uganda and gave me a needed push to refine the first draft. Libby Bassett edited and produced the manuscript and while so doing designed a layout, photos and cover.

My student and research assistant Ruth Nsibirano assisted with the majority of the interviews (several of them in El Niño's drenching rain), met some of the respondents on her own and took on the laborious task of translating tapes into English. Nite Baza Tanzam interviewed Owino market women, and several of the progressive farmers and rural women at Kisa, and translated those tapes. Joy Kwesiga interviewed progressive farmers and translated also, and later critiqued the manuscript. Rose Kiggundu introduced me to the women of MWODET and provided basic information on credit. Peace Musiimenta found and interviewed the first woman bus driver on the evening before my final departure from Kampala. Frances Luwanga and Wiebe van Rij assured my access to documentation on the small- and micro-enterprise sector and Nardos Bekele-Thomas to UNDP documents. The Africa 2000 project provided a small grant for interviews with the progressive farmers.

Marilyn Carr kindly critiqued a technical chapter. Elaine Eliah of the East African newspaper took several of the photographs: Sarah Namusisi on the cover; Christina Nasuna and Margaret Ssajjabi of Chapter 2; Winnie Byanyima of Chapter 3; Olive Kitui and Victoria Muwanga of Chapter 5; Fang Min of Chapter 6. The interviewers photographed the farmers. The author took all other photos.

Fountain Publishers were very supportive. Thanks to Justus Mugaju, Pat Haward and most especially to Sarah Jones for her careful and creative final editing.

Thanks to everyone.

Illustrations

Market Traders (Chapter 2)

Informal Savings Groups (Chapter 3)

Progressive Women Farmers and Traders (Chapter 4)

Independent Entrepreneurs (Chapter 5)

Small to Large Enterprise (Chapter 6)

Also Pictured

Tables

East Africa

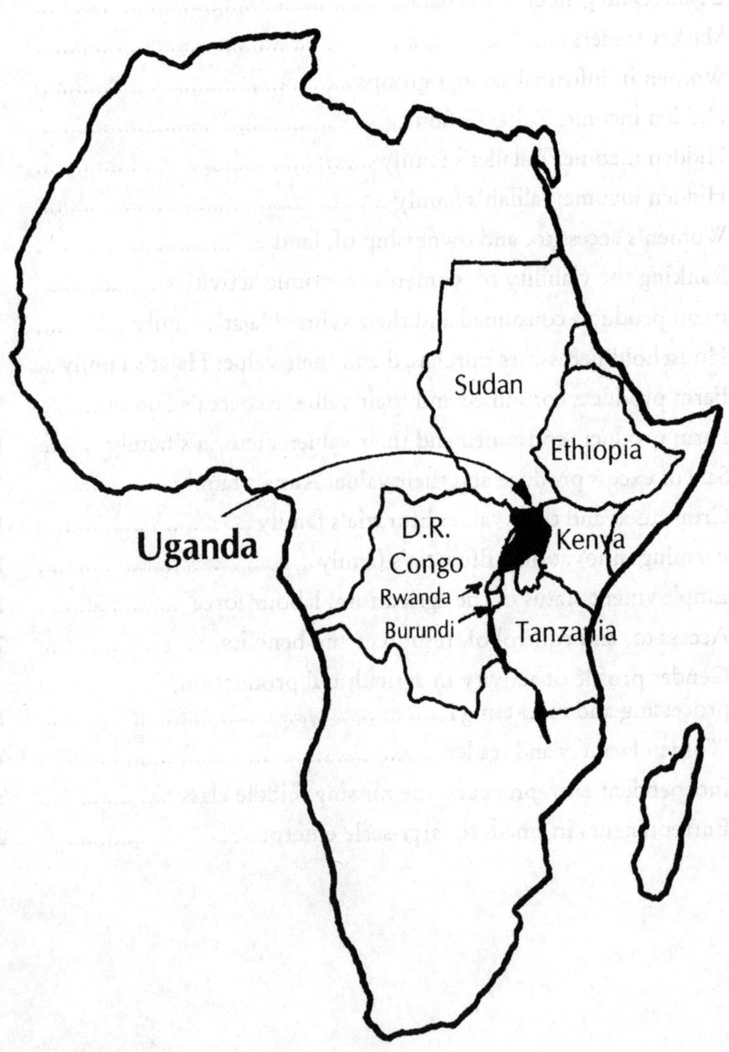
Sudan
Ethiopia
Uganda
D.R.
Congo
Kenya
Rwanda
Burundi
Tanzania

Uganda

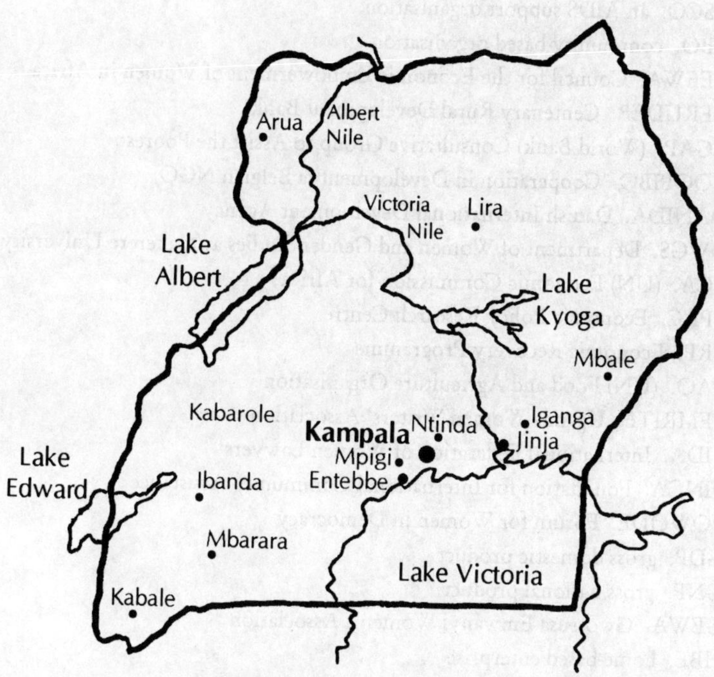
Arua
Albert Nile
Victoria Nile
Lira
Lake Albert
Lake Kyoga
Mbale
Kabarole
Kampala
Ntinda
Iganga
Jinja
Mpigi
Entebbe
Lake Edward
Ibanda
Mbarara
Lake Victoria
Kabale

Acronyms

ACFODE. Action for Development
AFWE. African Federation of Women Entrepreneurs
AIDS. acquired immune deficiency syndrome
ASCO. an AIDS support organisation
CBO. community-based organisation
CEEWA. Council for the Economic Empowerment of Women in Africa
CERUDEB. Centenary Rural Development Bank
CGAP. (World Bank) Consultative Group to Assist the Poorest
COOPIBO. Cooperation in Development (a Belgian NGO)
DANIDA. Danish International Development Agency
DWGS. Department of Women and Gender Studies at Makerere University
ECA. (UN) Economic Commission for Africa
EPRC. Economic Policy Research Centre
ERP. Economic Recovery Programme
FAO. (UN) Food and Agriculture Organisation
FEMRITE. Uganda Women Writers' Association
FIDA. International Federation of Women Lawyers
FINCA. Foundation for International Community Assistance
FOWODE. Forum for Women in Democracy
GDP. gross domestic product
GNP. gross national product
GEWA. Gwossusa Emwanyi Women's Association
HBE. home-based enterprise
HDI. human development index
HIPC. Highly Indebted Poor Country Initiative
IDRC. (Canadian) International Development Research Centre
IDS. Institute for Development Studies
IFWE. International Federation of Women Entrepreneurs
ILO. International Labour Organisation
IMF. International Monetary Fund
IMSENCC. National Co-ordination Committee for the Informal, Micro and Small Enterprise Sector
INSTRAW. (UN) International Research and Training Institute for the Advancement of Women
ISDA. Informal Sector Development in Africa

ISS. Institute for Social Studies
JASPA. (ILO) Jobs and Skills Programme for Africa
KCC. Kampala City Council
KDG. Kigulu Development Group
KMWF. Kasubi Market Women's Forum
KUS. Kampala Urban Study
LINT. Lwigule Idha Niwe Twegaite (farmers' group)
MFI. micro-finance institution
MISR. Makerere Institute of Social Research
MSE. micro and small enterprise
MWODET. Mpigi Women's Development Trust
NAWOU. National Association of Women's Organisations in Uganda
NGO. non-governmental organisation
NRA. National Resistance Army
NRC. National Resistance Council
NRM. National Resistance Movement
NTAE. non-traditional agriculture export
OAU. Organisation of African Unity
PAP. Poverty Alleviation Programme
PRESTO. (USAID) Private Enterprise Support, Training and Organisational Development Project
PSDP. Private Sector Development Programme
PSF. Private Sector Foundation
ROSCA. rotating savings and credit association
SAP. structural adjustment programme
SIDA. Swedish International Development Authority
SME. small and medium enterprise
SNV. Netherlands Development Organisation
SWRARP. Southwest Region Agriculture Rehabilitation Project
UAUW. Uganda Association of University Women
UCB. Uganda Commercial Bank
UEB. Uganda Electricity Board
UGIL. Uganda Garment Industries Ltd
UMA. Uganda Manufacturers Association
UNDP. United Nations Development Programme
UNECA. see ECA
UNFA. Uganda National Farmer's Association

UNICEF. United Nations Children's Fund
UNIFEM. United Nations Development Fund for Women
UNRISD. United Nations Research Institute for Social Development
UNSO. United Nations Statistical Office
UPE. universal primary education
URA. Uganda Revenue Authority
USAID. United States Agency for International Development
UWEAL. Uganda Women Entrepreneurs Association Ltd
UWFT. Uganda Women's Finance Trust
UWONET. Uganda Women's Network
VAT. value added tax
WETSU. Women Engineers, Technicians and Scientists in Uganda
WID. Women in Development
WIEGO. Women in Informal Employment: Globalising and Organising
WIRES. Women's Information Resource and Electronic Services
WWB. Women's World Banking
YWCA. Young Women's Christian Association

Preface

Women in African Economies comes at a very timely moment, with its profiles of women farmers, traders, merchants and other entrepreneurs who make significant but little recognised contributions to Uganda's economy. The reader not only hears their voices but also is given an up-to-date and systematic situation analysis of the environment they operate in. Uganda is its focus, but the relevance of this volume is wider because women's entrepreneurship, the obstacles women face and the potential they offer to create both wealth and well-being are a worldwide phenomenon.

After the chaos of the 1970s and early 1980s, the 1990s in general have been positive years in Uganda's history: The economy has grown and efforts are underway to institutionalise good governance. Women have become visible in the political arena, thanks to the affirmative-action programme of the ruling National Resistance Movement (NRM). Special seats for women in parliament, the requirement that one third of local councillors be women and other provisions in the 1995 constitution ensure, for the first time, that women's rights are recognised. These provisions have aroused women's interest in demanding increased participation and provided the impetus for them to join mainstream politics. This is a relatively well publicised process, both within and outside Uganda; affirmative action is debated from time to time, and women's organisations have documented the progress in reports and booklets.[1]

Surprisingly, the contribution and level of involvement of women in the nation's economy has not received similar attention. This volume therefore constitutes a breakthrough.

Drawing on her long-standing knowledge of the African continent, Margaret Snyder has collected and analysed a wide variety of women's experiences across the whole economic spectrum. All areas of the informal urban and peri-urban sector are explored, from marketplaces to roadside and home-based businesses, from relatively small enterprises to those of entrepreneurs who 'think big'. New areas for women, such as high-tech enterprise, taxi operation and real estate, reveal a shift from women's traditional domains of tailoring, bakery and catering. Women, individually and together, in rural and urban areas, have taken advantage of the Ugandan government's privatisation policy and opportunities to access credit; the role models featured in this book are only a sample.

One of the myths this volume casts doubt upon is the claim that women-specific projects do not easily change women's lives. In fact, this study definitively demonstrates that women smallholder farmers can successfully pursue both family well-being and sustainable agriculture. In dispelling the view that Ugandan women are not entrepreneurs in their own right, the author not only illustrates the extent to which they fund their families' well-being but also confirms that all of them aim 'beyond cabbage and tomatoes'.

These research findings fill the gap that has existed for nearly two decades, since Christine Obbo's 1980 pioneering work on the economic activities of low-income slum women in Uganda. As a development professional—at the African Centre for Women of the UN Economic Commission for Africa (ECA) in Addis Ababa, and as founding director of the United Nations Development Fund for Women (UNIFEM)—Dr Snyder has the advantage of analysing her Ugandan findings against a broader regional and international context. She has critically and effectively applied concepts about women and poverty, access to resources, and methodologies that are recommended and practised for the empowerment of women. This has led her to conclude that in Uganda, 'The opportunity exists to create a unique model of economic growth that tackles poverty at the grassroots level at a time when socialist models have failed and capitalist models are found wanting'.

If proof were needed, it was given when Tereza Mbire, one of the businesswomen interviewed in this book, was recognised by the Star Group (an international consulting firm) as one of 50 distinguished and leading women entrepreneurs of the world at a 26 April 1999 awards ceremony in Monaco.[2]

This study challenges entrepreneurs to influence economic decision-making bodies where they are not represented, and it challenges Ugandan-based researchers and activists to hasten the pace of publishing in this and other important sectors—especially the public sector, where women decision-makers could reinforce women's economic work.

Despite the hard life seen in each case study, women entrepreneurs are at a turning point in Uganda, and documenting their experiences is a source of encouragement. Not only is it rich in content, this account is presented in a captivating manner that urges one to read on and discover more.

Joy C. Kwesiga
Dean, Faculty of Social Sciences, Makerere University

[1] Among those documenting and publicising the political process are the National Association of Women's Organisations in Uganda (NAWOU), Uganda Women's Network (UWONET), Forum for Women in Democracy (FOWODE) and Action for Development (ACFODE). See also the chapters on political inclusion in Sylvia Tamale's (1999) *When Hens Begin to Crow,* on the role of women in parliamentary politics, and Aili Mari Tripp's (forthcoming) *Women and Politics in Uganda,* an analysis of the widening political field.

[2] 'Mbire wins global acclaim', *The New Vision,* 8 April 1999: 23.

Introduction

> **Micro and small entrepreneurs constitute the largest, most dynamic and most resilient element of the private sector.... Supporting them is central in combating poverty, creating employment and achieving broad-based economic growth.**
>
> Private Sector Development Programme 1997

This study cuts across the many sectors of Uganda's economy, reaching from the woman who sells her surplus beans and maize in the village market to the woman who creates an international air freight business. It is unique not only for its scope but also because the entrepreneurs themselves discuss the purpose of economic growth, priorities for investing their income and obstacles they face in business. Daisy Kayizzi, for example, has sat in the same small open space, in jua kali[1] ('burning sun') and drenching rain at Kasubi market selling matoke (cooking bananas) and Irish potatoes for fifteen years. 'I decided to stay here because at least you can get a shilling for your child to eat and go to school,' she explains. That she has done. Her eldest is married and the other four children are still in school. The views of these women farmers and entrepreneurs resolve the contentious issue of alleged competition between economic growth and human development as the primary goal of development. For them, growth is a means and peoples' well-being is the goal.

Entrepreneurs create wealth where there was none, and women entrepreneurs create it for themselves, their families and country, as this study demonstrates. Whether in cash or in kind, the product of their labour is used to eliminate poverty and foster the future labour force by investing in the health, education and shelter of the members of their households and communities and then in expanding their businesses. While doing that, they contribute measurably to the national income—the gross domestic product (GDP).

Women's rising entrepreneurial spirit makes it essential to a country's self-interest and development to recognise, measure, give a monetary value to, celebrate and support their economic productivity. Policies and actions to promote women farmers, merchants and entrepreneurs can multiply their capacities to counter poverty while strengthening civil society and advancing new forms of democracy from the grassroots. The opportunity exists to create a unique model of economic growth that tackles poverty at the grassroots level at a time when socialist models have failed and capitalist models are found wanting. Uganda is its focus, but the relevance of this study is wider, because women's entrepreneurship, the obstacles women face and the potential they offer to create both wealth and well-being are worldwide phenomena.

Roots of the entrepreneurial spirit

For decades, the colonial power favoured men in promoting cash crops, education and wage employment. After independence in 1962, one crisis followed another: President Milton Obote's socialism failed, the tyrannical Idi Amin's economic war drove Asian artisans and businessmen as well as Africans into exile, and subsequent regimes failed to bring peace or restore stability. All those events exhausted the society, and the economy—especially large enterprises—collapsed until peace arrived in 1986 and the rebuilding began.

Faced with hungry children whose fathers had fled or been killed, women moved into the cash economy as entrepreneurs. Short on capital, seldom owning land, but as committed to productive labour as their grandmothers had been, they brought income to their families in cash and in kind. In that process they faced even more responsibilities when conditions imposed by government agreements with international lending institutions reduced wage employment, health and education services, and directed scarce financial resources to large-scale business despite the country's dependence on agriculture and small enterprise—both dominated by women's labour—for some 90 per cent of its GDP.

Poverty still weighs heavily on 46 per cent of Uganda's people, whose annual per capita income was US$557 in 1995, even though the economy has grown at a world-class rate (averaging 6.5 per cent a year) in the past decade (UNDP 1998). That is why the Minister of Finance, Planning and Economic Development said, 'Reducing poverty must remain the overall and highest objective for public expenditure and action' (Ssendaula 1998).

A strong relationship is known to exist between poverty and the position of women. Women's poverty levels are worse than men's—a situation exacerbated in the colonial period when their unpaid labour began to enhance men's cash incomes. Today, there are growing gender disparities in education, employment opportunities and access to productive resources (UNDP 1997). The persistence of that situation challenges continuing economic growth when seen in the light of international research showing that, everything else being equal, countries in which the ratio of female-to-male enrolment in primary or secondary education is less than 0.75 can expect levels of gross national product (GNP) that are roughly 25 per cent lower than countries in which there is less gender disparity in education.[2] In Uganda the ratio for secondary school is 0.59 (World Bank 1997: 226).

A new agenda

Ugandan women are respected worldwide for their impressive political gains since 1986, when peace returned to their war-torn country. The 1995 constitution affirms: 'Women shall be accorded full and equal dignity of person with men' and they 'shall have the right to affirmative action for the purpose of redressing the imbalances created by history, tradition or custom.' Women are represented at every political level—from local government where one of every three councillors is a woman, to the national parliament where they are 18.8 per cent of all members. The vice president of Uganda is a woman.

Now that those instruments of political inclusion are in place, many Ugandan women see the economy as their second major challenge because, despite women's entrepreneurial achievements, it is more difficult to find evidence of gender equity in the economic realm than in the political.

Earning a living today

It is not easy to earn a living in today's Uganda. Opportunities for salaried employment in a growing population are few, and the lucky ones who get jobs often find they cannot stretch their income to meet family needs. Whether secondary school or university graduate, primary school dropout or illiterate peasant, the Ugandan knows few options for supporting a family or simply surviving other than self-employment as a farmer, merchant or entrepreneur. That is why President Yoweri Museveni advised university graduates to 'forget government jobs; go fish'.[3] The vast world of agriculture is the source of livelihood for 80 per cent of Uganda's labour force, and many families depend on the produce of rural or urban agriculture for the day's meals—produce that comes mostly from women's work although its money value is not attributed to women. Informal micro- and small-scale enterprises dominate the private sector of the national economy where the remaining 20 per cent of the adult working-age population are found.[4]

Finding cash income is more challenging for women than men because women, who comprise 'perhaps the majority' in the micro- and small-enterprise (MSE) sector (Republic of Uganda 1999) and provide some 70 per cent of the agricultural labour, have fewer assets and less access to productive resources than men. Because custom often works against them, they have less education, are less likely to own land to put to productive use or use as collateral for credit, have less information on markets, and bear heavy, time-consuming responsibilities for home, offspring and extended family. Although change has been coming in the last decade, those factors still limit women's capacities to maximise profits in any business they may undertake. Yet they are increasingly a major if not the sole source of support of large households—often providing half or more of the family income even when a spouse is present. They are the sole heads of 29 per cent of all households in the country (Ministry of Gender and Community Development and the Statistics Department, Ministry of Planning and Economic Development 1998).[5]

How do women add to their own or their husbands' meagre salaries, or find incomes to supplement the food they produce by their unpaid labour on the farm or in the backyard? Some start selling small items for a bit more than they paid and build a business that way. Others have initial capital in cash from a previous job, or an inheritance or loan from a relative. Still others stash away bits of cash saved from their household budget money until they have enough to make and sell matoke or mandazi (hole-less donuts), or take sodas or beer on consignment and pay for them after they are sold. They are micro entrepreneurs in the informal economy who work at home, at the roadside, in markets or other premises. The few women who have assets such as land to use as collateral—only 7 per cent of women in Uganda owned land before the as-yet untested Land Act of 1998—are entrepreneurs with their own premises who can borrow from banks or other private sources in order to move into new areas of business and agriculture and employ more people.

The concept and importance of the informal economy in Africa

Many of the entrepreneurs in this study work in what is variously called the informal sector of the economy, the peoples' economy, the second economy, the parallel economy or, as in Kenya, jua kali ('the burning sun'), so named because its 'offices', 'shops' and 'workshops' are in the open air. It usually embraces micro and small enterprises and is considered separately from the agriculture sector.[6] Most Africans find their livelihoods not in wage employment but in 'that smorgasbord of economic activities varying in size, products produced, levels of capital investment and gender', as sociologist Kinuthia Macharia describes it (1997: 38).

Such employment expanded rapidly with the economic downturn stimulated by oil price rises in the 1970s, the economic crisis of the 1980s and the introduction of structural adjustment programmes (SAPs), also in the 1980s, with such severe retrenchment of government employment that unemployment rose to between 30 and 70 per cent in Kenya as in other countries (Macharia 1997: 100). Attention turned to self-employment as governments were downsized, parastatal organisations privatised and thousands of employees declared redundant across Africa. Population growth, stagnant or declining employment in agriculture, and structural inadequacies, such as poor infrastructure and shrinking educational opportunities, also caused thousands of people to seek survival strategies in the informal sector (UN 1996: 11).

By 1991 informal employment accounted for 25 per cent of the total African labour force and 65 per cent of the urban labour force (UN 1996: 14). Statistician Jacques Charmes estimates that the informal sector contributes more than 40 per cent of Africa's GDP and more than 60 per cent of the non-agriculture GDP (1997: 177). The total number employed in the informal sector today (agriculture excluded) has more than doubled in a decade, to 40 million people who in turn support some 200 million of Africa's children, old and disabled persons. They include not only those whose total earned income comes from the informal sector but also those who have salaried employment and engage in business or trade on the side. Data gathered in Dar es Salaam found that women, children and elderly household members earned a remarkable 90 per cent of household income in 1988 while a tiny 10 per cent came from formal wages (Tripp 1997). Informal-sector work also contributes to reproduction of the modern sector—not an insignificant feature at a time when jobs and real wages are declining in Africa's formal economy (Charmes 1997: 173).

Today, for all those reasons, the informal sector stands out vividly as the 'most important labour sponge in Africa's labour markets' of the 1990s. The International Labour Organisation (ILO) Jobs and Skills Programme in Africa (JASPA) claims that in addition to contributing more than 40 per cent of GDP, this sector will provide 6 or 7 of every 10 new jobs on the continent (1993).

Women in Africa's informal economy

Who are those who contribute that 40 per cent of Africa's GDP? The United Nations says that it is women who constitute 'the principal labour force in the informal sector' and that their presence is widespread in Africa (1996: 11). Food and beverages, textiles, retail trade, pottery and cross-border trade are areas of female dominance, where trade constitutes half of all production in the informal economy.[7]

One must ask why women are clustered in the trade and services sectors of African economies. Macharia (1997) cites the paucity of capital available to them as the reason for their inability to enter fields demanding high start-up capital, a finding widely shared in research.[8] Tailoring, which requires a substantial initial outlay, is the exception, and he found women in this area were generally married or, if single, had previously worked in a public or private firm and consequently had the necessary start-up capital (Ibid. 1997: 150). In other words, he believes they obtained capital either from their husbands—something our findings in Uganda do not support—or from their own savings, as in this study. Anthropologist Gracia Clark found that in Kumasi, Ghana, only half the women traders received their start-up capital from kin, with only 10 per cent from spouses (1994: 182).

Because women are usually located in the trade and services subsectors, which are less lucrative than such areas as manufacturing, their lack of capital produces other inequities: less access to important information and longer work hours, despite their home responsibilities (Macharia 1997: 149). *Informal Sector Development in Africa* identifies lack of access to credit as the leading constraint for the small-scale entrepreneur, adding that it is 'particularly acute for women' (UN 1996).

Quantitative measurement of the contributions of female micro entrepreneurs to the GDP has been slow in coming. Existing data are not well known because they are not disseminated, statisticians say, even though they could be compiled and produce valid estimates (Charmes 1997). *The World's Women 1995* explains: 'The economic activity of women is often substantially understated because stereotypes held by census and survey interviewers and respondents lead to errors in the reporting and recording of economic activity.' Additionally, 'in many countries, women account for the major portion of persons engaged in those economic activities that are the most difficult to measure' (UN 1995). Further, the prevailing survey and statistical practice of using the household as the primary unit of analysis, thereby representing household income in a lump sum rather than disaggregating its various sources by gender, supports the myth that the male is invariably the provider.

Despite growing evidence of women's preponderance in the larger subsectors of the informal economy, 'the common trend in African countries has been the tendency to attach much lower value to informal activities dominated by women and much higher value to those dominated by men' (Macharia 1997: 85). A respondent for this study unwittingly accepts that devaluation of women's economic activity: 'My mother doesn't work; she just farms and makes crafts,' she says.

When the actual value of most rural women's labour on cash and food crops is added to their income from selling surplus food, their contributions to the rural family income at least match and often surpass those of men. There is evidence that the value of urban women's labour is equal to that of their rural sisters, but it too tends to go unrecognised. Whether from urban farming or the sale of home-baked goods, the value of women's productive labour remains as invisible as the value of their childcare and homemaking.

And because the likely source of women's non-farm cash income is the informal economy rather than salaried employment, it has been as invisible as the work of men in that sector. Thus women's work is doubly invisible: as 'women's work' and as productive employment in the informal economy.

But by no means are all women entrepreneurs at this very basic level of trade and commerce. There are growing numbers of women in micro-, small- and large-scale businesses who achieve on their own, with little access to formal-sector resources, and exceptional ones who achieve in the formal economy, making use of capital available from banks and other financial institutions. Their voices are heard in this study. One can only imagine the positive impact on national productivity if more women had greater access to the factors of production (land, labour and capital).

Defining micro and small enterprise in Uganda

In Uganda, 'micro-' and 'small-scale enterprise' are commonly used terms—the former fairly synonymous with 'informal sector'. The *Policy Paper on Micro and Small Enterprise Development* distinguishes between micro and small enterprises: '[M]icro enterprises are often related to self-employment and income generation while small enterprises are basically profit and growth oriented.'[9]

Micro enterprises, in quantitative terms, are defined as 'business undertakings employing less than 5 people, often family members; value of assets excluding land, buildings and working capital is below Ush 2.5 million; annual turnover is below Ush 10 million (about US$10,000 at the time of our interviews), which is the threshold for business-related tax'. Qualitatively, characteristics of micro enterprises are that 'they operate seasonally, usually they are not registered formally and hence have no access to formal services. They do not pay enterprise-related taxes and their management is rather weak in terms of both education and administrative capabilities' (Republic of Uganda 1999).

Small enterprises are defined as 'enterprises employing a maximum of 50 people; value of assets excluding land, buildings and working capital is less than Ush 50 million; annual turnover is between Ush 10 to 50 million, which is the tax bracket for one per cent business tax on annual turnover'. Qualitatively, 'they operate the whole year round, are formally registered and taxed, and owners/managers are educated and/or trained' (Ibid. 1999).

In its policy document, the government notes that those distinctions between micro and small enterprise (MSE) are not fixed and that entrepreneurs move from one level to another—some moving to medium and large scale. With less than a handful of exceptions, the businesswomen in this study are micro and small entrepreneurs. Although the distinction between the two categories is difficult to establish in a number of cases, an effort is made to classify respondents by MSE sector.

'The private sector in Uganda is dominated by the MSE sector which, though vibrant, is still very fragile and underdeveloped,' according to the Private Sector Development Programme (PSDP), which states that the sector provides an impressive 90 per cent of non-farm private-sector employment. The *Strategy for a Dynamic Microfinancing Programme in Uganda* finds that 'informal micro and small entrepreneurs constitute the largest, most dynamic and most resilient element of the private sector', and concludes that supporting them is 'central in combating poverty, creating employment and achieving broad-based economic growth' (PSDP 1997).

Despite acknowledging the importance of the informal sector's employment capacity and contribution to the GDP, and despite the sector's close linkage to the formal sector by providing goods and services, it was 1999 before the government formulated its policy on micro and small enterprise. Calling the eradication of poverty a matter of urgency, the minister of finance, in his June 1998 budget speech, had urged putting 'the right legal and policy frameworks in place regarding access to land and credit, support to micro- and small-scale enterprises, vocational training, environmental protection and disaster relief' (Ssendaula 1998).

While quantitative data on the sector in Uganda are scarce, the *Policy Paper on Micro and Small Enterprise Development* estimates that there are 800,000 non-farm micro and small enterprises in Uganda employing 1.5 million people—most of them poor by UN standards—and having an annual labour-force growth of more than 20 per cent (Republic of Uganda 1999). Impact Associates estimates that 80 per cent of them are located in rural areas, 10 per cent in large towns, and 8 per cent in the Kampala/Entebbe corridor (1995). Known facts and educated estimates about the sector include the following:

- About one third of all Ugandan households engage in some form of business, employing three persons on average;
- just over half of the enterprises have a net worth of US$53 or less. Commerce or trade account for 63 per cent, manufacturing 29 per cent and services 8 per cent; and
- six of every 10 enterprises produce at least half of household income and 27 per cent produce all of it, regardless of ownership (Ibid. 1995).

Entrepreneurs surveyed in the Impact Associates study reported that they selected their particular enterprise because of the limited start-up capital available to them—a common situation in Africa. However, they also felt they had the appropriate background and experience for their type of work and that it had market potential. Both men and women owners wanted credit and technical support, while admitting that 89 per cent of the credit they had accessed was from informal sources rather than banks or cooperatives.[10]

The significance of women in Uganda's economy: agriculture, micro and small enterprise

Women comprise 'perhaps the majority' of entrepreneurs in the MSE sector (Republic of Uganda 1999). The 1995 study by Impact Associates found Ugandan women doing most of the trading in food markets and heavily represented in tailoring, textiles, beverages, services and crafts. Women owners are more likely than men to be working at home or by the roadside; their enterprises survive longer than those of men. Women's tenure of premises is likely to be less secure than that of men, and women are more often found in semi-permanent, temporary and roof-only structures. Men are more likely than women to use banks, in all probability because they have access to far more capital than women, who are seriously constrained by limited access. Men belong to formal business support groups, while women are more prone to informal ones.

The *Uganda Country Gender Profile* (Keller 1996) describes the situation of the majority of women in the urban informal sector as follows:

> They are to be seen on the sidewalks selling cigarettes, groundnuts and newspapers, along the roadsides reselling milk..., and in the night markets, for example. The extent of night markets, and the ubiquity of food preparation and selling in open spaces behind office buildings and hawking of used clothes and other wares in offices are all indications of the importance of informal-sector incomes to urban dwellers. For women, these incomes do not come easily...; they work long hours, up to ten or eleven o'clock in the evening. They have their small children with them, in dangerous or unhygienic surroundings, or leave them at home in the care of a young relative or daughter, probably of school age but not in school.

But it is not just the poorest women who seek livelihoods as farmers, merchants and entrepreneurs. Ugandan women have many of the trading instincts that have long been attributed to their West African sisters. For example, a significant number of female entrepreneurs travel to Asia, Europe and the Middle East to purchase goods to sell from their houses, in public markets or in their own shops in both the informal and formal sectors. Several small- to large-scale business owners working in the formal economy are included in this study. The history of their entry into the business world parallels in some ways but is distinct from that of Ugandan men.

In summary, women farmers, merchants and entrepreneurs are critical to Uganda's economic growth because:

- Agriculture, the main source of GDP, is a female-intensive sector of production. Uganda's women farmers produce 80 per cent of food crops, 60 per cent of traditional farm exports such as coffee, tea, cotton, sugar and tobacco, and an impressive 80 per cent of non-traditional agriculture exports (NTAEs): maize, beans, cereal, vanilla and horticultural products (Elson and Evers 1997). That the labour of women continues to be unattributed or undervalued in economic terms and that control of production decisions, of income generated and access to factors of production is male-intensive results in failure to account for significant sources of current national wealth and its potential future increase.

- Women comprise 'perhaps the majority' of all entrepreneurs in the informal micro- and small-enterprise economy—the fastest-growing job-creation sector of Africa, accounting for up to 40 per cent of GDP (Charmes 1997). Although the sector is expected to provide 60 to 70 per cent of new employment and is also a growth point for the formal sector, its inclusion in government planning has lagged.

- Women reproduce the labour force both as mothers and increasingly as providers of a significant portion of the total family income: food, shelter, health and education. Their income is estimated as 50 per cent of total income in 2-spouse households and 100 per cent in the 29 per cent of households where women are the sole providers. In the countryside, that income consists of produce plus cash; in the urban setting the latter dominates.

- Priorities in allocating income show clear gender differences. There is hard evidence that in addition to their in-kind contributions of food and services, women's earnings are invested first of all in child and family requirements, including schooling and health care, then in expanding their businesses. Men tend first to retain a share of income for personal use (Dwyer and Bruce 1988; Snyder 1995). Thus the quality of the future labour force rests mainly with women.

- Women entrepreneurs offer great potential for the simultaneous increase of people's well-being and growth of the country's wealth, as long as their nation secures the peace and adopts appropriate policies society-wide. Wealth and well-being also depend on economic justice in a nation's relations with the global market. Issues include whether indigenous business and industries can grow under trade liberalisation policies and whether NTAEs deprive families of basic foods. The experiences of individual entrepreneurs are essential inputs to the formation of global market policies.

- The persistent poverty that stalks the growth of GDP in Uganda underlies the urgent need to broaden the economic base so that it embraces the 46 per cent of people who are poor, the bulk of whom reside in rural areas. Women's preferential investment in nutrition and schooling of the young, and their capacities to manage businesses when access to resources is equitable—as demonstrated in this study, confirm that poverty cannot and will not be eliminated without them.

Insufficient information

When truth is hidden, myths and partial truths abound, in Uganda as in every other country. One hears that 'women just supplement the family income men provide', that 'women's businesses are too small to matter to the national economy', that 'husbands give start-up money for their wives' businesses', that 'women who have money leave their husbands' and that 'no husband wants his wife to work'. Dispelling myths is difficult when, as earlier noted, despite all their economic activity, the substantial cash and in-kind contributions of women to household and national economies are unrecognised, as is their potential to augment that income and expand employment opportunities through increased access to capital, technology and training.

There are few data and only isolated case studies of women entrepreneurs to fill that knowledge gap. Among the serious consequences of that absence is that planners have insufficient information about the extent of women's capacity to create wealth, and women's investment in human capital, as contributions to the national and household economy (Stiglitz 1995). The policy and planning process is then distorted by a lack of sufficient evidence at a time when policy makers are beginning to be aware that the informal sector is the fastest growing source of incomes, and programmes to support it are being implemented.

This scarcity of information on Ugandan entrepreneurship generally and businesswomen in particular came to my attention when I taught in the Department of Women Studies at Makerere University during 1995–96. Government workers across the country were being retrenched, parastatal organisations privatised and the few formal-sector jobs women held were evaporating. All eyes turned to the private sector as primary, secondary and university students faced bleak prospects for salaried employment after graduation. Aside from the occasional brief newspaper article and often self-serving reports by donor agencies, little has been written about the experiences and views of self-employed Ugandans.

As a consequence, few role models of informal-sector employment exist to provide for youths examples of alternative employment, even though role models are often our best teachers: Their lives, words and actions bear witness to the influences of family, peers, the economic environment and national policy on their work. For these reasons, the voices of women entrepreneurs of many different types, classes and ethnic groups are heard here, sharing their experiences and insights as to what is needed to start a business, maintain it, make it profitable, expand it—and avoid pitfalls. They bring valuable first-hand, grassroots knowledge of the effects of the global economy, government policies and spousal relations on earnings in the micro- and small-enterprise areas of the private sector.

Finally, the cost of their invisibility is high among businesswomen themselves, many of whom must 'learn the Ugandan way—without capital'. They learn by risk and sometimes by loss. In the process they lose not just opportunities but also hard-earned assets. Learning mistake by mistake is clearly costly both to the individual entrepreneur and his or her family. But there is a less-recognised, even more significant consequence: National capital growth from investment in this huge section of the economy is forfeited.

In short, the absence of information about self-employed women has a high cost. The creation of individual and national wealth is slowed, as can be seen in the levels of poverty that persist in Uganda despite its impressive growth in GDP. In addition, the opportunity is missed to create a non-western model of economic growth and broad-based development that could be adopted by other countries.

Research methodologies

The selection of the 84 respondents interviewed between June 1996 and February 1998 was by the snowball method: one person leading to others. Entrepreneurs identified by donor groups—national or international—were avoided because such groups tend to focus on the better endowed and more successful recipients of supply-side assistance. The exceptions were participants in Africa 2000, because its approach through senior women farmers seemed especially challenging as a potential model for increasing farm production.

We chose a qualitative over a quantitative survey in order to provide a human dimension that statistics lack. To enable respondents to express themselves in their preferred languages, two senior Ugandan researchers conducted several of the interviews, and research assistants conducted or helped with many of the others. All interviews with entrepreneurs were taped to ensure accuracy of quotations. The author also interviewed representatives of relevant government and private organisations, who are listed, together with respondents, in Appendix 1.

Because it was not possible to visit every geographical area of the country, in order to broaden the base of the study several other studies have been woven into the text, many of them completed by staff and graduate students of the Department of Women Studies at Makerere University. Full use has also been made of other extant private sector reports, all of which may be found in the Bibliography.

In Chapter 1, all quotations are attributed by surname for the sake of consistency, because the chapter also includes a review of comparative literature, which ordinarily is referenced by surname. In all other chapters, given names are used. Note that while quotations from external sources are referenced, quotations from respondents to this study are not cited. Rather, interviewees are listed according to chapter and section in Appendix 1.

Throughout, some words, expressions and acronyms are used that may not be known to the reader; the words and expressions are defined in Appendix 2 and acronyms listed in the front pages.

The exchange rate of Uganda shillings (Ush) for US dollars at the time of the interviews—mid-1996 to early 1998—hovered around Ush 1,000 to US$1, and that rate is used in the text. In the few instances that a respondent has made reference to the old Amin money, it is futile to give a rate in dollar terms due to exchange-rate instability at the time.

Organisation of the study

Chapter 1 tells the story of the rise of entrepreneurial women in Uganda, which is also part of the story of a people's survival and recovery from civil war. The environment of peace that followed the war encouraged private-sector development and affirmative action; it emboldened women to organise themselves in civil society and ensure that their gender concerns were enshrined in the new constitution. Despite these achievements, women see a gigantic job ahead in overcoming the poverty that still afflicts nearly half of Uganda's people.

Adhering as closely as possible to the Ugandan definitions of micro- and small-scale enterprise, this study identifies five categories of entrepreneurs (Chapters 2 to 6), as follows:

- micro business in market trade, urban agriculture, home-based enterprise (HBE) and night markets (17 interviews);

- mutual support groups in the countryside and in small cities (11 interviews);
- farm-based enterprise (13 interviews);
- small enterprise in independent premises outside the marketplace (15 interviews); and
- small and medium enterprise (13 interviews), large enterprise (2 interviews) and managers (3 interviews).

A table in each chapter provides a socio-economic profile of each of the respondents.

Micro entrepreneurs who average 14 years in business in the urban informal economy—the marketplace, roadside, home, or backyard farm—are introduced in Chapter 2. Their levels of education, sources and size of start-up capital, availability of capital for expansion, motivation to enter business, and investment of income are discussed, as are the obstacles they face in business. Despite their differences, their choices for investing their earnings are markedly similar: They choose inter-generational change through education of their children, Uganda's future workforce.

Chapter 3 focuses on women's micro enterprises and their own finance institutions: the rotating savings and credit groups (ROSCAs) that are spreading like wildfire across the country. 'We are poor, but we can learn how to save money,' a farmer–leader says. And they do, at times in cooperation with MFIs such as the Uganda Women's Finance Trust (UWFT). They are seldom able to access capital from formal financial institutions such as banks, and the loans they get from MFIs are often insufficient to support business growth, even though their micro enterprises have the potential to form a broad economic base for expanding the country's economy and overcoming poverty.

Because it is beyond doubt that if progress lags in agriculture, Uganda will not develop, the voices of women farmers are heard in Chapter 4. The total monetary value of their work is explored by putting a value on the foods they grow for home consumption as well as those they sell. These producers of the nation's agricultural wealth, on whom the country depends for its food and the majority of its agriculture exports, tell how they respond to incentives that reach them directly (not through husbands). Their families enjoy a different lifestyle. As one farmer says, 'I estimate my farm and shop income as ten times what my husband and I earn as policeman and teacher.' Yet the vast majority of women farmers 'are effectively locked out of capital accumulation' at this time.

The independent businesswomen of Chapter 5 are small-scale entrepreneurs who have several common characteristics that define their class status. They fled wartime Uganda with their families or were sent out of the country to school and so were exposed to other cultures; they returned with an entrepreneurial spirit. One or both of their parents were community leaders; most of them had salaried employment as secretaries; most own land; they have husbands who contribute to family maintenance. They are the few businesswomen in the 'missing middle' group. Some have chosen non-traditional fields such as computer training, bus driving and book publishing. Most work in foods, flowers, textiles and wholesaling.

Small- to large-scale enterprise is the subject of Chapter 6, which pursues questions of capital accumulation and diversified investment. The significance of the size of start-up capital to the future prosperity of the business is discussed, as are the sources of working and expansion capital. Involvement of many family members as directors and workers becomes evident first within this group among those studied. These entrepreneurs are more highly educated than the small-scale entrepreneurs in Chapter 5; they are more likely to be single, widowed, separated or otherwise responsible for the whole household income. But the pattern of investment of their income is consistent with those found in earlier chapters of this book—the difference being that this group accumulates sufficient capital to reinvest or diversify their businesses.

Chapter 7 is quite brief. It presents theoretical and practical issues arising from this study in the light of businesswomen's potential as agents of national development and poverty alleviation. It then takes tentative steps towards a new development model, proposing policies and actions required by government and others to realise that potential and create a new, non-western, democratic model of economic growth.

This study and analysis of entrepreneurial activities provides role models for aspiring businesspersons and guidelines for the establishment and expansion of business. The study has additional, broader significance for policy makers: as an indicator of ways of making wealth more widespread and equitable. In other words, women's micro and small businesses augment GDP while they enhance individual and family well-being—the means and goal of development.

[1] Throughout the text, non-English words and phrases have been set in roman type, rather than the customary italic. Where needed, such phrases have been translated at their first appearance in the text; they are also defined in the Glossary (Appendix 2).

[2] Diane Elson (1998), quoting A. Hill and E. King (1995); the World Bank also cites this research. See the Bibliography for more complete citation information in this and other instances.

[3] President Museveni was speaking to 3,200 university graduates at Makerere University on 16 January 1998.

[4] The newness of interest in the informal sector is evidenced by conflicting data as to ownership of enterprises, size of economic sectors, etc. Most of the percentages used here are estimates from Impact Associates (1995).

[5] See also Bonnie Keller (1996).

[6] The ILO full-employment mission to Kenya in 1972 was the first to put the label 'informal sector' on a large portion of a nation's economy. The informal sector was defined in 1996 by the United Nations as 'any business or enterprise that is not formally registered with the national or local government', excepting money-making activities judged to be harmful to the society or the national economy, such as drug dealing, smuggling and armed robbery. Alternatively, it is sometimes defined in terms of size, rather than legality: as a business that 'employs no more than 5 to 10 persons, including owner and family and/or some apprentices ... [and] normally requires less than $100 in start-up capital and rarely up to $5,000' (UN Office of the Special Coordinator for Africa, 1996).

[7] Manufacturing (32 per cent), services (14 per cent) and transportation (4 per cent) make up the other 50 per cent. Data in Zambia confirm that women's informal earnings comprise 40 per cent of all earnings in the informal sector, and they are 48 per cent of earnings in trade, restaurants and hotels (Urdaneta-Ferrain n.d.: Table 3).

[8] Gracia Clark (1994); United Nations (1996); etc.

[9] Republic of Uganda (1999).

[10] The conclusions of the study omitted financial data on start-up capital, which was deemed by Impact Associates to be unreliable.

Chapter 1

The Surge of Entrepreneurship and Activism: From Crisis to Empowerment

[Those in exile] had to survive, and some of them had a very hard time. They returned home with an investment spirit as well as a popcorn or a dry cleaning machine.

Joy Kwesiga, dean, Faculty of Social Sciences, Makerere University

The contemporary story of entrepreneurs in Uganda is also the story of a country's experience of and recovery from civil war and its legacy of death, destruction and fear. A veritable explosion of Ugandan African entrepreneurship was born out of the need to survive amidst chaos and later encouraged by a government-created climate favouring individual economic initiative. Women who were often left to care for whole families during the years of chaos of the 1970s and 1980s became traders and entrepreneurs. Their entrepreneurial spirit was later nourished by positive attitudes and affirmative-action policies, to which they responded by institutionalising their concerns in political and economic arenas. They influenced the constitution of Uganda and ensured women's collective strength both in government and the civil society. Yet a gender gap persists and grows: Among its major causes are the human costs of structural adjustment programmes (SAPs).

The Amin and Obote years

Even before the unspeakable suffering of the 1970s and 1980s under Presidents Idi Amin and Milton Obote, Uganda's women farmers, like other African women, had lost status. When the colonial era began in the late nineteenth century, a cash economy was introduced, and men were singled out for education, paid employment and crop marketing. They thus gained power over women, whose unpaid labour enhanced men's cash incomes, and who were considered thereafter, legally, as minors. Christine Obbo describes these preferential policies used during the colonial period, using the example of coffee production in Baganda, where women's labour grew the coffee and dried it at home, and men got the income from it (1980). Despite such setbacks, women continued as providers in rural communities, where they were 70 per cent of the agricultural labour force.

Ugandans point to the tyrannical policies of Presidents Amin and Obote as forcing the growth of entrepreneurship, but its parallel rise in other African countries from the 1970s suggests that the immediate cause was the African economic crisis, made more complex by demographic and structural factors. What makes Uganda unique is that the crisis was profoundly deepened during the chaotic Amin and Obote regimes. More than 800,000 people died, 200,000 went into exile and millions were displaced from their homes in those years.

The tyrannical Idi Amin, who took power from Uganda's first executive president, Milton Obote, in a coup in 1971 declared economic war on Asians, who owned some 77 per cent of the nation's industries (Ministry of Planning, Manpower and Employment, 1989). The Asians had arrived to work on the construction of the Uganda Railway, and when it was completed, many of them stayed behind to take advantage of economic opportunities at a time when Ugandan Africans had little education or experience in modern business. Regarding Amin's expulsion of Asian businessmen, sociologist Arnest Wabwire writes:

> Far from furthering economic independence ... reinforced dependence as other foreign industrialists moved in [to replace the Asians].... The magendo (illegal trade) economy stepped into the vacuum created by declining commodity production ... [and became] a systematic black-market distributive system.... Industries ceased to function. (1996)

Winnie Byanyima, a National Resistance Army (NRA) veteran, member of parliament and founder of the Forum for Women in Democracy (FOWODE) says Amin's impact on farmers was catastrophic because 'he killed the cash-crop economy. Coffee growers could no longer earn money because the government had a monopoly on coffee but would not pay the producers. Farmers cut down their coffee trees. There was no coffee, no cotton to sell.'

Byanyima sees peasant women and workers as Amin's worst victims:

> [Women] were terrorised in the same ways as men but also had to endure rape. In fact, rape by soldiers became so common that a raped woman was often told she had only herself to blame for getting caught: Soldiers were rapists and women were expected to know how to avoid them. Corruption, which had started in the colonial period, reached epidemic proportions under Amin's rule. When poor

> women could not raise enough money to bribe corrupt officials [to obtain essential services such as health care], they were forced to pay with their bodies. (1992)

In 1981 the Government of Uganda negotiated with the International Monetary Fund (IMF) the strategy to revive the economy through financial assistance. The GDP rose thereafter, but industrial production fell even further and by 1984 had sunk below 1970s levels. In 1984 the economic impact of inflation was so great that the purchasing power of wages plummeted to one tenth of their 1972 value. Following the overthrow of Milton Obote's second presidency in a 1985 coup d'état, economic chaos set in: Inflation soared, the value of the shilling plummeted and real wages declined to a third of previous worth. Two years later industries were using a mere 20 per cent or less of their capacity. Wabwire notes, 'The significance of small-scale manufacturing emerged out of this crisis.' By 1989, small-scale industries were contributing about 20 per cent of GDP, fifty per cent of total manufacturing and over 80 per cent of wholesaling and retailing (1996). Legitimate enterprise not connected to the magendo economy had begun to grow, and women were central to that development.

The surge in women's entrepreneurship

Ida Wanendeya, who began her own business while in exile, notes that women's entrepreneurship started when men either ran away or were killed during the Amin regime, leaving women behind with the children. 'Women faced the challenge. If you have a starving child you are not going to sit and mourn when no one provides for it. You acquire a goat or cow and get milk or get money and buy milk for your child,' she says. Another respondent, florist Victoria Sebageleka, reports that women ran very big businesses in those days:

> Amin was very frightened by rich men, by educated men, by men who had their own minds and wanted to go on with business rather than get into politics. He started picking them up from their businesses and offices, so women started manning their husbands' businesses. That was the first time Ugandan women tasted running big businesses like dry cleaners, Bata Shoes—big, big enterprises. In my view, the businesses that were most successful in those days were the ones run by women when men were abducted or killed, and women stayed behind.

Dr Joy Kwesiga, former head of the Department of Women Studies and currently dean of the Faculty of Social Sciences at Makerere University, further explains that women were more adaptable than men at the time:

> They got small shops, they got beer-drinking places, stalls in markets. Remember Christine Obbo's description, 'candlelight markets'? Even if they put someone in the shop or stall during the day, they would go there in the evening, or they would start baking after work. A male senior civil servant did not see himself going into a tiny shop after 6 p.m. to start selling, but a woman would do that kind of work. Women became international traders, taking empty suitcases to London to buy clothes to sell back home. In the 1970s and early 1980s they began going to Dubai, and whatever negative views people may have of that, it was a venue for women to enter business. When they returned, they invested in shops to sell their goods, and many of them built houses, established other ventures, and paid school fees.

The irony, in Winnie Byanyima's view, is that the worsening economy strengthened many peasant wives in relation to their husbands. With the decline of men's agriculture in the 1970s, women, who urgently needed incomes, grew and traded more food. 'Peasant women came out of their homes to market their food and to look for paid work...; many became permanent workers or traders in the markets and towns. Widows and other female heads of households struggled, some for the first time, to support their families alone,' she says. Exploited economically and sexually, they learned to work outside the homestead. Even the wives of rich men looked for work when they were jolted into the reality that they might not always have husbands to depend on. 'The economic crisis enhanced the position of many Ugandan women, especially poor and peasant women, and weakened the basis for men's domination. Social security, widowhood and exile pushed more women into paid work,' Byanyima finds (1992).

Ida Wanendeya speaks from personal experience of exile during the years of chaos. Her whole family fled the country to live in Nairobi from 1975 to 1979. While there she had to find a way to survive, and fortunately a few friends like Mary Okello, then a branch manager at Barclays Bank, helped with capital to rear chickens. The business was such a success that poultry became her family's main source of income: She supplied hotels—the Intercontinental, the 680, the Jacaranda—and a few butchers. 'Through my women's meetings I found a home-delivery clientele. I was quite busy!' she says. On her return to Uganda, Wanendeya got involved in small business, then was appointed to the board of the Uganda Commercial Bank (UCB) and other companies.

Dean Joy Kwesiga also attributes women's entrepreneurship in part to the influence of those who went into exile:

> They learned so much outside the country—in Nigeria, South Africa, Kenya, Australia. They had to survive, and some of them had a very hard time. They either found paid employment or something to sell, and they returned home with an investment spirit as well as a popcorn or a dry cleaning machine. They did not want to come back with just the Bible they went with. That outside exposure, plus the fact that Ugandans are everywhere in the world these days, has promoted business ventures.

An environment of peace

In the view of those interviewed for this study, the 1986 victory of Yoweri Museveni and the NRA became a landmark because security improved, markets opened and traders came in. Kwesiga observes that women then started going further abroad—to Bangkok, India, Rome—and learned from others who were investing as privatisation took hold. Even as the NRA moved toward triumphant entry into Kampala in 1985 (assuming power in January 1986), the world's women were holding the 1985 Nairobi World Conference that closed the United Nations Decade for Women. A number of Ugandan women found their way to that conference on their own, apart from the official delegation. That experience was to transform their own lives and some of the directions of their country. They met women activists from nearly every country in the world and learned about their achievements in private and public life—achievements Ugandan women previously thought were far out of reach. The result was a resolve that they, Ugandan women, would do even better.

Byanyima also sees the change dating from the mid-1980s, when more women came out to do business. She relates it to the encouraging environment for women that came with having more women in leadership:

> The fact that a woman could sit on a government council was a statement that a woman has a public role outside the home. So there was growing acceptance of women's going out to earn independent income. The idea that a woman has a right to get out of the house and do something else sank into the minds of Ugandans.

Economic need was the most important factor, however. The Economic Recovery Programme (ERP), the first stage of a structural adjustment programme (SAP), was put in place by the Museveni government in 1987 under strong influence from the IMF, World Bank and bilateral donors. Its conditions included the usual ones—cuts in public sector employment, export promotion including non-traditional agriculture exports (NTAEs), and general market liberalisation. Government dependence on aid-flows increased and private investment was hard to find. Women farmers were quick to adopt NTAEs—forty-eight per cent of all women farmers did so by 1992—but the extent to which they themselves benefited from the proceeds is not yet clear (Elson and Evers 1997; see also Chapter 4).

'The overriding factor is that times became hard,' Byanyima says, referring to the economic restructuring that accompanied international credit. Jobs were lost when the parastatals were sold off and when public services were continually downsized. 'But even before the restructuring, there was a lot of wastage from pilfering in government,' she recalls. 'Families were slowly pressured by the need for a second income in the household. Men's incomes became smaller so women went out and earned, but they lacked skills for salaried jobs and in fact the jobs weren't there anyway so they found somewhere to set up a little stall and start selling.' When government cut its support of services, education became more expensive and health services that were suddenly cost-shared became prohibitive; a woman from Arua, for example, could not afford the Ush 200 (medical fee), so women simply took care of the sick at home and stopped getting health care for themselves.

The stability that created an investment environment in Uganda is another factor that pushed both men and women into business. In Kwesiga's view the 1986 peace (although it is still not everywhere) brought people a sense of security, so they started building houses and opening small shops. Before that time Ugandans who had money to invest bought houses in Nairobi or London. 'When Amin was toppled in the 1970s, there had been some hope that things would improve,' she says, 'but during the guerrilla war after 1980, soldiers were everywhere, taking peoples' cash and goods and even buildings, so there was general hesitation about investing. Stability is one factor pushing people into business today.'

Kwesiga speaks thoughtfully about the restructuring that fostered the reform of the civil service:

> It made all of us think about the future. Civil servants used to be settled in their jobs forever, so the retrenchment that cut jobs shocked many people. In that kind of environment, people look for alternative income. Now they say, 'I must have a shop somewhere to be able to feed the children or just to live'. They open a canteen in the university. They think, 'I may not always have a job, I may not always have a public position, and in any case I shall have to leave those positions sometime'.

Strength in numbers: women's activism

Women who remained in Uganda and those who went into exile during the years of terror knew that participation in wars of liberation did not lead automatically to their participation in the governments created by the winners. On the contrary, the experience of many African countries taught that men tend to exaggerate women's low literacy levels in order to ignore them when new governments are formed. It was clear that women would have to press for equity in the new Uganda: that human rights, including participation in local and national decision-making, would not just be bestowed upon them. There was work to do, and on return from the 1985 World Conference in Nairobi they started doing it.

Women's participation in the NRA liberation struggle, the lessons learned at Nairobi and the new environment of peace combined to foster the institutionalisation of their concerns in both government and civil society. They found innovative ways to ensure they were represented in governing, and they created a wide array of autonomous, development-oriented local and national women's organisations. It was clear that they had gained self-confidence and earned respect from men during the civil war years when they supported whole families and aided the revolution.

An example of the activist civil-society organisations women created is Action for Development (ACFODE), which was established in November 1985, just before the triumphal formation of a new government by the NRA. ACFODE sought to increase the participation of women and girls in social, economic and political arenas. They would 'break through the obstacles thwarting the advancement of women and their contributions to national development' in the words of current president Dr Ruth Mukama (ACFODE 1995). ACFODE immediately joined hands with the Non-governmental Organisations Committee and the National Council of Women to plan a week of celebrations for International Women's Day, 8 March 1986. Its climax was a ceremony officiated by the new President of Uganda, Yoweri Kaguta Museveni, who would hear much more from women in the ensuing months.

Concerned that the official delegation to the Nairobi conference had done little sharing with women back home, ACFODE organised a conference follow-up seminar at Mukono, just outside Kampala, to which 317 persons came, including 120 from rural areas.[1] Recommendations adopted and networks formed at that seminar would have a profound impact on Uganda for years to come. Women asked for change in the governmental institutions that affected their lives on matters such as employment, health and education.

Official action was fast coming. The Ministry for Women in Development was created in the President's office, merged with the Ministry of Youth and Culture in 1991, and was then renamed again as the Ministry of Gender and Community Development in 1994. In 1998 the ministry was consolidated once again as the Ministry of Gender, Labour and Social Development, but its two directorates, of women and community development, were reduced to a Department of Gender and Community Development, with a very small staff (*The Other Voice,* June 1998).

Announcing the creation of the ministry, President Museveni stated that government policy 'aims at strengthening the position of women in the economy by raising the value and productivity of their labour and by giving them access to and control over productive resources' (Kwesiga 1994). However, the ministry—like similar institutions worldwide—was never funded to accomplish the tasks set out for it. Typical was the government's 1994–95 budget, which apportioned just one tenth of one per cent to the Ministry of Gender and Community Development, a total of $595,000, compared to 20.9 per cent for the Ministry of Finance and Economic Planning and 25.1 per cent for security, including defence and police. Donor support, most generously from the Government of Denmark, supplemented the ministry's meagre allocation.

Among the ministry's accomplishments is *The National Gender Policy,* adopted by parliament in 1997, that 'gives a clear mandate ... by prescribing the basic principles for mainstreaming gender in all sectors', as Minister JanatBalunzi Mukwaya states in its preface. Target areas are set for action at national, sectoral, district and community levels. 'The ultimate objective of this policy ... is to evolve a society that is both informed and conscious of gender and development issues and concerns,' the minister states (Ministry of Gender and Community Development 1997).

Another example of the institutionalisation of women's concerns is in education. After the Uganda Association of University Women (UAUW) failed in its first attempt to establish a Department of Women Studies at Makerere University, ACFODE joined the effort, enlisting the support of the vice chancellor and donors in its petition to the University Senate—with a victorious outcome in 1991. In 1990 the university senate had agreed to add an additional 1.5 points to those scored by any female applicant to the university. By 1998 women were 33 per cent of graduates; the department awarded 56 master's degrees in women studies and commenced an undergraduate course as well. Its students' theses have been in vital development areas such as cross-border trade, urban agriculture and non-traditional cash crops; several of them are quoted in this book. They and other published works are beginning to fill the research gap that grew during Uganda's lost years of the 1970s and 1980s—including the UN Decade for Women, 1976–1985—when money was abundant for women's research across Africa, but the country was at war with itself.

The ACFODE story shows how non-governmental organisations (NGOs) made common cause over certain issues—a form of action that continues through the Uganda Women's Network (UWONET) and the National Association of Women's Organisations in Uganda (NAWOU), the replacement for the ineffective National Council of Women. NAWOU today comprises more than 50 women's NGOs and one thousand community groups and, among other activities, imposes quality control to ensure that crafts are exportable.

Women have spoken out and mobilised over issues of child abuse, sexual harassment, rape and spousal abuse. The death of an Asian woman late in 1997 was followed by an autopsy in which there was an attempt to cover up and avoid blatant evidence of frequent beatings. It brought women's groups of all beliefs and races to instant action in public protest on the streets. They succeeded in delaying the cremation of the body and demanding a second autopsy; criminal charges against her husband followed. Delia Almeida of Delmira Travel and Tours comments: 'The lawyer for the husband asked the magistrate to stop the NGO women from coming; he said that [the] women were spreading false rumours. Those men were concerned about women who are so strong and tough they want to suppress them and groups such as the Association of Women Lawyers (FIDA) that are fighting for women's rights.'

Even as women's NGOs act cooperatively, each has its own specialised priorities. In professional fields, NGOs include FIDA, with branches across the country; Women Engineers, Technicians and Scientists in Uganda (WETSU); FEMRITE, for women writers; the Uganda Media Women's Association; the Forum for Women in Democracy (FOWODE); Medical Women and others.

In addition to these post-revolution organisations, many religion-based organisations that also have socio-economic goals have existed countrywide for nearly a century. The Mother's Union of the Protestant churches was established in 1908 and the YWCA in 1952. (Uganda has the largest branch in the world.) The Uganda Muslim Ladies Association was established in 1976 and the Uganda Catholic Women's Bureau in 1993, the latter as a coordinating body for long-existing women's groups in individual parishes throughout the country. Those organisations and others such as the Girl Guides had shared common cause within the first National Council of Women that was established in 1964 and later abolished by Idi Amin.

Political representation

The front on which women and their organisations have worked most successfully is the political one. The ministry concerned with women organised seminars across the country so that women's voices would be heard on matters related to a new national constitution. The Constituent Assembly that debated the Odoki draft constitution had 18 per cent women among its members, its Vice Chairperson Victoria Mwaka was chosen for that post subsequent to serving as the first head of the Department of Women Studies at Makerere University. Women delegates were sensitised on gender concerns and parliamentary procedures; they formed a Women's Caucus to lobby for their issues. NAWOU set up a Gender Information Centre for them at the International Conference Centre where the Constituent Assembly met. The result is a constitution that is widely hailed across Africa as the first to be truly gender sensitive. Among its provisions:

> Women shall be accorded full and equal dignity of persons with men ... the state shall provide the facilities and opportunities necessary to enhance the welfare of women and to enable them to realise their full potential and advancement ... women shall have the right to affirmative action for the purpose of redressing the imbalances created by history, tradition or custom ... laws, cultures, customs or traditions which are against the dignity, welfare or interest of women or which undermine their status are prohibited by this constitution. (*Constitution of Uganda,* 1995, Chapter 4, Section 33)

There are other signs of progress in political affairs: At independence only two women were in a parliament of 88 persons; when the NRA took over, it grew to 39 of 263 (15 per cent) and after the 1996 elections, fifty-two of 276 (18.8 per cent).[2] The Resistance Council local-government system of the National Resistance Movement (NRM, the government successor to the NRA) includes a Secretary for Women's Affairs at each of its five levels of governance (village, parish, sub-county, county and district), and since 1993 Women's Councils have been set up also at each of those levels. Only Uganda among African countries has a woman vice president: medical doctor Speciosa Kazibwe. President Museveni was first elected in 1996, when women 'cast their votes for peace' by choosing him, as was often stated. Table 1.1 shows women and men in top decision-making positions in Uganda during 1994–1996 (*Uganda: Yearly Review 1997:* 45).

Table 1.1. Women and men in top decision-making positions in Uganda (1994–1996)

POSITION	1994		1995		1996	
	W	M	W	M	W	M
President	0	1	0	1	0	1
Vice President	1	0	1	0	1	0
Ministers	2	18	1	20	2	19
Ministers of State	1	11	5	24	4	27
Deputy Ministers	2	8	—	—	—	—
Parliament	46	219	46	219	51	226
Presidential Advisors	—	—	3	13	3	13
Ambassadors	2	22	2	22	2	21
Electoral Commission	3	4	3	4	3	4
Uganda Human Rights Commission	—	—	—	—	4	3
Judicial Service Commission	—	—	—	—	1	7
Public Service Commission	1	8	1	8	1	8
Teaching Service Commission	1	3	1	3	1	3
Supreme Court	—	—	—	—	0	8
Judges of the High Court	—	—	—	—	8	15
Permanent Secretaries	8	35	8	35	7	29
Under Secretaries	17	50	—	—	7	23
Directors	—	—	3	29	4	29
Commissioners	—	—	—	—	28	83
Chief Magistrates	—	—	—	—	6	14
Local Authorities	24	101	4	73	12	105
TOTAL	108	480	78	451	145	638
Percentage of women and men	18.4	81.6	14.7	85.3	18.5	81.5

Source: Ministry of Gender and Community Development Resource Centre. As presented in *Uganda 1997/98: Yearly Review*, 'Women in Uganda', by Joy Kwesiga.

The challenge of economic empowerment

The surge in women's entrepreneurship in the 1970s and 1980s brought with it the need for support systems for economic empowerment, so women created community-based and non-governmental organisations. Four discussed at various points throughout this book are briefly introduced here. The earliest of them are the autonomous rotating savings and credit associations (ROSCAs) formed by small grassroots groups of mutually trustful persons. Rooted in tradition, they fell from favour during the decades of mistrust and violence, then resurfaced once there was peace. Their uses are many—from business to burial—although the scale of savings is most often quite limited.[3]

Second, the need for capital to start or expand a business is acute for women whose dependence on male relatives leaves them without land of their own or other property to use as collateral for credit in the formal banking system. That need led to creation of the Uganda Women's Finance and Credit Trust (later renamed Uganda Women's Finance Trust—UWFT) in 1984, which became operational in 1987 as an affiliate of Women's World Banking (WWB).[4] With a mission to economically empower low-income women, UWFT offers savings and loan facilities, training in entrepreneurial skills and business counselling. As of 1997, over 10,000 clients were saving through it, and more than 1,000 loans, of up to $1,000 each, were listed at its ten branch offices.

Third, the Uganda Women Entrepreneurs Association Ltd (UWEAL) was formed in 1987 as a forum for women who own or manage commercial enterprises of various types and sizes. The recognised body of women in business, locally and internationally, UWEAL's members are also members of the Uganda Manufacturers Association (UMA) and the Chamber of Commerce. The Association is also an affiliate of NAWOU. Its objectives include researching and maintaining a database for promoting women's enterprise, facilitation of training in business administration, working with financial institutions to promote women's access to credit, and soliciting financial and material support. By 1998, UWEAL had about 200 members in several branches.

The fourth instrument to empower women economically arose from discussions of the African economic crisis at the regional NGO Forum in Senegal in 1994. Women decried the often negative impacts of economic 'reforms' such as structural adjustment programmes (SAPs) and the deterioration of women's social status they caused. The Council for the Economic Empowerment of Women in Africa (CEEWA) was formed 'to articulate regional and country-specific strategies to address causes of poverty and lack of economic empowerment'. The Ugandan chapter of CEEWA, whose members work in the economic areas of government ministries and the private sector, selected four priorities: control over land; micro-finance delivery methodologies, participation of women in economic decision-making and agricultural extension services (CEEWA n.d.).

Characteristics of organisations

A careful look at Ugandan women's activism and at the organisations women have formed since the mid-1980s reveals three important characteristics. First, women's activism is spearheaded by women whose convictions in areas of social and economic justice make them risk-takers: Miria Matembe, Maxine Ankrah, Cecilia Ogwal, Mary Okurut, Joy Kwesiga and Winnie Byanyima come to mind. 'Women are so strong, especially here in Uganda,' entrepreneur Delia Almeida believes.

Second, women's activism is invariably developmentally focused. NAWOU reports a shift beyond a welfare to a developmental, empowerment and advocacy thrust evident in FIDA and ACFODE's joint approach to the Ministry of Justice about legal reform on domestic relations. The UWFT seeks Uganda's economic growth through women's empowerment. For Kwesiga, this process indicates 'a shift in ideology, from women's welfare to women's empowerment, from women being regarded as minors to the position of adults'.

Finally, women's organisations are increasingly non-sectarian. Rose Kiggundu of CEEWA expresses a view often heard, which has special significance in a country with a history of ethnic and religious strife. 'One of the most important characteristics of the [savings and credit] groups is their mix of ethnicity and religion. You find women from different parts of the country, some of them Christian, some Muslim, pursuing their common concerns and trusting one another in their groups.' Political scientist Aili Tripp speaks of this characteristic of women's groups as inclusiveness, pointing out that of 150 women's groups whose members were interviewed in Kampala, 'less than a handful were formed strictly around ethnicity'. She adds, 'Clearly, the main organising principle was economic survival and mutual support rather than a primary affinity' (Tripp 1994). This non-sectarian characteristic is essential for a civil society that represents issues, rather than ethnic identities.

A gigantic job ahead

Despite women's activism and the positive attitudes and changes it has ignited, the situation of the majority of women calls for change. The United Nations Development Programme's (UNDP) 1997 *Uganda: Human Development Report* sets out the paradox of women's having economic responsibility without adequate economic power:

> [E]ven a cursory analysis of Uganda's gender profile demonstrates widening gender disparities: a dichotomy between women and men as regards access to productive resources, poverty levels, education, employment opportunities and participation in the political process. It is noteworthy that while the preponderance of the agricultural labour force is women (70 per cent of the total) and the bulk of food production (70–80 per cent of the total) is undertaken by women, only 7 per cent of women own land. And gender disparities cut across all social indicators, capability indices and indicators of political and economic participation.

To many observers and analysts, the growth of that gender gap, while due in part to traditions and colonial influences, is severely exacerbated by Uganda's debts to overseas lenders and by the punishing programmes of economic reform and structural adjustment agreed with IMF, World Bank and bilateral donors. Acceptance of SAPs conditions the availability of new credit—and much of the national income goes to pay debt and debt interest. While perhaps functional in the short run, retaining these conditions over years has proven dysfunctional, exacting a heavy toll on human development due to cutbacks and cost-sharing of essential health and education services. SAPs tend to channel resources to big business—often foreign-owned—to the neglect and disadvantage of micro and small enterprise which, as we have seen, is the largest future employer, expected to provide 60 to 70 per cent of new jobs in Africa.

Moreover, SAPs fail to foster a strong future labour force; instead they prolong poverty among the majority of people—poverty that afflicts women and children most adversely, as innumerable studies have shown.[5] For example, women's workloads are 'grossly increased' (Kyamureku 1997) when production of NTAEs is encouraged, because women are the agricultural producers of the food exports such as maize and beans that are needed for family consumption. Women's studies lecturer Mary Mugyenyi calls for addressing the 'structural rigidities in the country's socio-economic institutions that curtail women's full production', adding that 'women subsist at the margin of the poverty line and any further impoverishing policy package, however noble in its long-term objective, is unacceptable' (Mugyenyi 1992).

Even when they market the products themselves, women are at a disadvantage: Researcher and parastatal manager Esther Kapampara found women earning less income than men by almost 50 per cent when selling maize and beans. She explains:

> [W]omen produce for trade and use the income to meet household needs, increasing men's net profits at their own economic peril. The women thus get poorer while men get more affluent, enhancing not only economic inequality but also social inequality between men and women.... This situation is bound to translate into decreased agriculture output at individual, community and national levels as the women producers, who form 70 per cent of the agricultural labour force, are discouraged and do not aspire to better the situation perhaps perceived as their destiny. (Kapampara 1996)

Workloads increase for other reasons as well. Women must take on the added tasks of paying for education and health now that cost sharing of those services has been introduced; often unable to pay, they are forced to care for the family's sick themselves. To its credit, Uganda recently introduced universal primary education for four children in each family—at least two of them girls—with assistance from the World Bank and the United States Agency for International Development (USAID), but it remains to be seen whether the project is successful, and whether boys and girls will actually have equal chances to go to—and stay in—school.

Besides workloads, another increase widely perceived in countries around the world as a product of poverty-provoking economic adjustment is spousal abuse, which subsides when women have independent incomes (Dwyer and Bruce 1988, Elson 1995, House-Midamba and Ekechi 1995, Snyder 1995).

Recapitulation

Ugandan women showed extraordinary resilience during the Amin and Obote years, the 1970s and 1980s. Whether in the countryside, the village or the city, they took over men's businesses or started their own despite the unspeakable violence, including rape, they experienced with their families. Some fought alongside the rebels, while others left the country with families they often had to support in exile. When a blessed peace came in 1986 they organised to battle against poverty and ensure a peaceful political future. Through the creation of new NGOs and representation in public bodies such as the Constituent Assembly, they helped put in place a democratic institutional framework supported by civil society, including a constitution that is path-breaking worldwide for its gender sensitivity.

Today Uganda's economy, impressive in its growth at the macro level, is still punishing for the 46 per cent of her people who are poor.[6] So, despite their extraordinary achievements, Ugandan women are far from satisfied. They bear the brunt of poverty and ironically are also its potential eradicators. That is why they emphasise economic empowerment now that their political agenda is in place.

'The job remaining is still gigantic,' Kwesiga says. That makes the life stories and advice of experienced women entrepreneurs very important. And that is why they tell their stories in the following pages.

[1] The United Nations Development Fund for Women (UNIFEM) was among the sponsors of the conference.

[2] Uganda's figure of 18.8 per cent women in parliament puts the country just below the (1998) figures of 24 per cent for South Africa and 23 per cent for Mozambique, but well above most African countries.

[3] The UN Economic Commission for Africa (ECA) studied ROSCAs in eastern Africa in the 1960s.

Table 1.2. Uganda and gender: basic data

ITEM	NUMBER	PER CENT	SOURCE
GENERAL (1995)			
Population	20 million		
Urban (% of total population)		13	DP
GNP per capita	US$240		DP
Poverty: people below the poverty line (1998)		46	Ssen
Land area, sq. km.	241,138		
HEALTH (1995)			
Life expectancy at birth, in years			
Female	41.4		DP
Male	39.6		DP
Fertility rate			
No education	7.0		UFF
Primary	7.1		UFF
Secondary	5.1		UFF
Women of reproductive age using contraceptives			
Any method		13.4	DP
Modern method		8	DP
Infant mortality per 1,000 live births (1996)	88		DP
Maternal mortality per 100,000 live births (1996)	506		DPKLA
Women age 15–19 who have borne a child			
Age 17		43.3	UFF
Age 16		22.1	UFF
AIDS cases per 1,000 (1996)	13.8		DP
Tuberculosis cases per 100,000 (1995)	129.4		DP
HOUSEHOLD (1991)			
Female-headed households		29	UFF
Household heads/rural			
Female		28	UFF
Male		72	UFF
Household heads/urban			
Female		33	UFF
Male		67	UFF
Hh. income fr. women (in cash or agro-produce)			
Female-headed households (29% of households)		100	UFF
Male-headed households		50	WAE
EDUCATION			
Adult literacy rate			
Female		50.2	DP
Male		73.7	DP
Gross primary enrolment: female as % of male		85	DP
Combined 2nd and 3rd level enrolment ratio			
Female		34.2	DP
Male		41.9	DP

Table 1.2. Uganda and gender: basic data (continued)

ITEM	NUMBER	PER CENT	SOURCE
STRUCTURE OF THE ECONOMY (1995)			
Agriculture share of GDP		50	DP
Industry share of GDP		14	DP
Services share of GDP		36	DP
EMPLOYMENT			
Portion of total labour force (1990) in:			
Agriculture		85	DP
Industry		5	DP
Services		11	DP
Females as % of total labour force (1995)		48	DP
Women's labour share of total labour (1993–95) in:			
Agriculture		75	Elson
Food crops		80	Elson
Cash crops		60	Elson
Non-traditional agriculture exports (NTAEs)		80	Elson
Industry (overall)		15	Elson
Services		32	Elson
NATIONAL BUDGET (1990)			
Public expenditure on health as % of GDP		1.6	DP
" " on military as % of health + education expenditure		18	DP
DEBT (1995)			
Debt as % of GDP		64	DP
Total external debt	US$3.6 billion		DP
Debt service as % of exports (goods + services)		21	DP
WOMEN IN PUBLIC OFFICE			
Parliament (1999)		18.8	MP
Ministerial level (1995)		10.7	DP
Local government: district level (1999)		33 +	MP

Key

WAE Snyder, Margaret, 2000, *Women in African Economies: From Burning Sun to Boardroom*, Kampala: Fountain Publishers

DP UNDP, *Human Development Report, 1998,* New York: Oxford University Press

DPKLA UNDP, *Uganda: Human Development Report, 1998*, Kampala: UNDP

Elson Elson, Diane, and Barbara Evers, 1997, 'Gender aware country economic reports: Uganda, Manchester, UK: University of Manchester

Ssen Ssendaula, Gerald, 12 June 1998, *The 1998–99 Budget Speech,* Kampala: Ministry of Finance

MP Members of Parliament: personal information to the writer, March 1999, New York

UFF Ministry of Gender and Community Development and the Statistics Department, Ministry of Planning and Economic Development, 1998, *Women and Men in Uganda,* Kampala: Ministry of Gender and Community Development

[4] The idea of Women's World Banking is attributed to Ghanaian Esther Ocloo, attending the World Conference for International Women's Year, Mexico City, 1995. An international group of which the author was a member carried the idea into reality (see Snyder and Tadesse 1995).

[5] Some of the most respected studies on the effect of SAPs on women and children are: Munene, J.C., 1996?, *Empowerment, Poverty and Structural Adjustment in Uganda*, Kampala: Friedrich Ebert Foundation; Semboja, Joseph and Ole Therkildsen, 1995, *Service Provision Under Stress in East Africa*, Kampala: Fountain Publishers; Mamdani, Mahmood, 'Uganda: Contradictions in the IMF programme and perspective', in D. Ghai (ed.), 1991, *The IMF and the South: The Social Impact of Crisis and Adjustment*, London: Zed Books; Himmelstrand, Ulf et al. (eds.), 1994, *African Perspectives on Development*, Kampala: Fountain Publishers.

[6] Absolute poverty is defined as 'having an income less than that needed to meet basic requirements for food and other essential goods and services' (Permanent Secretary, Ministry of Finance, Planning and Economic Development, quoted in *The New Vision*, 13 July 1998).

2 Market Traders

Jane Namayanja owns two shops selling beverages and sundries

Christina Nasuna wholesales fruit and vegetables

Betty Nakiganda deals in cassava

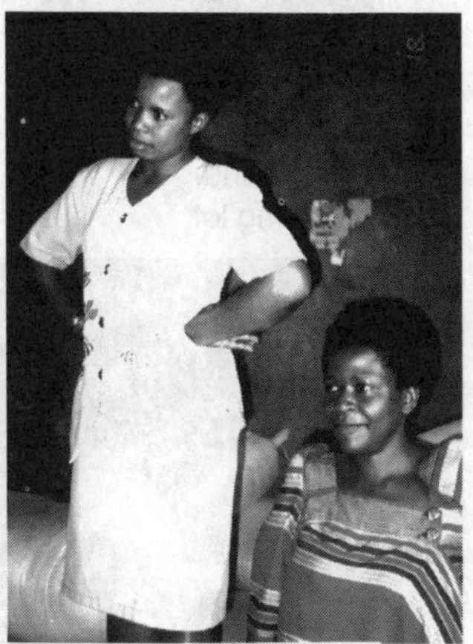

On Sena Women Veterans buy and sell dried goods

Miriam Nakalyana sells matoke

Teddy Birungi wholesales beer, soda and whiskey

Daisy Kayizzi sells matoke and potatoes

Margaret Ssajjabi owns 27 market spaces and a parking lot

Frida Obua sells vegetables

Rose Gawaya is an entrepreneur for the poor with the Slum Aid Project

Madina Nampijja sells potatoes

Chapter 2

The Urban Informal Economy: Marketplace, Roadside, Home and Backyard Farm

If you have a little capital you get a little profit, but if you have much capital, you get big profits. That is our dilemma.

Daisy Kayizzi, a foodseller in Kasubi market

Traders and buyers meet in an almost infinite variety of marketplaces in towns and cities. There is the bustling area designated by local authorities, where tightly packed stalls and tiny plots are allocated to individual merchants who must apply in writing and pay monthly fees—sometimes offering 'tea', or chai (a bribe) to assure one or several places. Tiny plots in open areas near markets can be costly too because they are in high demand. Then there are the often dangerous roadsides and the cluttered sidewalks where seated or mobile merchants ('footloose traders') peddle their wares. Many of those locations are illegal to start with or become illegal overnight when new laws are passed or old ones suddenly enforced. When the sun is setting, 'candlelight markets' appear, illuminated by a streetlight, candle or paraffin lantern, for those who are unable to obtain a stall or who have inadequate daytime jobs. Urban agriculture, practised in the backyard, or on vacant lots or along the roadside by some 36 per cent of Kampala households, yields food for the family; the excess is offered for sale or for barter in yet another urban entrepreneurial activity. Finally, there is the invisible home-based enterprise (HBE)—a small corner of living space set aside for manufacturing or sales. Of course there are also innumerable illegal activities, notable among them the commercial sex work of women.

The informal economy is estimated to account for 40 per cent of Africa's GDP, yet it remains invisible to those responsible for counting the national wealth. Informal commerce and trade engage 63 per cent of Ugandan entrepreneurs, who nevertheless survive in a vacuum largely devoid of government policy or practical support. More than economic, the marketplace is political, too. The immediate need may be mouths to feed, clothing to buy, rent to pay. But the market exists ultimately because political pressures and decisions, and the resultant economic structure, determine where opportunities will open for income and personal empowerment. When formal-sector wages are low and jobs are scarce, people turn to the informal sector for supplementary—and sometimes primary—family income, as they did during the Amin–Obote years. For those having little or no education, it is usually the only option.

For women, the informal economy is even more complex and fraught with obstacles than it is for men. 'Women's problems are dictated by forces outside their control,' says historian Nakanyike Musisi. Among such forces in Uganda are the political storms and economic crises of recent decades, the impact of SAPs and increasing ties to the global economy, compounded by 'gender disparity that has roots in the unequal access to resources and their distribution' (Musisi 1995). Ugandan researcher Elizabeth Agitta studied women traders in Lira and came to a conclusion universally applicable: 'Market trading with its meagre profitability was the only source of earning a livelihood. Women's activities were viewed as marginal and their earning role temporary and only supplemental in nature to family income. Consequently, women's contribution was regarded as welfare service rather than economic undertaking' (1990).

Some market women thrive, going from strength to strength. Others seem to stand still in their spaces, living day to day and sometimes debt to debt, close to bare subsistence level where a slight loss can mean personal and family catastrophe. But a slight gain is captured: Profit is invested in children's education, a plot of land, a small house and, circumstances permitting, reinvested in their business, as the stories that follow testify.

This chapter introduces traders in the Kasubi, Wandegeya, Kalerwe, Nakivubo and Owino markets of Kampala, and then moves to candlelight markets, urban agriculture, home-based enterprise and sex work, before profiling the businesswomen and discussing the following issues:

1. *Does the level of an entrepreneur's education influence the type and size of her business?*

2. *What are the sources of start-up capital, and how does its size influence business growth?*

3. *What motivates market traders, urban farmers and home-based workers to become entrepreneurs?*

4. *Is capital available for business expansion?*

5. How do women in urban marketplaces invest their income? What trade-offs are involved?

6. What external obstacles do traders confront?

Kasubi market: scorching sun or torrential rain

Just west of the turning from Makerere Hill Road to Hoima Road at the edge of Kampala and before you reach the Kabaka's Tombs, the Buganda kings' final resting place, Kasubi market sprawls, facing the university, down a hillside to a broad valley. Hundreds of people find their livelihoods there, in protective stalls, on postage-stamp-sized spaces of ground, or just hawking along roadways and paths that are slippery with mud. Trucks loaded with matoke and cassava slide along roads narrowed by pedestrians, bicycles and carts and made dangerous by drainage ditches that are sometimes straddled with boards, sometimes used as selling space. Heaps of bananas, potatoes, tomatoes, cassava are everywhere—on tiny tables or on cloths on the ground.

On the left as you enter the marketplace the stalls are roofed against the burning sun and drenching rain (torrential this year from El Niño), where one trader's fruits and vegetables are on the top of a table and another's underneath. Fresh meat covers a long table behind which three butchers service customers. The best locations are nearest the Hoima Road and close to the access roads.

Men sell, but women dominate Kasubi. Esther Nankumi is a market leader and secretary of the Kasubi Market Women's Forum (KMWF), which she represents at the Savings and Credit Association of the UWFT. She explains how the civil war, when men lost their lives, thrust women into the marketplace to support their relatives and their own needs. There are many AIDS- and war-orphans to be supported now, she adds.

Esther observes that when wives work, spousal abuse declines, and that fact is a strong motivation for women to 'go full swing into the market'. The other side of that coin is that when their wives work, husbands become lax about supporting their families. Many men work, but they have relaxed and are no longer as strong in business as in the past. Men now let women meet the domestic requirements, in Esther's assessment. That view is widely shared. 'But more women have education now, and even a little education helps a lot. Whether they have a little or a lot of money, they are good planners—better planners than men,' she believes.

The importance of education and start-up capital is evidenced in interviews at Kasubi with Margaret Namuga, Teddy Nakasumba, Betty Nakiganda, Madina Nampijja and Daisy Kayizzi, all vegetable traders. They and 44 others—twelve of them men—belong to KMWF. They save and obtain individual loans from UWFT, whose loan-repayment period is very short—four months with a possible two weeks of grace. The KMWF has strong constitutional provisions that keep male members from overpowering the women, and 'if the men cannot be led by women, we leave them out,' Esther says.

Margaret Namuga (46): 3 years secondary school; widowed with 5 children; sells vegetables

KMWF member Margaret Namuga sells tomatoes, greens, eggplant, other vegetables and banana leaves from a covered stall located beside the path to the butchers; she started 18 years ago selling the very same produce from the very same stall she occupies today. A 46-year-old widow with 5 children to look after, she is blessed with 3 years of secondary education. With business profits she purchased a plot and built a 3-room house in Kawala. 'Everything is on me,' she says. 'I care for my children's education, health, clothing and food. My eldest child is now in the fourth year of secondary school.'

Margaret started supporting herself and her family by baking mandazi and frying pancakes. Saving slowly and carefully, she was able to move to Kasubi market and stop selling cooked foods. She had to pay Ush 4,000 to the City Council for the stall, which is permanently hers, and used another Ush 4,000 as initial capital. 'I started with a few goods because I had little money. I used to pick a few cabbages, but now I buy a whole bag. I buy a whole box of tomatoes. But you have to start small, save slowly, slowly. When you save enough you can start something,' she advises young entrepreneurs.

El Niño's unseasonal rains are on Margaret's mind, as with everyone in the market. 'At times even God does not help you,' she says. During the rains, smaller markets spring up and capture customers. 'People won't bypass the small sellers to go long distances to visit this large market during the rains,' she explains.

Margaret's first loan from UWFT through KMWF was Ush 100,000 (about US$100) with weekly repayments, including interest. She took it out in February 1997 and repaid it within 4 months. The second loan, obtained a few months later, has been hard to repay. 'This season is dead, lost. Things are in pieces. Rains spoiled the harvest. So when you sell, the price is high, beyond what a consumer can afford.' It is in her interest to repay the loan and continue working and make a profit in order to care for her children, but that is very difficult now. 'We continue to repay even though we have no money remaining. Work has become more difficult and less rewarding.'

If she had enough money, Margaret would find someone to run her business and start a trade in non-perishables, such as dried maize and beans, because even if they are expensive to buy they can be sold later at a better price.

'My business should not have been in this state, but the items to sell are scarce; that is the reason for my small stock. Now a tin of fresh green pepper is 5,000 shillings; eggplant is 3,000, a sack of cabbage is 15,000, and banana leaves 2,000 for a heap.' In the past she traded groundnuts but now cannot, even though her brother gave her a grinding machine. She recalls that things were not so expensive before transport became a very serious problem with the roads ruined by rain; what little produce gets through from the farms is now very costly.

Are men better at business? Not so, Margaret believes: 'We buy the same goods, sell at the same price. We can do anything that men do.'

Teddy Nakasumba (34): 1 year secondary school; married with 6 children; sells vegetables

With Ush 50,000 as capital, Teddy Nakasumba can buy only one sack of potatoes and half a sack of cassava. The potatoes come from Soroti or Ssingo, depending on the season. Teddy started trading 10 years ago and is ready to trade a larger stock, but because she sells from under someone else's table (Margaret's), storage space is minimal. Born in Kawuku in 1964, she had 1 year of secondary school. The younger of her 6 children are still with her and her husband. 'I have been able to help my children and get what my husband cannot give me,' she says. 'That is why I continue to work, even though he might prefer that I don't.'

Some days Teddy would like to switch to a different business. She has problems getting supplies and scarcity drives up prices both for her and her buyers. 'But it is not really bad,' she says. 'Working means that you cannot fail to get enough to eat and to support yourself.' She never took a loan, yet has saved enough money to buy a plot of land.

Betty Nakiganda (48): widowed with 8 children; sells cassava

Betty Nakiganda sits closer to the road, with a metal roof overhead. Born in 1950 in Masaka, she is the proud mother of 8—the eldest studying at Makerere University. She has sold cassava since investing Ush 600 capital in 1982, the year after her husband died. She has never sat at home since then. 'I eat and drink from my business. I built a house so that I no longer rent. I bought my plot from cassava [earnings]. I have been able to educate my children. That is very important—an even better achievement than building a house.'

Betty's problems are not with customers but in getting the cassava to sell. Sometimes farmers bring it to the market and other times she goes to the village herself so that she can make a better profit. She has not taken a loan through KMWF because she has a sick child, so cannot meet UWFT's loan criteria of mandatory saving with UWFT, and in any case could not repay a loan. Nevertheless, she saves money with a unity group, or ROSCA,[1] of 15 members. In her group, a member is supposed to get Ush 450,000 in the month when her turn comes up, but sometimes only Ush 300,000 is available, because someone has failed to pay-in for her friends' turns.

'The world is now difficult,' Betty observes. 'When you think of changing work, as I would have liked to do, you have to look for more money. Once you settle into a business it is difficult to change, especially if you have a loan to repay and could lose that money.' Her advice to a young woman going into business is first to get a place to work and have enough start-up capital. She adds that trading demands a happy disposition, kindness and good sales promotion.

Madina Nampijja: 1 year secondary school;
married with 4 children; sells potatoes

KMWF member Madina Nampijja sits placidly by the side of the road holding a huge striped umbrella to protect herself and her produce from the drenching rain. She too was born in Masaka, where she studied up to secondary level. Her husband, who approves of her working, sometimes helps with their 4 children. They have a plot but have not yet built their house. The market is Madina's second job; she previously sold clothing. In 1994 she began selling Irish potatoes in heaps, with initial capital of Ush 20,000. Prices are volatile: this week she bought from the farmers at Ush 20,000 while last week it was 25,000.

Madina got a loan for Ush 50,000 through KMWF, repaid it in a month and will get a second one of Ush 100,000. She says that she has managed to stay in business through such loans, and she looks forward to a larger one that would allow her to fetch the potatoes from the countryside herself. 'Our big problem is the rain,' Madina says.

Daisy Kayizzi (38): single mother with 5 children;
sells matoke and Irish potatoes

Daisy Kayizzi has about 2 square metres of ground in front of a row of small shops near the market entry road where she sells matoke and Irish potatoes purchased from wholesale trucks through costly middlemen. 'If you go to the villages to buy for yourself, you may spend a month out there with these rains, so we wait here. In addition, while you are out there, you incur more losses. Your produce ripens and rots,' she says. A bag of Irish potatoes costs her about Ush 25,000; she will get a profit of Ush 2,000 to 3,000 from resales over 2 or 3 days.

Daisy operated a hotel in Katimba years ago, after which she sold plates and saucepans, but was robbed and lost everything. Now 38 years old, she has been sitting and selling in her small open space for 15 years, paying Ush 10,000 a month and in addition a Ush 3,000 monthly tax to the Baganda government.[2] Building is forbidden in her space because it is too close to the road. 'I decided to stay here despite the limitations,' she says, 'because at least you can get a shilling for your child to eat and to go to school.'

Her initial capital was very small—Ush 150,000 in the old currency of Idi Amin. Her first business loan was Ush 100,000 through KMWF and her second will be repaid at the end of next month. Like Margaret, she finds the second loan more difficult than the first, which was easy, she says, before inflation set in. 'We don't know what will happen if we fail to repay, so despite the hardship we always struggle to repay. We are hard-working.' Daisy thanks the loan officers while appealing to them to find ways to reduce the 30 per cent interest—a big strain. She once tried a ROSCA but found that people did not agree with one another so their mutual trust was minimal.

Problems at Kasubi are many in Daisy's view. People no longer have money so they do not buy. Matoke gets over-ripe, potatoes rot and transport persistently fails. 'You have to know a lot of tricks in this trade,' she says. 'If my potatoes rot, I peel them and sell them that way. Here in Kampala people do not want to throw away garbage so I peel bananas for them and when I get a bag of peelings I sell it at 300 shillings. No extra charge for peeling!'

Born in 1959 in Mubende, Daisy is a single mother with 5 children; the eldest, a daughter age 20, is married. The rest are still in school so they do not help her at the market; she is proud to be able to look after their health care and schooling. She does not want to change her business: 'I previously did 2 other jobs, but because of my health and my age I no longer find it easy to strain myself. Here you can sit in one place. Vehicles bring matoke right here.'

Daisy offers her wisdom, born of years of trading: 'My long experience in business tells me that I cannot fail because even if you incur losses, you see to it that you start afresh. If you want to work you cannot fail, because even with Ush 10,000 you can work as long as you plan well. The most important thing about selling food is that you can eat. That is what keeps us here. When the bananas ripen, I take them to my children so that they are not badly off here in town.' She concludes: 'If you have little capital you get a little profit, but if you have much capital you get big profits. That is our dilemma.'

Wandegeya market: starting with very little money

Wandegeya area was annexed to Kampala in 1938. In 1962 its market and the one at Nakasero were the only ones in the capital that 'were properly set out and built up, with plantains and sweet potatoes laid on the bare ground, spread out or heaped' (Mukwaya 1962). Wandegeya market lies at the confluence of Makerere, Bombo and Mulago Hill Roads north-west of Kampala, just a 5-minute walk from Makerere University campus. You can buy almost anything at its fixed-price shops and market areas, from food to electrical supplies, clothing, medicine, take-aways, pots and pans. Most numerous are grocery and baked-goods shops, and enclosed areas with covered stalls for fresh fruits and vegetables. The many restaurants and bars of Wandegeya's 'Bermuda Triangle' are famous weekend gathering places for students and intellectuals. While socialising there you can have your umbrella fixed, your shoes resoled, or your car washed. Fleets of matatus (minibuses) and small taxis gather at stands blocked out for them and overflow into the carparks. Hawkers of newspapers and foods abound. Since the university student population multiplied to some 10,000 in 1997, the roadside leading uphill to the campus has become a market annex for haircuts, cookies, baskets, peanuts, fruits and candies.

Wholesaler Teddy Birungi's business is by far the largest of the Wandegeya group interviewed for this study. Margaret Ssewanyana sells in the fruit and vegetable section; Jane Namayanja has two retail shops; Frida Obua's vegetable stall is through an archway from Teddy's shop; Miriam Nakalyana works from the separate matoke section.

Teddy Birungi (36): 2 years secondary school; married with 5 children; wholesales beer, soda and whiskey

'This shop is mine. I sell right from here,' says Teddy Birungi, who started her first Half-Jamaica Store in 1991, when the shops were being constructed. It cost her about Ush 1.5 million, and because it is under city council supervision she has 15 years before paying rent. With 10 workers, her business is classified as a small enterprise in Ugandan terms.

Teddy's wholesale shop is tucked in behind others in Wandegeya market. Its open front reveals crates of beer and soda and boxes of whiskey stacked to the ceiling; there is barely space for two people to shelter from the drenching rain. She sits at a small table with her back to the narrow footpath that separates the shops. Above her, just inside, a television is suspended nearly out of reach, and a soccer game is in progress. Passers-by stop to catch the score. Teddy is counting money on this Saturday morning after the neighbourhood bars have taken their stocks from her. Her daughter Sophie Nagawa is there to help and to learn the business. Teddy tells how she got started as an entrepreneur:

> I started business with very little money—about 500,000 shillings—after I began trading in the market and built up trust there. Businesspeople would lend goods for you to sell and then pay them,

> and you keep the difference. Once they know you are trustworthy you can do as I did—sell cups, plates, glasses and spoons in the closed-market section at Wandegeya. The people who eventually gave me loans of beers and sodas used to see me working in that area. I would sometimes buy from them and other times ask them to lend the merchandise. They knew they would get their money.

After some time of buying from friends, Teddy went to the depot herself to purchase wholesale. Presently her average sales are 200 crates of beer and 500 of soda each week. The highest demand comes on hot days, when it is not raining. Her problems at Wandegeya and her 2 branch businesses in Nansana are mostly due to breakage of bottles and even crates. Once she was held up at gunpoint and another time her money was stolen. She never had a loan from a bank, but wants to get about Ush 3 million from UWFT to expand her business. She joined Obumu Women's Group for the purpose of borrowing and doesn't belong to any other groups.

Teddy was born in Masaka in 1962. She and all 4 of her siblings were educated, but only to the early years of secondary school because her father died in 1971 and her mother, who is still living, was left with many other children to educate. 'I went as far as second year of secondary—not very far,' she says, adding, 'In our family there was no favouritism based on sex: Boys and girls were given equal opportunities to be educated. Now I am married with 5 children—all of them in school.'

Although she has no problems working as a married woman because she and her husband agree to it, Teddy finds that 'business is hard'. Even though she counts profits every day, she must pay her workers and put away money for her trading licence. Fortunately, should unforeseen problems arise, her business can be entrusted to her husband and some of her reliable workers.

Teddy views the business accomplishments that enabled her to invest the profits in her family with great pride. 'Through my business I have achieved a lot: I managed to construct a house, buy things for it, buy a vehicle and open two more shops like this one. I believe that unless a woman does not know what she is doing, there is nothing men can do that we cannot do,' she says. 'I appeal to fellow women to work so that they are self-sufficient and need not desire anything.' Her future plans? 'Ah, I wonder. I aim to build for my children, prepare them well for life, but you cannot know.'

Margaret Ssewanyana (45): 3 years secondary school, married with 3 children (plus relatives); serves as chairperson of the Obumu Women's Group; sells fruit and vegetables

Margaret Ssewanyana, chairperson of the Obumu Women's Group, started working at Musicraft assembling radios when she was 25. 'While I was on leave my auntie asked me to come here to Wandegeya market to assist her, and soon I found the market more rewarding than the office! In 1980 my aunt left me in full control—her stall is now mine.' Margaret started with Ush 4,000—her entandikwa (start-up capital) with which she bought sugar canes and two bunches of ndizi (apple bananas). Her capital kept on multiplying, and she managed to get many good things, she says.

Margaret sells pawpaw (papaya), pineapples, tomatoes and other fruit and vegetables that she buys from Nakasero market or from farmers who bring bananas to Wandegeya. Nakasero goods are expensive—the biggest pawpaw costs Ush 1,000 and small ones 400 or 300, she says. Her first loan, from UWFT, was easily repaid and she currently uses another. She wants to develop her business more, with growth capital of about Ush 500,000. Margaret faced the problem of the rains and the spoilage they cause by selling dry vegetables like groundnuts and maize. Another problem she solved is that of debtors who take produce on credit and fail to pay; she reduced the number of customers to whom she gives credit. Previously she had 10 defaulters; now there are only 2.

Born in 1953 at Katikamu in Luwero district, Margaret was one of four children, two of whom have died. She had three years at secondary school. 'My husband, who is a businessman, found me here when I was already working so he cannot stop me from working now. He helps with the children, but I provide their school requirements and health costs. The husband will say "I have no money", so the wife finds money to treat a sick child,' she explains. From her earnings, Margaret constructed a house in Nabweru where she keeps her own three children and some of her relatives. And she looks after her aunt who gave her the business.

Her advice to someone who wants to start in business is first to ask: Do you have capital? If you have none, how will you start? She will agree to pass on her experience to someone who is realistic about the need for capital. 'Start slowly,' she says, 'with things that do not rot. Or sell goods everyone needs—whether a big earner or small—so they move fast, such as tomatoes.'

Jane Namayanja (36): 5 years secondary school; widowed with 3 children; serves as treasurer of the Obumu Women's Group; owns two shops selling beverages and sundries

Jane Namayanja is treasurer of the Obumu Women's Group at Wandegeya. She has two retail shops: One sells everything from dolls to fruit drinks, while the other, inside the 'Bermuda Triangle', has beer and soda. She has 3 employees and buys her stock of drinks from Teddy at Half-Jamaica. 'Of course sales are subject to the weather: If it rains, I sell few beers or sodas and more waragi (Ugandan banana gin). But if the sun shines, I sell very strongly.'

Jane doesn't recall just how much capital she started with but knows it was very little. She actually started as a tailor with 3 sewing machines, but they were stolen so she put what savings she had into the shop. A 6-month, Ush 100,000 loan from UWFT was easily repaid, and she is using a second one.

Like other entrepreneurs, Jane faces problems daily. Some people run away without paying for their beer and others steal bottles and glasses. Still others just walk off with the bottles when they join friends passing by. She has become extra observant in order to avoid such losses.

Jane was born in a peri-urban area near Kampala called Ntinda in 1962 in a family of 9 children, all of whom went to school. She reached the fifth year of secondary school. A widow with 3 young children, she has been able to buy chairs, a refrigerator and a telephone as well as put metal roofing sheets on her home. She plans to construct houses when she expands her business.

'In my view, women do well—in fact better than men—in business because men spend their money on other things. Women do not like to waste money; they want to add to it. But business is not easy', in Jane's view.

Frida Obua (40+): 1 year secondary school; married with 8 children; sells vegetables

Frida Obua was working at National Insurance in 1972 when her mother came from Kenya to stay with her. The Wandegeya market stall was originally for her mother to sell fruits and vegetables, but Frida took it over when her mother died. The child of a church minister, Frida has 2 siblings and has completed 1 year of secondary school. Because Wandegeya is owned by the kabaka (king) rather than by Kampala city, she pays rent of Ush 3,400 per month for the stall and an additional 3,000 for electricity.

She says, 'All of my produce is perishable so when it rots that is money. Sometimes customers are few and you cannot sell everything, and when it rains as much as it has this year, produce tends to spoil. Capital can be a problem too: If you do not have enough, your business cannot grow. If I can get capital, I will enlarge the business and put in non-perishables like beans and rice.' Frida has never taken a loan but is planning to join a savings group in order to get one. She is sole owner but is helped by a niece. 'A newcomer to marketing must have capital, then a plan so as not to waste her money. If you just rush into business, your money will perish,' Frida says.

Frida has eight children. The eldest studies engineering; the second, architecture; another is in teacher training and another studies management. Three younger ones are in senior secondary school and the little one in primary school. 'Of course I contribute to the household,' Frida says, 'but my income is small so my husband, who is a police officer, contributes the most.' She believes that spouses should have separate bank accounts and make independent decisions about spending. She buys food and sometimes the children's clothing. She looks to the future: 'Within a year, things will be better for me, because in June, four of my children will graduate, and my expenses for school fees and other necessities will be cut down.' She adds, 'My husband also pays fees—they are his children too!'

Miriam Nakalyana (45): learned reading and accounting from a neighbour; separated and supporting 4 children and 13 other relatives; sells matoke

The matoke section of Wandegeya market is on its own with each seller having a small area on a large cement block rather than a separate stall in the main vegetable and fruit market. Miriam Nakalyana, a matoke seller, has probably done better than most in providing for family needs. Neither she nor her only sister had the education they would have liked; their father simply did not send them to school. She feels fortunate that a neighbour woman taught her to read the Bible, count money and do costing and accounting.

Miriam is 45. When she was 17, she started as a housegirl near her home in Mukono in order to get capital, then in 1968 took a job cooking for some teachers there. The attraction of the city was compelling; she left for Kampala 3 years later to help a friend who got her a waitressing job in a hotel, then worked with some women at the university. Three months of selling tomatoes 'defeated me', Miriam says, 'so I now sell matoke here in Wandegeya market. Starting my matoke business was hard. I started with 2 bunches of bananas and went on from there. In 1973–74, I progressed—sold 100 bunches.' The market then weakened, especially with the opening of Kalerwe market nearby in the 1980s. 'It took many of our customers,' she says.

Miriam pointed out a woman who had just bought 5 bunches of bananas—a big sale. Other customers buy 3, 2, or just 1 bunch or a heap that she sells for Ush 500. Businessmen bring the matoke from Masaka; she has found no women who sell wholesale. The wholesale price ranges from Ush 2,000 to 3,000 a bunch. Her main problem is selling on credit rather than cash. She explains, 'When I give you my accounts-book you will see that I have over 700,000 shillings. But in reality I do not even have 200,000 shillings. Some customers pay later, others pay in bits. Still others do not pay at all. But whatever little I get, I put back into my business.'

Miriam tried a unity credit group, but some of the members didn't contribute regularly, so it broke up; she never tried to get a loan. Nevertheless, she has drawn great benefits for herself, her own family and others from her business.

> I managed to buy a plot with a title and even build a house on it. I have a plan for the future. At home I have a neighbour who has a water tap. I also want to have water to sell because you can make money from that. I want to keep poultry and to put up a shop to sell firewood and charcoal. I cannot do it now because I have four children, and I support ten others for my sister who didn't get the chance to do business. She married, but her husband got spoilt with alcohol; even her second marriage was like that. I have been helping her ever since. I also have other people at home whom I support, like my aunt and a grandchild, in addition to my sister.

Other matoke sellers have similar burdens. Miriam's friend has to pay rent for her house and look after her children. 'I am lucky; I am not renting,' she says. 'You know men,' she adds. 'They are all different. Some are drunkards. Some are not drunkards but still do not look after their children, so the woman has to take responsibility for that.'

Kalerwe: winning with patience in a poor man's market

Kalerwe market, the one that captured some of Wandegeya's customers, is just five kilometres along the Gayaza Road north of Kampala. Not yet annexed by the city, the area is free of city council taxes. Kalerwe throbs with life: Kiosks or roof shades over neatly laid-out piles of vegetables crowd every inch of space. Buyers and sellers bargain everywhere for bananas (green and sweet), potatoes, cassava, fruits and green vegetables. Like central New York City, the market is often negotiated fastest by foot. Alternately dusty and muddy, Kalerwe is known as the 'poor man's market'. Yet it attracts not only its poor neighbours from the slums of Katanga, Makerere Kivulu, Old Mulago and Makerere Kikoni but also people who arrive in big cars, who know that this is the cheapest market in all of greater Kampala.

Margaret Ssajjabi (52): 6 years secondary school; separated with 6 children and brothers' 19 children; owns land with 27 market spaces and a parking yard and sells water

Margaret Ssajjabi is a prominent woman in Kalerwe and one of its most successful entrepreneurs. At 52 years of age, she lives with her children in the market area where she owns some 50 decimals of land (about one quarter of an acre) with 27 market spaces that she rents out. Some of the tenants build stalls; others sell from the open ground. There are hairdressers, electrical repairmen, purveyors of beans of all kinds, matoke sellers and cooks. In addition, Margaret has a parking yard where up to 50 vehicles can safely spend the night. She sells water to local residents at Ush 50 per 20-litre jerrycan. Four watchmen and 2 security guards are in her employ. In the future, she wants to build more shops.

One of a family of 43 children and living with her divorced mother, Margaret reached the second year of secondary school when her father told her there was no more money for school fees and took her to join the police. Dissatisfied with police work, she got some technical training and joined the Uganda Electricity Board (UEB) as a telephone operator. She explains, 'I was still not contented, so after marrying in 1974 I left UEB and started a business selling soda, beer, Omo soap powder and other things at Ntinda, near the the Jinja-Kampala Road. In the beginning, my husband helped me with transport but not money. I would get the goods on consignment and pay the distributors when I sold them. I was able to hire some girls to help in the shop. Determined to develop myself, I saved money and bought this land—the business plot for 800,000 shillings and the residential plot for 1 million shillings. I also have land in Bujjuko where my mother stays, about 15 miles from town, and I rent out 2 houses in Ntinda.'

What business problems are specific to women? Borrowing money, Margaret says. Men get loans from fellow men, through banks or privately, but not many women have money to lend. She managed to get a bank loan and repaid it. Now, she and 9 other women save together in a ROSCA, each paying Ush 3,000 daily. Each member gets Ush 189,000 after 9 weeks. Margaret built the cement block walls around the parking area with that money. The Kalerwe women she knows do not have contact with women's groups outside of their savings clubs so she has just organised a new savings group called Kitikyamwogo.

But women traders need more than money. Margaret believes they also want and need business education. Uganda's wars and the scourge of AIDS have left many orphans, so women have urgent financial needs. Margaret supports 6 of her own children and has supported 19 others—her brothers' children. The young people visit during school holidays and help with the market work, washing vehicles or collecting rents. Some of the children now earn on their own, but they help when Margaret is sick. Children should be taught to work, she says. Girls need to respect cooking but also not have the attitude that market work is beneath them. They, like boys, can collect money and bank it. That is what she is teaching her daughters.

What about marriage? 'It is easier to work when alone, not married,' says Margaret, who is separated from her husband. 'Men want you to be lesser persons, to wash their clothes. They see themselves as the ones who "understand". There are very few women who are married and working. It is hard to convince men to allow women to work.'

What advice does this risk-taker and successful businesswoman have for women who are coming up in business? 'Be patient. When you are patient you can win. And you have to be confident. Develop the skills of your trade and don't beg off and say, "I am just a woman".'

Kaveda market: undercapitalised young army veterans

The image of retired army privates, corporals and sergeants may be of middle-aged men, but such is not the case with a group of 10 retirees who have been in business together just 6 months, buying and selling beans at Kaveda market. Most of these On Sena Women Veterans Association members are in their 20s and 30s, were educated through primary school, spent about 8 years in the army and are married with children. Their initial capital was small—Ush 1 million—but it enables them to buy their produce either in Kampala or directly from the villages. They already have a storage lockup at nearby Owino market for the charcoal and second-hand clothing they will sell. Two of the members have their own separate businesses, while for the rest the joint business is their sole income. The group averages about Ush 60,000 income a week, from which they pay office rent and draw subsistence allowances, for transport and food for members, of Ush 2,000 for each meeting.

Chairperson Sergeant Alice Mugabekazi (Rtd) explains that the veterans' family responsibilities led them to join forces to earn a daily living. Their director, Oliver Ntale, is not a veteran but 'has been a mother to us'. She and the group's patron, John Calami, are both businesspeople who teach the group members. The Uganda Veterans Assistance Board helps too.

Alice grew up in Ntungamo, was educated in Mbarara through junior primary school and in Jinja through secondary school, and in 1985 joined the army. Now 32 years old, she dealt privately in soda and beer for one year, selling about 50 crates of beer each week before she joined the veterans' produce group. Her earnings go to family upkeep.

Oliver also hails from Ntungamo; she studied business and then joined the Produce Marketing Board as an assistant accountant for 13 years, during which time she was able to save out of her salary. She has dealt in produce over the past decade. It is she who encouraged the first 2 women veterans to join forces and gave them a start-up loan. 'I believe that business takes determination, efficiency and trustworthiness,' she says, then adds thoughtfully, 'A determined woman can succeed.'

Oliver explains the women's dilemma—a universal one for women who would be entrepreneurs: 'Our biggest problem is where to go for a loan. When you go to financial institutions seeking funding, they ask you to open an account first so that they can see how you run it. But how do you run an account when you don't have money?' She cites examples, explaining that since starting they have looked in vain for funding. 'Either the agencies do not listen to us, or they listen and then do not fund us. You can't save when you are not making anything, but we hope to save, then join savings societies or even form our own society.' The On Sena women joined the National Chamber of Commerce but not UWEAL because it seemed to be 'above them'. They visited the government's Poverty Alleviation Programme (PAP). One day, they hope, they will get capital to inject into their business.

The On Sena group called patron John Calami, a businessman in Owino market and executive secretary of the National Chamber of Commerce, Kampala district, to assist them in running their business. He is impressed: 'They are self-sustaining despite having little capital, very little capital. They have a meeting room, share a storeroom for their bags of beans and now have the lockup at Owino. They have been clever enough to seek the knowledge they need as traders.' John believes there is a very big difference between businesswomen and men, that women are more honest and less extravagant. But they are undercapitalised, which adversely affects their businesses, and they lack the collateral to get loans.

Echoing Daisy Kayizzi's words, both Oliver and John articulated the would-be businesswomen's biggest obstacle—lack of access to enough capital to start off on a scale sufficiently large to allow growth.

Nakivubo market: a husband invests

Monica Bateganya: 6 years of school;
married with 4 children; sells curtains

Monica Bateganya sells curtains from a table at Nakivubo market. She had 6 years of education in Namusisi–Kibulu, Iganga district. All her 4 children (2 boys and 2 girls) are in school, and she says that she treats them equally. 'I am a businesswoman,' she asserts proudly. She trades in nets (curtains) purchased from wholesalers, a business she started in Nakivubo market in 1991 with about Ush 50,000 from her husband. 'I chose this as my first job because I could get income from it. I manage to run it and pay the rent by keeping good records and accounts, and subtracting expenses like eating and children's needs,' she explains, noting also that she has no employees. Problems arise when nets are lost or during a season when people do not buy.

She took and repaid a loan from a group located in Kansanga that specialises in credit for women. Praising the group, she explains: 'If they give you 250,000 shillings, the interest is 30,000 shillings over 6 months—so you can get profits and repay.' To expand her business by buying her own bales of curtains would require something like Ush 3 million, she says. 'If I could get big capital, I would change from this business to one that paid better.'

Monica first got her husband's agreement that she work. In her 7 years of trading, she has managed to buy a plot of land and cattle. Her husband, an insurance company employee, contributes the most at home, but she pays for household needs. She comments, 'Men do better than we do. Women can cry for money, but men will have it in 24 hours.' She urges young women going into business to learn how to keep capital and not lose it; accounting makes the difference. 'For example, I bought at this much, I made this much profit and so I can eat this much,' she explains.

Owino market: 21,000 women vendors

Owino market has 30,000 vendors—21,000 of them women—up from only 669 in 1990 when the market was new (Manyire 1992). Long before you approach the market entranceway, salespersons are everywhere. Inside, stalls may be open or covered. Porters lug huge bales of goods on their backs out of or into overnight storage. Women vend 'previously enjoyed' (used) and new clothes, fresh and dry produce, raw food and cooked, and almost anything else you may dream of wanting.

Owino traders—men and women—actively defend their rights. For example, when the Kampala City Council (KCC) abruptly raised monthly dues for vendors in Owino, Nakasero, Nakivubo, Nateete and other markets, Owino vendors marched to City Hall in protest. It was said that '[f]ierce clashes with police took place en route'. A 5-hour meeting between 20 of the vendors selected by their colleagues, the town clerk and other city officials led to suspension of the new rates. Some 1,000 of the 4,616 dealers in second-hand clothes participated in the protest, calling the threatened rise in rates from Ush 8,050 to 12,075 per month an injustice. Vegetable stall dues were to be raised from Ush 4,600 to 6,900 and store charges from Ush 34,500 to 51,750. Some vendors also were angered by the stall-allocation system (*The New Vision,* 5 July 1997). In addition to righting these injustices, they sought dismissal of the market chairman, who was perceived as corrupt, and who said that he would not stand for another term of office later that year, yet was still in that post in May 1998.

The Owino Women's Group—registered with the National Association of Women of Uganda (NAWOU)—brings traders together for mutual support and common causes. Some also are associated with the Uganda Veterans Assistance Board. Owino Women's Group members Margaret Nalwoga, who deals in second-hand clothing; Jacent Nakayemba, who sells vegetables and new clothes; and Deborah Kyalusi, who deals in dry produce, discuss their trade in the following paragraphs, after Market Chairman Godfrey Kayongo gives his views about them. 'To my knowledge, since 1971 when the market was established, none of the women has had any formal financial assistance,' says Kayongo, whose impressive office is off the balcony near the major market entry gate. He claims that women do not face any problem getting market stalls because they are very hard-working and more trustworthy than men; it is easy to recover money lent to them. Women are also consistent, he says. They stay in the same business for long, unlike men who keep on changing from one business to another. Some women have very good businesses—they build houses and buy taxis. 'Women are industrious despite lacking the boost to enlarge their businesses' he concludes.

Margaret Nalwoga: 2 years secondary school;
single mother with several children; sells second-hand clothes

The chairman's words are confirmed by the women's own stories. Margaret Nalwoga sells second-hand clothes (kunkumura, or 'shake and see', in Luganda). Born in Buwaya, she is a single mother who went to school up to junior secondary two. The most educated of her family is a sister who is a professor at Makerere University. Before moving to Owino, Margaret was a wholesaler of beer and soda, but the capital required to make a reasonable profit was too much for her, she says.

> Out of the profit I make in this business I have been able to build a house and educate all my children. My eldest child got a diploma in computer science. Since I started in 1990 I have [saved] about 500,000 shillings. The stall where I work is my own so I just pay tax. I decide what to do with my money because my husband died. My biggest problem is lack of capital to inject into my business or to diversify it.

Margaret's views are echoed by another dealer in second-hand clothes, who adds that the government sought to ban their business in order to protect local textile industries. 'I think they should consider this very seriously, because people cannot afford new clothes, and without the second-hand ones some people would go naked,' she says. This is a dilemma for poor countries: whether to protect their own nascent industry by imposing tariffs on imported goods or to let those industries die off by allowing cheap imports of second-hand, previously enjoyed and discarded goods from industrial countries. The issue—discussed in Chapter 5 of this book—in the case of textiles is compounded by the persistence of poverty.

What do the second-hand merchants advise someone who wishes to enter their business? 'Handle finances correctly—keep basic accounts—otherwise you will soon go bankrupt! For instance, if your start-up capital is 10,000 shillings, you should not spend more than the 10,000 shillings. Come prepared to pay taxes, work hard and save. Know that sometimes the clothes you get will not be of good quality,' they say.

Jacent Nakayemba: 4 years secondary school; married with children; sells vegetables and clothes

Jacent Nakayemba also sold second-hand clothes for a short while, then switched to vegetables and new clothes that she irons and puts on hangers. She was born, studied up to senior four and married in Mpigi district. During the seven years that her marriage lasted she sold vegetables and staples from a small stand at her home. Due to high rent and other problems, she stopped working from home and started selling tomatoes, avocados and greens in Owino market. Pointing to the kinds of uncertainties she must cope with, she explains that fresh produce is a risky business because you must purchase only the amount you can sell in the day. With no refrigeration it will go bad.

Jacent believes a newcomer in the business needs about Ush 200,000 and that it is better not to inject a lot of money at the start because things might fail. Today, one buys a bag of produce at Ush 50,000 and tomorrow it is 100,000 so it is important to have a financial reserve, although admittedly that is not easy to do. She started business in Owino in 1990 with Ush 300,000.

'I am married and my money is mine, although I contribute to home expenses,' Jacent says. 'With my earnings I have been able to pay school fees and the upkeep of my family. I tried to get a loan from one bank but failed because I had no collateral. I am not a member of any revolving fund. In fact I fear joining groups because some people I know have been cheated,' she says, expressing a view that was common not long ago but has begun to recede as the environment of business confidence grows and women gain entrepreneurial experience.

Jacent advises that before a woman starts a business, she should make a survey of the area she wants to operate in: how much money is required, what is the most suitable location, and so forth. 'For instance, locating a clothing stall near a maize mill is simply stupid! Newcomers should [also] know that most women who fail in business do so because they don't keep proper account books. They fail to separate capital from profit. I advise women to get training. I have personally benefited a great deal from seminars like Improve Your Business.'[3]

Deborah Kyalusi: 4 years secondary school then worked in government; sells dry produce

Deborah Kyalusi deals in dry produce such as beans and maize, which she and others see as one of the easier businesses although it requires more start-up capital. She stopped school at senior four, worked in government for 20 years and then used her pension money to start her business, preferring self-employment. She started with Ush 1 million in 1987, and by 1997 her business had expanded fourfold so that she could build a shop. 'We are cheated a lot,' she says. 'In order to survive in business, you must give credit, but many times people don't pay and you take a loss. We need assistance because dry produce necessitates a lot of capital that I don't have. But dry products are the only business I know, and I fear to change.'

Deborah advises persons who want to go into business to have patience, be trustworthy and practise proper bookkeeping, to ensure that capital and profit are separate. Join savings groups, she says, and before you start, seek advice from experienced traders. 'I appeal to women to go into business to get incomes, because most women must cater for all the basic needs of their children, from education to food.'

The Owino Women's Group members want to start supportive projects, but to date have failed to get the needed money. The group approached UWFT, which offered Ush 150,000, but that amount was not sufficient so they declined the offer. NAWOU can give only minimal help because it is not a loan agency. The women have a plot for a daycare centre for their children. They wrote a proposal and took it to UNICEF, NAWOU, the Ministry of Gender and Community Development, DANIDA and the vice president of Uganda. The vice president offered them a building in 1996, but the matter continues to be frustrated by city council authorities, they explain.

How dependency weakens women: a wholesaler's view

Christina Nasuna (45): 6 years primary school; separated with 8 children (plus her brother's); wholesales and retails matoke, dried fish, Irish potatoes and cowpeas

Where she lives in Mengo–Kisenyi, they call her 'mama'. Christina Nasuna is a hard-working woman who is determined to succeed and prepare for her future despite her 45 years. She was born in Mukono district where her father traded in fish, using his Land Rover for transport to widespread markets. 'I am a businesswoman,' Christina says. 'I sell wholesale to traders in matoke that I bring to Kampala from towns such as Masaka and Mbarara. I have a retail shop too.'

She insists on making up for what she lost when she conceived and had to drop out of school at primary six, as all pregnant girls were forced to do by government regulation. She is the firstborn of eight children of a father who had other wives besides her mother and many children he initially wanted to educate. Christina's pregnancy disappointed him, and he lost interest in educating the other children.

After she conceived she started teaching and marketing clothes in her home village right away. 'I wanted to work on my own so as to meet my needs,' she says, 'not rely on charity.' She found a husband, but unfortunately he was like her dad—he had many other women and many children. She pleaded with him to take her to the village because of the hard conditions in town, but he refused. 'So I separated from him. He left me with all the children and refused to take care of them. I determined to support myself and my children,' Christina says.

She became a tailor but found business unprofitable, so she got two bunches of matoke and started selling it. She kept on increasing the amount—an approach she calls mwaga mwaga, meaning 'pour and pour'. Learning by trial and error and unwilling to fail, Christina joined other traders to hire a lorry to transport the bananas but soon realised it would be more profitable to go directly to the villages to get them herself. She hired a vehicle for Ush 100,000 and went to Masaka but learned that the rental cost can go up to Ush 500,000 in bad weather. Finally she entrusted a friend to buy and bring the produce, and another friend to help retail it.

Christina learned the hard way that the matoke business is difficult. Her major problem—transport—is the one most market women must endure when dealing in perishable commodities. 'At times you hire a lorry, not knowing that it is in poor mechanical condition. Because of the load and the poor rural roads that are ruined in the rainy season, it breaks down and the matoke gets spoiled by the sun even if it was okay at the start. It is best to buy bananas that are cut and loaded in the morning ... [but not] transported [until] the evening to avoid the day's heat. Otherwise, by the time you reach Kampala you could have 100 bunches out of 400 overripe—a great loss because one must sell them cheaply and your working capital shrinks.' Another problem is thieves, but so far she has been lucky with her loads.

Problems are partially solved by diversifying stock and markets. Christina now takes small dried fish to Kigali in Rwanda and returns with Irish potatoes, cowpeas and matoke. The future can be bright, she says, if she can get a big company to whom she can supply matoke twice a week, and not sell anything on credit.

Christina's 8 children are now independent; she is especially proud of her firstborn (in 1965), a teacher whose husband recently died of AIDS. Christina has become responsible for her brother's children since his wife died, and he too will die soon. She got Ush 200,000 from the Christian Children's Fund to help pay school fees, and paid it back in small amounts over five months, without interest. She has a loan of Ush 400,000 from the Foundation for

International Community Assistance (FINCA) that she will pay back. She never tried to borrow from banks.

Now that she no longer has to support her children, Christina has opened a bank account and plans to get land in town, where she will build a house and shops and rooms for tenants so that she can stop going long distances because of her age. 'I am now 45 years old, so my future is to settle in a permanent place. My son, who completed 2 years at Makerere College School, can soon take over my business.'

Christina joins other entrepreneurs in advising young girls that capital and record-keeping are very important. In her view, women are hard-working and, if they are determined, they can be more successful than men. 'But, unfortunately,' she says, 'many women think that men will give them money. The feeling of having to depend on someone to support you weakens women.'

Marketing by streetlight, shoplight, candle or lantern

Less well off than the women selling fresh and dried produce and clothing in official market areas like Kasubi, Wandegeya and Owino are those who sell cooked food in the markets of last resort—the 'candlelight markets' (Obbo 1980). Toninyira mukange (TM) is a Luganda phrase that means 'step not in mine' and refers to the roadside markets that appear in the suburban and poorer areas of Kampala and other cities and towns along pedestrian routes, at road intersections and matatu stations, bars and other locations where people pass or gather. The vendors are not usually licensed and often sell cooked food from makeshift tables or mats. The most intense hours are eight to eleven in the evening when both men and women sell. It is these markets that attract illiterate women and those who have very little primary education, according to a recent study by Nakanyike Musisi (1995). A third of the women she interviewed were widows, orphans or persons displaced by war or AIDS. Another third were separated or divorced, and the final third were either single or refused to reveal their marital status. Most are sole supporters of their families; some supplement husband's incomes.

Paying or sharing the rent of a single room and meeting school fees are their major concerns. More than 75 per cent of those surveyed opened business with only small amounts of capital; about 37 percent had worked as porters or in other low-status occupations to save enough capital to start their own businesses; about 12 per cent were financed by relatives, friends, husbands or partners. Very few had inheritances or had borrowed money to start their businesses.

Among the problems night-market vendors face is the time-consuming nature of their work, which demands shopping, cooking, then vending. In addition, tough competition forces prices down; roadside conditions can be unhealthy; and petty thievery and robbery are quite frequent. Women endure this life because income frees them from dependency; they can support themselves and their families. Musisi says, 'There is no question that TM has enabled some women to achieve some semblance of freedom from dependence on male relatives. In this way, it has liberated them from some of the unnecessary social controls that emerge from economic dependence.' Besides paying rent and school fees, the women use their earnings to meet daily needs of their households for food, soap, oil and the like, as well as buy clothing and obtain health care.

Women usually manage to get spaces on the well-lit streets and near to other women, usually female relatives. Men and boys work the more lonely streets. Men trade in luxury goods by day or evening while women sell foods raw or cooked—the latter following ethnic preferences. Two thirds of those selling cooked foods are women, who range in age from 15 to over 70, while most of the males are young boys who can't pay school fees; the few men who are older than 40 seek to supplement their meagre incomes from day jobs. Musisi finds a 'stunning gender bias' in explanations as to why most TM vendors are women: '[T]hey cook good food, they lure customers persuasively, and they have more patience than men, it is said. Some men even accuse women of coming into the market to find lovers so that they can retire from poverty.'

Despite its hardships, 'TM is a very empowering experience for the women who participate in it,' Musisi concludes. Her researchers found the market women 'very aggressive and very money minded'—a fact that she attributes to the emergence of a 'minicapitalist spirit'. The women 'behave as if they were men, they are very aggressive [and] cannot be easily threatened like women in the old days.' That is a dramatic transformation in women's lives. 'Yet they are still able to accommodate their indigenous social, cultural, political and economic frameworks,' she adds (Musisi 1995).

Eviction of streetside traders

The threat of eviction earlier mentioned is constant and can be a sudden reality for traders in candlelight markets or on the streets. The case of Kikuubo is illustrative. In February 1996, women vendors prepared foods for 1,500 people who could buy generous portions of chicken and matoke for Ush 1,200 to 1,500, and beans and matoke for Ush 700. That was until the KCC stepped in and confiscated the women's crockery, utensils and stoves, accusing them of using premises illegally (*The Crusader*, 1 March 1996). In one Kampala study, 12 per cent of entrepreneurs reported eviction as their major problem in the past year (Impact Associates 1995). Petty streetside trades and some business stalls were instantly ruled illegal by the KCC when the Local Government/ Resistance Council Statute of 1993 decentralised functions, powers and responsibilities, giving KCC new power over the markets.

Those evicted were hawkers and footloose vendors, the lowest classes of traders, known for their 'survival and micro enterprise businesses' (Ssonko 1997 quoting Mensink 1995).

They were angry. 'It is not only foreign investors who matter in Uganda. What about us who honestly put our savings together to be self-employed?' Charles Katende complained. Jane Mweddle added, 'I accept that we delayed heeding the KCC order, but that is no excuse to rob and assault us like criminals. I have a family to feed. Don't these people understand that?' (*The New Vision*, 23 Nov. 1995). The male evictees traded in handkerchiefs, glassware, plastics, shoes, bags, suitcases, cosmetics, clothes, bedsheets, towels, sugar, salt, cooking oil and soap. It was only women who sold cooked foods (Ssonko 1997: 39). Most of the women were young—between 20 and 30 years of age, married with dependants and had at least primary school education. Relocating after eviction, they tended to move to legally designated areas in evening markets, while the young men turned to hawking.

Commercial sex work: Is it economic enterprise?

Another difficult way for jobless women to survive with their families is commercial sex work. The sex sector, as it is sometimes called, has long been internationally classified with drug dealing, smuggling and armed robbery as doing little for the national economy and thus is not considered part of the productive informal sector—until now. A recent study by the International Labour Organisation (ILO) takes a different stance, identifying the sex sector as 'flourishing economic enterprise' whose revenues are 'crucial to the livelihoods and earnings potential of millions of workers beyond the prostitutes themselves.' Prostitutes in Thailand, for example, send the equivalent of US$300 million to rural relatives annually, and overall annual income from prostitution is estimated by experts as between US$22 and $27 billion (*The New York Times*, 19 Aug. 1998).

Some trace the sex trade in Uganda to returning World War II veterans who had learned about prostitution overseas, while others trace it to the Indian workers who built the Uganda Railways in the early twentieth century (*Arise*, Jan. 1997). In recent years, international peacekeeping troops that passed through Entebbe Airport and stayed in the best hotels of Kampala en route to Rwanda enhanced the trade. Writer Mary Okurut explains that at the time, the police cracked down on the sellers of sex as criminals, but not on the buyers, and in the process bargained with the women to give them sex too

(*Arise*, 1997: 24). Whatever its origin, prostitution thrives in Uganda as elsewhere today. In Kampala, charges range from Ush 1,000 to 40,000, varying with the location of the seller and the customer's ability to pay. Young, unemployed women find that they can earn enough to pay their rent, eat and dress well. In Kampala they turn to locations such as Kabalagala, the Speke Hotel and the Ange Noir night club. It is said that university students are among those working in the sector.

A prostitute is defined as 'a person who in public or elsewhere regularly or habitually holds himself or herself out as available for sexual intercourse or other sexual gratification for monetary or other material gains.' With that definition, prostitution was made illegal in Uganda in 1990, although, as women comment, its criminalisation has not solved the problem. On the contrary, it appears to have increased, and 'the legal status of prostitutes causes them incredible suffering. Prostitutes can be raped or robbed by clients and have no legal recourse.' ACFODE sees the cause in the socio-economic circumstances that women find themselves in, and has called on the public to 'tackle that root cause' (*Arise*, 1997: 2).

Josephine Ahikire, lecturer in women studies at Makerere, reminds colleagues that prostitution is a social act: 'Once there is a seller there is definitely a buyer.' She asks why the buyer of the services is 'always placed in oblivion' (*Arise*, 1997: 13). Mary Okurut asks, 'Who is the prostitute and who is not?' She names the law enforcement officer as a prostitute too, and sees the escalation in prostitution as a symptom of an ailing economy: 'The World Bank may say the economy is improving, but it is improving for a small section of our community. The rest live in abject poverty. The SAPs have impoverished a big chunk of our community, especially the women. Thus, so many women who were running small kiosks effectively have been thrown out of business' (Ibid. 1997). She adds that under the bite of poverty, young men do not wish to take on the responsibilities of a family, and since they 'cannot afford a girlfriend', they turn to prostitutes.

Women who live in slums like Nakulabye, near Kampala, are among those who sell foods, raw and cooked, in the night market and find their incomes too small in the face of the big roles they play as mothers and housewives. The Slum Aid Project, an NGO formed by five Makerere University students in 1991, works in seven Kampala slums, finding ways to help people help themselves out of their poverty.[4] The Slum Aid Project's coordinator, Rose Gawaya, explains that the capital they have is very small so growth is hard. 'A few women get money from their husbands and of course some thrive from prostitution, which sometimes looks like the only way out.'

Recent studies by the Slum Aid Project of Kampala and a smaller northern city, Lira, are the first in Uganda to document child prostitution. In Lira, where a striking 28 per cent of girls have sex by the age of 10, young prostitutes say that economic conditions drive them into the trade. In Kampala a prostitute can earn anywhere from Ush 1,000 to 40,000 from clients. She is likely to be illiterate (64 per cent) and have no dependants (*The New Vision*, 20 Jan. 1998). The Slum Aid Project offers counselling, training and revolving credit so women can open hair salons and other shops, and organises sports, dance and drama for the younger girls.

Rose Gawaya and her colleagues are entrepreneurs for the poor, using training and credit funds to help women lift themselves out of the slums. Some have been able to meet the aspirations of all the women in this study—and purchase land, build houses and send their children to school.

The country in the city: urban agriculture

Most of the entrepreneurs interviewed for this study are found in markets or shops or seen along the streets. But there are women and men whose informal-sector economic activity is less visible while not less valuable to them. They are the urban farmers and home-based workers among the 65 per cent of Africa's labour force who find their livelihood in the informal economy, producing foods or goods, for sale or barter, or simply for the family to eat.

In the early 1960s many Kampala workers grew at least part—probably as much as two thirds—of their food (Mukwaya 1962). By the early 1990s, estimates were more refined: Thirty-six per cent of Kampala households were believed to produce nearly half (45 per cent) of their food needs through urban agriculture. In fact, some 20 per cent of Kampala's total food supply—including most of the chickens—is produced right in the city. Beans, maize, cassava, sweet potatoes, bananas and vegetables are grown, and chickens, rabbits and cows are reared, in the city; more than one quarter of Kampala land is farmed (Maxwell 1992 in Musiimenta 1997).

The practise of farming within Kampala's city limits multiplied like other informal-economy activities when jobs were lost during Idi Amin's economic war and when the structural adjustment initiated lay-offs occurred a decade later. People's response to those crises was to produce their own food in their backyard, their front yard, on the roadside or any other open space in the city. Speaking of the IMF's SAPs and their effects, development researcher Emmanuel Nabuguzi explains:

> Urban agriculture developed both as a means of survival and as a fully-fledged commercial activity.... An informal distribution network

> operates among families participating in urban farming—for example, a medical doctor receives gifts of food. (Nabaguzi 1994)

Even though urban agriculture meets food needs, there is some strong disagreement about its value and propriety: '...the ruralisation of urban areas through the invasion of cities and towns by subsistence agriculture and rural poverty euphemistically called urban agriculture symptomises ... decay,' says Jossy Bibangambah, who adds, 'The argument by several writers that urban agriculture has an important contribution to make to Africa's economic development is unhelpful.... If it is as backward and trapped in vicious circles of poverty as rural agriculture which also provides food and self-employment, it is no answer to our search for sustainable development' (Bibangambah 1992).

The Urban Authority Act of 1972 made urban agriculture illegal, but the Kampala Urban Study (KUS) plan for 1994–2008 reversed that decision, proposing that guidelines be issued for city farmers. As of 1996, neither guidelines nor a permit system existed (Musiimenta 1997). Few city farmers have security of land tenure, so most are squatters whose farms are on their landlords' premises, along the roadside or on vacant lots. There is always the threat that tomorrow such farms will be abolished, as they were when Pope John Paul II visited Uganda and roadside produce was pulled up for security reasons.

Who are the urban farmers? Educator Peace Musiimenta tells us that women—two thirds of whom are married and between ages 25 and 44—provide 81 per cent of the labour in crop cultivation and 75 per cent in livestock. Even when they have husbands present, the crop and livestock decisions are almost always theirs. Substantial numbers of them combine their cultivation with related small enterprises: food kiosks, restaurants and bars, market stalls and maize roasting. More than half have primary or secondary education; only 1 in 10 has none (Musiimenta 1997 quoting Maxwell 1993 and Camillus 1993).

What draws women to city farming? For most, the motivation is economic. Because they can save the cash that they would have spent purchasing food, the vulnerability they and their children face during times of economic crises is reduced. One of Musiimenta's interviewees testifies to her responsibility for household survival:

> I have many children, and the salary of my husband is not enough. I cannot sit and watch my children starve or go to the streets. Therefore I had to look around for any survival strategy. I would have preferred business, but where could I get capital? The only alternative at my disposal was to use the compound for cultivation.

Another says:

> Life in Kampala has become so hard that some men are at a standstill and seem not to think any more. So as a woman I had to do something in order that my children and I would not sleep hungry. Apart from digging or keeping chickens what else can I do together with teaching?

Men's interests are in commercial urban agriculture, like poultry farming, and they sometimes step in with support when they see their wives succeed. But for women 'any agricultural activity, whether large or small, is enjoyable because it improves their socio-economic status in society.' Productivity also earns women the respect of their husbands—also a motivation of the market women of Kasubi: '...[W]hen men say that women's decisions in urban agriculture are authentic, it reflects the respect they have in women as equal partners in the upkeep of the family' (Musiimenta 1997).

Despite problems such as land security, women urban agriculturists identify lack of capital as their biggest problem. Without capital investment they are unable to diversify, to augment household income or hedge against inflation. Lack of credit results in high failure rates, low yields, limited capital inputs and keeps urban agriculture at a subsistence level, according to Musiimenta, who urges urban farmers to form themselves into associations so that they may acquire low-interest loans and entandikwa (start-up capital) and establish their contributions to the economy—contributions that are essential to the survival of urban populations.

When years of experience with urban agriculture allow women to relax a bit, they take great pride in their gardens. One woman waxes poetic:

> Most of the crops we grow in the city are treated like flowers. I just feel proud and love to look at my small garden of beans and maize in my compound, especially in the evening when I am relaxing from the day's routine work. (Musiimenta 1997: 73)

A less visible economy: home-based enterprises (HBEs)

In most socio-economic literature, the home is seen simply as a reproductive unit. Home-based workers defy that definition, making it an economically productive place even to those who do not yet consider household work as economic. The opportunity to work while remaining at home and watching over children—achieving some measure of economic independence—seems ideal for young mothers, among them women of Kampala. It also defies the view that the man is the sole breadwinner.

Worldwide, millions of women work within the privacy of their homes in a variety of kinds of paid employment. Their invisibility has disadvantages.

Home-based workers are out of the reach of protective legislation, a fact that has led to the formation of HomeNet, an International Network for Home-based Workers. HomeNet lobbied for and achieved the adoption of a convention by the ILO, which recognises that women working out of their homes are in fact workers who should have the same protection and rights as other workers.[5]

Like other types of informal-sector activity, home-based enterprises (HBEs) mushroomed in Kampala in the 1970s and '80s with the macroeconomic disequilibrium and consequent destruction of wage-earning opportunities. It is estimated that 21 per cent of Kampala's women-owned enterprises are home-based (Impact Associates 1995). The trade and sale of cooked foods dominate business conducted from home, but many women sell charcoal, cold drinks, fresh foods, meats and sweets. They also brew beer, make clothing and crafts, and farm; one in 10 engages in services such as baby-sitting, hairdressing, providing basic health care, and operating small nurseries (Mbaalu–Mukasa 1996).

Half of the interviewees in the study by women studies researcher Maureen Mbaalu–Mukasa had never been employed, but the other half were able to use their own personal savings as start-up capital. A third of them got initial capital from their spouse and just 15 per cent from other informal credit sources. Credit, when needed, was almost always (95 per cent) from informal sources—friends, relatives, and shopkeepers. Just over half (52 per cent) of the HBEs have received any credit at all. Less than a third had informal groups for credit or mutual support, among them a few ROSCAs.

The most common motivation for women to start an HBE is the same as other informal-sector employment—economic need. They are pressed to increase the household budget, or face a calamity, such as separation or the death of a spouse. An HBE can be initiated with little capital—the main reason for selecting it—and it allows for simultaneous pursuit of domestic responsibilities; compared to the market or other outside employment, it has limited overhead costs, such as rent and transport.

A serious problem—one that all but wealthy entrepreneurs face—is the drain of profits to household and family expenses. This usually leaves little capital for reinvestment in the business and thus eliminates any possibility of growth: Forty per cent of the householders interviewed derived all—and another 29 per cent at least half—of their income from their HBE. Those financial constraints also leave women working on their own: Eighty-seven per cent do not employ any labour, not even family members.

The Mbaalu–Mukasa study found that income from an enterprise is determined by the initial capital investment, the capital base, the educational level of the entrepreneur and the proportion of household income that is taken from profits. The level of pre-business planning and record-keeping also made a significant difference. Each of these factors, which influence the availability of capital for reinvestment, appears often in this book. Of note also is that many highly successful entrepreneurs whose interviews are presented in subsequent chapters got their start working from home.

Today's market trader: a profile

As seen in Table 2.1 at the end of this chapter, most of the 17 entrepreneurs interviewed in Kampala markets for this study are in their 30s or 40s, as are the urban farmers. A wider age range—from the very young to the very old—is found in the night markets, which also absorb young women evicted from illegal trading places.

The businesswomen interviewed have been in their current businesses for many years—two for more than 20 years—and those who have fewer than 10 years (none less than 4) previously engaged in other businesses. By contrast, among the HBEs, four out of 5 have less than 5 years in their business and half have never been employed before—confirming the likelihood that a number of them will move into small- or medium-scale business.

When the experience and advice of all of the entrepreneurial groups are compiled, the findings of the HBE study are confirmed, namely: that the level of education of the entrepreneur and the amount of start-up capital are important indicators of future income, as is the proportion of profits drawn off for family responsibilities rather than reinvested. Business-planning and bookkeeping are considered essential.

Issues raised at the beginning of this chapter can now be discussed:

Education: a head start to success

1. Does the level of an entrepreneur's education influence the type and size of her business?

The evidence of this chapter is that socio-economic class—strongly influenced by education—is a very evident determinant of one's position and one's profit in the marketplace. The Kampala market entrepreneurs interviewed for this study are literate, and most entered secondary school although many dropped out before completing it. Most home-based entrepreneurs have had primary education, one in five has had secondary and only one in ten none at all. The majority of urban farmers also have had primary or secondary and only one in ten have had none. The night-market women, in contrast, are either illiterate or have had little primary education.

Education also has a bearing on the amount of initial capital one has or can accumulate in a relatively short period. Workers in the night market have had little if any education and start with little capital; they have to run fast to stand still and, even worse, their daughters follow them onto the same treadmill: Some 62 per cent of the candlelight marketers had mothers in the same business, and 40 per cent dropped out of school due to pregnancy. That contrasts sharply with entrepreneurs who have enjoyed even primary, and more likely, secondary, schooling, whose children attain far higher levels of education than their parents.

Entandikwa: start-up capital as indicator of future earnings

> 2. *What are the sources of start-up capital, and how does its size influence business growth?*

'If you have little capital, you get little profit, but if you have much capital, you get big profits.' That observation holds true for home-based entrepreneurs whose 'petty business produces meagre incomes that cannot enable women to have substantial savings for reinvestment' (Mbaalu–Mukasa 1996). In the HBE survey, start-up capital was small: Two thirds used less than Ush 100,000 and most less than 20,000, indicating that capital base significantly determines level of profit. With a bare minimum of capital, the night-market women remain mired—as do many of their daughters—while the children of entrepreneurs having more education and more start-up capital become a new generation, surpassing their parents.

Teddy at Wandegeya and Deborah at Owino exemplify the rule that the size of start-up capital is a predictor of earnings. Their initial investments were significantly larger than the others. Teddy, who had worked several years and built up trust among those from whom she purchased goods to sell, paid Ush 1.5 million to construct her wholesale shop and in return is free from rent for 15 years; others pay Ush 3,400 a month for a stall and an additional 3,000 for electricity. She added Ush 500,000 to purchase initial stock—bringing the total cost of setting up her business to Ush 2 million. Deborah's government pension became her initial capital, and she smartly invested that Ush 1 million in dry, non-perishable vegetables like peas and beans, then later built herself a shop from the fourfold expansion of her earnings.

Kalerwe market's Margaret Ssajjabi is a major exception to the rule about the size of initial investment: she has thrived from a smaller capital base and is without competition—the most entrepreneurial of all the market women interviewed for this study. After working with the police and the UEB, like Teddy, she got goods on consignment and started selling soda, beer, soap powder and the like. She saved her money and bought land—and more land.

She has put roofs over her mother's head and her own and still rents out 2 houses, 27 market spaces and a yard for parking 50 vehicles. Margaret has supported her own 6 children and 19 children of relatives. Her business philosophy is succinct: 'Be patient. When you are patient you can win. And you have to be confident. Develop the skills of your trade and don't beg off and say, "I am just a woman".'

Men get initial capital from moneylenders who are their relatives or friends, but 'there are not many women who have money to lend,' says Margaret. Researcher Kinuthia Macharia found the same in Kenya's informal sector: 'Because traditionally they have had no access to capital, women to this day cannot offer each other the same financial support to start a business as men do' (Macharia 1997). Henry Manyire, a women studies lecturer studying Owino and Jinja markets, found as we did that 'few husbands provided start-up capital' (Manyire 1992).

Financial success like Margaret's is unusual in any country. But success in terms of the capacity to create wealth to care for the children and others for whom you are responsible can be within reach, as the lives of these market women testify. Very, very few of them had any hand-out or loan to get going. They started, saved and worked—little by little—to build their businesses. They built reputations for being trustworthy. Wholesalers knew they would get their money when they gave goods on consignment. Daisy at Kasubi expresses the vision of many of her fellows: 'My long-time experience in business tells me that I cannot fail because even if you incur losses, you see to it that you start afresh.'

Motivation: human development as a different measure of profit

3. What motivates market traders, urban farmers and home-based workers to become entrepreneurs?

While the level of initial capital can be a predictor of future growth in business and a significant determinant of the level of profits, the achievements of many of Kampala's market entrepreneurs testify that profits are not always evidenced by a growth of the business. Rather, they show up in investments. Margaret and Betty in Kasubi are among those whose investments are impressive. Margaret began business baking mandazi and frying pancakes, then accumulated Ush 8,000 as initial capital for her fresh vegetable business. She has clothed, fed and educated her children, and in addition purchased a plot and built a 3-room house on it. Betty, another widow, started with a meagre Ush 600: She has built a house and the eldest of her 8 children attends university. These women surely are not wealthy, but their high motivation led them to create wealth where there was none and bring a good life not only to themselves but to many children and other dependants.

Jacent at Owino started with Ush 300,000 and with her profits has paid school fees and the upkeep of her family. The widowed Margaret at Owino has a house and has also educated her children; her current capital is Ush 500,000. Teddy at Kasubi, who started with just Ush 50,000, says that she has been able 'to help the children and get what my husband could not give me. Working means that you cannot fail to get enough to eat and to support yourself.' Daisy echoes this sentiment: 'at least you can get a shilling for your child to study, to eat.' How different these views are from those of the respondents to Manyire's queries, whom he records as saying 'yes' when asked whether women traders neglected their children (Manyire 1992).

At Wandegeya, Miriam started business with just 2 bunches of bananas. She began working as a housegirl in her teens, with no formal education whatsoever. Now she has a plot, a house and a houseful of dependants including children, sister, aunt and a grandchild. Monica, in the second-hand curtains business in Nakivubo market, was given just Ush 50,000 entandikwa by her husband and has prospered well enough to purchase a plot and cattle, among other assets. Margaret at Wandegeya, who took over her aunt's fruit and vegetable stand and added Ush 4,000 of her own capital to buy sugarcane and 2 bunches of ndizi, also has a house filled with extended family, including the now elderly aunt. She is proud to have met the school requirements and health costs of her children. She reflects the views of many: 'The husband will say "I have no money" so the wife finds money to treat a sick child.'

Urban farmers ensure family food availability and hedge against inflation by producing their own food. Theirs is largely an occupation for married women, who comprise 68 per cent of Musiimenta's sample. Substantial numbers of them sell, or process and sell, the foods they produce (Musiimenta 1997). HBEs also benefit not only from opportunities to combine domestic responsibilities with cash income but also from very low overhead—neither rent nor transport to a workplace. They too put their earnings into household maintenance: Some 40 per cent provide all of the household needs; another 29 per cent provide half or more (Mbaalu-Mukasa 1996).

Yet one of the greatest challenges facing women in the marketplace is actually back at the household: the families they—and more frequently they alone—must support even when a husband is present. That responsibility eats up profits that might otherwise be reinvested in businesses, and their limited access to capital locks them into that pattern.

The credit dilemma: when capital isn't enough

4. Is capital available for business expansion?

Undercapitalisation is the curse of entrepreneurs. Their commitments to 'family first' use up potential reinvestment capital, and market women are severely constrained by sparse opportunities for obtaining credit to expand their businesses. When credit does become available, as is occurring with the global upsurge of interest in micro enterprise and MFIs (sixty of the latter in Uganda; see Chapter 3), interest rates are formidable. Even non-profit organisations charge 30 per cent or more a year on a 4-month loan. As a result, very few of the market women interviewed have taken loans from formal or informal finance institutions, and the situation of night-market women is worse: Just 12 per cent have external finance, and what they get is from friends or relatives. Urban farmers identify lack of capital as their biggest problem, despite other difficulties they face, such as crop security. Just over half of the HBEs get any credit at all, and those who do find informal sources: friends, relatives and shopkeepers. Getting goods on consignment remains a primary means of credit for many entrepreneurs who have built up reputations for reliability; the possibilities it offers ought to be more widely disseminated.

Three members of Kasubi Women's Forum repaid loans of Ush 50,000 to 100,000, but 2 of them are having difficulty with their second loans. The unseasonal rains from El Niño that drenched Kampala day after day and an economy that is not increasing jobs fast enough to keep potential customers from cutting back their household budgets suppress demand. For example, Margaret repaid Ush 6,800 weekly for 4 months in 1997. A year later, she says the season is lost because rains spoiled the harvest. She continues to repay her loan but has to deny her family in order to do so. Betty did not take a loan through the Forum because of expenses for a sick child; she joined a ROSCA and saves about Ush 30,000 a month.

The chairperson and treasurer of the Obumu Women's Group in Wandegeya market each repaid their first loans with ease and are repaying the second one from UWFT. Monica in Nakivubo, finding the 6-monthly interest rate of 12 per cent agreeable, praises the group that makes the loan. The women of Owino are less successful: Jacent failed to obtain credit from a bank because she has no collateral, and the Owino Women's Group failed to get enough money to meet their needs; Ush 150,000 was too little, so they refused it.

Oliver Ntale of the Kaveda Army Veterans poses the catch-22 dilemma her group and innumerable others face: 'When you go to financial institutions seeking funding they ask you to open a bank account first so that they can see how you run it. But how do you run an account when you don't have enough money?' The veterans searched in vain for an organisation to help them. Either the agencies do not listen to them, or they listen politely but do not fund. But their hopes remain high to get capital to inject into their business one day.

Economic empowerment: some trade-offs

5. How do women in urban marketplaces invest their income? What trade-offs are involved?

'Onions are my husband,' a Ghanaian market woman says (Clark 1994), meaning that she depends on her business rather than on a husband to meet her needs for money. Marketer Margaret Ssajjabi explains why she too holds that belief: 'It is easier to work when alone, not married. Men want you to be lesser persons, to wash their clothes.'

The market entrepreneurs in this study are about equally divided between those living with husbands (the term 'husband' is undefined) and single heads of household, who are widowed, separated or single mothers. More home-based entrepreneurs are married—fifty-eight per cent; in contrast, at least 4 of every 5—and maybe more—night-market women are self-supporting. All have children living with them, both their own and those of relatives. The married businesswomen still have a very strong measure of economic empowerment. Margaret Ssewanyana notes that if you are working before marriage, the husband cannot force you to stop; Teddy Nakasumba says that her husband allows her to work but does not strongly support it. Those women continue to work. Manyire says that 74 per cent of his respondents found men 'suspicious of wives who were traders', and nearly two thirds of them said they would quit trading if their husbands wanted them to. That was 1990, and times seem to have changed.

Esther at Kasubi market identifies a reason for the growing presence of women in markets: When wives work, spousal abuse declines, and that is a strong motivation for women to do business. In the case of urban farming, Musiimenta finds that women's productivity earns respect from their husbands. To women worldwide, with evidence from Peru to India, that is a very important value (Snyder 1995). The other side of that coin is that when wives work, husbands become lax about supporting their families, as numerous respondents say. There is some question, however, whether men actually carried full responsibility for the home; it may be that a myth was created by society to keep marriages in place.[6] Esther's assessment is: 'In reality many men are working, but ... they are no longer as strong in business as in the past. Men now let women meet the domestic requirements.' That view is widely shared.

One Owino entrepreneur has strong views about what she perceives as men's radically changed attitudes toward their families and households: 'Most times, when a man knows that you earn some money, he relegates the household upkeep to you and just remains as a figurehead of the family. If he pays school fees for the children, he considers that a lot! In fact, when a woman sees that the burden of keeping the household rests on her, she may prefer to stay on her own.' Night-market women are said to hold that view and seek freedom from dependency on male relatives: '[Marketing] has liberated them from some of the unnecessary social controls that emerge from economic dependency.... They are very aggressive and cannot be easily threatened like women in the old days' (Musisi 1995: 20). Matoke wholesaler Christina adds a caveat that some women who are not strong continue to expect men to give them money. 'That attitude weakens them,' she says.

Whether spoken or left unsaid, market-women's attitudes have changed profoundly since the Manyire study, actually completed in 1990, when 87 per cent of respondents said that it is man's obligation to provide for the family. While 4 of 5 also had no objection to women's involvement in trade, some 62 per cent said then that a housewife is more respected than a trader. That view is transformed today, when large numbers of women of all classes are both housewives and businesswomen.

Obstacles: women's work isn't work

6. What external obstacles do traders confront?

Women's willingness to pay household expenses when they work in the market is an obstacle they themselves create, but it should not come as a surprise. It is easiest to comprehend by observing the wide variety of unpaid labour in which women engage, thinking it a necessary contribution to the household—as 'women's work'. Personal labour and income are thus interchangeable, and women expect to meet household needs. Therein lies a contradiction: If labour and income are interchangeable, it is absurd to count as work only that labour that is paid in actual currency. Because 'what is not counted does not count', as scholars often observe,[7] the failure to give women's labour a monetary value leaves them out of national accounts and planning. It denies them access to resources that would boost both their own and the national productivity and income. This missed opportunity suppresses national economic growth.

Nowhere is that truth more vivid than in the field of agriculture, urban as well as rural. Peace Musiimenta sums up the contradiction: 'Urban agriculture carried out largely by women is vital to the livelihood of a significant proportion of the population, on the one hand, and is treated as less important on the other.' The same holds for women's domestic work, which 'is neither paid nor regarded as work'. Even though HBE transforms the home from a reproductive to a productive unit, because the productivity takes place behind closed doors it is left uncounted (Musiimenta 1997). Yet agriculture, animal husbandry, childcare, household maintenance and home industries can all be remunerated on the market.

That irony of women's making important contributions to the family economy while men get the credit as head of household is described by Hilda Tadria:

> A man who earns cash is highly regarded even if he cannot feed his family, whereas a woman who is 'merely' a subsistence producer is undervalued even if she feeds her family. It follows ... that with the existing division of labour, a man is highly regarded and not the woman because [even if she is earning cash] she is essentially a dependent (Tadria 1987 quoted by Musiimenta 1997).

Musiimenta's conclusion that urban agriculture is a step toward women's empowerment and recognition of their work rings true with this study's findings. It reduces gender inequality since 'the practice empowers women to contribute to their families' livelihood...'. Women make most of the decisions on production and thus improve their socio-economic status. The choice of economic autonomy over spousal dependence is a trade-off women seem increasingly willing to make even when it means that their capital base and personal earnings remain small. They prefer to control their own earnings and have less spousal abuse (including physical violence) although it means that they must take greater financial responsibility for the children and other domestic requirements when men become lax about supporting families.

More obstacles: beyond personal and sometimes even human control

'At times even God doesn't help you. Even when you are able to get wholesale produce, you fail to get buyers because of the rain,' says a Kasubi vegetable trader. Another says, 'If you go to the villages to buy for yourself, you may spend a month out there with these rains. And while you are there your produce ripens and rots, or the lorry breaks down and your produce gets spoiled by the sun.' The size of many market-women's businesses and their consequent fragility make them highly susceptible to forces beyond their control: The combination of monsoon-scale rains, poorly constructed and maintained farm-to-market roads and worn-out trucks is devastating for the fresh food vendor. But economic hard times can be the most devastating of all.

'People don't have money these days,' a vendor laments. That may mean selling on credit. Some pay later, others don't pay at all. Sometimes thieves steal the produce en route from the countryside. Urban farmers lose it to passers-by, right from their fields, for it is nearly impossible to make them secure if they are outside your own compound. Petty thievery and robbery are not unknown to any marketer, day or night. And many traders are totally insecure: They have no legitimate place to vend their wares; they are the footloose and transient traders who may be subject to the will and whim of the city council any day as new laws are passed or old ones suddenly enforced.

'The world is now difficult,' Betty tells us. Competition threatens profits when SAPs require retrenching civil servants, and economic insecurity characterises all wage employment. As a result, better-educated people take up part-time entrepreneurship, competing with full-time marketers and driving individual profits downward at a time of shrinking demand, when purchasers' pocketbooks are empty. SAPs bring extra burdens to women, who must use their own time and energy for family health care when they can't pay the shared costs the government introduced, even while clinic and hospital services decline.

Society needs to clarify and redefine 'investment' and 'consumption' when used concerning gender, initially by avoiding use of outdated western stereotypes that identify men as investors and women as consumers. It is very often the woman who invests—both financially and in unpaid labour—in future growth, starting with human development. Consumption for personal purposes not infrequently characterises the male spouse's use of a significant portion of his profits. The irony here is that a man has more profits because he is better positioned to add to his start-up and growth capital through loans from fellow men or from the formal banking system (Macharia 1997). This current scenario reflects a neo-colonial image: It perpetuates man's priority access to and control over resources rather than fostering a democratic access that would broaden the base of development. The family and the nation are the losers.

Recapitulation

The night traders are on the lowest rung of the socio-economic ladder with home-based entrepreneurs next; urban farmers and entrepreneurs in established markets are the best off. Key variables that significantly influence the financial growth potential of an enterprise are the level of education of the businesswoman, the size of her initial capital and the extent of family responsibility that affects her ability to reinvest profits in the business. Three of the 17 market entrepreneurs interviewed for this study were highly successful on the basis of those variables: They started large enough enterprises to have income for family responsibilities while retaining a surplus for reinvestment in the business. Others also created wealth, but not to the extent that significant business expansion was possible after meeting family responsibilities.

There is another success to be measured, however, besides business profits. That is inter-generational change: the extent to which an entrepreneur invests her profits in the education and well-being of children—Uganda's promise and future labour force. From that perspective the achievements of the urban market women, farmers and home-based workers are impressive despite the overwhelmingly difficult working conditions and heavy responsibilities many of them must endure. Their priorities shine through their life stories: to provide food and healthy lives for the children and others who depend on them; to educate their children to the extent possible—well beyond their own formal learning; and to possess a plot of land with their own home on it. However humble that home may be, it is a family's social security. Most of the women interviewed for this study had achieved that much.

Clearly such a choice—to invest in human well-being—is a trade-off with the accumulation of wealth when it constricts reinvestment in business. Investment in human development also contrasts with immediate consumption of profits, which respondents and others say many men choose, namely, to take another woman or wife, or to enjoy socialising. Those patterns call into question the internationally received wisdom that women are consumers; men invest.

The entrepreneurs interviewed for this study average 14 years in business. Their record of repaying the loans they get is excellent, and it appears that after surviving in business so many years they know how to manage. What is unclear is why there are so few sources of capital available to them that are commensurate with their capacities: why there is so little credit and venture capital to invest in their businesses for the sake not only of their families but of the nation's economic growth.

[1] ROSCA, for rotating savings and credit association, is an autonomous type of savings group rather than an organisation with branches.

[2] Several districts of central Uganda formerly comprised the Kingdom of Buganda, ruled by the kabaka (king) and enjoying a special land-use system under colonialism. Taxes are still paid to the kabaka in some areas.

[3] Entrepreneurship and skills-training seminars for micro and small entrepreneurs offered by the PSDP. MFIs such as UWFT offer similar courses.

[4] The Slum Aid Project is commonly known by the acronym 'SAP'; however, to avoid confusion, the full name of the Slum Aid Project is used in this text, and the acronym SAP always refers to structural adjustment programme.

[5] See http://www.gn.apc.org/homenet/ilo.html.

[6] Lynn Khadiagala's ongoing study of women in Kabale suggests that women always contributed much more to the household than was overtly recognised.

[7] The United Nations Statistical Office (UNSO) has a series of publications on counting women's work, some of them co-sponsored with the UN International Research and Training Institute for the Advancement of Women (INSTRAW). See, for example, United Nations, 1993, *Methods of Measuring Women's Economic Productivity*, also United Nations, 1990 and 1995, *The World's Women*. Author Marilyn Waring takes an iconoclastic approach to the subject in her 1988 publication, *If Women Counted: A New Feminist Economics*.

Table 2.1. Market traders

Name	Margaret Namuga	Teddy Nakasumba	Betty Nakiganda	Madina Nampijja
Age	46	34	48	40ish
Education	3 yrs secondary	1 yr secondary	—	1 yr secondary
Marital status	widowed	married	widowed	married
Dependents	5 children	6 children	6 children	4 children
Previous employment	sold cooked food	none	sold clothing	—
Business	sells vegetables	sells vegetables	sells cassava	sells potatoes
Employees	0	0	0	0
Spousal reaction	N/A	limited approval	N/A	approves
Amount of start-up capital	Ush 8,000 in 1980 = ± US$1,143	Ush 50,000 in 1987*	Ush 600 in 1982*	Ush 20,000 in 1994 = ± US$20
Source of start-up capital	self, from home budget	—	self	self
Source of loans/credit	UWFT; KMWF	—	ROSCA	KMWF
Owns land?	yes	yes	yes	yes
How income invested	education;health care; clothing; food; land; house	children's needs; education; land; land	house	land
% woman pays of household expenses	100%	—	100%	—
Major problems	heavy rains; repaying	scarce supplies sick child	suppliers; second loan	rains
Memberships	KMWF	—	ROSCA	KMWF
Advice	start small; save enough to start something	—	acquire adequate start-up capital	—

* **Note:** Up to 1980, Ush 7 = US$1. During 1981-87, the exchange rate was unstable; thus, no equivalent is given here. At the time of this study, Ush 1,000 = US$1.

Table 2.1. Market traders (continued)

Name	Daisy Kayizzi	Teddy Birungi	Margaret Ssewanyana	Jane Namayanja	Frida Obua
Age	38	36	45	36	40+
Education	—	2 yrs secondary	3 yrs secondary	5 yrs secondary	2 yrs secondary
Marital status	single	married	married	widowed	married
Dependents	5 children	5 children	3 children + relatives	3 children	8 children
Previous employment	operated a hotel; sold housewares	sold household items	assembled radios	tailored clothing	National Insurance
Business	sells matoke, potatoes	wholesales beverages	sells fruit and vegetables	owns 2 retail shops: variety, drinks	sells vegetables
Employees	0	10	0	3	0
Spousal reaction	N/A	approves	agrees	N/A	—
Amount of start-up capital	Ush 150,000 in 1983*	Ush 2 million in 1995 = ± US$2,000	Ush 4,000 in 1980 = ± US$571	little	—
Source of start-up capital	self	bought on consignment	self	self	self
Source of loans/credit	KMWF	none; wants UWFT loan to expand	UWFT	UWFT	none; plans to join a savings group
Owns land?	no	yes	yes	yes	—
How income invested	education; children's needs	family; house; car; trading license; 3 shops	education; health care; house	household; telephone; roofing	food; education; children's clothing
% woman pays of household expenses	100%	—	pays school, health care costs	100%	less than 50%
Major problems	acquiring capital; transport; spoiled produce;	bottle & crate breakage	—	pilferage	spoiled produce acquiring capital
Memberships	KMWF	Obumu Women's Group	Obumu Women's Group	Obumu Women's Group	—
Advice	plan well	aim to be self-sufficient	start slowly, w/ goods everyone needs	—	set up a bank account; acquire capital; plan

* **Note:** Up to 1980, Ush 7 = US$1. During 1981-87, the exchange rate was unstable; thus, no equivalent is given here. At the time of this study, Ush 1,000 = US$1.

Table 2.1. Market traders (continued)

Name	Miriam Nakalyana	Margaret Ssajjabi	Alice Mugabekazi	Monica Bateganya
Age	45	52	32	—
Education	home-schooled	2 yrs secondary	secndry. graduate	6 yrs school
Marital status	separated	separated	—	married
Dependents	4 children + 13 relatives	6 children + 19 of her brother's	—	4 children
Previous employment	employed as housegirl; cook; waitress	worked as policewoman; telephone operator; sold non-perishables	employed with Uganda Army; sold soda and beer	none
Business	sells matoke	rents out 27 market & 50 parking spaces, sells water	buys and sells beans	sells curtains
Employees	0	6	—	0
Spousal reaction	N/A	N/A	—	approves
Amount of start-up capital	—	consignment goods + Ush 800,000 in 1974 ± US$114,286	—	Ush 50,000 in 1991 = ± US$50 =
Source of start-up capital	self	savings	Mrs Oliver Ntale	husband
Source of loans/credit	none	bank; ROSCA	—	Kansanga women's credit group
Owns land?	yes	yes	—	yes
How income invested	business; land; house; children's needs	3 plots of land; 2 homes; 2 rental houses; family	family upkeep	household; land; cattle
% woman pays of household expenses	100%	100%	—	less than 50%
Major problems	credit deadbeats	borrowing money	getting a loan	—
Memberships	—	ROSCA	On Sena Women Veterans Assoc.,	Cham. of Comm. —
Advice	put profits into business	be patient and confident; develop skills; teach girls to bank earnings	use good accounting practises to keep capital	—

Table 2.1. Market traders (continued)

Name	Margaret Nalwoga	Jacent Nakayemba	Deborah Kyalusi	Christina Nasuna
Age	—	—	—	45
Education	2 yrs secondary	4 yrs secondary	4 yrs secondary	6 yrs primary
Marital status	single	married	—	separated
Dependents	several children	children	—	8 children + her brother's
Previous employment	wholesaled beer and soda	provided home grocery;sold second-hand clothes	worked for the government	taught; sold clothes; tailored clothes
Business	sells second-hand clothes	sells vegetables and new clothes	sells dry produce	wholesales matoke, dried fish, potatoes, cowpeas
Employees	0	—	—	2
Spousal reaction	N/A	—	—	N/A
Amount of start-up capital	—	Ush 300,000 in 1990 = ± US$300	Ush 1 million in 1987*	two bunches of bananas
Source of start-up capital	—	—	government pension	self
Source of loans/credit no collateral	—	none; failed to get bank loan:	—	Christian Children's Fund; FINCA
Owns land?	yes		—	—
How income invested	education; building house	school fees; family upkeep	building a shop	children'sneeds
% woman pays of household expenses	100%	school fees, health care	—	100%
Major problems	lack of capital	spoilage	credit deadbeats	transport, spoilage
Memberships	Owino Women's Group	Owino Women's Group	Owino Women's Group	savings group
Advice	keep basic accounts:pay taxes; work hard; save	plan; get training; keep good accounts;	seek advice of experienced traders;keep good books; join savings group	acquire adequate capital; keep records

* **Note:** Up to 1980, Ush 7 = US$1. During 1981-87, the exchange rate was unstable; thus, no equivalent is given here. At the time of this study, Ush 1,000 = US$1.

Irene Kalikwani is a printer

3 Informal Savings Groups

Sophia Nababi Nalongo is co-founder of Mpigi Women's Development Trust

Agnes Kityo organised the Twezimbe Women's Group, which runs a maize grinding mill (her story is told in Chapter 4)

Goreth is involved in a second-hand shoe cooperative in Jinja

The Hon. Winnie Byanyima is member of parliament for Mbarara

Sylvia Musoke owns a second-hand clothes shop

Chapter 3

Capitalising Micro Enterprise: Informal Savings Groups

There was that combination:
women not confident enough to face the banks,
and banks not taking women seriously as entrepreneurs.
Ida Wanendeya, co-founder, UWFT

'Women are aware they can improve their livelihoods through women's groups,' Parliamentarian Winnie Byanyima says. That is why ROSCAs 'spread like fire' in the 1990s, after the explosion of entrepreneurship among women that began in the chaos of the Amin/Obote decades of the 1970s and 1980s. The obstacles women face in getting capital and the enormity of their financial and personal commitments—to household and nation—have led to collective action.

'We are poor, but we can learn how to save money,' Deborah Nyanzi, a group leader, says. A striking characteristic of the women's ROSCAs now thriving across Uganda is their democratic approach to decision-making and management. 'Grassroots women keep democracy going,' says Professor Kavetsa Adagala of Kenya, as they do across Africa (Snyder and Tadesse 1995). Everyone participates in decision-making, and each must take responsibility to pay in order to have a turn at the kitty. That is not to say that all ROSCAs are without fault. There are examples of leaders taking the cash and of members failing to contribute regularly. But with experience, systems are evolving to avoid those weaknesses and to make women's businesses more efficient—to the benefit of the entrepreneur, her family and nation.

Well-managed savings and credit groups can and do serve as intermediaries with financial institutions, as the Mpigi case will illustrate. That model is worthy of study for the potential it offers for nation-wide replication: The formal banking system is tapped to release its resources to fight poverty, putting them at the disposition of grassroots women who create new wealth through their enterprises and invest it in the future labour force of Uganda—their children.

Both foreign and indigenous micro-finance institutions (MFIs) are multiplying in Uganda, seeking to promote business ownership among the poor—especially women. They are becoming controversial even as their proponents multiply, as the experience and advice of the entrepreneurs interviewed reveals. Tied with the institutional question of MFIs are the issues of savings, the predetermined amounts and scale of capital available and national policies about micro- and small-scale enterprises to foster the new model of democratic grassroots development that is arising.

This chapter begins with explanations of two dominant types of financial instruments—ROSCAs and the Uganda Women's Finance Trust (UWFT)—and their history, then moves to the towns and cities of Mpigi, Ntinda, Mbarara and Jinja to meet groups of entrepreneurs in action. These four issue-oriented questions are addressed:

1. *Since micro entrepreneurs, even when working in groups, seldom access capital from formal financial institutions such as banks, can federations of ROSCAs forge links between formal credit institutions and grassroots productive groups, and in the process promote economic democracy?*

2. *What new features of ROSCAs deserve widespread replication in creating a new, non-western economic development model?*

3. *The 1990s—the micro-finance decade—have seen a proliferation of MFIs with international funds to lend. Their loan cycles and repayment records are known, but have they been adequately evaluated as institutions in relationship with other strategic components of equitable economic growth?*

4. *Recognising women's solidarity and commitment to entrepreneurial activities, might expanded or new institutions for venture capital and commercial banking be used to capitalise their businesses, filling the gap between micro- and large-scale credit?*

Capitalising micro enterprise: ROSCAs, banks and NGOs

The ROSCAs found in the markets at Wandegeya and Kasubi were common in East Africa, and in fact across the world, decades ago. Sometimes called unity groups or merry-go-rounds, they are spreading 'like fire' across Uganda, says Rose Kiggundu of CEEWA. A study sponsored by the then Ministry of Women in Development, Culture and Youth entitled *Women's Informal Credit Groups* identifies 3 common types—all with 4 to 30 members (Guwatudde et al. 1994). Most common is the rotating savings group which creates a central pool of money contributed by members in specific amounts each, say Ush 1,000 (about

US$1) daily or weekly, and periodically allocates the available sum to each member in rotation until each has benefited. The proceeds may be put to any use the recipient chooses. The second type is the loan savings group, with a pool of money generated in the same way as the rotating savings, but money is lent to members with interest requirements—although it may be granted to a member for compassionate reasons. The third type is group investment savings, which also creates a pool of money, but in this case the group makes collective investments in an enterprise. Many ROSCAs specialise in one of the three categories, but they are increasingly a mix of two or three of them, as is the case with the Mpigi Women's Development Trust (MWODET) discussed below.

Small-scale credit started to be a popular concept in the 1980s, according to Joy Kwesiga, 'The idea had been pushed, for example, when government operated the Rural Farmers Scheme through the Uganda Commercial Bank (UCB). It wasn't all that successful, but it created awareness about credit.' There were other groups at the time, like the Centenary Rural Development Bank set up by the Catholic Church to make loans through parishes at the grassroots, not just to persons of the Catholic faith but to anyone located near a local branch who could get community guarantors. The Cooperative Bank also gave loans. 'Today, government's widespread Entandikwa ('a beginning', or start-up capital) scheme gives you something to start off a business. People criticise it, but it is creating knowledge about saving and borrowing in order to make money,' she explains.

A pioneer among MFIs, UWFT was the first to focus on women entrepreneurs. Two founding members of UWFT, Ida Wanendeya and Tereza Mbire, explain its origins. The idea was spearheaded by Christine Kwoba Abungu, a banker with many good connections, who organised a meeting at Makerere University to discuss women's access to credit. The original founders were 3, then 13. Tereza, one of the few entrepreneurs among the founders, speaks respectfully of the late Christine, explaining that after her travels abroad for seminars where she met women from around the world, she felt it necessary for Uganda to affiliate with WWB to have international connections and possibilities of assistance.

Although first conceived in December 1983, UWFT was not officially registered with the government as an NGO until August 1984 and even then did not have money. The preparatory expenses were met by contributions from the pockets of individuals who were committed to the idea—in the same manner that WWB got its start as a global organisation in the late 1970s. 'Many of us had to leave the country, and those who remained had to live quietly because we didn't know who we were dealing with at the time, so we actually started operations in 1987,' Tereza says.

Ida had entrepreneurial experience before UWFT was created. In the late 1960s, the Ugandan government decided that in order to encourage indigenous Ugandans to enter business, it would put aside certain business lines to be handled only by them. Wines-and-spirits was one of those, and Ida, together with her husband and two others, was appointed in 1967 by the then National Trading Corporation to be an agent. She actually operated the business because her husband worked for the Coffee Marketing Board until 1975 when they fled the country. That experience, together with her knowledge of finance as a director of the Uganda Commercial Bank (UCB), helped her be useful to UWFT.

Ida remembers a lot of discrimination at that time. Because top management in all banks was men, women had no say in decision-making. She recalls:

> That made it really difficult for women to access credit. We also realised that women lacked confidence to face the formal banks, mainly because of the type of businesses they were in: petty trading enterprises which bankers, male bankers, would not take seriously. They looked at women as people who wanted 'income-generating activities' just to top up the husband's pay, in order to buy an extra loaf of bread. At the time nobody thought a woman would buy an enterprise or run one profitably. So there was that combination: women not confident enough to face the banks, and banks not taking women seriously as entrepreneurs. We who were in finance, plus lawyers and other professionals, realised that we could play a role in accessing credit for women.

They looked for ways and means of putting a mechanism in place that would change those perceptions and recognise women as customers.

UWFT's vision was to reach as many women as possible to help them alleviate their poverty and become self-sustaining. Tereza, a boardmember from the beginning until she resigned in 1997, says, 'In the early years, we had some bottlenecks in that our debt collection was a bit down. The staff didn't act as much as we would have wanted them to do. And of course some women would not turn up for meetings.'

After buying their own premises with the help of a grant from the Danish International Development Agency (DANIDA) and other donors, UWFT's banking system was opened to members. 'That was pioneering!' Tereza exclaimed. Not only was it a banking system but it also had a training section—something other credit organisations did not do at the time. To qualify for a loan, applicants had to train in bookkeeping and other subjects. Field staff monitored women's business progress. Today UWFT has 10 branches in urban centres across the country and its loans range up to US$1,000.

There are about 60 non-bank MFIs in Uganda today, including indigenous and foreign NGOs, government ministries and grassroots micro-finance structures (PSDP 1997). There are also organisations that assist entrepreneurs and MFIs with feasibility studies and training courses. Kwesiga says:

> The good thing is that unlike in the past, when at times money was not returned because people thought it was a donation, people now know that you don't just get the money, that you have to train borrowers about saving and create a culture of repayment. Borrowers know that if you do not repay, you cannot get bigger money.

As ROSCAs mature and the banks and MFIs working with them gain experience, more sophisticated approaches to savings and credit schemes are evolving. MWODET draws on the experience of UWFT and its worldwide affiliates in WWB. The Faith Outreach Group in Ntinda started in 1996 with an innovative purpose and enterprises. Women's groups in Mbarara have much to teach, as do entrepreneurs in Jinja. Each of those savings groups is introduced hereunder.

The Mpigi Women's Development Trust (MWODET)

Business starts with problems, not profits.
Sophia Nababi Nalongo, MWODET co-founder

The Mpigi Women's Development Trust (MWODET), an umbrella organisation of 600 members, is based in Mpigi district, a mostly rural area about 20 kilometres from Kampala. A voluntary association, it was started by the late Theresa Kattaa, member of parliament and woman activist, whose colleagues speak of her with great pride. Aware that many grassroots women in Mpigi district were undertaking scattered initiatives to lift their standards of living, she mobilised women leaders to start an organisation that would promote entrepreneurship. A board was appointed and responsibility assigned; for example, a good farmer would become the group's director for agriculture.

The group's coordinator, Rosern Segujja, speaks glowingly:

> Theresa was a great and unique woman. She wanted to understand the needs of grassroots women and to see them assisted. She wanted every girl educated and every girl to have a job. She wanted every woman to have an income. She inspired many of us—some who had graduated university—to work as volunteers because the organisation had no money. She had goodwill and knew how to handle people.

Theresa married late, but unfortunately her husband soon died. She died the month her son sat for sixth-year secondary school exams. Today, Rosern says, 'That boy is an entrepreneur even though he is the son of a rich woman and could have whatever he wanted. After finishing university he started a bakery, got an old car on loan and delivered his bread to the villages.'

Sophia Nababi Nalongo speaks of her own association with Theresa Kattaa: 'Our founder called me first and told me, "We want to work, to earn. Why can't we start something like the women in Mugongo have—a very active group. Why can't our ladies in Mpigi come together like that?" I told her that I would try to get others.' She contacted Rosern Segujja to be the coordinator. Rosern told her that to get women together you have to offer learning opportunities. 'So we had a tie and dye course for 3 months until we were qualified. We each paid transport and an allowance for the teacher. The founder was then paying most of the group expenses so we decided to ask each member for Ush 5,000. That's how we began.'

MWODET started out well, but when Theresa died the impetus slowed. Rose Kiggundu of CEEWA was called in as adviser and undertook a situation survey with the members to find out how they felt about the organisation and what they wanted to do. Members were found in very high spirits and said the group should move on. A planning workshop was called to design a 3-year programme for MWODET, to establish: 1) a women's development centre; 2) a productive project for growing passion fruit and indigenous vegetables for home consumption and for sale; 3) collective marketing to secure better markets in Kampala for the farmers and entrepreneurs in the organisation; and 4) a nutrition project to train mothers, children and everyone within households.

Rose Kiggundu still finds the group stimulating: 'The exciting thing is that all of the women in the organisation are doing business of some kind. It is not an elitist organisation, it is a grassroots, self-help organisation.' Most members are rural women who do business at their homesteads. They keep animals and grow vegetables. Rosern, an Mpigi resident herself, wants to do more in the zero-grazing of animals and find opportunities for selling vegetables and small animals as rural-urban migration increases.

Each member belongs to a small group of 15 to 20 people, who come together under the umbrella of MWODET. The subgroups market together through middlepersons who transport farm produce to the city although, Rosern says, MWODET eventually wants to have its own vehicle and do its own marketing. Currently, each subgroup contributes Ush 20,000 for MWODET membership, and each has a bank account. Every member is required to save weekly and that amount is banked. Members may apply to borrow money to start or enlarge their projects, then repay the group.

The groups meet in a two-room space amidst a row of shops near the centre of Mpigi. What ordinarily would be the back room of a shop is used for the office; it has a large desk, several chairs and a telephone. Files are neatly stacked on a shelf. The front room, facing the road, has a large table and walls plastered with posters of women's activities from Beijing to Kampala.

Four of the 600 MWODET members spoke about themselves and their group activities:

Catherine Ddamulira: 4 years secondary school; married with 3 children; practices midwifery in her own clinic

Catherine Ddamulira was born outside Mpigi district, completed the fourth year of secondary school, then trained as a midwife. Some of her brothers went to Makerere University and others to training institutions; four of her sisters are nurses—among 24 children in all. Catherine was working in Masaka Hospital when she met her husband, who worked with UEB in Mpigi, so she moved there. Her household consists of 6 persons: herself, her husband, three children and a housekeeper.

'I am a full-time professional, a midwife running my own maternity clinic,' Catherine says. When she and her husband built their house they added a garage that will be her clinic. At the moment she uses the family sitting room as her workplace. After her husband was retrenched from his job, she paid all the household expenses by treating patients and selling drugs. Now her husband is setting up a bakery business—baking cakes—so both spouses will contribute to the household again.

Sophia Nababi Nalongo: married with five children; co-founder of MWODET; grows and sells mushrooms and other vegetables

Sophia Nababi Nalongo was born in Jinja and was in form three at school when money became a problem for her parents, so she left school and married a man from Mpigi. Six of her brothers and sisters are educated, but most stopped by the fourth year of secondary school. Three went to nursing school; two failed and one became a nurse, and others are running their own businesses. She has five children. Now her household includes six persons: a daughter, her husband, his sister, her sisters and herself. Sophia explains:

> I started my business slowly, slowly. When I went to the market with the money my husband gave me, I would economise and keep a balance of at least Ush 200 each day until I got Ush 1,000, then 5,000.

> Then I bought a bottle of oil and some flour and cowpeas to start baking sambusas (triangular pastries filled with vegetables or meat) and began supplying shops—one at a time—until my business enlarged and became big at last. I kept Ush 5,000 a week from my business to use for other things for my home. By that time I had twins and no maid so I could not go very far to do business! I added on baking crisps; the business grew so that I could save Ush 10,000 a week.

Sophia exchanged experiences with other women, who gave her the idea of taking a course in mushroom growing. She started commercially two years ago, selling to local people and to restaurants—the business is not yet big enough to sell to hotels. In addition to growing mushrooms, she uses the compound around her house to grow vegetables. The money saved from selling mushrooms was used to start a group to tie and dye fabric, but because some members failed to attend dying sessions there were delays in filling orders. 'Since in a group each one must contribute or you will cheat one another, we decided to do individual projects,' she says. 'I kidnapped the tie-dye business. I now supply three to five pieces a week to Maria Fisher shops, but my income is small from that.'

Because her husband's income for the family is small, Sophia spends most of her own earnings on the family and helps her widowed mother too. She saves, but her savings have decreased because of current expenses.

Deborah Nyanzi: married with 4 children at home plus 5 other dependants; farms and sells milk

Deborah Nyanzi was born in Mubende district; she also came to Mpigi when she married. She completed three years of high school, then went to a commercial school and qualified as a copy-typist. Her sisters had less education than she; one of her brothers works with a printing firm in town while the other is a farmer. In addition to her husband, she has nine in her household: her own four young children (the others have grown and are working), two nieces and a nephew, and two housekeepers.

'My business is progressing well,' Deborah says. 'I am a farmer. I grow greens and other crops—avocado, banana, some cassava, beans—for the family. I have two cows and sell their milk. I spend my income on my home because I have to buy everything for the house.' Her husband pays the children's school fees. But the value of Deborah's contribution to the family is much greater than it seems:

> If I were to sell my produce at the market rather than feeding my family, I would be very rich because there is a lot of money in that food. But when you do not use cash from the pocket to buy food, your contribution is not counted. If I could have sold everything, I

> would have enlarged my business. I would have a larger income than my husband.

How productive groups organise

Catherine and Sophia, both members of the Mutundwe Twegame Women's Group, explain how they are organised. Catherine says:

> There are 15 members in our group. My friend Sophia grows mushrooms, another processes wine from fruits, another supplies food to schools and raises chickens. Another raises rabbits—in fact, four of us raise rabbits on a small scale. One has a roadside market selling fruits and vegetables. Another sells only charcoal. Everyone is supposed to save every day, totalling not less than Ush 1,000 a week. That money is given to the group treasurer who deposits it in the bank the same day. (We give her transport money to go to the bank). Our group also has activities like helping orphans, and we help widows by digging the compound for them, as a wife would do.

Sophia explains that their group is doing well, that five members have borrowed money. She has not yet taken a loan herself because she is the chairperson, and leaders don't take the first loans because it does not set well with the others. They start with loans to members, and the group executives come last. They are looking for a communal business in which to invest their savings and plan to employ someone to look after it, to avoid anyone being cheated by working too much. Membership fees, like school fees, are used to run the group—to buy paper for record-keeping, pay transport to the bank. Each member has her own savings passbook, and the treasurer has to be sure all the books are correctly kept.

Catherine joined Mutundwe Twegame after it started, so she learned its procedures from the members. By the time she came, they had finished the courses in tie-dye, mushroom growing and compost manure. 'I have stayed and become active in the group because it is well organised,' she explains.

> Sophia is our chairperson, and the treasurer is from Kenya—a very nice lady. In Africa, and maybe all over the world, the person whom you trust is the one who can keep your money. Because we have individual savings books, even if some members cannot save very much weekly, everyone is still sure that whenever she needs money she will be able to withdraw her savings. That is very, very important.

Members must be active, so they visit one another's businesses, inspect the account books and record their comments about the business in a visitor's book kept by each member. 'You have to know whether your friend is actually selling charcoal.' They want to be sure that when a member borrows money she will be able to repay it. The period of each loan depends on the project; for example, keeping chickens does not allow early repayment.

Deborah chairs the Mutima Women's Group of 35 members: Some have retail shops or outdoor markets and others are farmers. Some do poultry farming, others zero-grazing. They started with 5 women who learned about saving, then expanded to 20. Having chosen their leaders, they made some by-laws and objectives, then opened an account with the UWFT in Kampala. Deborah says, 'I told them, "We are very poor, but we can learn how to save money. For example, if you get Ush 100, use 90 and save 10".' Every member saves at least Ush 2,000 a week and, after 4 months, they were delighted to find Ush 1 million in their savings account. They set about deciding how to use that money, devising regulations for loan applications and setting interest rates at 7 per cent for a 3-month loan. About 30 members have taken loans and repaid with interest to date. After that experience with their group savings, they began borrowing from UWFT itself, even though interest is high there; they requested that it be lowered.

Justine Lwanga-Budo: married; sells vegetables

Justine Lwanga-Budo joined MWODET, she says, because her husband is at home, without a job. 'I am now the man in everything. I take care of the children and everything else.' Justine's group has 17 farmers, including girls, widows and married women of different religious beliefs. They grow vegetables, raise rabbits and chickens, and sell eggs. Like the others, they have both individual accounts and a group account. Each uses her income in her home, and members can borrow from the joint savings account used as a revolving loan fund—for 4 months at 10 per cent interest. The vegetables they sell help them buy school and home needs for orphans and transport AIDS patients to hospital.

MWODET is also involved with gender sensitisation. Members went to all of the local primary schools to train the teachers in gender concepts and the evaluation of gender issues so that they in turn could teach gender skills to their pupils. Students were asked to visualise concepts of femininity, masculinity and the sexual division of labour. With a grant from the Netherlands Development Organisation (SNV), they produced a calendar with pictures drawn by primary school pupils in a Gender Art Competition they organised. The competition and calendars were new ideas in Uganda. In addition, exercise books and a gender desk diary also were published.

Advice to aspiring entrepreneurs: Start business with problems, not with profits

What advice do MWODET members have for others? Catherine says that, first and foremost, she would tell aspiring young entrepreneurs that it is very difficult. 'One has to ask: "What kind of business can I run?" And then be patient. It may take two to three years to realise a profit because you have to invest in fixed assets and other inputs that vary with the nature of each business.'

Sophia adds:

> When you start a business you must have respect for it—really love it. There are some businesses, like mine, which demand dirty work—digging, working with oils and the like. If I did not love it, I would want someone else to do the dirty things. You start business with problems, not with profits. You must put in a lot of effort and patience because when you first start you may lose.

For Deborah, doing business means that, in addition to being patient and devoted to the work, one has to be polite. 'You have to be patient to win; you will not learn everything the first day.' Justine adds that business is very demanding for her age group, and one must be willing to work very hard. 'Young persons wanting to go into business should come and see what we do. They will get energy and encouragement from us,' she says.

Problems MWODET members face

Marketing is the biggest problem for many group members. As Sophia expresses it, 'You must have a convincing tongue to sell something if you are going to convince other people to buy what you have. For example, in my mushroom business I must explain first because there are people who don't even know what mushrooms are. And you must produce quality goods. My sambusas must be very good!' However, Justine cautions, 'Profits can be very low when inputs are expensive. Feed, seeds and fertilisers are very expensive now.' And Catherine warns that no matter what, 'There are people who will go and speak ill about you.'

Start-up capital is a problem that concerns Catherine:

> The major problem we have in our society is capital. You will find it difficult to persuade a husband to contribute start-up capital for your business. Maybe that is because some men hear from their fellows about wives going to work, that working wives lead to family breakdown. When women want to start a business like piggery, poultry, rabbit rearing that they can do at home, the husband still believes that a wife who earns money will not respect him. Whether

> the stories are true or not, they are believed. That is the major problem women have.

As a result, women in her group negotiate with their husbands. Catherine says:

> If your husband gives you the chance to work, you should not hide your money from him. You must be sincere, tell him about your problems. For example, with my midwifery a mother will bring a child who is very sick so I must give the treatment; in most cases it must be on credit because the husband has already left when the time comes to pay. Sometimes people pay you and sometimes they don't. That is how you work. So once your husband has allowed you to work, you tell him about those problems—about the people who are not paying you, about marketing difficulties. It is good to be transparent with your husband because sometimes he can give you more money when he finds that you have had a loss.

Lack of training is yet another problem for entrepreneurs. 'And many of us never try to get it,' one member notes. Some women running businesses cannot keep accounts, she says, for they want to do things alone, 'and when you have no advisors, you are in darkness and you will have losses.' Trained entrepreneurs join organisations and learn from each other. Members value MWODET and their groups, Sophia explains, because 'you learn a lot when your friend visits to advise you. She may say, "The display should be here", or give you ideas on marketing. What I like about the group also is the different people who visit us. Once a lady from ... UWFT helped to train us. Today we have a writer who will tell our story to the world.'

Rose Kiggundu believes that ROSCAs could not have 'spread like fire' in Uganda a short while ago, but now that civil unrest is years behind them, women can trust one another. In addition, systems are improved: The fact that members can access their money in their own bank accounts at any time is very appealing. Because the groups are self-managed, overhead costs are low and interest rates can be kept down. In some other areas, interest charges add up to 100 per cent a year.

Ntinda Faith Outreach—widows who no longer fear

> **A widow has nowhere to start, no source of income.**
>
> Sophia Nababi Nalongo, MWODET co-founder

'What pains me so much these days is what happens when women, so many of them mothers, lose their husbands,' Sophia says.

> A widow has nowhere to start, no source of income, especially if she is in the town. She depended completely on the husband—she was a housewife waiting for daddy to bring money—and when he is gone she has to look for [help from] sisters and brothers-in-law or parents-in-law, and she becomes a burden to the family. That is bad. We need seminars to motivate people to overcome that problem. Men are the first to go, and they leave you in a big clan with so many children, so many problems. But if, when you lose your husband, you already have work of your own, you are prepared to support the family. When you are working, you forget your problems and bring up the children.

Another entrepreneur, Pauline Ofong, spoke of a group called Faith Outreach that she mentors; most of its members are widows and single mothers: 'The single woman and the widow are disadvantaged because we women still shun them. We see them as second-class among women. When the Outreach group called, I asked them one question, "Do you feel disadvantaged?" One of them said, "No, I have opportunities like every other person".' Pauline liked her spirit: 'A widow should not feel that she is no longer a woman, no longer a human being. If she has her own money to support herself and her children, she will have self-confidence.'

Faith Outreach is a new ROSCA based in Ntinda, a suburb originally designed for the better-off (Miner 1967).

Ruth Twesigye: widowed with 4 children;
raises and sells poultry and rabbits

When Ruth lost her husband in 1994, she was left with 4 children—the youngest 8 and the eldest 18—and she worked as an accountant in the Ministry of Education. Her salary was insufficient so she started a small business with her sister and brother-in-law selling timber. They soon had problems getting the timber so she switched to raising poultry and keeping rabbits at the home her husband left her. After consulting Pauline Ofong, an experienced entrepreneur, Ruth Twesigye started the group in 1996 with 15 women, most of them widows fearful of joining other women's organisations. Ruth says, 'I started with women who were close to me. Most of us were supporting our selves and our families after losing our husbands.' She is now also a full-time volunteer worker with Faith Outreach.

The group started in a modest manner, using membership fees to pay the costs of renting an office where trainers from the Private Sector Development Programme (PSDP) hold training courses weekly. A course called Improve Your Business, for example, includes record-keeping, transactions, exchange of money, daily cash records. In other words, everything from planning to sales.

'The future of Faith Outreach is really bright,' Ruth says. The group has a revolving fund, keeps books and is saving at the Cooperative Bank, where they get interest. They decided to charge members 10 per cent interest for a 6-month loan and are discussing affiliation with UWFT. In addition to individual projects, they want to start a tree nursery and sell manure. Later they will open branches in surrounding areas.

Jane Wanyama: 4 years secondary school; widowed with 8 children; deals in waste paper

Faith Outreach member Jane Wanyama, widowed in 1992, was left with eight children, ranging from a son now at Makerere University to three children still in primary school. Her eldest daughter passed away last November. Jane considers herself fortunate to have studied up to the fourth year of secondary school; her siblings also went to school in Jinja where their father was a teacher. Jane tells how she got into an unusual business:

> I deal in waste paper. In 1981 I started making medical envelopes for a second income when I was working at the East African Steel Corporation, and life had become so expensive that my husband's income was not enough to buy milk for the children. Some men would not like their wives to be involved in business, but my husband did not refuse my wish. Even if I had to go to Jinja he did not mind.

Just after her husband died, Jane went to UWFT but was unable to get a loan. This did not dissuade her, and when, in 1994, she learned about a factory in Jinja called PAPCO that uses wastepaper for toilet paper, duplicating paper and the like, she supplied it to them for recycling. But they went out of business. Jane's biggest problem now is transport. She could drive a vehicle herself and collect 100 kilos of paper a week from all over Kampala from government offices and printers then take it to Kenya for recycling, but she needs to have 15 tons to make the trip worthwhile. 'If I had enough money, we could build a recycling machine and open our own plant right here,' she says.

Jane works alone except when the children are home from school. It is sometimes difficult for her to pay school fees because her money is locked up in the paper business; the children can return to school when she accumulates enough paper to take to Kenya. For extra income she rents out part of the house her husband left her to a school and uses other parts to store waste paper.

Faith Outreach now has 26 members who each contribute Ush 2,000 a week from their own businesses. Some members keep hens or rabbits; others have bakeries. 'We come together, work together and learn from one another. We want to make jobs for young girls in future,' Jane says.

Mbarara: local government leaders' support

If I fail to pay, my goat can be taken.
ROSCA member

Member of Parliament Winnie Byanyima says that some ROSCAs in her constituency, Mbarara town, are similar to those in Ntinda and Mpigi. She says:

> Women are aware they can learn to improve their livelihoods through women's groups. So literally every woman belongs to some group. They all want to improve their families. When I organise a drama festival, for example, they almost always do a play or a song to demonstrate how poor, ignorant and powerless a woman is if she does not belong to a women's group.

While some of the ROSCAs—in Mbarara called bika oguze, meaning 'save and borrow'—are successful, others are less so. To start, there have been frustrations when women come to learn a skill, only to be told that they should do a project together. 'You would find 20 women all farming one plot of land that was too small to meet their family needs. I encouraged them to learn together but to have individual projects,' Winnie says.

Mbarara has registered 37 groups—many of them new. Winnie gave them a little money to begin with and offered training workshops for leaders, in management skills for savings and credit associations. The more successful groups share their experience with the less successful ones. 'Bika oguze are probably the most empowering activity at the grassroots because a woman can find some money to borrow and start an income-raising project,' she says.

> There is peer pressure to pay back money borrowed, and of course members of a group are from the same village, and each cares about how the others see her. Many groups use the local government system to enforce the laws so that when you join a group you have to say, 'If I fail to pay, my goat can be taken.' Successful groups usually do that. The clever ones insist that they take something that is not one's husband's.

Winnie describes a group that called her because one of their leaders had failed to pay. They thought she was well off and just refusing to pay, because she had used her refrigerator as collateral. They went to claim it, only to find that it was a piece of junk. It was worthless! They spoke with local government leaders, who talked to her, and she paid up. But mistrust remains. For grassroots enterprises, the local government system is important. 'People are not afraid to lend to each other when there are ways to bring a defaulter to account,' she has found.

In rural areas, the effect of years of political disruption has worn off, and people are not afraid of each other anymore. 'But there have been people who professed to organise women for credit and savings who would disappear with the money,' Winnie says. Fears based on that kind of experience were revealed at the first workshop on credit that she organised.

An obstacle for grassroots women is that the money they have to pool and lend to one another is quite small—from Ush 20,000 to 100,000, and after a while successful ventures need more than that. A woman who once used Ush 100,000 or 200,000 now needs 500,000, and her group doesn't have it. 'Sooner or later they need a bigger injection of capital,' Winnie says, 'and sometimes an international NGO can lend them money.' That is happening in Mbarara, where an NGO called Pride Africa can lend up to Ush 1 million. They start with Ush 150,000 and move in steps to 1 million.

Jinja: waiting for investment in Uganda's second city

The money is not enough for our business, but because it is what it is, we take it.

Sekabira Nakakoza, beautician

Jinja, Uganda's second-largest urban centre, lies on the shores of Lake Victoria at the source of the White Nile. Only 80 kilometres from Kampala, it was once the industrial heartland of Uganda, thanks in large part to the Madhvani family. When the Asians were evicted from the country in 1971, industrial employment in Jinja collapsed and whole families became poor. The town became a relic—its stately park-centred main street saw fewer cars and more potholes.

Today businesses are being revived in Jinja as the Owen Falls extension dam is constructed, employing 1,200 directly and more in support services. Nyanza Textiles Ltd (NYTIL) reopened, and Kakira Sugar Estates and Nile Breweries are back; new hotels under construction will cater for tourists visiting the source of the Nile and Bujagali Falls. The Asian-style buildings with their rain and sun shelters over the sidewalks are undergoing face-lifts.

In this environment awaiting capital investment, the informal sector is people's lifeline. For example, there are said to be 6,000 members of the boda boda (bicycle transport) association, whose bicycles carry passengers on their cushioned seats or goods tied front, back and sides. Buyers visit the central market and the shops. The micro entrepreneurs interviewed for this study, who rent small shops collectively or alone in central Jinja, are getting along, but chances of expanding in the near future seem few. Like other women, they have family obligations. And like other entrepreneurs they take the loans the MFIs offer, not always because they are adequate but because they are there.

If women get money they do not misuse it

Goreth: 4 years secondary school and some computer courses; married; in a partnership selling second-hand shoes

On Iganga Road in Jinja town, one man and eight women have a partnership selling second-hand shoes. Goreth speaks for the group:

> We each have our own stock, but we give one another mutual support. We rent the store and pay a watchman to guard it at night. We buy bags of shoes from importers, open and sell. If you do not have enough money, you can go back and pick from the bag one pair of shoes at a time and sell them. If you sell all of them, you can get a good profit of Ush 50,000 or 40,000. It would be better to have a lot of capital and a bigger profit, but these days shoes are expensive. But even though imported shoes are costly, one has to remember that shoes made here in Uganda are gone after 2 months' wear. Our old shoes, the second-hand (mivumba) ones, have strong soles and good leather. So, if you maintain them properly, they can serve you for 2 years.

Goreth says the Iganga Road partnership originated in their churches where the members shared interests. They are all in the Catholic Church except the gentleman. If one is sick, the others sell the shoes and take the money to him or her. They make business decisions together and contribute money as necessary.

Shaban (Mr): married; in a partnership selling second-hand shoes

The partnership appears to work well. They do not demand identical views on the subject of gender. However, Shaban, the only man, has strong and not atypical opinions about working women: 'I don't discourage women from working, but they become too proud and extravagant when they get money. They do not budget for it—they just buy anything they think of. We men spend money on a minimum scale. I encourage my own wife to work so that she understands the difficulties of getting money and learns how to spend it so that she will reduce her demands at home.'

Shaban continues, 'Men endeavour to meet the major economic responsibilities of the home. For example, I pay the rent and the school fees while my wife pays for small things like meat and vegetables. Sometimes when I go home, she has bought a kilo of meat, and she is happy because her economic situation is a bit high—better than that of the man.' Asked specific questions, his tone becomes moderate. 'Yes, a man will take an allowance for himself from what he earns before giving money to the family,' he says. 'And some men do tend to neglect their families. They are irresponsible and can go a whole year without buying anything for the woman.'

He believes that the money a wife earns is important, estimating that at least four out of ten wives carry the responsibility of the home, while six out of ten spend their money on other things. 'Before they began working they didn't know the value of money,' he asserts.

Goreth has firm, divergent views on how men and women spend money:

> Women are doing better than men in Uganda, and government supports them [the women]. Actually, the more you stay with a man, the more your headaches. The little money you get from shoes, he may take away. He might go looking for another woman, and problems are created. You have no meal tonight. So sometimes it is better to stay alone. Do I tell all women to remain single? No. Do not stay single, but work very hard for three or four years, then decide to have children. It is useless to marry a man who does not manage money well. He may say to you: 'If you have money, why don't you buy things for your house? Why don't you pay for the water and the electricity?' Men can be really irresponsible in their homes.

From those profoundly different perceptions, Goreth draws conclusions similar to those of Shaban: 'As a woman, you must earn your own money. If your spouse doesn't give you anything, you can buy what you need. Take care of yourself and make sure you don't have many children.'

Invited to do so, Goreth speaks of herself. After completing four years of secondary school she became a stenographer, then took computer courses and worked for Peoples' Transport, where she got a loan to use as initial capital. The repayment was deducted from her salary monthly. She finds entrepreneurship more suitable than wage employment because she gets money on a daily basis to support her family. Goreth has been in business for a decade on a small scale and wants to expand. She just started the shoe business. Earlier she bought maize and supplied it to grain millers, but that is a seasonal business and at times it was difficult to get the maize so she had to switch to something else to keep going. She has two children of her own to support after helping some of her siblings to go to school. She is the only member of her family to be self-employed. 'I have a man,' she says, 'but we are not properly married. We help each other, but the bulk of the family support comes from me because most of the time he is not there. I pay the school fees for the children, shoes, school uniforms and food.'

Most of the partners have accounts with UWFT, at its branch office on Iganga Road in Jinja. They explain that the amount borrowed depends on the amount saved with UWFT. If you save 10 per cent of your earnings, for example, you can get a loan of up to Ush 1 million. The partners in second-hand shoes know that they could save as a group, but most of them prefer individual loans.

A group of 28 women, chaired by Goreth, is approaching the Foundation for International Community Assistance (FINCA) to obtain loans to their businesses. Their personal expenses are mounting, and even though Uganda's newly elected President Museveni has promised free primary school education for 4 children in every family (at least 2 of them girls), that system was at time of writing just starting. In any event, they must buy uniforms and books, school shoes and lunches. 'We will have to do it,' Goreth said.

And then there are taxes. At the time of the interview, a new value added tax (VAT) was awaited, and they were organising to learn about it. 'We do not know how we shall be affected by VAT,' they said, 'but we fear it.'

What advice do the second-hand shoe sellers have for young women? The consensus is: It's better to do business when you are still young—because when you have children, you have very little time to be with them. You leave them before breakfast and are not with them at lunch. Most of your time is spent on business, making sure you sell the merchandise and running up and down on errands, such as going to the bank. So start your business when you are young. The partners believe that having their own business is better than office work as long as there is start-up capital. One says:

> My husband refused to let me work. We disagreed and separated, and I am doing my own work, my own business—I pick shoes one by one. I care for my two children; it is better to be living alone with them. I would advise young women coming into business to take care of their own money and children. It may be different for women who are in a proper marriage—in fact, they might give me advice.

How do the shoe merchants see the future for young women? They agree young women can get jobs, but the problem in Uganda is that wage jobs are not paying well now. A month's salary is not enough to pay your house rent or to buy a dress. You can't even afford transport by car to your place of work, or pay electricity and water. So it is not going to be easy for young women, in their view. Business is more competitive these days, they say. More and more women and men are entering the shoe business in Jinja so the field is getting crowded with shoe salespersons—even people who come from Kampala in the morning and return in the evening. 'The competition is big,' a partner comments, 'but we can still make a living because we sell a better quality [shoe] than others.'

The partners are proud of the female entrepreneurs of Jinja, where most shoe and clothing merchants are women. 'If men get money, they think of going to love other women, or to drink their money from morning. But if women get money, they do not misuse it. They get shoes, sell them, and use the profit to buy a cake for their child, milk, ... meat or fish for the family.'

Second-hand clothes and thieves

Sylvia Musoke: 4 years secondary school; separated with one daughter; owns a second-hand clothes shop

Sylvia Musoke's shop is small and dignified, located near Jinja's main street.

> I have sold second-hand clothes since 1992, when I dealt in both women's and men's clothing—even children's. Very beautiful clothing. You could sell and sell. [At the time] I bought by the bale from a woman who imported from Germany. But after thieves broke into this shop, I have too little capital to buy a whole bale of clothes. Now I deal only in expensive women's clothes. Customers come in every day, but most of them are window-shopping.

A while ago Sylvia could sell ten dresses a day, then go back for more. Now she sometimes sells just four dresses in a week, or just one, or none at all. At Christmas time, she thought she would sell a lot, but she never got the clothes to sell. The wrong clothes were available in the bales—clothes for casual wear, not holiday wear.

Sylvia started her business in a shop on Lubas Road after a friend introduced her to a man who would become her business partner. When he died, she went on her own in a shop given to her by her father. She had to start slowly, buying 2 pieces of clothing, selling them to friends and buying again. 'If you had Ush 2,000 you could buy a blouse and a skirt, then sell them at 1,500 each.' That, she says, is how she accumulated capital.

> In those days I used to fear loans because I did not know how—or whether—I could pay back. But after the thieves broke into this shop, I went to FINCA, the group from America, and they gave me a loan of Ush 100,000 with a one-week grace period and 4 months to

> repay in weekly instalments. It is a very small-scale loan. I need about Ush 300,000.

Sylvia supports her small daughter and an elder brother who lost his job when the long- established NYTIL textile factory in Jinja closed down. The closure was said to be due in part to the competition created by government's lowering of import tariffs as part of its structural adjustment programme (SAP) and the consequent influx of second-hand clothes. Her brother has re-applied to NYTIL, which is opening under new management, but does not know if he will get a job. Most of her other siblings attended university, but Sylvia stopped after four years of secondary school. Her family is spread across the world, living in Australia, England and Uganda's capital, Kampala.

Because Sylvia lives in a tiny room, her brother stays with their grandfather. She doesn't make enough to support her child as she would like. 'The money I earn is not enough, yet it is something. But it is hard when someone is sick, or you don't have food at home. There are times when you find it very difficult to cope ... with your situation.'

These days she is worried. Recently, a friend offered to get clothing for her to sell, but she couldn't afford the airport tax so the idea flopped. She says, 'I don't know how the future will be if things go on like this. I am praying [to] God that things will change.'

Sylvia is caught in the dilemma of many women entrepreneurs:

> The little capital we businesswomen have isn't enough to help us to solve our problems. You can solve little ones, but then you find times when you don't sell, and you still need money. Maybe you have a patient to care for or don't have food at home. We often encounter such problems, but we normally move on. There is no other way.

Because of poverty, Sylvia says, women have learned to support one another. Recently, she and some friends started a ROSCA. She collects Ush 1,000 weekly from each member. Each week, one member takes all the money and pays her share the following week for another to take. Sylvia says the idea came from a friend. They hope it will go well and eventually that they will get more capital.

But life is uncertain. Sylvia worries about the possibility of having to abandon her shop for a smaller place or for a stall in the market where she would have to share with someone else— because a stall is expensive, almost as expensive as the shop she has. And on top of that, she has to pay license and tax. Yet she hasn't considered changing her business. If she could get enough money, she would buy a bale of clothing and sell it in her own shop. 'Because it's what I started with. I would just continue this business,' she says.

Sylvia advises young women to seek advice from others before they select a particular type of enterprise, in order to learn how to deal with profit and loss, and how to manage. 'At times you may get a lot and at times get a loss,' she says. She has learned the hard way. Although she has not found a business advisory group in Jinja, she is grateful for one very good friend who gives her advice.

She speaks poignantly: 'At month's end you may have some little money, but you have to pay rent for the shop and for the place where you stay. You have to buy food again, to look after your little people. In doing business, you find that if you do not think twice, you will lose. You must be very careful.'

Sylvia has a unique idea about getting help through women parliamentarians—and a venture-capital fund that better-off women could establish:

> The women being elected to parliament are mostly businesswomen so they know the hardships we go through. They could help us with ideas—better ones than we now have. In the rural area you find women who have capital and nothing to do with it. The parliamentarians could talk with such women and get them to invest in their fellow women. As women go up to parliament, they ... can show us how to use money, how to budget it in order not to go back to the poverty world.

Women can be just as successful as men

Irene Kalikwani: high school certificate and secretarial school; married with 2 children; printer

'Ugandan women have always been interested in business,' Irene Kalikwani, a Jinja printer says. 'My mother still buys cloth to make gomesi (busuti), our national dresses, and goes to the village to sell them. Then she returns to buy more. She also joins many groups that give ... money to look after their families, because my father does not work.'

Irene is the fifth of eleven children, and all went to school except the lastborn, who was premature and cannot matriculate. After getting her high school certificate she attended secretarial school, but there were no secretarial jobs. She was a shopkeeper for four years, but it did not pay well. Then, in 1986, she joined her brothers in the printing business; when they left it, she and a colleague took over.

Her business is not steady; it comes on special occasions. 'Right now we are printing posters for contestants for parliamentary seats. When school is open, we print receipt books, bank slips, etc. We sometimes print T-shirts, but that is not steady either. So I do not employ people on a regular basis—they just help when I get a job, and I pay them for that. We do not normally get big jobs.'

Irene and her colleague rent a small place with two desks and walls covered with samples of their work. They run the business together and bank over their two signatures. Her two children are grown—one has completed high school, and the other is beginning it. She shares household expenses with her husband, especially by paying the school fees. The family lives in a rented house where the landlord expects his money six months in advance.

'The banks in Jinja only give credit when you have a big business and a surety like a land title,' she explains. 'You cannot get credit just because you have an account. So, to keep our business alive I joined FINCA and borrowed money for business materials. But what they gave us is not enough—only Ush 100,000 at first. You are supposed to pay that back within 16 weeks, and then they will give you more. This time we will get 150,000. So, over time, I could expand my business. If I got enough money, I would buy a printing machine for about Ush 8 million. There are people here in Jinja who could repair it. But I could only purchase such a machine with a loan.'

Women in Jinja save together in a merry-go-round (another expression for a ROSCA) and in the burial groups that many join. (Burial groups are savings groups, similar to ROSCAs, that assist members with costs of funerals and burials.) 'They are helpful,' Irene says. 'I joined one. You get money when it is your turn. We are 30 people, so after 2 weeks we bring Ush 10,000 each, and give the 300,000 to one member who brings gifts like cups, plates or clothes for you. In time you can build a house and put things in it.'

How do the women use their earnings? For most, their first priority is school fees, then buying or building houses, Irene says. When she was working in a shop, she managed to buy a plot but has not constructed anything. Whatever she gets she uses for her children's education.

'Women who do big business are the ones who are building. If you get money, you can build houses to rent, then build a bigger house for yourself.' Irene believes, 'It is best to start with the small ones, for renting, so you get money every month.'

But it takes money to get money for building. Some women go to Dubai, Irene says, although tickets are costly, and you need cash to buy goods there to sell to shop owners in Jinja. 'You supply them and you are paid a big sum, but you can't start with small money.'

The future? Irene says, 'Some day my daughter should take over my business. Women can be successful in business. They are very hard-working. They can be just as successful as men.'

Paying family expenses equally

Sekabira Nakakoza: 7 years primary school; married with 6 children plus her brother's 4; beautician

'I have been plaiting hair since my childhood. As you know, children play games plaiting grass. That became my profession,' Sekabira Nakakoza of Saloon Masabena says. She started plaiting for money at home, then moved to a saloon on Main Street, then to Saloon Masabena in 1994. 'I required capital to buy threads, Vaseline and other items. Sometimes two or three people come per day. Business is good on big days like holidays, but on other days you can sit and no one will come. That is a problem. Yet I would advise a young woman to come here and learn the business,' she says.

Sekabira's father worked in a sugar factory in Miyana until the Madhvani Corporation transferred him to Kakira. She says:

> People of old times were not like us. One could not rent a house; you had to buy. My three brothers, two sisters and I were born here in Jinja. There were many other children my father produced outside of marriage. My mother did not work; except for crafts and farming she had no job. We went to school until our parents could no longer pay. I went up to primary seven. When my father died, all of us were taken back to the countryside where we stayed until we grew up. Mother stayed in Jinja because as a widow she could not go with her children.

Sekabira's biggest problem is that some customers cheat. After their hair is plaited they say, 'Let me come back to pay,' and then they do not return. How to solve that problem? 'One could make people pay before plaiting, but that is difficult because you cannot know who will cheat and who will not. And if you ask for money before plaiting, some women get annoyed and ask, "Who do you think I am, a thief?" Yet,' she adds, 'when you have no work and people come, you may still decide to do work on credit and take a chance, rather than just sitting.'

So far, her income is not sufficient for her needs. FINCA said it could lend Ush 100,000 and more. She says, 'The money is not enough for our business, but because that is what it is, we take it. They also teach us how to save—voluntary savings, which are paid on top of the loan repaid, but the savings are your own.'

Sekabira intends to expand her business in future and build a house rather than renting as she does now. She has no property because she invests in school fees for the three of her six children who are in school—two in secondary and one still in primary. The other dependants she has helped have grown up, but her brother, who died recently, left four children with no one to support them. She will have to help because her remaining siblings have no jobs.

'My husband, who drives a taxi, does not object to my business. He and I contribute everything we have to our home and family. We pay school fees and other home expenses—equally,' she says.

Not every family situation is so egalitarian. A difficulty expressed in Mpigi and heard elsewhere is that of husbands who take wives' money when they come across it. Or they take it indirectly by saying, ' "Get that from the shop (if you have a retail shop), and I will pay." ' 'After five months your capital is down: Soap, salt, sugar stocks are gone. So, after all your work, your money is finished. That is how we fail in business,' some women say. 'We lack support.' They add a complaint often heard: When a woman is working, the man feels he can abandon all the home needs—everything—even school fees.

Informal savings and credit groups: summary and a broad look at issues

We are poor, but we can learn how to save money.
Deborah Mutima, ROSCA member

Collective action and mutual solidarity in the face of pressing personal and family needs underlie the formation of ROSCAs. Deborah Mutima's group saved a million shillings in four months. The group improves women's access to productive resources—namely, skills and credit, which make them self-reliant in enterprises they can control, the Guwatudde study by the Ministry of Women in Development asserts. One group sums it up: 'Unity is strength.'

As seen in this chapter, group loyalty goes all the way from sharing a shop, as the shoe merchants in Jinja do, to contributing savings to one another in time of emergency. Although some entrepreneurs are still wary of ROSCAs, the mutual trust that wavered during the crisis years in Uganda is returning. The ministry study says it too: 'Groups instilled in their members the spirit of group work and discipline. There was no evidence of such vices as quarrels and internal conflicts' (Guwatudde et al. 1994). Sharing the same values at church (the Jinja group), knowing that the local government will back a claim in cases of delinquency (Mbarara women) or simply seeking solidarity because you are widows or single women (Ntinda Faith Outreach) serve to strengthen that trust.

Interestingly, two of every five groups in the Ministry of Women and Development study were created on March 8th, International Women's Day, which celebrates the national commitment to women's advancement and economic empowerment. As Uganda's president said on International Women's Day 1988, 'Our policy aims at strengthening the position of women in the economy by raising the value and productivity of their labour and by giving them access to and control over productive resources. By productive resources I mean land, capital, credit....'

Formal credit systems: not now a source of capital

With this background, we can address the four issue-oriented questions raised at the beginning of this chapter:

> *1. Since micro entrepreneurs, even when working in groups, seldom access capital from formal financial institutions such as banks, can federations of ROSCAs forge links between formal credit institutions and grassroots productive groups, and in the process promote economic democracy?*

Behind that question is another: Why do women form ROSCAs? One reason is they have difficulty accessing capital—at times because they don't know how formal credit organisations such as banks and cooperatives work. A not insignificant reason to stay away from banks is the belief that some people—especially directors—in banks are known to be corrupt and self-serving. 'Malpractices in the formal lending systems discourage women who have meagre savings...,' the ministry study says.

Formal credit sources such as banks discourage micro entrepreneurs because they find small-scale loans costly to administer. In addition, few women own land or a house or have salaries—the usual collateral to guarantee a bank loan. The facts are stark: Only 7 per cent of Ugandan women own land and 8 per cent have leasehold. Even when women are eligible for formal credit, the cost of borrowing—interest rates that can reach 40 per cent, payment for paperwork, fares to travel to the bank and the time necessary to consider and close a loan—are totally discouraging to the small borrower. The description in Chapter 2 by the veterans group of women's dilemma is appropriate here: Financial institutions want you to open an account before they give you money so they can see how you handle it, but if you don't have money you can't open an account.

Another deterrent to women's borrowing is the location of banks or credit institutions: Distance from home or the workplace makes travel an obstacle, but the new postal bank system should help relieve that problem. In addition, preconditions set by credit institutions, such as costly improvements in the workplace or even proposals that applicants switch to another business, inhibit women and so do superstitions. In the Busoga area, '...the idea that borrowing should be kept secret is still prevalent. Most women said that borrowing was shameful and degrading' (Guwatudde et al. 1994, quoting Tibikoma 1994).

Bank demands that husbands co-sign any loan agreement are also off-putting for many women, who fear that the money will no longer be theirs or that their husbands will refuse to agree lest they lose their own capital assets in the case of default. In some ROSCAs, mistrust of husbands is so strong that members chose an unmarried woman as treasurer, assuming that a woman on her own is unlikely to embezzle the group's funds (Ibid. 1994). The delicacy of many marital relationships is on the minds of the Mpigi women, who stress the importance of keeping men's confidence and support by telling husbands about marketing and other problems they must face.

Unable or unwilling to seek funds from banks or other formal credit institutions, women turn to one another to meet their needs for capital. The ministry study found that 73 per cent of the ROSCA members were married market-vendors, brewers and craftspersons (married in the social sense of a woman and man living together or having children), with an average of 7.8 dependants—although just 3.6 of their own children on average were still living. They clearly have heavy household responsibilities. As a member of one group says, '...men need women when it comes to family obligations' (Ibid. 1994).

ROSCAs: a grassroots source of capital

2. What new features of ROSCAs deserve widespread replication in creating a new, non-western economic development model?

Membership in informal credit schemes is attractive because it depends on character rather than assets to be used as collateral. A member should be willing to assist and be assisted, and regular and timely contributions are expected. For those reasons employment or residence near one another is the custom. While membership is determined by sex, some groups invite a few men to join in order to 'dispel any suspicions' that might lead men to cause trouble for the women's groups—a custom found in Kasubi market too. Shaban, the male member of the Jinja shoe cooperative, may serve that purpose.

Mutual trust and cooperation are fostered among the Faith Outreach widows as a specialised group and in the Mpigi officers' decision that they should be last to receive loans—features that deserve replication. They are also evident in Jinja, where the cooperative of second-hand shoe merchants handle one another's goods in the absence of the owner. Unwritten but binding regulations demand commitment to the operations and activities of a group, according to the ministry study: In addition to having a few trusted officers, all members participate in major decisions. Resignation without good reason means forfeiting one's contributions. Hearsay about members is unacceptable, and 'rumour mongering is prohibited', as one group says. ROSCA members are aware that sometimes chairwomen 'help themselves to funds' that Local Councils reserve for women's groups. That problem and the need for mutual trust underlie the Mpigi women's 'officers-last' policy for loans.

The structure of MWODET appears to be a model for ROSCAs. It is carefully designed to help members move toward economies of scale while retaining democratic governance. The individual 15- to 20-member ROSCAs are federated under the MWODET umbrella and can readily access credit, training and other programmes through it. Yet small-group autonomy and democratic management structures are retained by each ROSCA, which sets its own interest rates, and whose members visit one another's businesses to advise and, not incidentally, check the accounts. They keep their joint bank-savings account that is used for loans separate from their individual ones, and a member may withdraw money from the latter as needed—a highly motivating factor that the ministry study apparently did not uncover and deserves consideration for replication.

The Mbarara women add another dimension to group governance: When peer pressure is not effective, they turn to locally elected officials for assistance in getting loans repaid. 'People are not afraid to lend to each other when there are ways to bring a defaulter to account,' says their MP Winnie Byanyima. So, when necessary, they make use of the local government system to ensure loan repayment. Their motto: 'If I fail to pay, my goat can be taken.' Successful groups ensure that whatever is used for collateral belongs to the woman herself.

Failure of some members to pay promptly can pose problems among participants in ROSCAs—anecdotes of incidences abound and discourage some potential members. Contrary to common belief, however, the groups in this study, as well as that of the ministry, keep careful records and choose their leaders well: One does not need a high level of education to be a responsible member. The Mpigi women have brought member and group record-keeping to a high level of competence, and their desire for frequent training and technical advice attests to their wish to continue in that vein. The Ntinda women agree: Members take a course offered by the Private Sector Foundation (PSF) once a week for six weeks, to learn or brush up on planning, production and bookkeeping. Marketing is a priority subject for training—the highest priority for some Mpigi women, who discussed the need for proper displays and good public relations.

The ministry study argues that informal credit groups 'address the needs of the poor where formal financial institutions cannot reach' because of their small size and their avoidance of formalities. It found an information gap between groups and the local authorities, suspecting that those authorities do not take women's informal groups very seriously; because they are born of meeting domestic demands, they remain a mystery. The Mbarara women have faced and overcome that obstacle by making the local authorities allies in times of default.

Start-up and working capital—a scarce resource

Catherine is neither the first, nor the last, person in this book to identify capital as the major obstacle for her group. Most women's meagre start-up capital is accrued through their own trade while a few members have savings from household budgets or previous wage employment. Most women in the ministry study do not have land for agriculture or horticulture, and the amounts of money they can save are insufficient to purchase necessary raw materials. Although the ministry study says that quite a number of ROSCA members get their initial capital from their husbands, the comments from Mpigi on this subject make one wonder if 'from their husbands' means the tiny savings women stash away from a household budget which then become an independent income to be used as start-up capital. Sophia and many of her friends in Mpigi became entrepreneurs that way.

The major constraint associated with ROSCAs is evident: Capital is small and not expandible. The ministry study found the average operating capital for credit groups to be Ush 323,000, or 21,000 per member; the rotating or deferred-savings types averaged Ush 112,000 per person. 'Our capital cannot expand because it is that miserable amount we borrow from and do all our activities from,' one member says. The money they pool and lend to one another is quite small, ranging from Ush 20,000 to 100,000. That is why the Mbarara women welcome the NGO credit groups that offer larger amounts—up to Ush 1 million—once an enterprise is firmly on its feet.

MFIs cannot escape the constraints of the small-capital issue either. Lending all businesses the same amount in cookie-cutter fashion makes for ease of administration of the MFI, but it can make repayment difficult when businesses cannot expand and earn enough to repay the capital plus 30 to 40 per cent interest, and sometimes even additional fees. Recipients of such credit may have to run fast to stand still. As Irene in Jinja says, 'Business can be good when you have money.'

MFIs: a critique

> *3. The 1990s—the decade of micro-finance—have seen a proliferation of MFIs with international funds to lend. Their loan cycles and repayment records are known, but have they been adequately evaluated as institutions in relationship with other strategic components of equitable economic growth?*

ROSCAs have limitations—the most serious being the small amounts of capital they can access, which in turn constrain the growth of members' enterprises. But they can be stepping-stones to other sources of credit, as the Mbarara women are finding through MFIs there. However, MFIs, many of them foreign rather than locally based, need thoughtful analysis, as the *Strategy for a Dynamic Microfinancing Programme in Uganda* (PSDP 1997) proposes. The *Strategy* finds that locally based MFIs, such as UWFT, 'derive their mission more specifically from the needs of the community' than from their own needs and 'are more committed to financing all types of profit-motivated farm and off-farm activities, including agriculture production.' Foreign NGOs, in contrast, focus on petty trade and commerce mainly, and most of them exclude farm production and processing, as PSDP points out.

The *Strategy* adds that the emphasis of most foreign MFIs is 'skewed towards building sustainable financial institutions at the cost of building a more sustainable enterprise sector'—a view we heard from several Ugandans. The new international credit programmes have made the 1990s the decade of micro-finance and, like the World Bank-chaired Consultative Group to Assist the Poorest (CGAP), are designed to perpetuate that trend, according to the *Strategy*. Even the local MFIs come under criticism for too much dependence on donor funding, thus suppressing local savings mobilisation and consequently limiting national economic growth. In a country such as Uganda, where 85 per cent of the population derives its livelihood from the land, where 90 per cent of rural women and 53 per cent of rural men are engaged in agriculture, and 50 per cent of GDP comes from agriculture, that criticism is relevant.

The secretary-general of the United Nations raises some of the same issues. He notes that 'microcredit programmes skyrocketed to prominence in a decade [the 1990s] of lowered expectations for the public sector' and decreasing foreign aid, and adds a warning about MFIs. Studies he cites affirm that 'the use of credit as an instrument for poverty eradication' has its limits and explain that many countries have high interest rates—that can reach to 30 to 50 per cent—with additional stiff premiums that add to charges for the use of credit (UN 1998). This study records similar costs in Uganda.

Of great importance, the UN study criticises the many microcredit schemes that are 'stand-alone operations', meaning that they lack support services and linkage with public-sector activities, such as land reform, which may condition their success. The secretary–general urges that micro-finance be considered 'one component of an overall strategy to foster small-business enterprise.' The larger strategy would include savings mobilisation and access to land, appropriate technology, markets, housing, education and nutrition. Uganda has lacked a policy framework for small-business enterprise, and the entrepreneurs' search for capital continues, as will be discussed together with micro-finance issues in the final chapter of this book.

Filling the capital gap

> *4. Recognising women's solidarity and commitment to entrepreneurial activities, might expanded or new institutions for venture capital and commercial banking be used to capitalise their businesses, filling the gap between micro- and large-scale credit?*

Two creative ideas in this chapter begin to respond to that question:

The first comes from Sylvia, second-hand clothes merchant in Jinja, who suggests a venture-capital system among women. 'We women are far behind,' she says, 'but some of us have money. In the rural area you find a woman who has capital and nothing to do with it. The parliamentarians could talk with such women and get them to invest in their fellow women.' The Zimbabwe Progress Fund (Private) Ltd is a venture-capital company that may be a model for Uganda. It provides equity capital and management support for the development of new businesses and the expansion of existing ones. In the Zimbabwe case, the objective is facilitating transfer of ownership of productive assets to indigenous management and employees. Nonetheless, its structure, investment and shareholder patterns provide a useful example of the relevance of venture capital to women's entrepreneurship.

The second creative vision for women's finance institutions comes from Ida Wanendeya, one of UWFT's founders:

> I would like to see WWB-affiliates, such as ... UWFT, go beyond the survival level women now deal with. I do not see why they cannot be developed into real banks. As we are now running them, we are going to be donor dependent for a long time. But if they were commercial enterprises or part of them became commercial, then at least they would be able to make money and serve more women. Depending on donations has its limitations. How are we going to upgrade them? It is time for a new look.

Into the twenty-first century

MWODET offers potential as part of the new grassroots, democratic development model that is arising. However, two important issues remain outstanding in this chapter.

The first issue is ideological: Women still fail to see their non-monetary work as productive labour deserving to be counted and valued. 'My mother did not work,' Sekabira says, 'except for farming and crafts.' Deborah is one of the millions of women who contribute in-kind to the family and 'would be very rich' if she sold the food. 'When you do not use cash from the pocket to buy food, your contribution is not counted,' she laments, while estimating that if it were counted, she would bring in much more money than her husband does. Daisy at Kasubi market (Chapter 2) sums up the realities: 'The most important thing about selling food is that you can eat. That is what keeps us here. When the bananas ripen, I take them to my children.' This issue of women's non-monetary incomes is considered in detail and given monetary value in the chapter on women farmers that follows.

The second issue is logistical: The poorest women often remain out of reach. 'Without a continuous source of capital, the poorest women are still difficult to target under informal lending,' the ministry study says. This study also suggests that the issue of the size of loans available to micro entrepreneurs be reconsidered so that the entrepreneurs may have chances to lift themselves out of poverty rather than recycling it as so many must do through microcredit. The ministry study proposes that ROSCA groups emphasise saving, rather than consumption, in order to expand their capital, and that they find means of linkages between groups for mutual learning. As regards savings, Deborah's statement should ring in our ears: 'We are poor, but we can learn how to save money.' Referring to linkages, the MWODET model offers lessons for groups everywhere.

Perhaps the most important lesson of this chapter is about leadership. The Hon. Theresa Kattaa of Mpigi and banker Christine Kwoba Abungu risked creating financial institutions (thereby also risking their personal credibility) and led others to share their visions of economic empowerment for ordinary women. Neither one had enough years on earth to know that their dreams of MWODET and UWFT would be realised.

Recapitulation

Following women's entry into entrepreneurship in the 1970s and 1980s, their awareness that they can improve their livelihoods through savings and credit groups has brought about a near-explosion of ROSCAs. Unable or sometimes unwilling to make use of the formal banking system, women entrepreneurs turned to one another for support and for capitalisation of their enterprises. This has led to a good deal of innovation in the structure and management of savings and credit groups in the 1990s, at times in cooperation with UWFT, as evidenced in the Mpigi, Ntinda, Mbarara and Jinja case studies of this chapter.

The major constraint that entrepreneurs face is capital—both start-up and working capital. What ROSCAs can generate is small and not expandible. The newly proliferating MFIs address that limitation by offering microcredit. Despite their merits, however, their limitations are several: the often high and prohibitive cost of borrowing; their lack of linkages with other elements of support to small business; and, possibly, suppression of indigenous savings that are essential to Uganda's progress over the long term. A Ugandan study suggests that locally based MFIs, such as UWFT, are more responsive to community needs than are foreign ones (PSDP 1997).

Another study found what we learned from the market women in an earlier chapter and from all the women in this one: Women entrepreneurs set priorities for use of their profits that put children and family first, land and home second and business expansion third. Entrepreneurs in that study, and this one, buy property and livestock, build a house, start up a poultry project and/or recapitalise their business. Paying rent on time, supporting innumerable dependants, providing school fees and clothing for the children, purchasing a mattress, bicycle or radio, become possible. In Mpigi, Catherine supported the household after her husband's retrenchment until he started a bakery and contributed again. Justine says flatly, 'I am now the man.... I take care of the children and everything else' because her husband is unemployed and at home. Whether married or single, the women have numerous dependants and a strong commitment to family well-being. These priorities suggest that a new development model should emphasise building healthy citizens and a strong labour force as of greater importance than the immediate growth of the GDP. They also suggest that improving women's access to training and credit makes sense as a sound basis for overcoming poverty and lifting the GDP from a far broader base by promoting grassroots economic growth.

Irene in Jinja sums it up: 'Business can be good when you have money.'

Table 3.1. Women in informal savings groups

Name	Catherine Ddamulira	Sophia Nababi Nalongo	Deborah Nyanzi
Education	4 yrs secondary school	3 yrs secondary school	3 yrs secondary school + commercial school
Marital status	married	married	married
No. in household, including herself	6: 3 children, husband, housekeeper	6: daughter, son-in-law, his sister, her 2 sisters	9: 4 children, 2 nieces, 1 nephew, husband, 2 housekeepers
Previous employment	Masaka Hospital	cooked food	copy-typist
Name of group/position	Mutundwe Twegame Women's Group	Mutundwe Twegame Women's Group/Chair	Mutima Women's Group/Chair
Business	midwife in her own clinic	grows and sells mushrooms & vegetables	sells milk from her own cows
Spousal reaction	supportive	—	positive
Amount of start-up capital	—	Ush 5,000	—
Source of start-up capital	self	household savings	—
Source of loans/credit	—	—	her group's savings; UWFT
Owns land?	yes	—	—
How income invested	household; building house & clinic	family needs; widowed mother	all household needs
% woman pays of household expenses	portion	most	100%
Major problems	acquiring capital; obtaining training	marketing; obtaining training	—
Memberships	MWODET	MWODET	MWODET; UWFT
Advice	realise difficulties; be patient; talk business with husband	love your business; produce quality goods; be patient	be polite & patient to win

Table 3.1. Women in informal savings groups (continued)

Name	Justine Lwanga-Budo	Ruth Twesigye	Jane Wanyama
Education	—	—	4 yrs secondary school
Marital status	married	widowed	widowed
No. in household, including herself	—	4 children	8 children
Previous employment	—	accountant; sold timber, poultry and rabbits	East African Steel; made medical envelopes
Name of group/position	ROSCA	Faith Outreach	Faith Outreach
Business	sells vegetables	raises and sells poultry and rabbits	deals in wastepaper
Spousal reaction	—	—	was supportive
Amount of start-up capital	—	—	—
Source of start-up capital	—	—	—
Source of loans/credit	her group's savings account	—	UWFT declined
Owns land?	—	yes	—
How income invested	school & home needs; orphans; transporting AIDS patients	—	business; school fees
% woman pays of household expenses	100%	100%	100%
Major problems	cost of feed, seeds, fertiliser	—	transport
Memberships	MWODET	Faith Outreach	Faith Outreach
Advice	be willing to work very hard	—	learn accounting

Table 3.1. Women in informal savings groups (continued)

Name	Goreth	(Mr) Shaban	Sylvia Musoke
Education	4 yrs secondary school; computer courses	—	4 yrs secondary school
Marital status	co-habits	married	single
No. in household, including herself	4: partner & 2 children	—	2: 1 child + brother
Previous employment	Peoples' Transport; sold maize	—	—
Business	second-hand shoe partnership	second-hand shoe partnership	second-hand clothes dealer
Spousal reaction	—	positive	—
Amount of start-up capital	—	—	Ush 2,000
Source of start-up capital	loan against her salary at Peoples' Transport	—	—
Source of loans/credit	Peoples' Transport; FINCA	—	FINCA
Owns land?	—	—	no
How income invested	school fees; family needs; business	family needs; business	family needs; business
% woman pays of household expenses	most	about half	100%
Major problems	overcrowded business field	—	thieves; lack of capital
Memberships	church; FINCA; UWFT	—	FINCA; ROSCA
Advice	start young; earn your own money; have few children	women should work if they can	seek advice from others to learn management

Table 3.1. Women in informal savings groups (continued)

Name	Irene Kalikwani	Sekabira Nakakoza
Education	high school; secretarial school	7 yrs primary school
Marital status	married	married
No. in household, including herself	4: husband, 2 children	9: husband, 3 (of her 6) children + 4 of brother's
Previous employment	shopkeeper	—
Business	printer	beautician
Spousal reaction	—	supportive
Amount of start-up capital	—	—
Source of start-up capital	took over brothers' business	—
Source of loans/credit	FINCA	FINCA
Owns land?	yes	no
How income invested	school fees; other needs	school fees
% woman pays of household expenses	portion	50%
Major problems	inadequate credit available	non-paying customers; lack of capital
Memberships	FINCA; merry-go-round	—
Advice	advertise; do quality work	—

4 Women farmers and traders

Regina Nalongo Kabanda grows and sells vanilla, beans, heifers and pigs

Efurazia Bamuturaki grows and sells vegetables, milk, forestry products and prepared food from her farm (below)

Christina Night Bekunda sells milk and sorghum–honey beverages she makes; she also trains in appropriate technology

Paskazia Zalibugire grows and sells trees and vegetables

Women farmers in Ibanda formed an economic group

Chapter 4

Women Farmers and Traders

In many cases male privilege overrides the development agenda.

Aramanzan Madanda, M.A. thesis, Makerere University

'I am known in this village as a professional farmer,' Zulaika Mutumba told us. Indeed, the farmers of Uganda are mostly women, but in peasant economies the world over they are likely to be called 'farmer's wives' or 'unpaid family workers', even among themselves. The facts belie such descriptions. Nine out of every 10 Ugandans live and work in the countryside, and an estimated 90 per cent of women, compared to 53 per cent of men, engage in agriculture—making it by far the most important sector of the national economy. Women's labour produces 80 per cent of the country's food, sixty per cent of traditional farm exports, such as coffee, tea, cotton, sugar and tobacco, and an impressive 80 per cent of non-traditional agriculture exports (NTAEs), including maize, beans, cereal, vanilla and horticultural products.[1] That is not all: Women are ever more frequently expected not only to provide the household food as their mothers did, but also to meet health, education and other cash-demanding family costs.

It is beyond doubt that if progress lags in the countryside, Uganda will not develop, and that progress in agricultural production depends heavily on women farmers and entrepreneurs. The limited perception of women not as farmers but as wives of farmers is unrealistic and, as the women in this chapter tell us, also risks suppressing productivity. 'Trickle down' and 'trickle over' theories—that the one who does the farming need not be addressed directly or command decision-making power over the factors of production—make no sense when human development and economic growth are a nation's stated goals.

While the division of labour and power differs from region to region in Uganda, what is generally true is that men own the land and sons inherit it, leaving women owning only some seven per cent. Men also determine the use of their wives' and children's labour, and as landowners they control the products of that labour. Thus men sell the crops, and the women, who do most of the work, have little control over the income. National planners identify women as 'unpaid family workers' while men are regarded as 'self-employed' (ILO 1995).

Discouraged by these practices that impede their (and national) development, women farmers often fail to respond to incentives to increase production, such as higher prices or markets for crops. They are also known to resist intensifying their economic efforts because they are already overwhelmed with responsibility for the well-being of their husbands and other family. When husbands have sole control over all family earnings, they may use income to acquire a new wife, consequently decreasing household income for the welfare of the first family—wife and children—and failing to reinvest in productive activities.

That scenario is changing slowly as women advance 'from dominating non-monetary activities to venturing into monetary activities' (Bafokuzara 1997), as seen in previous chapters of this book. When that happens, husbands often have greater respect for their wives, spousal abuse subsides and wives are even encouraged to make greater use of productive resources. A positive cycle of change begins.

In this chapter, women farmers explore the total monetary value of their work by pricing foods produced for home consumption as well as those sold. By giving market value to food consumed at home, it is possible to see the total worth of the farm production and women's contribution to it—a sum which, if the whole value of the national economy is to be assessed, ought to be more visible.[2] An additional evidence of women's economic activity would be a market value on their reproductive activities (and those of men as appropriate): caring for children, cooking, collecting water and fuel. Because others have often proposed such valuation,[3] we do not delve into it here, except to state that the time spent on activities associated with reproduction of the labour force can be priced and should be part of the national product. Also in this chapter, the extent to which women farmers invest any cash income in the family—especially the health and education of their children—is compared with that of entrepreneurs in markets or at home, in the town or in the city, who are the subjects of earlier chapters of this book.

The country's largest economic sector—agriculture—and in particular the smallholder family farmers, who number some 2.5 to 3 million men and women in Uganda, are the subjects of this chapter. The theme addressed herein, as in the foregoing chapters, is how—at one and the same time—to promote economic growth and human development. Peasant farmers and progressive agribusinesswomen who were identified by service and credit providers as the senior family farmers were interviewed, with the goal of making an initial assessment of the wisdom and effectiveness of programmes targeting them as agents of rural change.

Four questions are expanded upon in the final section of the chapter:

1. *What is income? Is the estimated two thirds of the food produced that is eaten at home part of the national product?*

2. *Who are the actual household breadwinners and how is their income used?*

3. *Does the current practice of considering the household as the basic unit of analysis lend transparency to the source of income in cash or in kind that is produced by each household member?*

4. *How can incentives reach the main producers of the nation's agricultural wealth in such a way that Uganda's development will be expedited? In other words, how should access to the factors of production figure in macro and micro planning and practice?*

Iganga district: progressive farmers

Generally, in the village men have control over everything.
Zahara Kasolo, progressive woman farmer

Iganga district lies along the northern banks of Lake Victoria in south-eastern Uganda, near the Kenya border. Predominantly rural, it is the most densely populated district in the country. All three progressive women farmers interviewed there received assistance from the Africa 2000 Network financed by the UNDP.

Zahara Kasolo (34): one year secondary school; married with a household of 14, including her 8 children; grows vegetables and rears cattle

'I have been a farmer all my life,' Zahara Kasolo says. She grows bananas, pineapples, cassava, sweet potatoes, groundnuts, maize, beans, soy, greens, tomatoes and cabbage, and rears cross-bred cattle. At 34, Zahara is married and supports 12 children, eight of them her own, contributing about 50 per cent of the household cash income in addition to the family food she grows. She is the most educated of her own 8 siblings, having completed a year of secondary school in Jinja, where her parents were in business. When they retired and moved back to the farm, she could not continue schooling for lack of fees, then married a farmer that same year.

Zahara bought her land together with her husband, and they built the house jointly too. She earns an average of Ush 10,000 a week from sales of produce to spend on household things like books and school fees for the children, sugar, salt and paraffin. 'I would value my business at about Ush 2 million,' she says, adding, 'I am partners with my children and husband, and we all work on the farm. I usually hire one worker, too.'

Zahara credits her surplus of food—a surplus she now markets—to the training in sustainable farming methods that the Africa 2000 Network brought to her district, and to her membership in a farmers group called Lwigule Idha Niwe Twegaite (LINT), meaning 'It is open, come join'. Her husband is one of their coordinators. The farmers use sustainable agriculture methods: They manure, mulch and spray but use no chemicals. The mulch helps to retain water in the soil, minimise weeding and improve soil fertility. Trenches are dug to trap water and stop soil being washed away. Explaining how the new methods improve their lives, Zahara says, 'We now have a more sustainable banana plantation, and the bunches are very big. Generally we have a lot of food, and the surplus for sale has increased, but I have not yet tried any new tools.'

Debt is to be avoided, in her view, so she has not tried to borrow any money. In October of 1997, she started selling bananas to buy vegetable seeds. After building a cow shed using money from the sale of crops, she was given a cow by Africa 2000. 'My biggest problem has been the cow. The calf it delivered died, so milk production is very poor,' she says.

Zahara explains that the family generally has plenty of food and usually eats bananas, sweet potatoes and cassava. The average amounts consumed from the farm and their value are calculated in Table 4.1.

Table 4.1. Hidden income: Zahara's family

Item	Quantity/week	Price (Ush)	Amount/week (Ush)	Amount/year (Ush)
Bananas	5 bunches	5,000	25,000	1.3 million
Sweet potatoes	2.5 tins	1,500	3,750	195,000
Cassava	2 tins	4,000	8,000	416,000
Pineapples	5	100	500	26,000
Cabbage	3	300	900	46,800
Greens	—	—	1,300	67,600
Tomatoes	—	—	2,000	104,000
Bitter tomatoes	—	—	300	15,600
Onions	—	—	250	13,000
Passion fruit	—	—	500	26,000
TOTAL	—	—	42,500	2,210,000

That is the family's hidden income—Ush 2,210,000 a year in produce they consume to improve their nutrition and keep them healthy.[4] It is considerably more than the Ush 10,000 she uses each week to buy staples. 'When I get income, my husband and I discuss how to use it. Before we sell off any food we have to first ensure that the family needs are adequately catered for. It is always a joint decision,' Zahara says. She plans to expand the business in future, to build some shops with residential units behind for renting. She would also like to buy more land for agriculture.

Asked who would take over the farm in the future, she replies, 'Because daughters usually go away when they marry, I want one of my sons to take over the farm when I am no longer able to run it. Girls usually drop out of school, because even when money is available, parents value them for their marital worth.' That is a view heard often in the Ugandan countryside.

Zahara has noticed a difference in the way women and men do business. Women usually try not to misuse money, she says, while men are 'easy spenders'. Generally, in the village men have control over everything. But women working in groups are becoming aware of their rights and beginning to control their income.

I am known in the village as a professional farmer.
Zulaika Mutumba

Zulaika Mutumba (35): secondary school; married with a household of 14, including her 3 children; grows and sells rabbits, bananas, beans, coffee

'I have been a farmer all my life, although it is only for the past 11 years or so that I have become known in the village as a professional farmer,' Zulaika Mutumba says. 'I am also a mobiliser of the masses. My parents were mobilisers too, besides being the most prominent farmers in Bukoona village here in Iganga district. My father was also a chief in the village,' she explains. Zulaika started secondary school but, like Zahara, dropped out because of lack of money for the school fees. The most educated of her 4 siblings reached the second year of secondary school. At 35 years old, she is married with 3 children—one girl and 2 boys. She provides about half of the cash income for a household of 14 people—including her own children, her mother and her mother-in-law. All the children are in school.

Zulaika started her agribusiness in 1994, using as initial capital the proceeds from sales from the farm. She rears rabbits and grows bananas, beans and coffee in partnership with her husband and son. However, all family members do the farm work together. Because of the improved methods of farming adopted, her production has increased and she has more surplus for sale. 'But the weather over the past 3 years has limited our farming to few tangible benefits,' she says. Nonetheless, she earns about Ush 20,000 a week, which she allocates for casual labourers, maintaining the home, paying health and school fees, buying scholastic materials, clothing, and for other needs. When she gets income, she and her husband decide together how to use it. It is a joint decision.

Zulaika's biggest problem is under-capitalisation; she tried getting a loan but failed despite the fact that her business is worth about Ush 1 million. In order to be able to open large tracts of land, one needs additional capital to either hire more labour or use a tractor. Currently she hires on average 5 people on 8 acres that are cultivated. Those acres belong to her husband and she has 4 more acres herself that she inherited from her father. 'My husband and I built our house together,' she says with pride.

The foods grown for the family—especially bananas, maize and beans—could sell for about Ush 3,649,000 each year if marketed. That is more than is earned from cash sales, which add up to some Ush 20,000 a week, or Ush 1,040,000 a year. The family food, the hidden income that is put on the table, can be assigned a market value as seen in Table 4.2.

Table 4.2. Hidden income: Zulaika's family

Item	Quantity/week	Unit price (Ush)	Amount/week (Ush)	Amount/year (Ush)
Bananas	14 bunches	4,000	56,000	2,912,000
Sweet potatoes	3 tins	2,000	6,000	312,000
Maize flour	0.5 tins	2,000	1,000	52,000
Eggplants	—	—	2,000	104,000
Tomatoes	—	—	3,000	156,000
Onions	0.5 kg	500	250	13,000
Beans	—	—	—	100,000
TOTAL	—	—	70,173	3,649,000

Zulaika adopted new methods of farming that have made a marked difference in her quality of life. She uses compost manure as mulch and double digging and trenches to trap water and nutrients.

> The problem with these practices is that one needs expensive farm implements other than the hoes, pangas, forks and buckets. I have not used modern equipment. I do not even own a spade to clear trenches of eroded soil. I tried using an oxen plough, but one of the

> cows died and we have not yet got a replacement. We got the cows and the plough from the vice president of Uganda, Her Excellency Speciosa Wandira Kazibwe.

Zulaika is indeed a mobiliser. She is vice chairperson of both Local Council I (LCI) and LCII. In 1991 she formed LINT, to which she and her husband belong, and she has served as its chair ever since. Initially the group was only for women, but they decided to open it up for men, to get their advice, after realising from their gender training that women's issues are of concern to both women and men. She has gained a lot from the group—ideas about sustainable farming, intercropping and the like. LINT gets help from Africa 2000 Network and the Kigulu Development Group (KDG) in the form of training and credit. (KDG is an indigenous voluntary association of which LINT is a member association.) Zulaika belongs to other groups as well and intends to join the Uganda National Farmers Association (UNFA) because it improves farmers' access to inputs, provides them with market information and helps them market collectively.

'In the future, I hope my business will expand so I can put some money aside for my children's school fees. If I got a lot of money, I would bank it to use for their education,' she says. 'I would also like to get a cow and buy more land. I will leave my business to a boy because the girl is likely to get married and go off.'

Some women in this village—especially those who have joined groups—now have access to credit and to an income.

Jalilah Galiwango, progressive farmer

Jalilah Galiwango (35): two years secondary school; married with a household of 10, including her 6 children; grows and sells vegetables, bananas

Another Iganga farmer, Jalilah Galiwango grew up in Namasiga village, about three kilometres east of Jinja, in a family of six—four boys and two girls—all of whom went to school. She left high school in her second year because of pregnancy, then married. She describes her mother as a strong Christian and her father as a builder. Both were church elders.

Now 35, Jalilah is a farmer, married to a staff member of KDG and Africa 2000; they have 6 children—four boys and 2 girls. She supports a household of 10 people—two adults and 8 children—and provides about half of the household's cash income in addition to the food she grows for the family.

Jalilah started farming in 1991 after getting training from KDG. She grows maize and sweet potatoes—the most important family foods—as well as bananas, beans and greens. She has one heifer and one goat. 'Before I sell off anything,' she says firmly, 'I ensure that there is sufficient food for the family.'

Estimates of Jalilah's hidden income—the food consumed from the farm by the family—add up to about Ush 2 million annually, as can be seen in Table 4.3.

Table 4.3. Hidden income: Jaliah's family

Item	Quantity/week	Unit price (Ush)	Amount/week (Ush)	Amount/year (Ush)
Sweet potatoes	7 tins	2,500	17,500	910,000
Maize	4.5 kgs	500	2,250	117,000
Beans	3.5 kgs	800	2,800	145,600
Greens	—	—	1,400	72,800
Cabbage	3 heads	200	600	31,200
Tomatoes	—	—	1,400	72,800
Eggplants	—	—	100	5,200
Bitter tomatoes	—	—	700	36,400
Pumpkins	—	—	500	26,000
Milk	21.5 litres	500	10,750	559,000
TOTAL	—	—	38,000	1,976,000

Jalilah adopted sustainable methods of farming just as Zahara and Zulaika did. For instance, she double digs, removes suckers from around the bananas and prunes them in order to get bigger bunches. Her initial capital from Africa 2000 Network was seeds and a cow. She faces the same problems with adoption of sustainable methods that others experience: They are 'simply too labour-intensive', and she has not tried new tools to alleviate that. However, she finds a welcome difference in the quality, quantity and variety of food they eat.

Although their land belongs to her husband's family, Jalilah and her husband are constructing their house together. 'The business is mine, but family members, including my husband, help me with the work,' she says, adding, 'My biggest problem is under-capitalisation. Some of the inputs are expensive and of course not all are readily available. I have no workers; I can't afford any.' She values the enterprise at about Ush 2.5 million.

Jalilah joined the Paidha Farmers Group, an association of both men and women, and is also a member of FINCA, a credit organisation that she joined as a trader. 'I have benefited from Paidha most—they give a lot of training through agriculture extension services, exposure to new ideas and a grant from Africa 2000 Network,' she says. She sees very little difference in the way men and women conduct their business, 'especially at this level, where you have to do nearly everything yourself'.

And like Zahara and Zulaika, Jalilah says that her boys will inherit the business when she dies or for some reason is unable to continue. 'Leaving the farm to a girl wouldn't make much sense because girls usually marry into other families,' she says, echoing the accepted practice, which in fact reverses daughters' chances as future farmers of Uganda.

'Traditionally, in this community at least,' she says, 'women did not have access to credit, extension services, income, technical inputs or cash employment.' Women have been prized mainly for their reproductive role, as mothers, and they have worked primarily in the subsistence sector, where with rudimentary tools, the hoe and the panga, they are expected to produce enough food to cater for the family's needs. Jalilah says, 'The situation in this village has not changed much. However, some women, especially those who have joined groups, now have access to credit and to an income.'

Eventually, if she gets enough money, Jalilah will expand the farm. 'I would first have to plan carefully, but I think, given favourable weather, farming is a very profitable investment. At this rate, I see the future as bright.'

'Stealing food supplies stealthily'.

Quoted from *The Monitor* newspaper, 11 August 1998

The three progressive farmers interviewed above ensured that family food came first, before the surplus was sold, but other women farmers in Iganga region have considerably less power, according to recent research on food security reported in a local newspaper. In that report, Iganga women farmers said:

> The men wait for us to go to the well or fetch firewood, and take advantage to sell food either from the house or from the garden. Because they do it in a hurry, and stealthily, they do not bargain for a fair price. They are also afraid that we might catch them. It seems like a household stealing from itself for the sake of money.[5]

Another recent study (Madanda 1997) found both men and women engaging in domestic family food thefts—the women stealthily selling some food to buy household necessities when their husbands failed to provide them. Men, however, would sell foodstuffs 'to obtain money for a local alcoholic drink, etc.' Even children sometimes engaged in such thefts, which were most common in households characterised by conjugal conflict.

The newspaper report also described how traders not only pay low prices, but short-change the farmers, who report 'skewed weighing scales and tins that hold less than the volumes indicated on them'. Negative effects of the liberalisation of Uganda's economy under SAPs were cited: 'Emphasis on exports of both traditional and non-traditional cash crops has simultaneously meant decline in the production of foodstuffs consumed locally, both in amounts and in variety. This has consequently undermined food security.' This impact of the adoption of NTAE policies is widely recognised by analysts of SAPs and other globalisation-directed policies as a potential—and at times actual—threat to the nutrition and well-being of the young.

Mbale: women's access to the factors of production

**In essence women belong 'nowhere'—
which makes it difficult for them to access land.**
Aramanzan Madanda, Makerere University graduate student

Women farmers face similar problems feeding their families elsewhere in the country. Researcher Aramanzan Madanda reports on factors affecting food security in Mbale district: 'In many cases male privilege overrides the development agenda,' he says, adding that 60 per cent of the families he interviewed had faced household food shortages during the 3 previous months. Men made most of the decisions alone, even about food stored for the hungry season. 'Women do most of the work but do not control the fruits of their agriculture effort because control power is a function of land ownership, not a function of labour effort in the production process' (Madanda 1997). He explains that land inheritance is 'almost exclusively from men to men', as the progressive Iganga farmers stated.

A case study indicates the negative effects on production when women are excluded from the decision-making process:

> Wamage reported that during the last food-growing season she and her husband cultivated and harvested a considerable amount of food. Some of it was rice, which is also the cash crop of her village. Her husband sold the rice to put up a new brick house and buy a bicycle. As soon as the house was completed the husband married a second wife 'who was brought on the bicycle I worked hard to buy', she adds. 'I cannot put in more effort in cultivation because the harvest can as well be used to marry a third wife.'

When the issue was put to the other members of the focus group, the women raised a chorus in agreement with Wamage (Ibid. 1997).

Acknowledging women's resistance to increasing their productivity and recognising that 'whoever controls the household resources influences the household food situation', Madanda looks at the factors of production: land, labour and capital. Women and girls do not inherit land because daughters are expected to leave home with their husbands when married, and the family would lose the land. But even in their new situation, they cannot inherit. 'In essence women belong "nowhere"—which culturally makes it difficult for them to access land...,' he explains. And that, in turn, seriously affects productivity, as the Wamage case illustrates.

Those who own the land control its produce—a fact that often excludes women from the cash economy. Husbands leave their wives to work alone on the land they (the husbands) own, while they themselves seek wage employment as casual labourers. 'Women gave their labour as part of family obligations; the men did not,' Madanda says. Most women are 'confined to the traditional private and subsistence sector ... [and] locked out of the whole capital accumulation process'. Households having food security are those which are 'wife-headed': that is, where husband and wife live separately so the wife has access to and control over the factors of production at the household which she controls.

Arua, Lira and Kabarole markets

> **Most rural women subsist at the margin of the poverty line, and any further impoverishing policy package, however noble in its long-term objectives, is unacceptable.**
>
> Mary Myugyenyi, lecturer, DWGS, Makerere University

As seen in Table 4.4, Arua district data bear out Madanda's judgement that women 'belong nowhere' in terms of land.

In Arua district—where land is in short supply—cash crops, which are under men's control, were expanded, and women faced problems accessing land for food (UWONET 1994). Identifying food crops such as maize and beans as NTAEs creates yet another problem important to economic growth and development: the selling of food needed for family nutrition, as seen in Iganga.

When an economy is liberalised, the expansion of NTAEs and the pressure put on women to increase the quantity of export crops increases their already heavy workload at the same time that 'cuts in government health and education ... transferred the burden to women', as Mary Mugyenyi finds. She concludes that 'Most rural women subsist at the margin of the poverty line, and any further impoverishing policy package, however noble in its long-term objectives, is unacceptable' (Mugyenyi 1992). As evidenced by the farmers in this chapter, as far as possible, women resist selling food until the family is fed.

In Lira, in northern Uganda, researcher Elizabeth Agitta (1990) finds that market trading, with its meagre profitability, is the only source of earning a livelihood, yet women's entrepreneurial activities are viewed as marginal, to supplement the husband's income—a myth common to many countries. Henry Manyire does not find that type of gender bias. After studying gender constructs in agricultural markets in Kasese district, he concludes that the product market is the least gendered of all agriculture markets and that price considerations are impersonal (Manyire 1993).

Table 4.4. Women's access to, and ownership of, land

State of Ownership	Respondents—	
	Number	Percentage
Own land	0	0
Husband	46	74
Husband and wife	0	0
Late husband	7	11
Other male relative	9	15
TOTAL	62	100

Source: Arua District Fieldwork, May 1994, cited in UWONET, 1995, *Women and Structural Adjustment: A Case Study of Arua District*, Kampala: UWONET.

Esther Kapampara, a researcher and former parastatal manager, disputes Manyire's findings in her study of women's participation in the marketing of maize and beans in Kabarole district. She finds that 'despite liberalisation of marketing of non-traditional cash crops (NTAEs) there were gender differences in the marketing chain that disadvantaged women, hence disproving Manyire's conclusion that relations between buyers and sellers in the product market were impersonal and gender neutral.' She finds women earning less income than men by almost 50 per cent, and that women use their income for household needs formerly met by men, 'thus increasing men's net profits at their own economic peril'. The logical conclusion she reaches is, 'This situation is bound to translate into decreased agriculture output at individual, community and national level as the women producers who form 70 per cent of the agriculture labour force ... do not aspire to better the situation perhaps perceived as their destiny' (Kapampara 1996).

Survival strategies in Ibanda

If women stopped their economic activities, some homes would perish.

An Ibanda woman farmer

Despite the many obstacles some women in Iganga, Mbale, Arua, Lira and Kabarole face, women farmers endure stoically and find creative ways to earn income for family necessities, including children's education. Whether in the town or the countryside, they value spousal respect and are willing to take on additional responsibilities as a trade-off for a peaceful home.

A study by Angela Bafokuzara assesses the relative effectiveness of three economic survival strategies used by poor rural women in Ibanda, a sub-district of Mbarara in south-western Uganda. People there engage in subsistence agriculture and animal husbandry and grow coffee as a cash crop, although maize and milk are now emerging as non-traditional marketable produce. The three income-earning strategies women use are: selling their labour on the labour exchange, sometimes communally; engaging in crafts and petty trade; and participating in ROSCAs. Unlike the progressive farmers, they have no national or international NGOs to support their economic activities (Bafokuzara 1997).

Ibanda women farmers engage in communal labour to earn money to 'solve the problem of food shortage in their homes'. One in 5 of the women interviewed sells her labour either individually or in a group—even though it is viewed by many in the community as lowering women's status and their husbands' as well. Women receive Ush 500 to 600 a day while men earn Ush 700 for similar work. Sometimes they work in each other's gardens on a barter basis rather than hiring labour. Almost 80 per cent engage in petty trade, such as groceries (mainly household staples), second-hand clothes, farm produce, cooked food and local brews. About 30 per cent make handicrafts—baskets, mats and pots—to sell for cash, which they obtain as a group so their husbands cannot claim it. Many sell their handicrafts through middlemen rather than directly, thus reducing their profits. Some 42 per cent of the women are members of informal ROSCAs, of the several types described in Chapter 3.

Assessment of the viability of each strategy brought the results set out in Table 4.5.

As seen in Table 4.5, petty trade is the primary income earner, followed by the sale of labour, ROSCAs, communal labour and, lastly, handicrafts. Single women earn the most money, married ones a bit less, while the divorced and widows earn less still—the latter recalling the situation of widows in Mpigi and Ntinda. Despite the earnings disparities, all the women believe that married women earn more than unmarried ones. 'Two hands are better than one,' they say. Bafokuzara questions the consistency of such a statement, for when interviewed individually the majority of the women say they are running their economic survival strategies and other domestic chores single-handed: that is, without help from a spouse, and that married women have the most responsibility of all.

Table 4.5. Ranking the viability of women's economic activities

Economic Activities Per Month (in Uganda shillings*)	Average Total Cost	Average Total Revenue	Average Total Profits	Ranking
Sale of labour	Not costed	4,487.7	4,487.7	2
Communal labour	Not costed	3,327.3	3,327.2	4
Handicraft	5,351.5	7,569.1	2,217.6	5
Petty trade	27,181.5	36,602.8	9,421.3	1
Informal savings and credit schemes	4,834.7	9,282.6	4,447.9	3

* In 1996, Ush 1,000 = US $1.

Source: cited in Bafokuzara, Angela, 1997, 'Economic survival strategies adopted by rural poor women: A case of Ibanda sub-district', p. 45, M.A. thesis, Department of Women Studies, Kampala: Makerere University.

The author interprets this inconsistency as an indication of women's great respect for marriage as an institution. The women are 'reluctant to reveal the negative impact it has on their economic activities,' she concludes. This same interpretation may be relevant to the Iganga farmers met earlier, who consistently say that 'husbands and children helped with the agriculture work', but in the next breath speak of the labour as if it were mostly their own, sometimes together with hired labour.

Formal education is identified in the Bafokuzara study as an important prerequisite for managing economic survival strategies. Education means higher income: All women who have gone past primary school earn incomes above Ush 6,000 a month while only three fourths of those who attended primary only did. The author concludes, as others have done, 'Education is a necessity for improvement in the income-earning capacity of women.' The majority of the women who own property (defined broadly not only as land but as cows, goats, fowls and pigs) also earn higher incomes than those who do not. Of note in this regard is that in Ibanda, custom forbids a husband to sell off his wife's animals.

'Women tend to use all their resources for the improvement of their households'—for education, health, clothing and food, the author finds. They buy pigs, goats and fowls, provide medical care for their children and themselves, meet their children's school fees and buy scholastic materials. Nearly a third of them 'felt financially independent'. Other benefits of their survival strategies were: earning a living and saving; getting respect from the husbands and reducing family tensions; building self-confidence; having freedom of movement with more time to participate in economic activities; finishing digging in time; having plenty of food in the home; and gaining experience in business and injecting money into business and other investments, including contributions to their credit scheme (Bafokuzara 1997).

'Getting respect from the husband' brings us back to the market women of Kasubi who are willing to make a trade-off by paying household and schooling costs, because spousal abuse decreases when they have independent incomes (see Chapter 2). Those benefits are chosen by women worldwide (Snyder 1995) and will be revisited in this study.

Women farmers in less isolated locations—the environs of Entebbe and Kampala—are rich by comparison with those in Ibanda. Hajat Nabakooza Kalema, Agnes Kityo, Joyce Bwagu, Regina Nalongo Kabanda, Rebecca Njulungi and Victoria Nalongo Namusisi are among them. Their stories follow.

The farming environs of Kampala and Entebbe

Ask for Hajat the farmer.

Hajat Nabakooza Kalema

Hajat Nabakooza Kalema (45): six years primary school; married with a household of 13 (10 children); farms and sells rabbits, milk, coffee and surplus food

'If you come looking for me here, just ask for the Hajat who rears cows, rabbits and chickens. In other words, ask for Hajat the farmer. Besides the animals, I have a banana plantation, vegetables and fruits like avocado, passion fruit and oranges. I have been a farmer all my life. During my first marriage, I used to do some little farming. In the second marriage, I still had a plantation. However, I started serious farming here in 1989, growing bananas, sweet potatoes and vegetables for my family. Most of my crops are on a subsistence level—I sell off only the surplus. I'm 45 and married with 10 children—six girls and 4 boys.'

Hajat Nabakooza Kalema was born in Bongole village, Butambala in 1952; both her parents were farmers. Her father had 7 years of primary school and was a church catechist; her mother left school after 4 years.

> We were 11 children: two girls and 9 boys—most of whom died young. The most educated member of our family—a boy—got an A-level certificate. I went up to P6 then was forced to leave Buligo primary school to cook for my father and young brother after my parents had a misunderstanding and my mother left. Time came when men started asking for my hand in marriage, but my father refused, arguing that I was still young. Eventually in 1968 there was a man who came, quite an elderly man, and my father gave me permission to marry. My husband, Edward Kabuye, was a businessman, an agent for sugar and soap in the area. I gave birth to 3 children: one girl and 2 boys. When my husband died in 1972, I got many problems. That is when I first started thinking of doing business.
>
> [My] husband had enough money to support three wives—I was the youngest—as full-time housewives, but when he died his relatives grabbed the property. Fortunately, they left us the house, and we at least had enough food. But our life was difficult. I used to make mats. I had user rights to our late husband's land so I grew one acre of cotton and got Ush 3,000 from selling it in 1974. I used that money to start trading sugar, clothes, soap and oil in Kampala about 31 miles from home.

In 1975 she remarried, to Haji Musa Kwamira, a businessman dealing in the same goods she did, so she left her former husband's home for Kibiibi, a town situated about 37 miles from Kampala. There she was the youngest of 4 wives, and she continued working. She arrived at her new home with her children until one of her co-wives from the first marriage volunteered to look after them. 'I realised that the love was mutual so I let the children go stay with her, and I provided the school fees, clothing and all other requirements. I became like a second husband to my former co-wife, providing all her needs as well.'

In 1975 Hajat opened a bank account, and when she saved enough money, she bought a plot in Kawempe where, in time, she constructed houses to rent, mostly single rooms, then bought cattle and other animals. Inevitably, as she says, she realised that being married to a man with too many wives was risky. Although she was a working wife, her husband took care of all her domestic needs and the money she earned was her own to do whatever she wished with. But there came a time when he refused to allow her to work, saying that they had enough money. With her other fatherless children and three girls and a boy by her present husband, she could not risk not working. She moved to one of her Kawempe houses, brought all her children there and continued her business. Eventually when Idi Amin left power she moved her workplace to Luwum Street in Kampala—M.I. Enterprises—to sell shirts, trousers, children's clothes and shoes.

> When your first marriage is not good, you get a problem of getting another man. Oh, I got another man all right, but I chose not to move away from my home in Kawempe. My new (third) husband, Haji Abasi Kalema, who has other wives, traded in Dubai then and is now a businessman in town. He moved in with me. In 1987, I felt that it was necessary to have a plot near the city so I bought this land, four acres in all, with this house. The land and the house are mine and renovation of the house was my effort. I produced two children, a boy and a girl, with my current husband. All my children are in school—the lastborn in second year of primary.

None of her husbands has ever asked for her money. Hajat controls it and decides where it goes. She supports the 13 people in her household, including 8 children—of whom 6 are her own—without any assistance from anyone. Hajat and her household use the produce from their farm; if she sold it she would earn about 3.6 million shillings a year.

The food they eat is seen in Table 4.6.

Table 4.6. Farm products consumed and their value: Hajat's family

Item	Quantity	Unit Price (Ush)	Amount/week (Ush)	Amount/year (Ush)
Bananas	4 bunches	4,000	16,000	832,000
Sweet potatoes	2 tins	3,500	7,000	364,000
Cabbage	10 heads	300	3,000	156,000
Greens	—	—	3,500	182,000
Onions	—	—	1,400	72,800
Pawpaw	2	500	1,000	52,000
Avocados	28	400	11,200	582,400
Beans	10.5	900	9,450	491,400
Passion fruit	7 kg	500	3,500	182,000
Milk	35 litres	350	12,250	637,000
TOTAL	—	—	68,300	3,551,600

Settling into farming four acres, Hajat got training from Africa 2000 and adopted organic farming practices, which she, like the other progressive farmers, finds very labour-intensive. However, even when the labour is costed, organic manures work out cheaper than chemicals, she says, and the farm is more productive. She also uses natural pesticides, such as cow urine and ash, to control pests in banana plantations and vegetables. Chemicals are used only sparingly.

'I call myself a businesswoman because I sell rabbits, milk, coffee and surplus foods,' Hajat says. 'I started with 2 heifers in 1989, using as initial capital my savings from my former business. I bought each heifer at Ush 150,000 then constructed a proper shed for Ush 800,000 and spent another Ush 100,000 on growing fodder.' Hajat never tried getting a loan apart from the Africa 2000 Network grant, which is given to all group members. She is in partnership with all her 10 children, three of whom—a boy and 2 girls—help with the business as does one hired hand. Their business became more profitable when, on the advice of the Minister of State for Agriculture, Animal Industries and Fisheries, Dr Kibirige Sebunya, she started a clonal coffee nursery.

At present their farm includes the nursery of clonal coffee with about 10,000 plants, each valued at Ush 400; three cows producing 14 litres daily, each litre worth Ush 350; thirty rabbits, each valued at Ush 10,000; a quarter of an acre of vegetables and another of bananas; one acre of pasture, and fruit on a fence. In addition, her houses in Kawempe bring rent.

Household necessities purchased include sugar, water, meat, cooking oil, health care, electricity and clothes, adding up to some Ush 3.8 million a year, as shown in Table 4.7.

Table 4.7. Household necessities purchased and their value: Hajat's family

Item	Quantity	Unit Price (Ush)	Amount/week (Ush)	Amount/year (Ush)
Sugar	7 kg	1,100	7,700	400,400
Health care	—	—	30,000	1,560,000
Water	—	—	17,500	910,000
Meat	3 kg	2,200	6,600	343,200
Cooking oil	1 litre	1,500	1,500	78,000
Electricity	—	—	4,615	240,000
Clothes	—	—	5,769	300,000
TOTAL	—	—	73,684	3,831,600

'In future I hope to buy more land and expand my farm,' Hajat says. 'I also hope to modernise my farming, especially the coffee nursery, which is not up to standard as a money maker. I need to get a source of water nearby, now that I have the coffee nursery that uses a lot of water. When I am too old or sick to work, my children will take over—most likely a boy,' she adds, echoing the preference expressed by other women farmers who exclude their daughters from inheriting land.

When Hajat first moved to the village after the civil war ended in 1986, most people were poor and had suffered a lot. She decided to form a group to help farmers improve their condition and help herself to be accepted by the locals who at first viewed her as an outsider—an outsider who had not experienced any suffering. The Twegombe ('let's enjoy/imitate others') Women's Development Association, established in 1992, is the result of her leadership.

Hajat encourages women to join groups because it is much easier to access credit and be aware of and use improved technologies. Apart from farming, which members do individually, her association sponsors drama to earn money to construct a market. Hajat says the members' husbands do not decide for them how to spend their money—although some husbands do control women's money. Men own the land and in most cases allow women to use it, but when they see their wives becoming economically empowered from using the land, they sometimes withdraw their user rights. That fear of women's economic empowerment reflects similar attitudes identified by the Mpigi women of MWODET and others interviewed for this study, although once women bring money to the household, spousal violence often subsides and appreciation of wives' contributions begins, as Kasubi market women relate in Chapter 2.

Says Hajat the farmer:

> Africa 2000 Network gives our association members training for improving our productivity. It has also financed our rabbits, cows and pigs. We do not have access to the government's agriculture extension workers, but since we started putting into practice the knowledge acquired, our production has gone up. Marketing is our problem now. We decided to construct our own market because middlemen buy our produce at such very low prices. We have not thought of export marketing because there is enough market for our produce locally.

For Hajat, the future is bright, especially when produce can be marketed. She sees a difference between the way men and women conduct business. 'Usually women work with their men. But men want women to work for them,' says Hajat.

If I had a lot of money I would first thank God; then I would bank it as I think about what to do with it.
Aisa Nalongo, army veteran and farmer

Aisa Nalongo (56): four years primary school; widowed with eight children; army veteran; certified midwife/traditional-birth attendant; sells surplus food crops

Aisa Nalongo lives in Nabweru South village, not far from Hajat the farmer, although they live in very different worlds. Aisa's husband was killed in the war in 1982. A retired soldier herself, she worked as a children's nurse and taught nutrition to soldiers. Born in Lusanja Busiro village in Mpigi district in a family of 6 children, Aisa had 4 years of primary school, and most of her siblings went to high school. Now 56 years old, she has 8 children of her own—the eldest age 32 and the youngest finishing primary school. She says:

> I am a farmer. I care for a zero-grazed heifer and grow beans, maize, sweet potatoes, matoke and groundnuts, and sell my surplus to pay the children's' school fees. I am also a traditional birth attendant—something I learned even before becoming a soldier—and recently took a certificate course in midwifery. I am able to manage my three businesses because they are all at home—my farm is just around the house. My big boy and my nephew help with the farm.

Aisa got an in-calf heifer from Heifer Project International in 1997 as a member of the Uganda Veterans Association Board. Sadly, it is diseased with foot rot, and its calf, which she should have given back to the project, was born with it too and died after 4 months. 'Unfortunately, I get little milk from the cow; at first 10 litres a day but now only 2 litres.' She says there is a market for milk at Ush 600 per litre, but now the little they get is for family use. The 'only problem' she has is with the cow's disease; she has borne all the costs—feeding, drugs and all—without really benefiting. Milk production is low, the heifer is diseased, and she is not sure that the calf soon to be delivered will be free from the infection.

Aisa believes that women are more hard-working than men and advises those going into business to have patience, 'for without patience you cannot manage. You have to be prepared for loss,' she says. She knows.

The group's capital base is very small—not enough to do the needed.
Agnes Kityo, group leader

Agnes Kityo: owns cattle and a paraffin station; organised the Twezimbe Women's Group, which runs a maize grinding mill

Her house sits on the hillside near a small village called Wakiso on the Hoima Road, ten kilometres from Kampala. Below its main floor is a large, L-shaped and sparsely furnished sitting room, and down the hill sits a cattle shed on one side and a grinding mill on the other. This is the home of Agnes Kityo, chairperson of the Twezimbe ('let's build') Women's Group. She started in business in 1968 with a few shops and now owns a paraffin station. She is the proud owner of four full-grown cows and two calves.

In 1990 Agnes got the idea to alleviate women's poverty in the area by organising a group of more than 50 women. The Twezimbe Women's Group includes several women in their 20s, some in the 30s to 50s range, and one senior in her 70s. They come together to share an enterprise—a grinding mill. In addition, most have their own income-earning activities. Many members lost their husbands during the war so are entirely on their own to support their families and themselves. They grow fruits and vegetables—bananas, tomatoes, potatoes—primarily to feed the family. Surplus is sold, as are the maize, soya and pawpaw that they grow for the market to earn money for rent, school fees and household expenses. Those members who have husbands are thought of, not as women farmers, but as husband-helpers, when they do farm work.

In 1994, with their own money they constructed the cement block building that houses the maize mill where women from surrounding villages can bring their maize for grinding. Their key problem is an erratic electrical system that too often fails and keeps the mill idle; they desperately need a generator that will run on petrol. In addition, many women lack transport to bring their maize from the countryside to the village for milling. Finally, they are eager for specialised training for their individual businesses. Each member has a project—pigs, rabbits, goats, tailoring, etc.—and each one saves money. Beyond economic activities they enjoy music, dance and drama, together or performing for others.

Twezimbe Women's Group is affiliated with UWFT and NAWOU. They keep a ROSCA to lend money to their members for their individual projects. For example, Hadija Kagwa is a farmer who also sells sugar and soap. She borrowed Ush 100,000 from the group to begin raising poultry and repaid it in monthly instalments. Anet Nattambo is a horticulturist who also owns a piggery and could expand since she has land to develop. But the group's capital base is very small—not enough to give her a loan 'to do the needed.' She has nowhere to turn. The new Poverty Alleviation Programme (PAP) demands a deposit of 15 per cent of the million shillings Anet would like to borrow, but she doesn't have it.

The dilemma persists. It is difficult to get a loan if you have not already had one, to prove that you will repay. It is even difficult to get one on a guarantee of your peers, if they have never seen you use a loan.

It is more difficult for women to borrow money than for men.
Joyce Bwagu, farmer

Farmers in Kira

Kita village, in Kira, is not far off Jinja Road, near the famous Namugongo shrines of the young nineteenth century Christian and Muslim martyrs. There, two farmers are neighbours: Regina Nalongo Kabanda and Joyce Bwagu.

Joyce Bwagu (33): seven years primary school; married with nine children; sells surplus milk and produce

Joyce is 33 years old, married, with 9 children—six boys and 3 girls. She was born nearby and educated up to primary 7. The most educated of her siblings—a family of 10 girls and 10 boys of different mothers—had 4 years of secondary school then went for secretarial training.

A subsistence farmer, Joyce sells her surplus produce and is proud that in 1996 the YWCA made her a cattle farmer, with a cow that has a 4-month-old calf. Before receiving the cow she had to construct a shed and get enough pasture. She paid the YWCA Ush 50,000 and then spent more on the shed, which would have cost Ush 400,000 if she and her husband had not minimised costs by working on it themselves. Although the heifer was given specifically to Joyce, her children and husband assist with it. The YWCA is the only group she belongs to and she advises others to join.

'It is more difficult for women to borrow money than for men, especially when one does not have a regular source of income to pay back,' Joyce says. So she borrowed most of the start-up capital from her sister, the secretary, and some extra from her husband. Unfortunately, her sister died before she was able to repay the loan. A Cooperative Bank representative was scheduled to visit the neighbourhood to teach about banking savings, as Joyce intends to do.

'I do not get enough milk—only about 6 litres a day—because I do not have the money to buy the heifer feed. There are just too many problems—buying drugs, salt and other things. In addition, my supplier sometimes runs out of stock,' Joyce says, while adding that there is no problem with marketing the milk, nor with health officials. 'My husband bought the plot and built the house,' Joyce says. Each spouse contributes about equally to upkeep of their 11-person household. Her earnings average Ush 5,000 net profit a week, from a gross of Ush 25,000; the money from the cow goes to sustaining it.

If Joyce had enough money, she would try another business such as trading in foodstuffs, which she believes has greater market possibilities. Nonetheless the future is bright, especially if she can get more assistance with her farm.

If I got some capital now, I would not mind.
Most of my money is spent on the children.
Regina Nalongo Kabanda, vanilla farmer

Regina Nalongo Kabanda (47): six years primary school; married with eight children; grows and sells vanilla, beans, heifers and pigs

'I am in the business of vanilla and beans, heifers and pigs. I started my business slowly in 1993 with my husband. I needed capital but failed to raise it so I used my little savings. I began by rearing chickens but realised that it was not very profitable so I switched,' says Regina Nalongo Kabanda, who lives within a 10-minute walk from Joyce. Regina is 47 years old and married with 8 children, six of them girls. Born in Busiro in a family of 26 (12 girls), she went through 6 years of primary school, until her father died and she dropped out and got married. The most educated of her siblings is a veterinary doctor.

Regina spoke of her experience as a businessperson: 'In the past I did not earn enough to save. Now people are starting savings schemes, but I will not join because I believe they are unreliable. I have never taken a loan from a commercial source, but if I could get some capital now I would not mind so I may join the Cooperative Bank scheme,' she says. At present she does not belong to any organisation; she is too busy with children, home and farm.

Regina and her husband do all the farm work themselves, with help from the children during school holidays. Part of the land is theirs; the rest is rented. So far she has no problems with her vanilla plantation—fortunately, it does not need to be sprayed. Her acre of vanilla brought Ush 160,000 last season, and with time returns will improve. Her heifer is 6 months in calf. Her only problem is not enough cash to buy pesticides for the tomatoes.

'As far as money goes I am in control, although we decide jointly how to spend it,' Regina says. This season she expects about Ush 400,000 from the vanilla, Ush 300,000 from tomatoes. Since starting, her business has expanded a lot—perhaps a hundredfold. All the money is spent on their 8 children, all of them hers. Her youngest—twins—are 10 years old. Her eldest has graduated from college. Like other women farmers, she expects the sons to take over the business one day.

She advises women who want to be entrepreneurs to try their hand at vanilla farming because it is profitable and easy to grow; rain does not affect vanilla as long as there is sun during the harvest period. Initially, however, you have to be patient because it takes about two years to mature. She also advises women to give birth to few children—perhaps four.

With well-founded optimism, Regina says, 'I believe that our business will continue to prosper in future.'

My biggest problem now is insufficient capital. I want to expand production but cannot.
Rebecca Njulungi, progressive farmer

Rebecca Njulungi: four years high school: single and supporting 12 children (none hers); sells bananas and vegetables

Rebecca Njulungi is single. She lives in Mpigi district, on the opposite side of Kampala, with her mother and nieces and nephews, supporting 12 children—none of them her own. She provides about 75 per cent of the household income. Rebecca is in partnership with her mother, but all family members work on the farm, especially during the holidays for the school-going ones. They employ one hired hand, and 2 of her brothers, who did not get a very good education, assist; they will take over the business one day, she says.

'This land belongs to the kabaka of Buganda, but the plot and the house are ours. We have been here since the 1950s. Our land is not fully utilised because it is rocky, but we have 1.5 acres under bananas, one quarter acre under vegetables, 3.5 acres under sweet potatoes and cassava. We have one pig, 200 poultry and 2 cows that are in calf.

Rebecca was born where she now lives, in Budo village of Mpigi, where her father, who had five years of secondary school then left for lack of money, worked with the Ministry of Education as a senior office superintendent until his death in 1973. He belonged to the Father's Union and is still remembered in the village as someone who got jobs for people in the Ministry of Education where he worked. Her mother was a nurse until she married and started running the canteen in King's College Budo. A member of the Mother's Union and Gwossusa Emwanyi ('more than coffee') Women's Association (GEWA), Rebecca's mother still sits on the executive committee of the Mother's Union, Namirembe Diocese and is chairperson of Nateete Archdeaconry.

After completing 4 years at Kampala High School, Rebecca worked with the Departed Asian Custodian Board before joining the Cooperative Bank in Jinja from 1991 to 1997. One of 8 children—six boys and 2 girls, she is one of the 2 who attained 4 years of secondary education. 'The rest failed to go that far because our mother could not afford to pay their fees,' Rebecca says.

Following her mother's footsteps, Rebecca became a member of GEWA in 1991 and of Naggalabi Women's Group when it was formed in 1995. She was one of the first people to attend GEWA workshops on sustainable agriculture, then started commercial farming in 1992 after a study visit to Kenya. Because their area is hilly, the family depended on the market for nearly all their needs, hardly growing anything until getting the training from Africa 2000 Network. Now they are almost self-sufficient in food, with a banana plantation—quite an achievement in the area—cabbage, cassava, sweet potatoes, amaranths and other leafy vegetables. They grew until they were attacked by an unidentified disease. Tomatoes were not profitable, zero-grazing failed and five cows were lost 'from ticks and inexperience,' Rebecca says, but they do have a pig.

On average the farm earns Ush 50,000 per week, which is spent on feed and drugs for the poultry and cows, as well as salt lick, paraffin, sugar, salt and other domestic items. Some of the money goes for medicines and doctors when a household member is ill.

Table 4.8. Farm products consumed and their value: Rebecca's family

Item	Quantity/week	Unit Price (Ush)	Amount/week (Ush)	Amount/year (Ush)
Cassava	2 tins	5,000	10,000	520,000
Bananas	3 bunches	5,000	15,000	780,000
Sweet potatoes	2 tins	3,500	7,000	364,000
Beans	4 kg	800	3,200	166,400
Cabbage	3	300	900	46,800
Milk	14 litres	500	7,000	364,000
Eggs	1/2 tray	2,800	1,400	72,800
Greens	—	—	1,000	52,000
TOTAL	—	—	45,500	2,366,000

The main foods consumed by the family are bananas, sweet potatoes and cassava. However, recently the cassava was attacked by mosaic (a virus that attacks plants) and a prolonged dry season that have affected its yield. Farm products household members consume are valued at about Ush 45,500 a week, or Ush 2.4 million a year. They are shown in Table 4.8.

As a member of GEWA, Rebecca is eligible for grants to start commercial farming. 'In a group there is some special togetherness so that if one has a problem and it is within other group members' means to solve, they do help,' she believes. 'For instance, I first learnt about the advantages of intercropping from a group member. [Also, n]ow that women have formed groups, it is easier for us to access loans.'

Rebecca's initial capital was a grant of Ush 132,000 from Africa 2000 Network, then another Ush 150,000 to buy 50 birds, and a third grant of Ush 360,000.

Most GEWA members are heads of household, either widowed or never married, so the question of husbands' control of money does not arise. Rebecca does, however, know married women who have some control in their families. She believes there is a difference in the way men and women conduct their businesses: 'Women are more committed and with sufficient capital they make more profit than men,' she says.

Rebecca remains convinced about practising sustainable agriculture even though some of the practices are highly labour-intensive. She has been hard-hit by the prolonged drought, but if she manages to fight the termites with neem trees, she can keep the cows under zero-grazing. Water is a problem: She must repair the old water tank when she gets money. She concludes:

> Adopting the new methods has made a very big difference in our lives. We bought our foods at the market for about 20 years. Now we are almost self-sufficient in food. Our income increased, and the nutritional status at home improved. My biggest problem now is insufficient capital. I want to expand my activities but cannot. I tried to get a loan from ... PAP but have not yet succeeded.

I want to get a loan, but the interest rates are just too high.

Victoria Nalongo Namusisi, progressive farmer

Victoria Nalongo Namusisi (32): diplomas in journalism and business management; divorced and supporting 18 children (3 hers); raises and sells poultry, bananas and vegetables

'My father valued girls—he bought a plot of land for each of us,' Victoria Nalongo Namusisi says. Victoria has one diploma in journalism and another in business management with a specialisation in communications. 'Considering that communication is a very crucial element in the home and in business,' Victoria explains, 'I find my last diploma the most useful in my life.' Today she is a progressive farmer.

Victoria started farming as a business in 1989 when she found her salary as a journalist insufficient to meet her needs. She borrowed Ush 40,000 against her future salary and used it to clear land and make sweet potato heaps. She was encouraged by her first harvest, which sold for Ush 1 million. 'I do not have partners in business. It is just myself and my children. I care for 18 children—three of them my own. My son and I are both signatories to the business account. He is more aggressive than the girls, although they also help me in business,' she says.

Victoria was born in 1956 at Kisubi Hospital, not far from Nalugala village where she now lives. All 12 brothers and sisters were educated; the eldest became a consultant in international civil aviation. The second, who died in 1996, had a master's degree. The third is a Ph.D., heading the Geography Department at a Nairobi University. Her elder sister qualified as a secretary but stopped working when she married. Another brother stopped after 4 years of secondary school and joined her father as a fisherman.

'My father had four years of primary school and my mother had three. Although he was only a peasant fisherman, my father mobilised villagers to take their children to school. And unlike most men of his time, or even now, he did value girls,' Victoria states with pride. He bought each of his daughters plots of land—she received the land she farms today when she was only six years old. When she bore twins in 1983, he suggested that she give them to him to care for because the house where she stayed with her husband was rented, and he didn't like it. Unfortunately, her father died in 1996.

Victoria married in 1976 at age 20 but doesn't think she was ready for marriage then. She was studying journalism at the time and was a national athlete. Through athletics she met James Okoth, then general secretary of the National Council of Sports. The marriage lasted only 7 years, and she has remained single since then.

Victoria's first child was born in 1977 in Kenya. Besides her own three, she has adopted more than ten children, looking after them and paying their school fees. One is a Moslem girl she saved from a forced marriage. Her adopted children are at different levels of education, ranging from the final year of university to primary; all have education and training. During holidays they are all in the house.

> Some of my adopted children grow vegetables that we sell to maintain the household. They are like all children, who usually consider their mothers first and are found digging beside them. Except for that help I would call myself the sole breadwinner in the house. I am a mixed farmer, keeping poultry—both layers and broilers, growing sweet potatoes, pumpkins. I have been a farmer all my life. Since I was born it is the only way I know of making money. All our money for school fees comes from farming.

She earns about Ush 200,000 from the farm every week to spend on sugar, rice, posho, dry beans, cooking oil, telephone, electricity, school and medical fees, and clothing. She thinks that her business could bring in about Ush 15 million a year if she devoted full time to it. She has 3 workers—a herdsman, a house attendant and a gardener who also helps with the poultry. She owns both the land and the building. Because of her large family she sometimes uses all her income for school fees and so doesn't have any for agriculture, but she resolves that problem by asking her regular suppliers for credit.

In addition to her weekly cash income, Victoria has in-kind income from the farm: The food that household members eat is worth on average Ush

Table 4.9. Farm products consumed and their value: Victoria's family

Item	Quantity/week	Unit Price (Ush)	Amount/week (Ush)	Amount/year (Ush)
Sweet potatoes	5 tins	2,500	12,500	650,000
Cassava	1 tin	2,000	2,000	104,000
Bananas	2 bunches	4,000	8,000	416,000
Pumpkins	3	800	2,400	124,800
Cabbages	14	500	7,000	364,000
Greens	—	—	3,000	156,000
Tomatoes	—	—	3,500	182,000
Beans	seasonal	—	5,769	300,000
Eggs	20	100	2,000	104,000
Eggplants	—	—	1,000	52,000
Bitter tomatoes	—	—	2,000	104,000
Milk	35 litres	600	21,000	1,092,000
TOTAL	—	—	70,169	3,648,800

70,000 a week. The most important crops grown for the family are bananas, cassava and sweet potatoes. The family typically consumes the amounts shown in Table 4.9 from the farm, which have a value of Ush 3.6 million a year.

Victoria, like Rebecca, got a start on improved agriculture when members of her group visited Kenya:

> We learned how to prepare organic manure, conserve soil, intercrop and use other sustainable methods of farming as well as project-proposal writing. For example, I started growing bananas as a business in 1996. In the past, I only had about 30 plants and they yielded small bunches [and] I thought that my land was not good for bananas. But after 3 months of training, I started my first banana plantation using organic farming. I got a cow through Africa 2000 and 10 bags of cement for putting up the cowshed, in August 1997.

Victoria also grows vegetables like amaranths, cabbage, cauliflower, green pepper, carrots, tomatoes, several leafy green vegetables, sweet potatoes, cassava and, occasionally, Irish potatoes. She rears goats, cows, rabbits, pigs and poultry. One advantage of all those animals is that they are sources of manure, which she mixes with coffee husks to produce compost, and she uses animal urine mixed with pepper to control banana weevils.

Victoria too has left off using chemicals in favour of sustainable agriculture, practising intercropping to minimise the amount of weeding needed. Her family has not faced any serious problems adopting the new methods, which have brought about a marked difference in their lives. 'We can now afford to eat vegetables like eggplants, bitter tomatoes and sweet tomatoes every day. Production has increased. We still don't use new tools; I had wanted a tractor but couldn't afford it,' she explains.

'Getting loans can be complex for women. It is especially difficult for a single woman because she is asked questions like whether she was married in church or not. When a woman is not properly married, she is asked where they will find her should she default on payment. Yet when a married woman borrows money, the man has access to it and sometimes controls it. The interest rates are just too high in any case,' Victoria says, but if she could get a loan she would rear more broilers (currently she has 500) to market at the new hotels being built in and around Entebbe.

Victoria makes time to serve her community, particularly young girls:

> I joined Awake Pota, a project for teenagers, which works mostly with women as concerned mothers. I am also a member of Twekolere Women's Group and am its current chairperson and am the first Ugandan woman to encourage women to join scouting: I argue that girls should no longer only be Girl Guides—it is time for them to be Scouts. Now we have a number of women in scouting, and I am the vice chairperson of the Uganda Scouts Association. I benefit from all those groups myself as I share with women who are oppressed—especially those who think that they cannot survive without men. I show how a single woman can not only survive but thrive as a farmer and mother of children who need her.

Victoria wants to buy more land for mixed farming so that she may fence off about five acres where her cows can graze freely. The most important attribute for women entering business is to be prepared to sacrifice and to be patient, Victoria says. 'Families must be empowered economically—families that have lost hope in life, such as those who live with AIDS.'

The mountains of Kabale: gender partnerships

The climate of Kabale, a mountainous district in south-western Uganda, is favourable to agriculture, which provides a livelihood for most of its half million people, many of whom also engage in cross-border commerce with neighbouring Rwanda. But population density—one of the highest in the country—has left families with fragmented plots and has encouraged over-cultivation, with a consequent decline in productivity. Attempting to introduce improved farming methods and agro-industry, the district authorities administer the government's Entandikwa and PAP credit schemes. The former has dispersed few funds and its loan recovery rate is said to be over 70 per cent; the latter's recovery rate is said to be over 90 per cent. Africa 2000 is among the NGOs that work with women farmers in Kabale. Four progressive farmers responded to this study: Anna Ndoshore, Christina Night Bekunda, Paskazia Zalibugire and Efurazia Bamuturaki.

I estimate my farm income as ten times what my husband and I earn as policeman and teacher.
Anna Ndoshore, teacher and farmer

Anna Ndoshore (38): four years secondary school and teacher-training college; married with three children; school teacher, general store owner, sells milk and vegetables she produces

Anna Ndoshore's school expenses are not too high since her children are still at the primary level. But she dreads the day she will start paying for secondary school education. Very confident and outgoing at age 38, Anna is a schoolteacher and mother of three children, married to a policeman. She attended a teacher-training college and has taught since the 1980s but plans to resign to look after her farming and trading businesses.

Her house, built with permanent materials, is designed in two units, with a shop and sitting room at the front and bedrooms at the back. The kitchen is separate, to keep smoke out of the main house. The animals are kept at a good distance. Well arranged, properly mulched crops fill the garden. As Anna conducts a visitor around the homestead, her husband Jerome tends the shop while the older boy looks after the saucepans on the fire. There is a water pipe stand in the background, and the house has electricity. A pressure lamp is on standby in case power goes off, since customers come even in the early hours of the night.

The Ndoshores cultivate two acres within the Kabale municipality—a former brick-making area where topsoil was removed. They prepared the land well, and their small farm thrives, supplying the family with vegetables—bananas, beans, sweet potatoes, indigenous greens such as dodo (amaranths) and eshwiga, cabbage, onions, carrots and spinach, Irish potatoes, avocado, cassava, yams, pawpaw and 'a lot of beautiful flowers', the interviewer observed. There are useful shrubs and trees: greveria, alnus, bottle brush to treat animal cough, and others like nyarwehindure for treating malaria as well as omwetango for various ailments. There is also a daily supply of milk from two heifers that are zero-grazed and five goats. One heifer was provided by Africa 2000 on 19 December, 1997, after Anna had bought one with credit from PAP six months earlier. Anna's farm has food to spare for sale.

The basic family income comes from Anna's salary as a primary school teacher—Ush 75,000 a month plus some extra through the Parents/Teachers Association. Her husband's salary brings little because police officers are usually underpaid and must provide their own room wherever assigned.

Sale of excess produce from the farm brings the income shown in Table 4.10.

Table 4.10. Sale of excess produce and its value: Anna's family

Item	Quantity	Unit Price (Ush)	Amount / mo. (Ush)	Amount / year (Ush)
Cabbages	—	—	1,000	12,000
Milk	14 litres/day	320	135,000	1,620,000
Mushrooms (dried)	—	—	10,000	120,000
TOTAL	—	—	146,000	1,752,000

The mushrooms were a 1996 innovation. Anna works with the main mushroom farmer, Enid Rwakatungu, who supplies inputs and training, then exports the dried mushrooms abroad in bulk. Anna did not estimate the total income from her shop, but says that it helps pay school fees and provide family clothing and other household requirements. She sells takataka (odds and ends): soap, paraffin, safety matches, salt, sugar, maize, millet and wheat flour, candles, stationery, cutlery. Hers is a typical peri-urban shop.

Anna is not sure of her father's age, but he is in his 60s. Although he had no formal schooling, he learned to read and write at a church education programme. He is a church warden, Council I chairman and clan leader. Her mother, who passed away a few years back, could also read and write but had no formal schooling. She was a Mother's Union leader and treasurer of a revolving fund for women. The parents had 12 children—six girls and 6 boys. One boy became a cooperative officer after graduating from university. Five—including Anna—completed 4 years of secondary, and of those, one boy and one girl joined the police and 2 became self-employed. Two sisters finished 2 secondary years; one became a secretary and the other a businesswoman. A brother who completed 7 years of primary school, and a sister who finished 6, stay with their father.

Anna explains how she became a progressive farmer: 'When I joined the Africa 2000 scheme, I was already trained in better methods of farming as a member of Two Wings Agro Forestry Group, which operates in Kabale district. However, Africa 2000 polished me up, and through the extension service I get guidance on the spot, hence the greater yields.' The benefits are many: Her family income has increased to an estimated ten times the two spouses' combined wages. In addition, Anna buys only rice and meat but no longer any fresh produce. She regularly uses new technologies, such as fuel-saving cooking stoves, as well as a shovel and a bicycle. She explains:

> I am the secretary of our organisation called Karubanda Bakyala Tutunguke ('self-elevation of Karubanda women') which has 28 members. We operate a ROSCA, have borrowed Ush 5 million from the Poverty Alleviation Programme (PAP) and Ush 100,000 from Entandikwa—both government schemes—and have repaid the money. It is through this association that I got a second heifer with PAP money. The first calf produced has to be given to another member—mine is soon to be passed on.

Despite her achievements, Anna shares with other farmers an acute need for capital to expand her businesses.

> Basically, more capital is required to enable me to look after the heifers very well so that they can produce more milk. I also need more agricultural inputs than I can afford now—weed killers, fertilisers, etc. At present I am able to pay a full-time workman, and sometimes I use casual labour. My husband does some farming at the weekend as I do, but both of us are constrained by our full-time paid employment.

She needs to save for her children's education and improve her house, which is still unfinished. About Ush 50 million is needed to complete her home and business.

Exuding confidence, Anna urges women farmers to join women's groups and learn a lot. She advises government and other bodies to offer more training to women.

My mother is a great inspiration. A well-known businesswoman in the market, she gives us tips for our business.

Christina Night Bekunda, progressive farmer

Christina Night Bekunda (30): seven years primary school; married with five children; sells milk and sorghum-honey beverages she makes, trains in appropriate technology

Like Anna, Christina Night Bekunda lives in a peri-urban setting that is administered by Kabale municipality. It too is part of a brick-making zone where the top soil was removed and the level of re-fertilisation must be high in order to harvest anything. But, being a heavily populated area where land is scarce, whatever can be utilised is valuable, as Christina's family knows well. Their homestead consists of three buildings—the main house, a small one with rooms for rent and an animal house (chickens, goats and store). The houses are in a small trading centre on the main road from Kabale to nearby Rwanda.

At age 30 Christina is married with 5 children, all in primary school. Her husband Gershom, 41, quit after 2 years of secondary school to join the Army in 1975, worked on and off as a foreman on road construction projects and is now fully occupied with household production. 'My mother, now 55, is a great inspiration to me and Gershom,' says Christina. 'She is a well-known businesswoman who has had a stall in the municipality main market for a long time. She gives us tips on how to run [a] business. She is a very strong person both in build and character, whom everyone knows, and she has a lot of influence in the market. She is a church warden, a member of several credit schemes and a counsellor in the AIDS support organisation, ASCO.'

Christina and her five siblings were brought up by their widowed mother. As the eldest, she stopped schooling after seven years. The second-born—her sister—just completed her fourth year of secondary school; one brother is in third year of high school, and the other three are still in primary school. Christina's husband was a leader of the Young Farmers' Association in the sub-county and has served as a local councillor. His mother attended three years of primary school and has been a Mother's Union leader. His father was a businessman and a mixed farmer. His parents were keen to educate their children, and Gershom disappointed them when he ran away from school to join the army. He deeply regrets this because those siblings who remained in school are now better off than he is. His four sisters and one brother completed a minimum of four years of secondary education. His big sister is a very well known and well off trader.

Christina and Gershom plant less than half an acre around their home and have additional land on a distant hillside that Gershom's parents gave them. Their crops include vegetables—cabbage, carrots, dodo, eggplant, spinach, onions, indigenous greens (eshwiga, nakati, eshogi) and cauliflower. They also grow fodder—mainly elephant grass. They recently got 100 chickens, which have yet to reach laying stage; they own two rabbits, one heifer and a calf they named Kembabazi ('of grace'). Gershom's parents put aside a few cows for him too. Their town farm (0.4 acre) is supported by income from the rural one, which is quite far away and requires more growth capital.

At the moment the family income is derived from milk sold on a daily basis. The cow was received on 19 December 1997 from Africa 2000. 'Two litres of milk are reserved for the family and we sell 3 litres every day at 320 shillings each,' Christina says. 'We are trying our best to see that the milk yield is increased. Part of the income is used to pay for part-time help in collecting fodder. Other income is from the cold beverage I make from sorghum mixed with honey that is profitable but time-consuming. I also earn money as a trainer in appropriate technology: I go around the district demonstrating fuel-saving stoves and helping those who are keen to build them.'

To prepare for the arrival of the free heifer and set up other business activities, Christina borrowed Ush 400,000 from PAP through her women's organisation and will soon complete repayment. She worries about the 100 layer chicks and prays they do not die prematurely.

Christina finds community organisations very helpful. She belongs to a ROSCA with 19 other women, is a committee member in a kwezika (burial association), and is active in the Mother's Union at her local church. She is also vice chairperson of ASCO, whose 30 women and 3 men counsel patients, try to place orphans in homes and create awareness about HIV/AIDS within the community.

The various training programmes she has attended taught Christina to produce insecticides and manure (from cow dung, urine and fire ash) and plant a variety of fodder. With that assistance, despite her small farm and poor soil, Christina is self-sufficient in vegetables and a few other crops, while her husband prefers to concentrate on livestock rearing, especially cows, estimating they are more profitable. She would like to diversify, to have a small shop for general groceries and her home-made beverages, and cultivate her bigger pieces of land in the more remote area. But she must face the problem of transport: If it was available, the town farm would benefit from the rural land where more fodder and other crops could be grown. Her main challenge is getting enough money to buy drugs for the heifer and pay labour and school fees.

Although not yet earning a lot of profit, Christina and her husband have a sizeable number of investments that, she argues, point to a future with hope. Fortunately, the family is still young.

> **I am generally in charge of production. I know what to keep for the family and what to sell. I discuss these issues with my husband, but I am in charge.**
>
> Paskazia Zalibugire, progressive farmer

Paskazia Zalibugire: completed junior secondary school; married with eight children; grows and sells trees and vegetables

'The sweet-potato crop earns me the most. I get an equivalent of 600,000 shillings a year. I do not get it in cash; rather, I arrange with the secondary school (Rushoroza) to place a value on the crop and work out the equivalent in school fees,' Paskazia Zalibugire explains. She, her husband and family live in a village called Muyumbu on the outskirts of Kabale town. Her husband is a primary school teacher, and she manages the farm. The fifth in a family of 12 children, Paskazia completed junior secondary school and married at the age of 20. One sister is a Makerere University graduate and senior civil servant. Her eldest brother is a medical assistant, a sister completed secretarial training, and another is studying for a diploma in catering. Another sister got through primary 6, but 4 of the girls did not go to school at all—they learned to read and write at church. Paskazia's father, who died a few years ago in his 80s, was a local council chairman, treasurer of a savings group and elder of the village where many looked to him for advice and for settling disputes. Her mother, who is 78, had no formal education but learned to read and write at her church and to this day is an active women's leader.

'When my husband retired ten years ago, it became necessary for us to look for alternative income. Having eight children, I had to think hard,' Paskazia says. Most of the produce on their six-acre farm is for home consumption; some of the acreage is up in the hills where they grow potatoes and trees. Her most important crops are sweet potatoes, beans and vegetables. The family's annual income comes from their tree plantation. Eucalyptus and black wattle are used for firewood at home, and the surplus sold at about Ush 10,000 each year. They sell vegetables: carrots for two seasons, at Ush 30,000, cabbage at 10,000 a year. Other greens fetch an average of Ush 10,000 a year. The sweet potatoes she uses for school fees are valued at Ush 600,000. So the total value of the crops sold or bartered is about Ush 660,000. The rest of the crops are for home consumption. She has 3 sheep and a few chickens for feeding the family and grows fodder and firewood. For food she grows avocado, guava, mountain papaya, pineapple, soya bean and broad bean. And yes, some medicinal plants.

'My main focus now is on the cow,' Paskazia says, flashing a smile and referring to it as Patience Kashemeire ('the fine one'). 'I received it last December after training by the Africa 2000 group. I got intrigued with the farming methods used by Mrs Bitalabeho, a progressive woman farmer in a neighbouring village and consulted her from time to time until recently when I underwent my own training. Now I improve my yields through decomposing rubbish, grass and weeds for manure; utilising cattle urine as an insecticide; making manure from cow and sheep dung with urine and chicken droppings; and using better mulching methods and using trenches to halt soil erosion (fanya juu and fanya chini: 'Do it up' and 'do it down').

In the past, Paskazia hired part-time casual labour during peak seasons, but now she has one young man working for her full-time, in addition to the help she gets from her husband and the children. In the past, too, on rare occasions government workers at the District Farm Institute would address rallies on farming methods, but they didn't visit individual farms, so it was not so useful in her view. Lately the farmers' groups are visited by funders such as PAP, Southwestern Region Agriculture Rehabilitation Project (SWRARP) and Africa 2000.

A strong believer in the strength that organisations can give, Paskazia is a member of Muyumbu Bakyala Tweheyo Kukola ('Muyumbu women, let's work harder'), a women's community-based organisation formed in 1994. They have received several loans as a group: first Ush 300,000, then later another 500,000 for brick-making; both were repaid. They then borrowed Ush 60,000 from the Centenary Rural Banking Scheme and repaid that too. In addition, they have their own informal loan scheme they call Kushukirana—'refilling one another's basket'—whose members are 30 women and 3 men. She says that the men were interested and are helpful in tasks like supervising the brick-making. 'I am the treasurer of the group. I have gained from group association. If it were not for the group, I would have no heifer, because donor organisations prefer working with groups,' Paskazia says. She is also active in the nearby church—on its council and with the literacy programme—and is chairperson of the Women's Council I and secretary for women's affairs in the village (LCI) council.

Some neighbours are starting to come to learn from her. Many join groups as a result, 'although of course you will always meet a few negative people in life!' Paskazia comments. Her main problem is lack of money for her big family. She speaks with pride of her children: The firstborn, the only boy, is an information officer. The next—all girls—are doing higher-diploma, teachers-college and secondary exams, and the last two are still in primary school. But she advises young women to have small families, to utilise family planning services.

'We have made plenty of progress,' Paskazia says. She cites increased household income, food security with no famine threats, control of soil erosion, better yields and weed control. She refers in particular to her banana plantation, on which passers-by comment because it is usually thought that bananas cannot thrive in her part of the district. She uses a fuel-saving stove but is still confined to the panga and the hoe for farming.

> If it were possible, I would prefer to have my land in one piece—the scattered pieces are not convenient to farm. I want to read more books,

hear more radio programmes and see more videos about farming. There are other things to learn like making charcoal from banana peelings and rearing rabbits. There is a lot more to learn!

I have always been a businesswoman.
Efurazia Bamuturaki, progressive farmer

Efurazia Bamuturaki (40): completed primary school; married with nine children; grows and sells vegetables, milk, forestry products and prepared food

'I have always been a businesswoman,' Efurazia Bamuturaki says with pride. She has a small stall at the market yard where she sells prepared food weekly. 'It has contributed a lot to the family income, but I suspended this because of my new heifer. I am interested in business. If I had more capital, I would sell locally brewed banana and sorghum beer—convenient products that I could operate from home. Then I would open a small shop attached to the house. My main interest now is to make money to educate our children. My husband Filipo uses his capital to grow tomatoes that bring high profit so that we can build a better house.'

Efurazia's is a typical rural household in Kabale district although it now has an above-average income. Located in a village called Kishongati cell, Bukinda sub-county, the house is roofed with iron sheets, and the walls are of mud and wattle. Floor and walls are neatly plastered with a mixture of lime and cow dung. The farm is on a slope, as are many others in this hilly area where environmental degradation is widespread and any action to stop it is easily noticeable. The population pressure on land is intense since this is one of the most densely settled areas in Uganda.

The family is lucky to live near the main highway connecting Kenya, Uganda and Rwanda, which makes marketing easier. The sub-county has a teacher's college, two secondary schools, a health centre, a seminary and several primary schools that provide markets for produce. It is possible to have telephones and electricity in this area if one can afford them, but so far those are utilised only by the teacher-training college and the seminary. They are beyond the means of the surrounding rural households.

Efurazia and her 5 sisters all completed primary school; one brother reached senior 4 and the other got an engineering degree at Makerere University. Her father, a peasant farmer with no formal education, joined the 7th Battalion of the King's African Rifles during World War II. Her mother had no formal education either, but like the father learned to read and write at the Catholic Church. Her mother, now about 75 years old, is a farmer, housewife and trader specialising in salt and baskets, who sometimes barters, exchanging salt for dry peas, beans and other produce. She has been a woman leader in the church, 'and I have learned a lot from her', Efurazia says.

When she was 15, Efurazia married Filipo Bamuturaki, who had left school after 2 years of secondary because of the fees. She is 40, he 53, and they have 9 children, the eldest of whom, a girl, stopped schooling in her fourth year of secondary school; the next, a boy, is in teacher-training college. The older boys are in secondary school, and 2 girls are waiting for enough money so they can enter too. The rest are in primary school.

Filipo describes in detail the whole process of farming—the types of crops and livestock, the usefulness of the different shrubs and vegetables—while waiting for his wife to arrive from the field where she went to do a woman's job—weeding. An entrepreneur himself, he makes baking tins, bread bins and lamps, and repairs saucepans and big metal drums. He is the village artisan.

The Bamuturaki land is about 6 acres in total but composed of 11 separate pieces. Their livestock includes 3 goats, two sheep, two pigs, eight chickens, four rabbits, two heifers and 5 dogs (Filipo sells puppies). How their crops are used is seen in Table 4.11.

As seen in the chart, Efurazia realises more than Ush 544,000 a year from produce and gets an additional Ush 1 million annually from the daily sale of milk. She was selected as an Africa 2000 model farmer and trained as part of a group, after which extension workers visited individual farms to give guidance on the spot. The training lasted about 18 months. In contrast, official government extension workers from the District Agricultural Farm visit and give advice just once a year.

Innovations the family has adopted include those described in Table 4.12.

A friend of the family observed another transformation: the change in Filipo since the new methodologies were introduced to the family. 'Filipo has immersed himself in the family production as opposed to the many hours he and his colleagues used to spend consuming spirits. The physical change is visible.'

How did the family manage to make the costly improvements? Africa 2000 provided a free heifer that was in calf, but Efurazia had to look for money to build the cowshed, to buy required drugs and to prepare fodder before the heifer was delivered. They borrowed Ush 80,000 from friends and relatives: Ush 50,000 interest-free and Ush 30,000 that requires a monthly payment of 1,000 for every 10,000 of the loan. Efurazia emphasises that under the Africa 2000 scheme it is easier for the wife to borrow, but in consultation with her husband.

Like her mother before her, and like other progressive farmers, Efurazia believes in organisation. She belongs to an association known as Rukombe

Table 4.11. Crops used and their value: Efurazia's family

Item	Use(s)	Quantity Sold	Unit Price (Ush)	Amount (Ush)	Amount / Year (Ush)
Bananas	At home & brewing banana beer for sale	40 litres	—	5,000 / month	60,000
Cabbage	At home & for sale	8 sacks	1,500–2,500	16,000 twice / year	32,000
Spinach	At home & for sale	—	—	—	2,000
Onions	At home & for sale	—	—	—	200,000
Sweet potatoes	At home & for dogs	—	—	—	—
Irish potatoes	At home & for sale	2 sacks	15,000	30,000 twice / year	60,000
Sorghum	At home & for sale	—	—	—	50,000
Peas	At home & for sale	—	—	—	70,000
Beans	Mostly at home; also for sale	—	—	—	60,000
Tomatoes	At home	—	—	—	—
Indigenous greens	At home	—	—	—	—
Eucalyptus trees	At home & for sale	—	—	—	10,000
Agroforestry	At home: to demarcate land & treat maladies	—	—	—	—
Milk	At home & for sale	15 litres / day	—	—	1,000,000
TOTAL	—	—	—	—	1,544,000

Tukyengane ('trust one another') Agricultural Group, established in 1982 during a time of economic and political crisis, with 31 members—twenty-six women and 5 husbands, which she chairs. She says:

> The immediate cause for starting this group was our poverty. We lacked clothes, bedding, household utensils—everything. We sold our labour collectively. Sometimes we would get credit from a shopkeeper as a group and get basic things we needed. Sometimes we would plant our crops as a group and sell everything. This enabled us to buy a plot. We have now added a produce store and are constructing a shop

next door. The building is not complete—we are still raising funds. As a group we have borrowed money from two government schemes (SWRARP and Entandikwa) and paid it back.

Table 4.12. Farming innovations: Efurazia's family

Preparation of manure	Waste (e.g., peelings, plant stocks) that was previously discarded now is used for enriching soil
Control of soil erosion	Terracing and trenches dug in the banana plantation retain water, known in Kiswahili as fanya juu and fanya chini, or 'do it up, do it down'
Kitchen garden	Established to provide more varieties of vegetables for domestic consumption
Agro-forestry techniques	Including plants for fodder (some grown near the home so that children can feed animals), other plants to create good hedges and landmarks, and some to treat wounds, worms and growths on the skin
Dairy farming—zero-grazing	Bringing food to the cow so that it needs no pasture area
Banana plantation	Methods of spacing and mulching bananas have resulted in big bunches and softer bananas; passers-by and officials 'marvel at the change'
Energy-saving fuelwood stoves	Because the fuelwood stove is built economically, less wood is used and less attention is required during cooking.

Efurazia also belongs to Bafumbo Association (Catholic Mother's Union) and the LCI executive committee. She chairs the Nyezikye Association (a collaborative burial group).

> I have gained a lot from these associations as we hold periodic training sessions. We can borrow from the groups' savings, and other members act as your guarantors if one needs credit from shopkeepers. I have also gained a lot of confidence. I found it hard to address people before, but now I have no problem. I am also able to give guidance to other people. Even when I am not asked, I pass on to fellow farmers good farming practices.

Women: the senior family farmers

Women's labour produces 80 per cent of Uganda's food, and food crops account for 90 per cent of agriculture income in cash and kind. In addition, women's labour produces 60 per cent of traditional farm exports and an impressive 80 per cent of NTAEs, such as maize, beans, cereal, vanilla and horticulture products. It is beyond doubt that if progress lags in the countryside,

Uganda will not develop, and that progress in agriculture depends heavily on women farmers.

Yet, as described earlier, women farmers are not seen as the progressive farmers and providers that they are. Insufficient information as to the facts blocks women's direct access to productive resources and puts the brakes on development.

Table 4.13. Employment status of the agricultural labour force

Labour Unit	% Male Distribution	% Female Distribution
Employee	1.1	0.2
Self-employed	69.1	26.6
Unpaid family worker	29.8	73.2
Total	100.0	100.0

Source: 1991 Census, in ILO, 1995, cited in Elson, Diane and Evers, Barbara, July 1997, *Gender Aware Country Reports: Uganda*, Manchester, UK.

Table 4.13 makes that clear: In the agricultural labour force, 73.2 per cent of females are classified as unpaid family workers and 26.6 per cent as self-employed. In contrast, 69.1 per cent of males are considered self-employed.

The limited perception of women not as farmers but as farmers' wives, and the perpetuation of 'trickle down' and 'trickle over' theories that channel resources only to male farmers, are totally unrealistic, as the lives of women in this chapter testify.

The factors of production: land, labour and capital

Access to and control over land, labour and capital—the factors of production—form the framework for further analysis of the information in this chapter. Information provided by nine of the ten progressive farmers is summarised in Table 4.14, which reveals stark differences between regions in the country regarding control of production factors—land, labour and capital—and related resources and benefits. The data are grouped so that the three factors can be discussed separately.

Land

Men and women both have access to land, but only in Kabale is land control shared by husband and wife. An example of access without control is Hajat's

Table 4.14. Access to and control of resources and benefits

Resource/Benefit	Access*	Control*
Land	9 MF	6 M
Credit	6 MF, 3 M	3 MF, 6 M
Technical inputs	4 MF, 3 M	1 MF, 6 M
Extension services	5 MF, 4 M	3 MF, 6 M
Improved tools	7 MF	1 MF, 6 M
Transport	6 MF, 2M	8 M
Primary education	9 MF	3 MF, 6 M
Income	5 MF, 3 M	2 MF, 6 M
Cash employment	8 MF, 1 M	3 MF, 6 M
House	—	9 M
Health care	9 MF	4 MF, 5 M
Sons' labour	8 MF, 1 F	4 MF, 4 M, 1 F
Daughters' labour	7 MF, 2 F	3 MF, 4 M, 2 F

M = male, F = female, MF = male/female
* Where numbers do not add to 9, the respondents had no reply.

remark, 'Men own the land and in most cases allow women to use it. However, when men realise women are becoming economically empowered as a result of using the land, they sometimes refuse it.'

The nine progressive farmers stand out among their peers for their relationship to the land they till: They own or co-own it or have secure tenure. Ownership of land in Uganda has traditionally been mostly male: Sons, not daughters or widows, inherit it. When clarified and passed,[6] the Land Act of 1998 may change that reality, but as of 1998 women own only seven per cent of the land, and wives seldom inherit it even though anticipation of being thrown off the farm when one becomes a widow is a sure disincentive to improving farming practices. Some ethnic groups do, however, allow women to retain use of the land when widowed; despite the custom of relatives taking land from widows, Hajat and her co-wives stayed in the house and had user rights to the land for some time. Other exceptions exist—women who inherited or had land purchased for them by their fathers—that made a great difference in the capitalisation of their farms. Every Ugandan father who owns land ought to hear about those examples.

Of the 13 farmers, three received land from their fathers. Victoria, perhaps the most successful of all, says that her father, a peasant fisherman with just 4 years of primary school, was unique for his time—and for present times—

because he valued girls and, when she was only 6 years old, bought land for each of his daughters. Zulaika inherited her 4 acres from her father and farms the 8 acres belonging to her husband. Rebecca, a single woman living with her mother, has a plot and house on 5 acres of the kabaka's land (on which one has secure tenure rather than ownership) long occupied by her family. Rose, a Nanyonjo shop owner, whom the researchers met in Kira, also inherited land from her father, so was able to place her shop on part of it and sell the rest to get her start-up capital.

Others have purchased or been given land: Zahara bought it with her husband and they built their house jointly too. Her business is a partnership with her husband and children. Joyce lives and works on land and in a house her husband bought. Jalilah's in-laws own the land where she and her husband are building their house. Veteran and widow Aisa Nalongo owns her plot and home. Christina and Gershom have land given to them by his parents.

Women themselves take an understandable but disturbing view of land inheritance by their daughters—perhaps because they do not foresee change in what is often labelled 'the culture' and thought to be everlasting. Jalilah, Zahara, Hajat and others expect their sons to take over their agribusinesses because girls move away when they marry into other families. Speaking to the land issue in Mbale district, Madanda says that even after marriage, women cannot inherit land: 'In essence women belong "nowhere".'

Labour

Labour is the second factor of production. Access to and control over children's labour and related assets such as improved tools, technical inputs, health care and primary education are shown in Table 4.14 above. Both spouses have access to the help of sons and daughters, but control of that labour rests with men in Iganga, whereas in Kabale, control is shared by husband and wife, as is control of primary education. The two female household heads of course control all family labour, and Victoria comments from her experience that despite control by their fathers, children usually consider their mothers first and 'are normally found digging beside them.' Boys in Kabale are beginning to share in housework, such as washing kitchen utensils.

Even though some of the progressive farmers can hire more labour, most women's labour shortages are more severe than those of their husbands. In Mbale, as elsewhere, men as owners of the land command the labour and they own the labour product. In addition, there are gender-based price distortions in labour markets. In Ibanda, where women hire out their labour as one of their survival strategies, men receive Ush 700 for a day's work while women get only Ush 500 to 600. Women's competitive labour is sometimes even discouraged, reflecting the community view that women who hire out are of lesser status and they lower the status of their husbands, too.

Access to technical inputs and improved tools that enhance output and reduce time and energy burdens is a subject of importance to the respondents and an indicator of women's progress. Only Anna among the progressive farmers speaks of using a shovel and a bicycle. Most of the farmers find the new, sustainable agricultural methods very labour-intensive, although they admit that yields improve and family nutrition is much better too. 'I have more surplus,' Zulaika says. For a few women the improved yields and income offer the possibility of hiring labour or moving from occasional labour to a permanent worker, as Paskazia did.

Kabale women say that there are so few new technical inputs that the question of access and control is moot. As regards extension services, it would of course seem logical that the women, who do the bulk of the agriculture work, would be the recipients, but where these exist they too generally go to men—except in Kabale. NGOs such as Africa 2000 are beginning to break that pattern by extending services to women's groups and even to individual women farmers. Transport is in men's control although some farmers in mountainous Kabale comment that gender matters little as transport is either inadequate or inaccessible. Improved tools also are scarce, excepting fuel-saving stoves and some shovels. Technology is a male prerogative in six of the nine cases under review.

The farm women of Kabale displayed their labour- and fuel-saving stoves with pride. They are ceramic with fitted spaces for pots and stovepipes for ventilation, and were first introduced in the Sahel some years ago. Another technological improvement by one of the farmers was a pair of oxen to help with the heavy work, but that ceased when one of the oxen died. Otherwise, the day-to-day tools used by farmers—progressive or poor—are those that their grandmothers used.

Good health and education of the labour force are essential to a nation's productivity. Zahara's statement that 'Women are in control of health in cases of common ailments like fever and measles, while in emergencies and when transport is necessary the man takes over' describes the traditional division of labour wherein men control the cash. Respondents state that women's access to and control over health care is largely an irrelevant issue today. Such care at clinics and hospitals has become too expensive, when it exists at all, since the government cut health budgets and introduced cost-sharing by families when it undertook SAPs.

Table 4.14 also shows the opportunity for primary education—essential for a more productive labour force—as equally accessible to boys and girls with the recent introduction of universal primary education. Yet for two thirds of the women farmers, it is men who control rights to the education of their children—the exception once again being Kabale, where control is shared between spouses.

The division of farm labour between spouses and tasks assigned to children confirms the thesis that women are the senior family farmers. Information provided by respondents—the nine progressive farmers—is presented in Table 4.15.

Table 4.15. Gender profile of activity in agricultural production, processing and marketing

Activity	Women Participating*	Men Participating*	Children Participating
Land clearance	2	**9**	—
Land preparation	**8**	5	1
Fencing	2	**9**	—
Planting	**9**	4	8
Fertilising	**8**	4	5
Weeding	**9**	4	8
Bird scaring	3	—	8
Harvesting	**9**	8	9
Carrying	**9**	6	8
Sorting/grading	**9**	4	6 (mostly girls)
Threshing	**9**	6	5 (mostly girls)
Processing	**9**	5	5
Storage	**9**	3	4
Marketing	**3**	**6**	6

***Bold** indicates primary responsibility

Table 4.15 summarises information on the gender division of labour in the households of the progressive farmers of Kabale, Iganga and the environs of Kampala. Not included in the group is Anna, who is in effect the head of her household and responsible for all farm activities because of her husband's absence on duty as a police officer. Victoria, a single head of household, provides information on the general situation where she lives rather than on her own experience; it is included. Several respondents say that their husbands assist them on the farm, but their assessment of the gender division of agricultural labour raises several questions about the extent of that help, as the table shows.

The table shows a quite typical division of labour for eastern Africa, where men take primary responsibility for clearing the land and fencing it—and marketing the produce. The more tedious tasks—land preparation, planting, fertilising, weeding, harvesting, carrying, sorting, threshing, processing and storage of crops—are the domain of women, who at times have some help from men and children (particularly during the harvest). Scaring birds away from the crops is usually a task for children, though in Iganga women do it too.

That division of labour changes with marketing, where men take over and control the income; only in Kabale do women have major responsibility. Children also market small quantities of produce, especially when stalls are located at or near the home. Kabale women farmers also share control over the family income and cash employment, as is later discussed, but the trade-off they make is that their husbands do not participate in threshing, sorting or storage—tasks shared with their daughters, and 'men tend to monopolise the highly profitable resource: banana plantations'.

A more comprehensive picture of the whole of Uganda than those from our interviews comes from the Ministry of Women and Development, Culture and Youth estimate of 1994 that farm women in Uganda do the following work (Elson and Evers 1997: 17):

- sixty per cent of digging and planting;
- seventy per cent of weeding;
- sixty per cent of harvesting;
- ninety per cent of post-harvest processing; and
- one hundred per cent of hand-hoeing.

Capital

'Women are locked out of the capital accumulation process,' Aramanzan observes. Access to capital—the third factor of production—is firmly in the hands of men, as Table 4.14 shows under the categories 'credit' and 'income'. In the Kampala and Iganga areas, men generally have both access to and control of capital. All but one of the progressive farmers say that both men and women are free to accept work in return for cash, often by digging someone else's farm. But six of the nine farmers say that control of any income earned is with the man. Again, only Kabale is the exception. Zahara of Iganga states, however, that women are becoming aware of their rights and thus control their income 'to an extent'. This seems to be true of the family home as a form of capital; it is accessed by both spouses but under male control in all nine cases.

Victoria comments that accessing capital in the form of loans is not easy for women, no matter what their marital status. Single women are asked questions about their marriages and where they can be found in case of default. A married woman may find her loan controlled by her husband. Victoria's good fortune was to borrow against her future salary, and she now skirts the problem of financial credit by accessing it in kind from the suppliers of her farm inputs.

Rebecca's as well as Victoria's start-up capital was saved or borrowed from their wages—giving them a head start over those farmers who were never wage-employed. Some respondents told us they tried but failed, or they had 'not yet succeeded' in getting loans from formal sources. There are not only technical but at times also unspoken political qualifications for borrowers. Rebecca had no luck with PAP, and Regina also failed so she used her own savings. Efurazia solved her need for capital by borrowing from friends and relatives—some of the money on an interest basis and some free. Joyce borrowed from her sister and her husband. Zulaika would sell one crop and use the proceeds to invest in another after she failed to get a loan. Some, Hajat among them, simply do not try for individual loans; the prospect of getting into debt has no appeal to them.

The women of Ibanda adopted the strategy that 'is spreading like fire' across Uganda: the ROSCA. It is their favourite survival source, although it places between second and third on a scale of effectiveness in increasing capital (see Table 4.5, Ranking the viability of women's economic activities). The ROSCA is the basic method of savings and loans both in the countryside and in the city, because it is accessible, based on mutual trust, economically useful and open to everyone. Paskazia and Anna are treasurers of their ROSCAs. Other farmers are members; only one or two resisted joining them because of hearsay about failed ones. Curiously, there were no ROSCAs in the area studied by Madanda, and Aisa said there were no such groups in her village.

For most of the progressive farmers and others, access to capital is easiest through their local women's group, which at times allows a few husbands to join, because credit organisations—both governmental and non-governmental—prefer to work with groups that can on-lend to their individual members. Even in Iganga, Zulaika says, 'Women in groups now get more access to credit, technical inputs, extension services and transport.' All encourage their fellow women to join groups because it is easier to access credit and learn about improved technologies.

Innumerable community-based organisations (CBOs) serve as vehicles for training and credit organisations. Among the latter are government's Entandikwa and PAP, which are managed by local authorities; ; the YWCA; and the Uganda National Farmers Association (UNFA). Noticeably absent from the farms are the MFIs found in the urban setting (excepting loans for businesses in town), despite Uganda's including agriculture-related activities in its definition of the informal sector (see Introduction). Most foreign MFIs follow CGAP guidelines, noted in Chapter 3, which state that agriculture production and on-farm processing are not micro enterprises. The result is that 'the smallholder production sector at the grassroots is marginalised' (PSDP 1997). This must change.

The senior family farmers interviewed all say that their group loans have been repaid. Horticulturist Anet, who also owns a piggery, is a member of that group. She has land but needs capital to develop it. The group's capital base is very small, and members' individual financial positions are so delicate that they hesitate to guarantee others' loans. Moreover, some organisations, such as the PAP, demand deposits of a designated percentage of the loan—amounts that smallholders seldom have in cash.

Africa 2000 is unusual in giving grants instead of loans to the women's groups, some of which create their own revolving funds as a renewable financial resource. That approach allows women to build their assets and in due time turn to formal credit sources for additional funds. It is a technique worth watching because it does not saddle the farmer with debt at a time when her capacity to repay is limited—much less to repay with the very high interest and related borrower costs that prevail in Uganda banks and other credit institutions. Of note also are the refreshingly large amounts available, totalling Ush 642,000 in Rebecca's case, that MFIs often don't make available.

Under-capitalisation persists as a very serious obstacle to increasing productivity for those whose agribusinesses are well grounded. 'I have an acute need for capital to expand,' says Anna. Rebecca, Jalilah and Zulaika also face under-capitalisation. Efurazia needs a fresh supply of capital to open a shop in her home. Victoria avoids the problem by obtaining her supplies on credit from businesses she patronises regularly. Hajat earns extra capital from renting off-farm houses she owns.

The market

Four of every five produce-sellers in village markets are women farmers. Observers note that women sell there and get low returns while men travel farther to export markets that bring higher returns. Men command cash for both hired transport and bicycles. Recall that progressive farmer Anna was the first to use a bicycle. But Wamage of Mbale (Chapter 3) found that the bicycle bought by her spouse with income from the rice she grew was used to transport a new wife into the new house her earnings helped build—an incident that brought strong empathy from her colleagues. Such situations make many women wary of intensifying their productivity—and consequently constrain Uganda's development. The labour market also favours men—as the Ibanda study confirms.

Most of the progressive farmers do not cite marketing as a difficulty. Regina is the only one among those interviewed who consciously sought out the export market and grew vanilla for it, making a handsome profit. Hajat says that because local demand is strong, her group decided not to seek out export markets. Because middlemen buy their produce at very low prices, they decided to construct their own market.

Filling the void of insufficient information: questions raised in this chapter

Four questions were posed at the opening of this chapter. The following responses indirectly address the void of insufficient information about women farmers which in turn cause distortions in data used by government and private planners in formulating strategies to boost farm productivity, raise the national GDP and fight the poverty that prevents Uganda's progress.

1. What is income? Is the estimated two thirds of the food produced that is eaten at home part of the national product?

The value of the food produced for home consumption is counted into the national product in Uganda through Household Budget Surveys, as noted by the World Bank (World Bank 1993, Annex III). However, farmgate, or producer, prices have been used in the past and are understatements of the consumption value of the food. In the case of this study, we expect that the farmers also understated the market value of their produce. Our major concern, however, is that the value of the product be properly attributed to the women farmers rather than to 'the household', so that resources, as appropriate, are channelled directly to women to increase productivity and national income.

Women farmers' produce is used in two ways: to feed members of the household and to sell for cash. The latter being the usual definition of 'income', some examples of cash from sale of produce on the market are given first:

Anna, whose teaching salary is Ush 900,000 a year, brings in an additional 1.8 million shillings a year from her 2 acres in Kabale municipality from sales of cabbages, mushrooms and milk, not counting income from other produce or the shop in her house. Paskazia sells produce for Ush 60,000 and wisely barters her potatoes valued at Ush 600,000 as school fees for her eight children; she thus removes temptations to sell them for cash and leave the children outside the school door, as happened to 4 of her own sisters. Efurazia sells Ush 534,000 worth of vegetables, trees and beer annually, and expects a jump in income from selling the milk of her new cow. Christina's income solely from milk (after she reserves nearly half of it for the family) adds up to more than Ush 3 million a year.

Of special importance to understanding women farmers' total productivity and their share of GDP, the progressive farmers estimated the cash value of their in-kind hidden income from food produced for family consumption in addition to the value of surplus or cash crop food they sell. The two added together determine the total income women produce:

Hajat reserves about 50 per cent of the produce of her 4 acres for the 13 members of her household. She calculates the value of the food the family consumes at 3.6 million shillings a year and of that sold at 3.8 million—totalling Ush 7.4 million. Having saved enough earnings from trade, she bought 2 cows and built the sheds for them, and she recently planted a coffee nursery; both will augment her income.

- Zahara earns about Ush 520,000 a year from sales, and her family of 12 children (8 her own) consumes Ush 2.2 million worth of the food they grow annually—totalling Ush 2.7 million. Zulaika uses about Ush 3.6 million worth of food for consumption and sells 2 million worth of produce—a total of Ush 5.6 million.

- Victoria heads a household in Entebbe of 18 persons, including her own 3 children and 10 adopted ones; she values the food consumed by the family at 3.6 million shillings a year and her income from the sale of produce at 10 million, used for school fees and related costs, for a total Ush 13.6 million. Rebecca, who supports 12 children (none her own), earns some Ush 2.6 million in addition to consuming 2.4 million worth of produce from her 5 acres—a total of Ush 5 million.

2. Who are the household breadwinners and how is income used?

Besides the value of the food for home consumption that the women farmers provide and the income from sales used for school fees and general family maintenance, consider:

- The three progressive farmers in Iganga provide about half of the family's cash income—in addition to income in-kind that is the family's food. Jalilah's 10-person household consumes Ush 2 million worth of produce each year, and in addition she provides half of the family's cash income.

- The Ibanda women who were selected for interviews because they are poor and who have no support from NGOs other than their own ROSCAs, manage to earn from Ush 53,000 to 113,000 each year. Women use all their resources to improve their households, says Bafokuzara, echoing the universal findings of this study. Their 'banks' are the small animals that their husbands are forbidden to sell and that serve as insurance against 'men's habitual neglect of family responsibilities'. In Ibanda, a man would sometimes leave the family 'with no salt', they say, so women engage in economic activities. One respondent says, 'If women ceased their economic activities, some homes would perish' (Bafokuzara 1997).

- In Kira, Regina expects to get Ush 700,000 from her export crop, vanilla, and tomatoes each year (excluding the milk she sells). She and her husband jointly decide on expenditures, but she controls the money that benefits their 8 children. Hajat says that her husbands has never asked her for money. She controls it, supporting 13 people in her household without any assistance from anyone.

- Without exception the women farmers interviewed invest their income, be it monetary or in kind, in improving the nutrition, health and education of their own and other dependent children. People come first: Women make sure the family is well fed before selling off the surplus. Whatever the reason, 'Women usually try not to misuse money, while men are easy spenders,' Zahara states.

Bafokuzara quotes the National Council of Children (1994) observation that when women have incomes, 'nutrition in their families is improved because the more a woman gets, the more she will put into the family feeding'. She adds, 'A woman cannot tolerate having her child seated at home due to lack of school fees. She would rather use her last coin and put her child in school.'

Relevant here is a study which concludes that when women have control over family income and household resources the pattern of consumption tends to be more child-focused and oriented to meeting the basic needs of the household. Comparing households in seven countries, the World Bank found that those headed by women have higher school enrolment and completion rates than those headed by men.[7]

3. Does the current practice of considering the household as the basic unit of analysis lend transparency to the source of income in cash or in kind that is produced by each household member?

This study identifies women's in-kind share of household maintenance as hidden income, but the fact is that their cash income also is often hidden from policy makers and planners. The reason is that a typical household survey (*The Integrated Household Survey* and its annual updates in Uganda, for example) uses 'the household' rather than the individual earners within it as the basic unit of analysis. That methodology fails to capture the sources and uses of at least half and often much more of the family income. Why? The husband as 'head of household' is assumed to be the source of all income—the breadwinner.[8] The wife is presumed to be not the provider but the user of the resources the husband brings to the household. This chapter and this study as a whole remove the bases for such assumptions. Reformulating household surveys is a starting point for giving greater attention to human development.

By omitting the individual sources of income, the household survey methodology produces insufficient information (Uchitelle 1998 interview with Stiglitz) and sets off a chain of distortions and blockages to economic growth and human development. Resources that should be allocated to both men and women or to women alone flow mainly to men; benefits for children are given to fathers rather than mothers; and so forth.

The importance of attribution of income by gender is evidenced by the fact that the most successful women farmers and entrepreneurs—those who are most able to provide for their children while adding to Uganda's GDP—have assured access to the factors of production: land, labour and capital. Their income makes possible their support of large households—their own children and those of deceased relatives—a not insignificant achievement in a country afflicted with AIDS. Madanda calls for a food security policy whose framework should be geared to enabling women's secure access to important resources such as land, labour and capital—a proposal revisited in the final chapter of this study. As Bafokuzara does, he identifies girls' and women's education as a critical factor affecting their access to and control over those resources.

4. How can incentives reach the main producers of the nation's agricultural wealth in such a way that Uganda's development will be expedited?

The proper direction of incentives depends first of all on the knowledge base. Two recent studies remove the 'insufficient information' block that distorts planning. First, 'The gender aware country economic reports: Working paper number 2, Uganda' (Elson and Evers, 1997) provides an overview of the economy of Uganda and analyses economic structures, processes and policies from a gender-aware perspective using a macro, meso and micro framework. It identifies ways to remove imbalances in patterns of resource allocation to create sustainable and equitable economic growth that can only be achieved when human development is a primary concern. Second, *The Women's Budget, 1996* (Budlender 1996) is another useful document. It examines key elements of the national budget with a view to integrating human development targets in macro economic policies and programmes. FOWODE's design of a similar instrument in Uganda will place in proper balance the allegedly competing values of human development and economic growth.

At the field level, the package offered to women's and mixed farmer groups by Africa 2000 seems to contain critical elements of effective support to senior family farmers. There is group training for a year or more in advance of the services, then grants and credit in the form of a heifer or seeds or money, and follow-up extension services. Many of the community-based groups organised themselves some years ago so their cohesiveness is proven and mutual trust is strong. For example, Efurazia's group set about helping one another out of extreme poverty during the economic and political crises of the early 1980s by selling their labour communally. Africa 2000 deserves careful study as a model for creating incentives to increase productivity.

A variety of forms of community-based women's organisations and ROSCAs are operating in Uganda—most of them completely independent of one another but having the same goals. As enterprises grow, however, the capital a ROSCA can provide is inadequate. Organisations such as MWODET form ROSCAs into federations that can access additional resources—training and credit—from financial institutions such as UWFT and the Cooperative and Centennial Banks. The point here is to make training and capital available at reasonable cost and in sufficiently large amounts (often beyond micro) for farmers and entrepreneurs to expand their productive capacities as many of the respondents in this chapter have done and many others could do.

Class status and leadership

A final consideration is the class status of the progressive farmers, as indicated by land ownership, parents' status and the women farmers' education. As we have seen, several of them own land, and those who do not appear to have strong claim to the land they work with their husbands. That is of primary importance to their productivity.

Whether they were educated or simply literate, both parents of the progressive farmers studied were leaders in their communities. Paskazia's father chaired the local council; he and Anna's mother were treasurers of savings groups. Anna's father was a church warden and local council chairman. Paskazia described her mother as a women's leader. Both of Christina's parents were businesspersons and farmers. Zulaika's parents were prominent farmers and her father a village chief. Jalilah's parents were church elders, and her father was a builder by trade. Hajat's parents reached primary four and seven. Zahara's parents were the most educated—her father to secondary four and her mother primary seven; they were in business in Jinja. Rebecca's also were educated: Her father worked at the Ministry of Education and mother was a nurse. Victoria took special pride in her primary-four-educated father—a peasant fisherman with a very strong commitment to the education of all children in the community; her mother went through primary three.

Those humbly educated (but advanced for their time) community leaders produced daughters who are better educated—a firm generational step—and also leaders in their communities. All of the progressive farmers belong to women's associations and groups, and some were the founders of their respective groups. Their education complements their upbringing: Three enjoyed primary, six secondary, one teacher-training and another diploma-level education. The contrast with the education of the poor women in Mbale is sharp: Just 23 per cent of the women there have some primary and 17 per cent have no education at all; one in 10 reached junior secondary and one post-secondary. In Ibanda, thirty-three per cent of the women had no schooling, fifty-eight per cent some primary and only 10 per cent post-primary.

Advice to women who would enter agribusiness

Those women farmers who have the education and incentives that make them progressive farmers can and do have high aspirations. Asked how they would advise young women who wish to improve their agricultural output, most urged that they embrace the new sustainable methods and join farmers organisations; some would persuade their husbands to join too. The advantages include access to training and funds and the benefit of learning from others' experience. Anna speaks simply: 'Join women's groups; you will learn a lot.' Hajat advises women entering agribusinesses to have patience, be hard-working and be prepared for a full-time job. Almost everything needs daily inspection if you want returns, she adds, and women's farming is difficult because women have so many roles and so many associated problems.

Recapitulation

'Women contribute 50 per cent and often much more of the household cash income from their sales of fruits, vegetables, trees, beer and sundries. The market value of the food they produce and feed to a dozen related or adopted members of their households—the hidden income—at least doubles in value their cash income. In addition to the nutritional value of that food, the cash income is invested in human development— school fees for their own and others' children. Thus the evidence is overwhelming that whether a spouse is present or not, women are senior family farmers and not infrequently the mainstay of Uganda's rural households.

The importance of women farmers is not limited to their households and families, however. The country itself depends on them. Ninety per cent of Ugandans live and work in the countryside where 90 per cent of women, but only 53 per cent of men, engage in agriculture. Women are the vast majority of the farmers on whom the country depends for its food—and for its economic growth—for it is women's labour that produces a striking 80 per cent of the non-traditional and 60 per cent of traditional farm exports that earn foreign exchange.

The statement at the beginning of this chapter rings even more true from the case studies: It is beyond doubt that if progress lags in the countryside, Uganda will not develop, and that progress in agricultural production depends heavily on women farmers and entrepreneurs.

There is room for change, based on the following: Education and ownership—or permanent use of land—mean higher productivity, higher income and more produce for Uganda. Education—especially of daughters—is a major road to progress and the economic prosperity of a nation. Under-capitalisation haunts women farmers, and the systems that are evolving to enhance their access to capital call for policies and actions by government and the private sector.

Although the positive changes are relatively recent, there is abundant evidence that the progressive households enjoy a different lifestyle. But at present the vast majority of women farmers of Uganda are more akin to those of Mbale and Ibanda—those who are 'effectively locked out of capital accumulation'. That situation can change. In his budget speech for 1998–1999, the Minister of Finance conceded, 'Poverty levels are still unacceptably high' (Ssendaula 1998). The potential that senior family farmers and thousands of agribusinesswomen across the country offer for contributing to economic growth while simultaneously strengthening human development stands out as the greatest resource Uganda has for lowering those poverty levels.

[1] Food crops in Uganda account for 90 per cent of agricultural income in cash and in-kind, according to government and World Bank statistics (Elson and Evers 1997: 17).

[2] In *Uganda Growing Out of Poverty*, World Bank, 1993, Annex III, the World Bank notes that a market rather than a farmgate (producer) value should be used to calculate non-monetary agricultural income. In this study, the women farmer's own estimates

were used, and they are likely to have undervalued their produce. An additional point in this book is that women, not an anonymous 'household', produce that food.

[3] See Note 6 of Chapter 2.

[4] The reader is referred to studies of gender issues in farming systems research and extension, such as those of Joyce Moock and Robert Rhodes, 1992, *Diversity, Farmer Knowledge and Sustainability*, Ithaca: Cornell University Press.

[5] *The Monitor*, 11 Aug. 1998, quoting 'Draft report on the impact of agricultural market liberalisation on household food security in the districts of Iganga, Pallisa, Kitgum and Arua', by OXFAM, SNV and COOPIBO–Uganda.

[6] Women parliamentarians and the Uganda Land Alliance of NGOs proposed a number of amendments, including the 'co-ownership by spouses of land on which the matrimonial home is located and any other land from which the family derives sustenance', thus inhibiting irresponsible sale of land by a spouse, and ensuring the wife's inheritance. It was also proposed that half of the board, committee and commission members dealing with land titles be women. The argument set out by Parliamentarian Miria Matembe was cogent: 'In my district, I have seen women suffering. At their [biological] homes, land belongs to their father, then where [a woman] marries, she works on land. After 30 years, if a cruel husband chases her, she belongs nowhere. For safety of women, the bill should protect their right of co-ownership of land where they live or on which they depend for sustenance.' (*The Monitor*, 27 June 1998)

[7] World Bank, 1999, *Gender, Growth and Poverty Reduction in sub-Saharan Africa*. See also Dwyer and Bruce 1988.

[8] A Ugandan colleague reminded the researchers that this is in a country where banana-based matoke—not bread—is the staple food.

Table 4.16. Women farmers and traders

Name	Zahara Kasolo	Zulaika Mutumba	Jalilah Galiwango
Age	34	35	35
Education	1 year secondary	secondary school	2 years secondary
Marital status	married	married	married
No. in household, including herself	14: 12 children (8 hers), husband	14: 3 children, husband & other relatives	10: 6 children, husband & other relatives
Business	grows & sells vegetables, bananas; raises cattle	raises & sells rabbits; grows bananas, beans, coffee	grows & sells vegetables, bananas
Employees	1	± 5 casual labourers	none
Source of loans/ credit/assistance	Africa 2000 Network	Africa 2000 Network	Africa 2000 Network
Land owner?	jointly with husband	yes	no
How income invested	built house; school fees; household needs	built house; health care; school fees; household needs	building a house on husband's family land
% women pay of household expenses	50% of cash + Ush 2,210,000 worth of food	50% of cash + Ush 3,649,000 worth of food	50% of cash + Ush 1,976,000 worth of food
Spousal reaction	supportive	supportive	supportive
Major problems	health of cow	under-capitalisation	under-capitalisation; labour-intensiveness
Memberships	LINT	Local Councils I & II (Vice Chair), LINT (Chair); + others	Kigulu Development Group; Paidha Farmers Group; FINCA
Advice	—	—	—

Table 4.16. Women farmers and traders (continued)

Name	Hajat Nabakooza Kalema	Aisa Nalongo	Joyce Bwagu
Age	45	56	33
Education	6 years primary	4 years primary school; certificate in midwifery	7 years primary
Marital status	married	widowed	married
Dependants	13: 10 children, husband	8 children	9 children
Business	raises & sells rabbits; sells milk, coffee, surplus food	midwifery; sells surplus vegetables, matoke, groundnuts	sells surplus milk and produce
Employees	1	0	0
Source of loans/ credit/assistance	savings from former food and clothing business; Africa 2000 Network	Heifer Project International	sister and her husband
Land owner?	yes	yes	no
How income invested	built house and rental houses; bought cattle and other animals	pay school fees	household needs; cow
% women pay of household expenses	100% + Ush 3,551,600 worth of food	100%	50%
Spousal reaction	#2 (of 3) negative	—	helpful
Major problems	marketing; low prices from middlemen	health of cow	lack of money for heifer feed
Memberships	Twegombe Women's Development Association (founder)	Uganda Veterans Association Board	YWCA
Advice	Be patient and hardworking; inspect daily	Have patience	Join the YWCA

Table 4.16. Women farmers and traders (continued)

Name	Regina Nalongo Kabanda	Rebecca Njulungi	Victoria Nalongo Namusisi	Anna Ndoshore
Age	47	40s	32	38
Education	6 years primary	4 years high school	diplomas in journalism, business mgmt.	4 yrs secondary; teacher training college
Marital status	married	single	divorced	married
Dependants	8 children	supports 12 children, none her own	supports 18 children (3 hers)	5: 3 children
Business	sells vanilla, beans; raises heifers and pigs	grows and sells bananas and vegetables	raises and sells poultry, bananas and vegetables	teaches; runs general store; sells own milk and vegetables
Employees	none	1 + 2 brothers	3	1 + casual labour
Source of loans/ credit/ assistance	savings	wage-employment savings; Africa 2000 Network	borrowed against future salary as a journalist; Africa 2000 Network	PAP; Africa 2000; Entandikwa
Land owner?	yes, jointly w/ spouse	yes, jointly w/ spouse	yes	yes
How income invested	children; household needs	household needs; animal feed; drugs, health care	school fees; health care; household needs; clothing	school fees; finishing house; household needs
% women pay of household expenses	about 50%	75% + Ush 2,366,000 worth of food	portion + Ush 3,648,800 in food	most
Spousal reaction	helpful	—	—	supportive
Major problems	lack of cash for pesticides	insufficient capital	getting loans; interest rates	expansion capital
Memberships	none	Naggalabi Women's Group; GEWA	Awake Pota; Twekolere Women's Group; Uganda Scouts Association	Two Wings Agro Forestry Group; Karubanda Bakyala Tutunguke
Advice	Try vanilla farming; have few children	Form groups	Prepare to sacrifice and be patient	Join women's groups

Table 4.16. Women farmers and traders (continued)

Name	Christina Night Bekunda	Paskazia Zalibugire	Efurazia Bamuturaki
Age	30	51	40
Education	7 years primary	completed junior secondary school	completed primary school
Marital status	married	married	married
Dependants	5 children	8 children	9 children
Business	produces and sells milk and a sorghum-honey drink; trains in appropriate technology	grows and sell trees, vegetables	sells prepared food, vegetables, milk, forestry products
Employees	part-time	1	—
Source of loans/ credit/assistance	PAP; Africa 2000	Africa 2000; Muyumbu Bakyala Tweheyo Kukola; Centenary Rural Banking Scheme	Africa 2000; friends and relatives
Land owner?	yes, jointly w/ spouse	no	yes, jointly
How income invested	school fees; veterinary drugs; paying labourers	education; household needs	school fees
% women pay of household expenses	about 50%	about 50%	about 50%
Spousal reaction	supportive	supportive	positively transformed
Major problems	lack of capital	lack of capital	Lack of capital
Memberships	ROSCA; burial society; ASCO	Muyumbu Bakyala Tweheyo Kukola; ROSCA; Women's Council I; Mainstream Council	Rukombe Tukyengane Agricultural Group; Bafumbo Assoc.; Local Council I Executive Committee
Advice	—	Have small families; use family planning	Use good farming practices

5 The Missing Middle Class

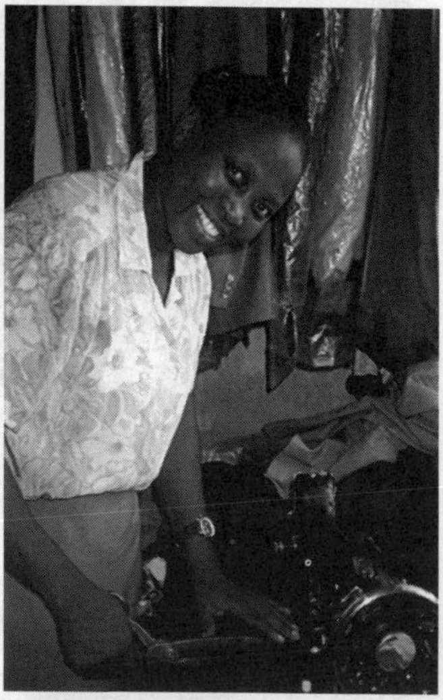

Olive Kitui makes women's clothes and sells them in her two shops

Mary Nsubuga owns two shops that sell sundries and food

Ida Wanendeya makes and sells various textile products; she also co-founded UWFT

Victoria Muwanga owns and drives matatus

Dr Florence Munduru founded and runs a private clinic

Angela Bazirake founded Computech Systems

Lilian Kahenano owns a supermarket

Cothilda Busulwa makes and sells women's clothes in her own shop

Joyce Rwakasisi manufactures and sells women's clothes, workwear and curtains

Chapter 5

From Wages to Independent Business: The Missing Middle Class

> **Women are aware that if you are going to make it, you've got to make it on your own.**
>
> Joyce Rwakasisi, owner, Solaire Fashions

A matatu (minibus) passenger bound for Ntinda from Kampala was deeply impressed with his driver's safety-consciousness. 'Drives carefully. Doesn't screech the brakes,' he commented as he moved forward to congratulate the driver. Astonished, he blurted out, 'Are you really a woman?'

Driver Victoria Muwanga is one of the micro- and small-scale entrepreneurs of Uganda who, like the progressive farmers in Chapter 4, are trying new ways to enhance their productivity and income. At times they are pioneers in fields of economic activity where few Ugandan women have yet ventured—bus driving, computer training—but they are always entrepreneurial pioneers as women, even when they deal in everyday needs such as clothing, food, plastic utensils, flowers or gifts.

Most of the businesswomen introduced in this chapter are women of wartime Uganda who fled with their families or were sent out of the country to school while the return of peace at home was awaited. Many had salaried employment for a number of years but were retrenched or retired, or they started a business on the side and in time found it more rewarding than their jobs.

Another common characteristic of this group is post-secondary education—a distinct advantage over the micro entrepreneurs and even the progressive farmers in earlier chapters of this book. Their ownership of land (more than a tiny plot) opens the doors of banks for loans and overdrafts. Most are married to husbands who contribute to household and family maintenance, freeing up some of the entrepreneurs' profits for reinvestment in their businesses.

In short, these entrepreneurs can be described as middle class in a society dominated by peasant farmers and micro traders. Nonetheless, as the reader will note, they work hard, take risks and face formidable obstacles, not least of which is surviving the terrors of civil unrest that brought looting soldiers to their doors. They leave no doubt that women are as able as men to manage more than micro enterprise—on condition, of course, that family and society make it possible for them to gain the knowledge, assets and opportunities to start and expand business.

There is another, inter-generational point to be made. The businesswomen in this chapter benefited from their parents' commitment to make a better life for their children than they had themselves. The lesson to be learned is to look to those parents of the current generation who invest in equipping their children with good nutrition and education to carry them into the future as developers of Uganda and to enhance their earning capacities through positive policies and support systems. There is no doubt that Ugandan women, like other African women, are such parents. The businesses described in this chapter are classified as small rather than micro enterprises.[1] They are profit- and growth-oriented, and their assets (excluding land, buildings and working capital) are estimated to be worth more than Ush 2.5 million each. Most of them employ five persons, are year-round businesses and are located in independent premises. Their owner–managers (in some cases joint owners) are educated at post-secondary level and are among the first Ugandan women to move from micro- to small-scale enterprise. As a middle group these women are few in number, arguably because their characteristics and assets are not yet common among women in Uganda. They are the few in the 'missing middle' (Gordon 1996: 142), most of whom got a generational head start. Understanding them should help identify ways to multiply their numbers.

Of the 15 women interviewed who moved from paid employment to entrepreneurship, three selected less traditional fields: computer training, bus driving and book publishing, and 12 opened restaurants or hotels, or started textile, dressmaking or other traditional businesses. After the women tell their stories, common characteristics are identified, with both expected and surprising results as regards parentage, education, start-up capital, previous employment and overseas experience. Significant issues are considered—among them the controversial land-ownership and trade-liberalisation policies. Women's continuing use of institutions to support their pursuits is seen through the professional organisation of UWEAL. Finally, these successful businesswomen offer their experience and advice to aspiring young entrepreneurs.

Respondents are grouped in four categories of business: non-traditional enterprises, food and lodging businesses, wholesale and retail shops, and textiles and clothing. In the final section of the chapter, the following questions are addressed:

1. What are the socio-economic characteristics of the 15 independent micro- and small-scale entrepreneurs interviewed, in terms of parental status, education, overseas living, land ownership and marriage?

2. To what extent does class status affect the capitalisation of middle-level enterprises (e.g., access to start-up capital, credit and loans)? Is the women's capital adequate for investment in family well-being and reinvestment in business growth?

3. Is middle- or upper-class status a prerequisite to reaching this middle level of entrepreneurship, and if so, what policies and actions might allow others the possibility of joining the 'missing middle' group of small- and medium-scale enterprises?

Non-traditional enterprises

To be female and a micro- or small-scale entrepreneur having independent premises and employing others is to break with tradition in Uganda. To drive a bus, train computer operators, publish books or be a medical doctor is even more path-breaking. Victoria Muwanga, Angela Bazirake, Robinah Kafeeke and Florence Munduru chose those professions.

Nothing is going to stop you from being a woman, a wife, a mother just because you drive a bus.

Victoria Muwanga, matatu owner–driver

Victoria Muwanga (44): secretarial school; widowed with four children; matatu owner–driver

Victoria Muwanga—Vicky—knows that driving the most common form of transport, the matatu—is labelled as a 'men-only' job in Uganda. 'You need to see the shock on peoples faces, especially men, who enter my bus unknowingly and later discover a woman behind the wheel. But now they like my driving,' Vicky says.

Vicky is Kampala's first woman matatu owner–driver. She is unwilling to be sidelined because she is a widow and determined not to become the burden to her family and community that MWODET member Sophia in Mpigi spoke of. When some men say that she is a muyaye (delinquent, unreliable or uncouth child)—a not uncommon jibe at widows who are found in the marketplace—her reaction is clear: 'I do not care because I know I am not a muyaye; I am just earning an honest living. I have to survive. Women should not fear what people say. It is what you think, how you carry yourself, that matters.

Nothing is going to stop you from being a woman, a wife, a mother just because you drive a taxi!'

Vicky was born in a family having only 4 boys among the 16 children of several different mothers. Both boys and girls in their peasant family went to school. Her father, who was educated in a seminary, never said, 'Victoria cannot do this because she is a girl.' If there was cooking to be done and it was a boy's turn, he would be in the kitchen. If there was shopping to be done in the town centre and it was the girl's turn, she would get on the bicycle and ride the 3 miles through jeers, cheers, shouts and whistles—because she was a girl riding a bicycle. 'But of course the onlookers would not harm us because my father was kind of a big man in the area as a medical assistant,' Vicky says.

Vicky was born in 1954 and grew up in Kyagwe but lived with a foster mother while attending Mengo Girls' School. She later stayed with a maternal uncle, a church minister with a Dutch wife who liked her and made her work hard and at times abused her, although she looks back appreciatively to those years of learning. Because she loved to watch her father in his clinic, he called her 'doctor', but after her father died, her uncle did not warm to her aspirations to become a nurse. He finally gave in and sent her to Nsambya Hospital for training with the Irish nuns. Brought up in a very strict and guarded atmosphere and tasting freedom from grown-ups, she and some other students ventured into a discotheque and were suspended from school.

Vicky's uncle was very disappointed, but being a 'forgiving parent', as she calls him, he sent her to Nakawa to train as a secretary. After Amin expelled the Asians, she got a part-time job in town after school, then a job with the Produce Marketing Board, from which she resigned in 1984 to try a restaurant business. 'I had grown tired of the "Yes, sir" kind of life expected of a secretary,' Vicky explains.

Why is she driving? Her husband died of leukaemia in 1992, leaving a small estate to his two youngest children—her daughter and a step-daughter who attended university in England. Vicky and her in-laws argued and eventually, with the help of lawyers, decided that the estate should be split into two, with the big girl getting almost three quarters while she got the rest. She tried farming and the food business for a while until a friend suggested she buy a minibus.

With the money from her husband's estate, Vicky entered the transport business with her own matatu and a hired driver. 'My God! I cursed myself,' she says. 'For a whole year I got no money while the vehicle became ramshackle. The hired drivers were using the vehicle to transport goats, matoke and other produce from many hundred miles away. She woke up one morning and said to herself, 'I am going to sell this thing. But I have to bring up my child. So why can't I drive it?' She recalled learning to drive as a girl staying at her uncle's place. She had persuaded his drivers to teach her how to drive and so learned on a Mercedes Benz. 'There and then I made up my mind—and here I am,' Vicky says. 'It is best to be your own driver.'

Vicky believes there is no reason not to drive instead of hiring young boys, most of whom have never handled a million shillings before. 'They can cheat an owner out of Ush 100,000, then think they are very rich, stay at home until the money is gone and then come crawling back,' she says. She considers her problems normal—getting tired, having sick children to worry about, having little time for the family. 'There is no time to do anything else; that is the main problem,' she says. She can save perhaps Ush 35,000 between Monday and Saturday, then get the vehicle serviced on Sunday. Because thieves may waylay an unsuspecting driver, she stops working by 7 or 8 in the evening.

She has no other business currently, although she wants to start small-scale farming to help her sister and save enough money to get a new vehicle. 'If God wills', she will have two. No longer 'green' as she was with the first vehicle, she knows that drivers can cheat the owner. Vicky has big children from her first husband: Her son, age 22, is studying hotel management and the daughter, 20, business management at Makerere University. 'I am now an old woman (age 44). Maybe I produced children too early. My first was born when I was 19,' she says.

The Rotary Club of Mengo recently honoured non-traditional employment for women and self-reliant widows by giving the pioneering Victoria Muwanga a vocational award. *The Sunday Vision* newspaper (13 Nov. 1997) described her reaction: '"I did not expect such recognition and respect from these young people", a visibly grateful lady said in her acceptance speech.' The recognition, Vicky said, has made some members of her family, who had been reluctant to accept her new profession, change their minds. 'My eldest son, who had insisted that his friends would laugh at him, is now happy with my achievement. The big girl had encouraged me from the start but had probably not expected such an honour in a short time.'

You find yourself working for the landlord who owns the premises.
Angela Bazirake

Angela Bazirake (50ish): B.S. and diploma in education; married; founded Computech Systems

Like Vicky, Angela Bazirake entered a non-traditional field of work for women. She created Computech Systems with start-up capital from her government retirement package. She offers classes in computer operations, sells stationery and photocopies, and organises secretarial and typing services. Course offerings include Introduction to Computers, Lotus, D-Base and Windows; specialised programmes are also developed, installed and taught.

Unlike Vicky, who had a technical skill—driving—before investing in her business, Angela entered the hi-tech computer world without personal experience in computer operations or business management. 'Sometimes the learning process is a bit expensive,' she says. She has a B.S. and diploma in education—an impressive achievement for the daughter of a peasant family that survived by subsistence in Kabale district, and all of her siblings have some education, although just one other has a university degree. Having taught for several years, she joined the Bank of Uganda, then took early retirement in 1994.

On her own in business in Mbarara town, Angela admits that while supervising her company she is taking computer lessons herself. She employs her daughter, who has a degree in computer science, to be her trainer, but the daughter will soon start a master's degree programme and have to be replaced at Computech Systems. There are two other employees, a cashier and a general worker—both women—since Angela is 'gender sensitive', as she puts it.

Without a continuing source of capital, Angela faces problems restocking. 'There are wastage and errors here and there which are not economical,' she explains. She's not sure how she can supplement her initial capital (the retirement package) so she doesn't see the future as very bright. Having borrowed from commercial banks and found the repayment expensive because of interest charges, she seeks alternative sources of credit. A second problem is the market: Merchandise sales are low, perhaps because her location is a little bit away from the centre of trade activity. 'The bright side of the business is the training; students are available and they pay,' she says. Angela would like to invest in a building of her own because rent is very high. 'You find yourself working for the landlord who owns the premises,' she says.

Angela shares family support with her husband, who takes most of the responsibility so that she can pay her employees and the rent. 'If I make a profit, I contribute to the food and other family expenses,' she explains. She is seeking advice on the future of her business.

I sold them an idea.
Robinah Kafeeke, publisher

Robinah Kafeeke (41): B.A. in humanities, Kenya Institute of Administration; life partner with two children; established a publishing house

Robinah Kafeeke is among the most innovative of entrepreneurs, providing a service to Uganda's education system. Described as 'elegant, bright and having a terrific sense of humour' (Kamugasa 1998), she established her publishing house—Rorash Enterprises—in 1986 after years of experience working for international publishers, Oxford University Press and Heinemann–UK. Her experience speaks volumes, making her a credible credit risk for both the Uganda government and a multinational corporation. And that in turn has helped realise her dream of publishing rather than importing books for Uganda schools. Her experience and training give her a distinct advantage over Angela, both in management know-how and in accessing capital.

Like other successful small-business entrepreneurs, Robinah has international experience—she lived in Ghana, Kenya and Zimbabwe—and has been a salaried secretary. Born in 1957 in Toro, she completed senior secondary school in Lira then went to Ghana to live with an uncle who paid her school fees. Returning to Uganda, she schooled in Jinja then was off to Kenya in 1975. Failing to get a job after training at the Kenya Institute of Administration, she took a secretarial course 'because secretaries had opportunities' (Kamugasa 1998). She was right. She worked at the High Court, then the World Bank, then a merchant bank in Kenya before reaching what would become her vocation—publishing—through a job with Oxford University Press in Nairobi selling their books outside Kenya. When work permits for Ugandans living in Kenya became hard to get, Robinah moved to Zimbabwe to earn a B.A. in humanities.

Back home in Uganda she applied for and received a US $100,000 grant from the government to import textbooks in 1990 and became a Heinemann–UK agent. She sold Heinemann the idea of helping her to set up a publishing house and registered Rorash Enterprises. With that start-up capital, her company became active in 1992, and its first books were published in 1996. Her comment: 'It was fantastic!' Her earlier administrative work in the worlds of finance and publishing had given her skills and the opportunity to learn from the mistakes of others, so to avoid having to make them herself at her own expense.

Although she started the company as its manager, Robinah's business is a partnership with her life partner, Rashid, a banker. Their business name—Rorash—includes their personal names. Robinah's son and daughter are at Makerere University and primary school at Namugunga.

Robinah's dream has come true, that 'at long last, a multinational is working with a local company to produce Ugandan texts' (Kamugasa 1998). She and Rashid share that dream with the community through the recently launched Rorash–Heinemann Educational Fund for the improvement of primary and secondary schools. Technical education, a wealth of relevant experience and a vision of self-reliance for Uganda make Robinah a pioneer among women and among Ugandans.

The biggest problem is time allocation.
Dr Florence Munduru, founded private clinic

Florence Munduru (46): medical degree, Makerere University; married with five children; opened a private clinic

Today, medicine is a recognised field of study for women and men, but in 1974, when Florence Munduru qualified as a doctor at Makerere University, such was not the case. Like Vicky and Angela, Florence is a pioneer in what was a non-traditional field for women. Like Robinah, her business contributes to an essential service—in this case, health.

Florence married a doctor and went to work for the government in Jinja where she became an innovator once again by opening a private clinic. At a time when services are in short supply in Uganda and bribes are on peoples' minds, Florence will neither ask for them nor pay them. A recent example of that honesty is when she was arrested by a police officer because her road license was three days overdue. Despite the fact that she understood what the officer wanted—money to keep her name out of the police files—she refused to be corrupt.

What motivated Florence to start the clinic? 'Earlier on, the conditions of government service were okay; the salary was enough. But demands kept increasing as my five children grew and times were harder economically in Uganda.' Like any other business, opening a private medical clinic required capital. Florence saved from her salary and her supportive husband gave her a hand by buying beds, mattresses and other equipment. The clinic is located towards the end of Jinja's Lubas Road, in a building that could once have been a shop. It is small but well equipped, with six beds for admissions and areas for treating outpatients, ante-natals and deliveries. Florence has two senior midwives who work in homes and handle deliveries in all but complex cases; an additional staff of three assists. Rent is steep and increasing, and the facilities are too small, but she has found no other place for her practice.

'My biggest problem is time allocation because I still work for government so must run around everywhere—come here to the clinic, look at home, go to the hospital. Occasionally the workload brings a lot of friction because my husband is adamant in wanting me to cook. Once in a while I do give him that treat,' she says.

Florence Munduru was born in the Arua district, West Nile (northwestern Uganda) the first in a family of six girls (the one boy had died) whose father was a schoolteacher and pastor and mother a schoolteacher, now retired. Five of the girls went through university and the sixth to business college. All married and live in different parts of Uganda, except one who lives in Nairobi. Now that her own children are getting through school—two of them already are in university—Florence thinks of going home to Arua to open a similar but larger clinic. 'We have built a house, have bought land, and I think it is time for me to retire from the government and go back home,' she says. 'I've never had a loan, but when I go there I have to find one. I need to know about women's groups that provide loans!'

Asked whether the women's movement makes any sense to people in the health sector, Florence replies in her soft-spoken way: 'They are not actively bothered about it.'

Victoria, Angela, Robinah and Florence came to their non-traditional professions with different types of preparation. Vicky had her driver's license and, perhaps more important, a father who encouraged his sons and daughters to abandon stereotyped roles. Robinah had post-secondary training, plus experience in management and previous employment with a publishing house. Florence trained in her field. Only Angela lacked both technical and management skills and only she has no continuing source of capital. Most creative in finding start-up capital is Robinah, whose government-financed project and partnership with a transnational corporation ensured her of capital adequate to her chosen business.

Food and lodging businesses

Two graduates of Makerere University and two teacher-training college graduates all owned land and were wage employees before venturing into the private sector. Sarah Kibuuka owns a butchery with her husband, Lilian Kahenano has a supermarket, Pauline Ofong a restaurant and Theresa Kayondo owns a hotel with her husband.

Growing a hundredfold with the market.

Sarah Kibuuka, co-owns a butchery

Sarah Kibuuka (mid 40s): economics major, Makerere University; married with three children; manages and co-owns a butchery

'We did not start as big as you see here. We have grown with the market. We started with one small building and no bank loan, but with our little [capital] we built up as we went along. As the customers increased, we went on expanding,' Sarah Kibuuka, manager and co-owner of a butchery, Ro-Sa Brothers Co., explains. In a large workroom with shiny aluminium equipment and cutting tables, four workers prepare cuts of meat for sale. There is a packing machine and a deep freezer where the meat of 30 animals can be kept. A smoker uses sawdust and husks to prepare the fish: tilapia and Nile perch. Six hundred kilos of meat, plus fish and baked goods, are sold weekly from the recently renovated, impeccably clean retail store.

Indeed, it was not always like this. Sarah, her husband and her husband's brother, Robin, who lives overseas, bought the land and the first building, now used as the retail shop, in 1974. It was only in 1984 that they started the butchery, using the property as collateral to buy their machines. They took a loan from the East African Development Bank that year.

The earliest years were not easy. The initial building had 4 shops: Sarah and her husband rented out 3 of them and kept the fourth as a general store of their own, to supplement the income from their salaries. But by 1980 soldiers came often and emptied the shop. 'We got fed up with the lack of security,' Sarah says. They asked themselves, 'What can we buy and sell within a day, so that the soldiers won't take all our investment'? It was difficult for people to get meat at the time, so they decided to start with 10 kilos. Only 3 kilos were sold, and the rest was used to feed the family. But word soon went around. People realised they could order the meat they wanted. When a specific order came in, the meat would be purchased, prepared and delivered. Soon a small freezer was needed. Their bakery opened about 2 years after the butchery on the idea that the one would complement the other—a customer might need something in the bakery to use with meat or fish.

How did Sarah come to be an entrepreneur? Born in Kampala, she went to Gayaza High School, then Makerere University, where she majored in economics. She married in 1973, a year after graduation, and soon had three children. Her husband worked as a financial director in a large company that imports cars and heavy equipment, and Sarah found employment with the Red Cross. She claims that she became a businesswoman as a hobby at first because she didn't know much about meat, except from her cookery book. She began by working with the butchery part-time, but soon realised that success depended on a higher financial investment.

Sarah left her job at the Red Cross when she and her husband decided that if they were going to put more money into their business, a member of the family must manage it. Supervision could not be left to an outsider. Her husband's job was more secure than hers and provided financial safety for the family in case the business did not work out. 'By that time I had become deeply involved in our project, which my mother-in-law assisted. Her death gave me the final push to become independent,' says Sarah.

Cookbook in hand, Sarah and two assistants 'started to work out which part of the meat was coming from where', as she expresses it. Business picked up and they learned as they went along, but she knew that professional training of her workers was in order, and urgent. Sarah approached DANIDA.

'Look here,' she said, 'we are trying to develop this business but what we lack is skilled manpower. Our people have never handled meat before, and they must learn to meet the market demand. Also, we want to begin our own meat processing—and none of us know about that.' A proposal for training fellowships was written and two of the best employees selected. 'We were lucky that DANIDA agreed.' In 1990 they sponsored the two staff members for three months in Denmark at a meat trade school, where they were taught to process sausage, smoke fish and many other things. 'Now they are training us!' she adds proudly.

Like other enterprises, Ro-Sa Brothers faces major problems every day. Two key issues for the company are competition and finance. For the first six or seven years there was no competition.

> We covered the whole range of meat: rabbit, duck, beef, anything. But in the last three years two people started bigger butcheries. At one time, we thought we were going to be wiped out because the competition was nearer Kampala. We could not move to town because we could not afford the rent for the space we need. If we had to rent this big space, we could not stay in business.

Their solutions? First: quality control. 'We are working frantically on our products—keeping product quality up to standard,' Sarah says. Second: assisting customers. 'We get customers of different nationalities, some of whom cannot express themselves in English. You either give them a chart so that they can show you exactly what they want, or you show them the meat itself.' Third: market research. 'We list our customers and depend upon them to tell us what they want. Now, when an Italian comes in, we know what he might want.' And fourth: image. 'We improved our retail area. You have to keep your place of operation presentable so when someone comes in they would not wish they were somewhere else.'

A second area of concentration is a persistently big problem for small entrepreneurs: finance. Finance is almost never adequate. 'Right now we are in a financial squeeze,' Sarah says. 'I think everyone is feeling it.' Ro-Sa is taking actions to ensure financial strength: staying on good terms with banks; keeping good records ('If you talk with someone about loans, they will want to see your records,' Sarah explains).

The third area of concentration responds to friends' queries. They may ask, ' "Why don't you do something else alongside meat?" Suppose I were to be involved in the butchery, bakery and some other lines,' she muses, 'then I would not be able to cope. Whenever I think of something else, my mind goes off what I'm already doing and things start going wrong. You must concentrate on how you will get from A to B, and what it will cost if you cannot pay on time.'

That leads to Sarah's fourth concentration point: keeping suppliers happy. 'That cannot be done if you default on payment, because then you won't get the support you need. You must know what you need, know when and where and how to go about getting your requirements.'

She does all the management, but her husband participates when needed. He has introduced new accounting systems and audits the accounts. At times when she is away, he monitors for her, making it unnecessary to hire someone from outside. None of their workers are members of the family.

> The children are still too young to be involved in the business—two of them are still in secondary school—so I do not know if they will come into business with me. The eldest, Rosemary, just finished a course in hotel management and may have an interest in the butchery. I hope so.

Sarah's wish for the future? 'We hope that one day, as this area builds up, we will be able to supply everybody from this end of the city, and they won't have to go past us to buy their meats in Kampala. That will be our happiness, for it means a wider market.'

Twenty loaves of bread were given us to start.

Lilian Kahenano, supermarket owner

Lilian Kahenano (late 40s): Cambridge School Certificate, secretarial school; married with one child; owns a supermarket

'Twenty loaves of bread were given us to start,' the owner of the Eight to Eight Supermarket explains. Lilian Kahenano and her colleague, Pauline Ofong, were in salaried office jobs (Lilian as a secretary) so they hired a woman to sell the loaves in an empty shop. When they returned in the evening they were excited: The bread had gone. That was the beginning, in 1992. They knew that someone buying bread would also want butter, tea, sugar and margarine, 'so we kept increasing our stock, slowly by slowly.' Today a customer can find literally everything, from soup to nuts, magazines to bottled water, and tumblers to put it in.

> After some time we thought we should go for a loan to advance our business. I had worked for a bank, so we approached a bank and got one million shillings, using Pauline's land title to secure collateral. Pauline left our partnership after two years to start her own business selling children's clothes.

Lilian was born in the mountainous western district of Kabale where her father was a priest in the Church of Uganda. She refers to him as 'a very hard-working man' whose nine children (she is the third) all went to school; one brother became a university professor, and four sisters went through university. Lilian completed the Cambridge School Certificate, then went on to secretarial studies. She was personal secretary to the governor of the Bank of Uganda for a long time—from 1973 to 1989.

> In the part of Uganda I come from, women are taught to work hard at family level. You might say that hard work is a cultural thing. Most of us had to work with our hands, then we were given good basic education by the missionaries, who taught us to think for ourselves.

In the early years of her bank career, Lilian met women who encouraged her to go into her own business. One of them, Tereza Mbire, an interior decorator, and the other, Alice Karugaba (see Chapter 6) would take Lilian's salary and trade with it, turning a profit for her. Those two inspired her to begin, but getting into business herself was an eye-opener. Lacking entrepreneurial training, she thought that owning a shop meant stocking its shelves well—that was about all. Neither she nor Pauline had ever taken out a bank loan, and they didn't know how to, even though Lilian had worked in a bank and was married to a banker. 'One of the problems women find is not knowing banking procedures. But even when you learn them, women will probably not have the collateral for a loan. We were among the few lucky ones,' she says. That she and Pauline had no legal partnership brought another shock: When they wanted to separate, they didn't know how to divide the stock and other assets. Accountants helped them resolve that problem.

Eight to Eight gets its name from its working hours: It opens at eight and closes at eight. There are five employees—none of them family members. One is a retrenched policewoman who is the security guard. Lilian tries to be in the shop most of the time, but is constrained by doubling as a housewife and looking after a family. 'It is preferable for the owner to be around, but you have to do purchasing both locally and abroad and go around looking at other shops to understand the competition and trends. As new shops are opened, one has to keep ahead in order to stay afloat. It's very exciting to think up a plan and carry it out so that you keep ahead,' says Lilian.

There are many problems to be faced at the supermarket: staff, customer and supplier honesty is prominent among them. Another is record-keeping: The accountants have sometimes been 'very unreliable'; one had recently 'left the books somewhere'.

Lilian appreciates the early women entrepreneurs who led the way for women like herself. She recalls that during the era of Amin and the wars, some men were killed and others ran away.

> So women found themselves responsible for very large families without any source of income. They had to send children to school so they sought means of family support. Most went into trade but now there is diversification into farming.

What of the future? Lilian wants to expand, but is faced with high rents in her central location in the city, on DeWinton Road, opposite the National Theatre, where she pays Ush 900,000 monthly for her space. In fact, she already owns a building in Kololo, in the suburbs of Kampala where her customers are moving, and which she rents to make money for its renovation, hoping to open a larger shop within a year.

Lilian and her husband have one son in primary seven, but they are also looking after a brother-in-law and a nephew whom they put through school. She considers herself very lucky that her husband supports her work. He doesn't work in the shop, but he also doesn't object to her going there or travelling abroad to procure items for sale or attend meetings. One bit of her luck comes from the time of their marriage when both of them worked at the Bank of Uganda, and her job with the governor kept her out of the house from early morning to late evening. So her business hours continue at Eight to Eight.

When she is not at home, her husband takes over. He helps the children with homework. Since she is a businessperson, she can afford to have two workers at home whom she instructs by telephone. But it is not easy to expect men to participate very much at home, she says.

> When men see women 'growing wings', as they say, when women have money and dress well, some husbands become jealous. They think that their wives will no longer be dependent and will no longer consider them very important. It is up to the woman to show that her husband is still important, that money is not more important to her. A woman has to be very persuasive at home. Money is just a tool and should serve to unite marriage partners because they are no longer poor.

Lilian urges young women not to despise work. 'You may take up one type of work while looking for something better, but at least work.' She lives by that advice herself, to the extent of helping to unload goods delivered to her shop. 'My upbringing and my education taught me about work. I think they have helped me to achieve, to know that one can do something if one is confident. Then it is easy to progress past the first 20 loaves of bread.'

Do what you are good at, what you are interested in.
Pauline Ofong, organiser, restaurateur

Pauline Ofong (50s): studied social science at Makerere University; separated with five children; owned a restaurant (later sold), makes candles

Pauline Ofong, one of Uganda's pioneering entrepreneurs, is a past-president of UWEAL. She has done a great deal since she and Lilian Kahenano dissolved their partnership at Eight to Eight. She opened an exclusive little shop on Kampala Road selling clothing for babies, children and mothers-to-be. It was a small shop but a smart one and the only one in town. She kept it until 1995 when the owner closed the building for renovations, and she found a wage job with the Uganda National Farmers' Association (UNFA).

In 1997 Pauline was invited to the USA, as a leader of women entrepreneurs, to study small-scale enterprises. On returning, she found herself without a job so looked around and opened a new location for a restaurant, in a place where owners of the buildings wanted an eating place to serve 26 shops. The restaurant, called Kembabazi Food Centre, is in a courtyard nestled among buildings that house pharmaceutical shops; a hairdresser and bridal salon were already in the courtyard. A brilliant green-and-white-striped awning protects 2 outdoor tables, and additional indoor tables seat 8 near the kitchen which occupies half of the space; a counter services her take-away business. Her 5 workers include 2 cooks, a waitress and 2 delivery persons.

Barely a week after Pauline opened her restaurant, the building burned down and took 3 months to repair. The struggle to regain customers began. Pauline's rent is Ush 500,000 a month, paid 3 months in advance. Her start-up capital came from her brother and sister, and a business partner at Wandegeya market area gives her ideas. Lack of capital keeps her from buying kitchen utensils and additional furniture, she says, but she prefers to start small rather than borrow more money.

'There is entrepreneurship in my family,' Pauline says. Of her five siblings, two brothers who finished high school and took technical training have their own businesses, and two sisters are in business; she thinks they are more successful than she is. Three of the family are university graduates and a sister completed secretarial studies in the UK.

Born in Kabale, Pauline lost her father when she was just eight, but with the support of the extended family she continued at Gayaza High School, King's College Budo and Makerere University. After receiving a social science degree in 1966 she worked at the Ministry of Agriculture as an assistant secretary, coordinating the Freedom from Hunger Campaign. In 1971 she left the Ministry to work at the Produce Marketing Board. 'That is where I picked up the entrepreneurship spirit,' Pauline says. 'I met several women who were trading in maize and beans, supplying produce to the Marketing Board. That's when I started. I got a little money and they would buy me maybe two bags that they sold in Kampala.'

She was still young then—about 30. During the Amin years she worked with a wood-industries corporation as administrative manager. But in 1984 the political situation became so bad that her managing director was taken away and everyone was scared. She left Uganda for Nigeria to teach history in a secondary school. Fortunately, her job in the Produce Marketing Board was still open when she returned in 1986, and she rose to the rank of personnel manager, all the while continuing trading as well as renting and selling houses, and selling land as she still does. In 1992 she and Lilian started Eight to Eight. Two years later she took a shot at politics, standing for the Constituent Assembly women's seat in Kabale. 'Of course I did not succeed, but it opened my eyes more. I got experience,' she says.

Pauline has five grown children—two girls and three boys. The first three are professionals, and the younger ones are at Makerere University and in senior secondary school. Another dependent who finished high school is the youngest son of her brother who died—'He is my son now,' Pauline says. Her husband, a Nigerian who studied at Makerere and worked at Makerere University Hospital, is now back home.

By April 1998 Pauline began a gradual pullout from her business. Hawkers on the streets outside had eaten into her market, and the high rent continued to constrain her. Her deep love seems to be helping to strengthen women's groups such as Faith Outreach and UWEAL. But she still has a small business: 'I make candles, by the way,' she says. 'I have tested the market, and I think it is good. That may be a lasting business.'

I retired from teaching because the money was not pleasing.
Theresa Kayondo, hotelier

Theresa Kayondo (40s): teacher-training college; married with eight children; owns a hotel and runs a printing press

Theresa Kayondo, known in her neighbourhood as Kayondo, the rich one, is also known for her kindness. She has room for everyone who seeks her advice, and women are proud to have her as chairperson of their newly-set-up savings group that keeps its money with UWFT to get loans to expand their businesses. An attractive woman, she defies both her age and the fact that she is also a powerful businesswoman who travels overseas, recently to Italy, on business. She runs a printing press in addition to the Roadmaster

Hotel she speaks of here. A strong Christian, she tends to downplay her own achievements.

Born in Busiiro in a family of 12 children, Theresa completed secondary school and teacher-training college. Her parents struggled to see that all of their children went to school, reaching as high as each could; one of the 9 girls went to university, another got a diploma in education. Theresa retired from teaching about 17 years ago 'because the money was not pleasing.' In 1985 she opened a 12-room hotel called Roadmaster jointly with her husband. At first there were no other hotels around and, since beer was only sold from hotels, their business did well. That situation changed as Kampala grew. Her solution to the competition they now face is to maintain high standards and low prices. A single room without breakfast is Ush 10,000, and a family suite with 3 beds Ush 20,000.

'I have four employees plus a lady who runs a take-away so that guests can get food,' she says. But business is hard. There are income taxes to pay and defaulters to deal with, though she solved the latter problem in part by having each customer pay before getting a room.

Theresa's husband is employed and is supportive of her work. 'I do not know why, but he wanted both of us to work. I have a village full of children—eight! The firstborn is 27. When they complete secondary school, they come and work here,' she explains. 'If I get enough money, I will look for a plot of land and construct a house.'

As seen in their profiles, Sarah the butcher faces competition squarely and deals with it through strategic planning: quality control, capital management, product concentration and prompt payment of suppliers. Theresa faces it with quality control and low prices for hotel rooms. Lilian's business is steady, and she plans to follow her customers by extending to the suburbs. Pauline, trying out a new business, endured first fire then competitive street food-sellers—and decided to leave her restaurant behind.

Shops: wholesale and retail

Household staples, gifts and flowers are diverse merchandise but Mary Nsubuga, Olivia Mwebeiha and Victoria Sebageleka share in common their secretarial training in Nairobi and employment as secretaries. One is married and two are widowed. Their fathers were, respectively, a school principal, a chief and an agriculture officer. Mary and Olivia both inherited land from their fathers, and Olivia got more land when her husband died. Victoria farms her deceased husband's land.

I started with a small shop in a very tiny building.
Mary Nsubuga, retailer

Mary Nsubuga (48): secretarial school; married with six children; owns two shops that sell sundries and food

Mary Nsubuga is among the first Ugandan women to trade internationally—the Dubai women, as they have been called. Thanks to a start-up loan from her husband in the early 1970s, she became an importer and wholesaler of textiles from Hong Kong—and costume jewellery, children's dresses, shoes and the like from Bangkok. A pioneer by virtue of being a wholesaler too, she shares with Robinah an early residence in Kenya and a special spirit of community service; she shares with Florence and Vicky the status of daughters of schoolteachers and other professionals.

Mary sells brilliantly coloured plastic pots, buckets and other articles, and retails basic food necessities from her two shops in Nateete town, a few kilometres from Kampala. A rather sleepy cross-roads a brief two years ago, Nateete now teems with life—cars, taxis, matatus, bikes, motorcycles, and porters carrying supplies on their backs or in wheelbarrows. A new covered market sits on the highest hillside, tucked behind rows of shops. One of Mary's shops is in that row.

Mary is nearly 49 years old. Educated through 4 years of secondary school in Kampala, she attended a Nairobi secretarial college where her dictation speed reached 100 words and typing 50. On her return to Uganda, she found a job in a government ministry, then transferred to other ministries as advanced positions opened up. She was stenographer/secretary in the auditor general's office; then in the Ministry of Public Service and Cabinet Affairs; in the National Curriculum Development Centre; and finally in the Ministry of Health.

She then decided to go into business—a decision taken with her husband as he was about to leave for a two-year overseas course, and her government salary could not meet their family needs. She bought stock with money her husband sent her and sold clothing in a very tiny building in Nateete town. When he returned, she opened a small business in Kampala where, in 1979, they invested in a building on Ben Kiwanuka Street that had been owned by departing Asians. 'That was when my husband lent me some money and I became an international importer,' Mary explains.

'When the new regime took over and returned property to the Asians, the rental prices started to rise so it became difficult for me to make a profit.' She decided to take bank loans, beginning with Ush 6 million, then purchased air tickets and went overseas to buy goods. The 6 million lasted a year, then she took out a bigger loan, for Ush 10 million in order to make bigger purchases.

Once cargo cleared at Entebbe Airport, she would start selling, and in 2 weeks everything—baby shoes, skirts, blouses—was sold.

'That was the time when airport taxes were not very high,' Mary recalls. Business was so good that she bought a small Toyota Corolla for herself and built a house with her husband. She purchased most of their furniture, chair coverings, cutlery, a pressure cooker and other household items. She was happy with her business until rents started to soar, so she changed to wholesaling and took the shop back to the small town of Nateete in 1995, then opened a branch nearby. 'Here you can rent two rooms for the price of two market stalls in Kampala,' Mary says.

Mary's best-selling items are from Nice House of Plastics. She orders, for example, 200 jerrycans, plates, toothbrushes, cups, dishes, basins and pails of different sizes. She also sells general merchandise including tea leaves and margarine, paying for orders on delivery with post-dated checks. The system works very well,' she comments.

Explaining the ownership and management of her enterprise, Mary says she and her husband are co-owners and she manages the money. But she always seeks his advice: 'I am going to do this. How do you see it?' she asks. He sometimes requests her to make purchases for the family from a small part of the profits. She banks money every day; the bank opens for her so that she does not have to keep Ush 200,000 or more in the shop or at home. 'It is too much,' she says.

Mary Nsubuga was born in Masaka town where her father taught primary school and then became principal of a teacher-training college—Gaba TTC—until he died in 1994. His land was divided among his eight children, each of whom cultivates and collects food from it. Their mother is 'just a housewife' but has pushed herself to do business. Mary says fondly, 'She is such a lady that you cannot believe she was educated only up to primary school. She speaks English and has visited London. We are proud of her. She now works with my sister in sales and even [makes] purchases from abroad.'

The oldest of Mary's six children is in second year at Makerere University, doing a bachelor of commerce degree. A daughter is in senior four, others in secondary and two still in primary school. A learning-disabled son goes to work and everywhere with his mother. The children help out in the shop during their holidays. Four cousins and her sister-in-law work for her, so she is free to go to town for purchasing and to the bank.

Mary and her husband each provide about 50 per cent of the family income. He pays school fees for the children and she pays for necessities such as school shoes, uniforms, soap. Sounding a bit like Florence of Jinja, she says, 'When there is no food at home, I cannot wait. I buy it. If there is a major thing to do for the house, he does it, like building a fence or a gate, but I provide the food, milk, bread, butter. From my business earnings I built a very small house for myself which I rent for Ush 25,000 a month. As you know, women are not always sure of the future—anything can happen. My husband knows about the small building of mine.' Mary expects her children to take up her business one day—perhaps the daughter who lives with her now.

Like Robinah the publisher, Mary gives generously to her community and her fellow women. She is proud to have been chosen president of MWODET in Mpigi to carry on the work of the honoured and much-loved Parliamentarian Theresa Kattaa (Chapter 3).

Business needs patience: Money does not come overnight.
Olivia Mwebeiha, gift and flower shop owner

Olivia Mwebeiha (50s): Kianda Business College; widowed with five children; owns a gift shop

Olivia Mwebeiha became an entrepreneur by trading in clothes and shoes from abroad, as Mary Nsubuga did. Like Mary, Vicky and Robinah, she began her working life as a secretary, heard of older women who opened small shops and decided to venture into trade herself. She sells crafts, artificial silk and plastic flowers imported from Hong Kong and fresh flowers in her gift shop at the Grand Imperial Shopping Arcade. People come to pick a gift to congratulate a mother for her successful delivery or another special occasion such as a birthday or wedding. Local people pay Ush 20,000 or more for a flower arrangement, but expatriates prefer crafts, she says.

The money Olivia inherited from her husband had to be used for school fees and other needs of her children, so her initial capital in 1994 was small—about Ush 500,000. She built her business slowly with it, and in that process discovered that business needs patience because profit does not come overnight.

Olivia explains her work:

> A shop like this is easy to run—it needs an attractive display. An owner's most important asset is the art of appreciating colours. At first I hired young women who knew flower arranging and learned from then. Selling clothing was too demanding—you have to move all through the shops, sorting and selecting what to buy—whereas with flowers you visit just one wholesaler to buy all you need. The fresh-flower growers deliver here so I do not have to go to select them. In the past two years my youngest son does the shopping, and I have four other workers. At my age I think this is the best business: It pays well and is not too taxing on my energy.

Taxes are Olivia's biggest problem. She buys her stock cheaply, but the taxes at the import clearing sites plus the 17 per cent VAT make them expensive. Rent is not much of a problem. The management at the Grand Imperial Hotel is reasonable, she says, and it depends on the shop's location. She has been able to get loans from banks because, fortunately, she has the security: a title deed for land she and her husband had bought; she inherited his share, and she inherited some land from her father as well. At times she finds it impossible to work without an overdraft, but that is not a problem during the 3 years she has banked with Greenland Bank.

Olivia was one of 12 children—eight girls—but she is the only one who inherited some of her father's land. As the seventh child, she doesn't know why she was so favoured, but it was in her father's will. He was a ssaza (county) chief in Buganda, and by the time he retired in 1965 was a magistrate. Because he was educated, he gave all his children chances for education. Olivia completed secondary school in Uganda, then attended Kianda Business College in Nairobi. She was a secretary for 15 years at the Kampala Water Board, then moved with her husband to Jinja and worked for Uganda Breweries before retiring.

Olivia has 5 children, with the lastborn in his third year at Makerere University and the rest working. She expects her daughter, who is abroad for studies, may run the business someday since she selects and sends the gifts Olivia sells. Her son—the one who buys the flowers and is studying law—could also run the business. 'If I can get US$10,000 or $20,000, I will start a cottage industry in crafts such as flower pots and baskets,' she says.

This is where most of our businesses fail: We treat profit as our money so we do not inject it back into business.

Victoria Kakoko Sebageleka, florist

Victoria Sebageleka (50ish): Kianda Business College; widowed with six children; owns a flower shop, also sells vanilla, milk and produce

'I started this florist shop for a very sad reason. My son Shani was born with a heart problem. I took him to Boston Children's Hospital, but he died after six operations. When we were there, my husband sent us flowers through Inter-Flora, and my son loved them—they made him very happy during the days he lived. As a young boy he used to pick flowers and give them to me. As a young girl I too had loved flowers.' That is why Victoria Kakoko Sebageleka, owner–manager of Jean's Florist at the Sheraton Hotel, opened her business in 1988.

When she returned home in 1986, she wanted to do something in her son's memory. She also wanted to be financially independent and to bring life to

Kampala, which was nearly destroyed by the civil war. Because her husband had spent a lot of money on their son's hospitalisation and treatment, she believed she should give him some kind of support. A flower business satisfied all those needs. During the years of turmoil in Uganda, when she lived in Germany and Britain, she had taken courses in flower growing and arrangement. At that time people used mostly potted plants with just a few flowers for decoration. So she became an innovator.

'I arranged the flowers at the Nile Hotel for our president when he hosted his first dinner for a visiting head of state,' she says. She started by using Ush 70 she saved from the household allowance her husband gave her—a lot of money at the time, soon after the currency reform of 1987, which entailed the demonetisation of the old shilling, then the conversion of the old currency notes at the rate of 100 shillings to one new shilling. With those shillings she bought flowers, put them in her own pots and made an impressive display for the presidential dinner. 'For the first time I made money, real money,' Victoria says, adding, 'I must have been paid something like Ush 300,000—a lot in those days. My husband just shook his head and said, "How did you do this?" '

That is how she started. Then the general manager of the Sheraton asked her to arrange flowers for the hotel, a 'very challenging and lucrative job'. Her flower exhibit at the Nile Hotel, and another at the Sheraton, won top prizes. She began teaching flower arranging and growing flowers too.

Born in Fort Portal, in Kabarole district, in Toro kingdom, Victoria is a member of the royal family of Toro. After studies in Ankole, she attended Kianda College in Nairobi but did not go on to university. She became one of the many entrepreneurs who would start her working career as a high-level secretary—a wage-earning career that was newly open to women at the time. The East African Community was in the process of Africanisation, and secretaries who had studied administration, business management and accountancy were much in demand.[2] Victoria's siblings went to school too: One of her sisters studied in Paris and another in Lesotho; her two brothers studied in Germany.

At the East African Community, Victoria was secretary to the chairman, then worked in the statistical department. She moved on to United Touring Company, a very big tourist agency in Nairobi. Annoyed with Uganda's President Milton Obote for removing the country's kingdoms, she returned to Uganda in 1971 after Idi Amin seized power. She transferred to the Kampala branch of United Touring Company, then joined the American Embassy, the UN Food and Agriculture Organisation (FAO) and the United Nations Development Programme (UNDP) before starting her floral business. Now some of her six children—her own and step-children from her husband's first marriage—help her. A daughter who studied accounting helps with the books and the youngest son sometimes helps to run the shop.

Victoria took a brief foray into politics in the late 1980s and early 1990s when she became a member of the National Resistance Council (NRC), then the equivalent of parliament. She was also the woman representative for Mukono district (her husband's area) in the Constituent Assembly, and is proud of her motion that every council should have at least one third women members. 'We lobbied a lot through the FOWODE caucus and came out with a good package for women in the constitution,' Victoria says. That view is widely shared.

Heady with success, she ran for parliament in 1996, not for a 'woman's seat' this time but against a man, thinking that she was politically mature so could tussle with men, as she said. Whether because she was a woman, a widow or simply born in another district, she lost. With that journey into political representation behind her, Victoria concentrated on the shop she designed herself at the luxurious Sheraton Hotel. The rent for Jean's Florist Shop is now very expensive, even though it includes parking space, telephone and electricity, she says, recalling that she paid no rent when she was the official hotel florist.

Victoria has survived some setbacks, like the interfloral service that collapsed because the person hired to run it could not cope, and she ended up paying a lot for inefficiency when orders went unfilled. She prefers overdrafts to loans because they do not need collateral. Having had a bank account since she was a teenager helps—being known means she can get a substantial overdraft—say Ush 3 million—just by signing a paper. For a big amount, say Ush 10 or 15 million, she says, she would take a loan. But to bridge a difficult period an overdraft is sufficient.

Women and men need to meet in professional associations, Victoria believes, so she belongs to the Uganda Florist Association, which organises exhibitions and trade fairs and occasions for exchanging views professionally, such as discussing how to price flowers. She also belongs to UWEAL, although it meets on Saturdays when she goes to her late husband's village to attend to the family. Owing to her commitment to the economic empowerment of women, many from her husband's area, Mukono district, frequently call on her for advice and assistance with their organisations.

Victoria's biggest problem now is the rent for her shop. The second problem is taxes, specifically VAT. Then there is the competition among florists, who, she says, 'are now all over the place. I have trained more than 70 florists in Kampala. They work with me a while, then go and open their own shops. There is a flower vendor about every 5 metres in this city!'

Victoria speaks with pride about the father who gave her a royal heritage: 'He was among the first agricultural officers in Uganda to study at Makerere University—he graduated in agriculture. I took my love for nature, for agriculture, for flowers from him. Actually, I am still a farmer now.' She has a few rabbits and ten cows and is constructing a poultry shed. She grows vanilla, matoke and a lot of vegetables, including a big plot of sweet potatoes. 'Much of what I grow is for my own use, except the vanilla, which is for export, and I also sell some milk. I sell matoke and vegetables to friends—so it is partly commercial and will be more so when I start the poultry.'

About women entrepreneurs, Victoria says:

> We women were latecomers on the scene, and that made us work to perfection. When a woman is an entrepreneur she means serious business. She will think twice and think very hard before taking a bank loan. Yet we find ourselves to be good debtors: When a woman owes money to a bank she will do everything to pay it back—even pay it early. But for men, it is as if society expects them to have debts, society expects them to take a second wife, society expects them to do things that a woman would not venture to do.

Because they are landowners, Mary, Olivia and Victoria all have access to bank loans and overdraft privileges. Mary pays half of the household expenses; Olivia and Victoria—both widows—pay all.

Textiles and clothing

Joyce Rwakasisi, Cothilda Busulwa, Olive Kitui and Ida Wanendeya are all in the clothing business, taking a variety of approaches to competitive imports. Each has enjoyed above-average education—two were schooled in Nairobi and one in the UK. All but one—who started as an entrepreneur—had previous salaried employment. Three have husbands who are partners or helpers.

The spirit of entrepreneurship has come.
Joyce Rwakasisi, owner, Solaire Fashions

Joyce Rwakasisi (40s): B.A., Makerere University, secretarial course, teaching diploma; separated with three children; makes women's clothes, workwear, curtains

Joyce Rwakasisi, owner-manager of Solaire Fashions, started tailoring 'in bits and pieces', as she says. She made clothes for her friends at university, and made her own clothes, curtains for her home and soft furnishings for her room at university. After graduating in 1971 she worked in the private sector for some time in Nairobi while doing business informally, and after marriage in 1974 she sewed for her family. It was only when she returned to Kampala from Nairobi in 1988 that she incorporated her business making ladies wear, and over time branched into workwear and curtains.

Joyce started small, with a sewing machine in her house, working from her dressing room. Eventually she borrowed money from the bank and moved into rented premises in Uganda House, where she set up a small cottage industry with three industrial machines and three tailors. 'I couldn't afford much more at the time because I had to pay rent, electricity, allowances and salaries for the staff,' she says.

She does not find ROSCAs useful because the amounts they can lend to members are too small to have an impact on her business. She needs larger sums of money—US$1,000 to $2,000 that one can get from a bank and repay in 6 months without problems. 'Interest rates were not as outrageous when I got my first loan as they are now,' she says. She has taken a series of loans from the same bank.

Solaire Fashions is a sole proprietorship with three permanent and some part-time workers. Joyce reduced the number of permanent staff because she could not afford to retain and pay lunch and transport allowances to many people during economic hard times; she observes that business contraction is the general trend in 1998. It is hard to get loans because banks demand property—houses or land—as collateral, and the land has to be in an urban rather than rural area where it would be less valuable. Fortunately, she had land inherited from her father to give to the bank as security. At the bank, she can take an outright loan or an overdraft. For her, it is easier to service an overdraft than a loan because the loan requirements are very strict and hard to abide by. In any case, loans are for a longer period.

Imported second-hand clothes that have poured in under the SAP policies of trade liberalisation are one of Joyce's main problems. Second-hand clothes are 'some kind of abstract competitor,' she says. They are fairly good, and the economic condition in Uganda being what it is, men and women go in for cheaper ready-made clothing. In response, Joyce is finding her own market niche: 'We still have a small section of the market, because when I realised that I was having a problem from the competition created by the second-hand dealers, I decided to get out of the box, as they say, and venture outside my original plan.' She started doing workwear in mass production and curtains for individual homes and institutions in the small workshop next door to her office.

A local textile industry is trying to discourage the flood of second-hand garments and textiles into Uganda that has come about since import taxes were lowered under the government's SAP. Jinja Fabrics, or NYTIL, a newly revived firm that originated in colonial years, finds the cheap imports to be stiff competition. Consequently the firm cannot expand the variety of their output, so entrepreneurs such as Joyce cannot satisfy all their requirements for fabric locally.

In addition to imported second-hand clothing, stiff competition also is coming from tailors and garment manufacturers setting up business throughout Uganda, so she must face up to the need for advertising and other publicity, Joyce says. Then there is the problem of shortage of recurrent capital to run the business, because when you want to expand you must bring in a new market and new equipment, and the money is never readily available, she explains. 'It is very, very difficult,' she says.

One way to broaden the market is to export.

> Within UWEAL we have a small caucus in the garment industry, exploring the possibility of exports to Europe or America. I have visited India, Taiwan and Thailand and find it very, very difficult to compete because, especially in the Far East, the use of local raw materials makes their production costs much lower than ours. In our case we have to import everything, and when you finish making a garment it is not competitive. And you must produce in quantity, which demands a lot of capital to meet strict deadlines. We are moving slowly, and hopefully getting there soon.

Joyce was born in Kampala and educated through Makerere University where she got a B.A. in political science and public administration and a public administration diploma. She moved to Nairobi for a secretarial course and a teaching diploma, but has no formal training in the industry she is involved in now. Having learned all the basics of sewing from her mother, who retired about 20 years ago from teaching domestic science, she taught herself the rest. Her brother is an orthopaedic surgeon in South Africa, and her sister is married and living in Winnipeg, Canada. Their father was an administrator in the then-governor's office. In addition to being the volunteer secretary of UWEAL, Joyce belongs to UAUW, but finds herself too busy to join other organisations.

Joyce supports her family on her own—one hundred per cent. Her children help when they are on holiday, she says. Her daughter, who just finished secondary school, has not yet indicated whether she will follow her mother's footsteps. 'Let's wait and see,' Joyce says.

She believes that times have changed, and women now realise that they must stand on their own feet and no longer depend on husbands or fathers or other relatives.

> Women are aware that if you are going to make it, you've got to make it on your own. You have a home to look after. Some married

women find that they can handle a career—not just nursing or teaching but also in the private sector. Women are more hard-working, more committed, and the banks find them better borrowers because they are very serious about repaying loans. The spirit of entrepreneurship has come hand-in-hand with the general development the country is undergoing. So long as political stability can be guaranteed, I think the future is very, very bright. It is a question of stability and hard work. The sky will be the limit.

Today there is a lot of unemployment, so there is no money, no business.

Cothilda Busulwa, owns and operates Suzie Fashions

Cothilda Busulwa (50s): studied nursing, secretarial course; married with ten children; makes women's clothes, sells in own shop

The liberalised economy is hitting Suzie Fashions hard. 'Today there is no money and no business. Imported second-hand clothing has totally destroyed the market,' is the view of Cothilda Busulwa, whose business survived the years of instability and looting in Uganda only to face these new problems.

Along Gaba Road a new two-storey building belonging to Cothilda and her husband is set on a rise. She operates Suzie Fashions from there, with a shop on the main level and a workshop upstairs—where bridal gowns, bridesmaid wear, confirmation dresses, veils and casual wear are made. Customers look through pattern books, select the styles they like and place their orders.

Cothilda resigned from her government secretarial post and started developing a career as a dressmaker in 1976, making clothing for her friends and her children. People brought the cloth to sew because she had no capital at first. Her reputation spread when she started making school uniforms, and capital accumulated so that she could buy tape measures, scissors and pattern books. 'Then I could start a real business,' she says proudly.

One day a bank manager brought his children, and she made dresses for them. As they talked he said that he could change her business by financing it. They went to his office and he lent her Ush 30,000 at first, then more. She repaid as quickly as she could in order to minimise interest costs. When the work accumulated, her husband proposed that they look for a place somewhere else. She worked in Mengo until getting a shop in the UCB building in the centre of Kampala in 1978. Planning for the future, she and her husband bought land on Gaba Road and over 12 years built enough space for 3 large shops. Suzie Fashions is a family business, a limited company, so parents and children sit together to decide how to spend its income.

Reflecting on the ups and downs of entrepreneurship, Cothilda sums up:

> During the years of instability I lost a lot because of looting, so instead of moving forward I had to start again. Then another looting came, and we started yet again. Things became much better, but today there is a general problem—a lot of unemployment—so there is no money and no business. Another problem we face is [the] electricity failure that makes it impossible to finish our contracts on time in the workshop upstairs. I used to have 20 workers, but at the moment I have only 4, having reduced them because the work reduced. When there are fewer workers, they work harder and get more money.

Cothilda finds the trade liberalisation policies a serious threat to local industry. Tax is a major concern because high taxes make locally produced goods very expensive, not competitive with imported ready-made clothing. Cothilda believes that second-hand clothing has totally destroyed the market. 'Local people complain to government, which controls imports, about the problem of marketing their goods. Buyers do not care whether a garment is new or old, so long as they can wear it and it is cheap. When the money is not there, they go for the cheapest, not only clothing but also shoes and other goods.'

Getting loans is another obstacle for entrepreneurs, especially women. Even if the presentation passes muster with the bank manager, 'you can apply for one today and get it in about six months.' But meanwhile, she says, 'You lose business.'

Cothilda was born in Makindye county and studied nursing at Nsambya, not far from her present location. She taught aspiring nurses, worked at Mulago Hospital, then at Makerere University sick bay before going to Britain for a secretarial course. On return she worked for the Ministry of Education as a stenographer secretary, then a personal secretary, and later became confidential secretary at the East African Examinations Council for some ten years, where she was sent to West Africa to learn about the examination work there.

'I think I was the lucky one in my family; my two step-sisters had very little education. Here we do not usually say how many children we have, but I have ten of my own. They are grown—only two are still in school. One daughter did personnel management and works at the revenue authority. Another is a doctor,' Cothilda says with pride.

She joined UWEAL and UMA, where she is in the small-scale-industry section and finds these organisations very useful. 'They run seminars in planning, management and bookkeeping that help you account for your money. They also assist you to prepare feasibility studies, and give you advice on getting loans and even about taxation.'

Asked how she sees the future, Cothilda says she really cannot tell because the business climate is deteriorating instead of improving. 'Even food merchants are complaining.'

Second-hand clothes cost less.
Olive Kitui, clothing manufacturer and retailer

Olive Kitui (40): Evelyne College, Kenya; married with seven children; makes women's clothes and sells them in two shops

'Formerly we were very busy but of late, maybe because of poverty, tailors are getting fewer customers. Second-hand clothes cost less. Tailoring a simple dress will eventually cost not less than 40,000 shillings. You cannot compare that with 3,000 shillings! We cannot charge cheaply because of rent,' Olive Kitui says.

Olive has a production and sales shop on Luwum Street not far from Nakasero market and a retail outlet in the new taxi park, where she hangs clothes for sale, sharing the rent with an aunt who sells Dubai clothes. The Luwum Street place is a small room with sewing machines lined up on one side next to the wall. The customers, who include brides, only come inside to have their body measurements taken, then wait outside where she has three benches, all usually occupied. Relatives, friends and fellow tailors flock to her place so that a visitor can hardly get to talk to her for five minutes without interruptions. Olive is both a tailor and woman activist.

Born in Mbale district, in the hills of Budadiri county in 1958, Olive was the first of eight children whose parents are still alive and married. She completed four years of secondary school in Iganga in 1976, then, thanks to an aunt who headed the secretarial department at a commercial college, she took certificate courses in design and textiles at Evelyne College in Kenya.

Not unlike publisher Robinah, Olive was steeped in training and wage work related to her professional field before becoming self-employed. On her return from Nairobi in 1978, she started working with Uganda Garment Industries Ltd (UGIL) designing ladies clothing. After three years she tired of the design department and changed to the stores department, then to costing, where she priced raw materials and supervised other workers. Single at the time, she found the salary—Ush 620 a month—'little but meaningful'. Gomesi (national dress) material then cost Ush 250.

'It was easy to learn on the job at UGIL, and I was ambitious—I wanted to learn more!' Olive resigned in 1983 to serve in Mbale as general manager for some companies belonging to the former Minister for Rehabilitation. When a new government took over, she lost out and returned to Kampala towards the end of 1987 to join her husband, who had been coming to Mbale for weekends. That was a turning point in her life.

Thanks to some friends who got her a space on Kampala Road, she started her small cottage industry with four machines—two purchased when she was still at UGIL and the others bought cheaply with her savings from some Europeans who were leaving. Her work became known, slowly, after she displayed some dresses. Competition was high in dressmaking at the time, but she attracted many customers, who still come to her.

> My initial capital was my machines, but that was not all. When I needed money for rent, my husband gave it to me—Ush 25,000 a month. I thought of getting a loan. I think it is difficult for women to get loans because they fear the repercussions. You may get the money, but it does not work out properly.

When the building Olive occupied on Kampala Road opposite Biplous was wanted for other uses in 1991, she moved to Luwum Street, where she could make enough to pay school fees for her children. Transport was easy because her husband worked with an embassy and had to come to town, but rent—Ush 150,000—is a big problem, so she shares the space with others. She employs and trains 3 girls, but they leave after training and try to start on their own. Training girls who are stranded, many of them school dropouts, is Olive's duty, she believes. Even though they run away, many of the trainees return when they feel defeated; they call her Mummy.

Olive is interested in politics, especially for the economic empowerment of women. She is a mobilising secretary for the Kampala Women Tailors' Association and Women's Council II of Kampala Central, the area where she works. Working with Parliamentarian Margaret Ziwa, she helps resettle women, especially tailors who are displaced, from the streets.

Even though Olive is personally ambitious, as she says herself, and uses every chance that comes her way, she is also very helpful to others—a characteristic that draws many people to her. She attends seminars organised by women councillors on how to borrow, how to spend, how to pay back loans. They have a ROSCA, part of which was given by President Museveni when he visited Kampala Central and part by Vice President Kazibwe. She applied and is confident that she will get a loan from the Ush 10 million available. She has a dream about developing her business. 'I have been thinking about Ugandans. We import school bags, and when I look at them, they are not really very wonderfully made. I have a dream that sometime I might start an industry—there is none of this kind.'

Olive has seven children—three boys and four girls. Her firstborn is in his fifth year at Makerere High School doing arts. She boasts that her children—

especially the girls, but even the boys—can mend their own clothes. During their holidays they work with her on her machine at home. All of her siblings went to school, although the sister who follows her got pregnant when she was in her first year of secondary school and dropped out. Another sister is a teacher in Wavamuno School for the Disabled, and a third works at Speke Hotel as chief cashier in the restaurant. Olive says proudly, 'All the relatives who have ever stayed with me know how to mend their clothes. I keep occupying everybody.'

Expenditure at home depends on the situation there. If Olive's husband cannot manage alone, she contributes. She works even though married because her husband helped her start the business and her income helps meet family expenses that would be a burden to him. 'He is cooperative and gives me a lot of support where I fail,' she says.

'I have achieved a lot,' Olive says. 'I have managed to pay [school] fees for my brothers and sisters, even to help my parents, who are peasant farmers. I also helped my husband to put up a house. Right now we have a heifer, and I am building a poultry shelter to improve our diet, not for money. I have three acres of land, one of them planted with grass for the cow.'

Twenty per cent is the borrowing rate, but for savings you are lucky to get 5 per cent—so where is the 15 per cent?

Ida Wanendeya, co-founder, UWFT

Ida Wanendeya (50s): married; co-founder of UWFT, makes and sells various textile products

Ida Wanendeya had entrepreneurial experience before she helped to create the Uganda Women's Finance Trust (UWFT). In the late 1960s, the government decided to put aside certain lines of business only for indigenous Ugandans. Wines and spirits was one of those product lines, and Ida was appointed by the National Trading Corporation to be an agent, starting an enterprise in 1967 with her husband and two friends. 'I actually operated the business because my husband was employed by the Coffee Marketing Board. I did that until 1975 when we had to flee the country,' she says.

On return from exile, Ida spent a year or two in politics, working for the then-ruling party, the Uganda Peoples' Congress. (She did not stand for election, and has never done so.) Because of her business experience, she was appointed to the Board of the UCB from 1980–1987, and boards of other companies. She also served on the Makerere University Council during the same period.

Mona Enterprises Ltd, a very small industry, is Ida's current business. 'It wouldn't keep me going if I didn't have other work,' she says. She has five fabric weaves, of which the most common is the kikoi—a multi-purpose cloth that can be used to cover yourself, a table or a settee. She also makes bed-spreads and table mats using cotton yarn, although she is trying sisal, rafia and raw wool that she hopes to import from Kenya or Ethiopia. The undyed yarn is Ugandan, but she has to import dyed yarn from Kenya because local textile mills have run down and are only now being reactivated.

Ida is an entrepreneur who believes in give and take, teaching and learning. In addition to UWFT, she is a member of UMA, UWEAL and UAUW. She also joined NAWOU and is a founding member of the national branch of Soroptomists International. She is a member of both the African and International Federations of Women Entrepreneurs (AFWE and IFWE) and the Association of Women Managers in Eastern and Southern Africa—the latter not very active.

Ida speaks warmly of :

> We started in June 1993, and I was privileged to be a vice president. Apart from the fact that the idea of Africa is still too big for many of us, whenever we meet we have useful exchanges of ideas, experiences, addresses. We gain market. For example, now I have a very small market for my kikoi in Ghana. AFWE will soon have a meeting at ECA in Addis Ababa, and of course we will have an exhibition, take our products there. It is the West African custom: You never travel without your merchandise.

Reflecting on the past and the future, Ida says:

> Here in Uganda we lost a lot of time—from 1971 when Amin took over for some 15 years, we were busy trying to survive. Now we are trying to catch up—at least I feel so. I had programmed myself to retire at a certain age, but now I feel that I am just starting life. I must run and make up for the lost time. Women feel that way. We have had a lot of exposure and are realising that if we share information and work together we do better. So you find that each women's organisation is trying to market its ideas, and there is a lot of competition among organisations. If I want my organisation to be known, it has to deliver something, and if it doesn't, it might not survive. So the reasons for women's involvement come from a combination of factors.
>
> Today women have the low-paying jobs—especially in the civil service, where they work as teachers, secretaries, nurses and the like. But the cost of living does not discriminate between the highly paid and the lowly paid. Everyone pays the same amount for a loaf of bread.

> So women have to say, 'Okay, how can I afford it?' So they become entrepreneurs.

Ida's hope is to see more women move into high-level business rather than the low and middle businesses they are in. She would like to see more women in production—other than just agricultural production. She would like to see a corporation owned by women. She recalls that in 1994 a group thought of an African bank for women. 'We had a consultant and reviewed the first draft, but somehow the idea went to sleep,' she says.

The most difficult field for women manufacturers in this era of globalisation is textiles and clothing. Trade liberalisation policies include eliminating protective tariffs, thus opening import doors to a flood of second-hand clothing and jeopardising local business. Ida has kept her market because she produces kikoi which, like kente in Ghana, is not (at least not yet) produced in western countries. Joyce is finding alternative markets for uniforms, and with other UWEAL members is exploring export possibilities. Cothilda and Olive had not yet moved in those directions at the time of the interviews.

A profile of the entrepreneurs

What does it take to be a successful small-scale businesswoman? Based on these discussions with successful entrepreneurs, we can now answer the questions posed at the beginning of this chapter:

> *1. What are the socio-economic characteristics of the 15 independent micro- and small-scale entrepreneurs interviewed, in terms of parental status, education, overseas living, land ownership and marriage?*

A profile of the businesswomen interviewed, who average 10 years of self-employment, reveals that most of them came to entrepreneurship with middle-class status: Their fathers were teachers, priests and administrators; only three were peasant farmers. They had an above-average education for their time: Eighty-two per cent post-secondary and 20 per cent university. Before they became entrepreneurs, two thirds had 'seen the world' outside Uganda—in Kenya, Nigeria, South Africa or the UK. A striking 87 per cent had salaried positions before launching their private-sector enterprises. More than a quarter of them, twenty-seven per cent, inherited land from uncommonly visionary fathers, and a total of 60 per cent own land, either by inheritance or purchase, some jointly with husbands. Two thirds are currently married, and 20 per cent were widowed with an inheritance; only one is on her own.

The socio-economic status of this group of businesswomen is thus clearly higher than that of most of the market women, the informal savings group members and several of the progressive farmers studied in Chapters 2, 3 and 4.

> *2. To what extent does class status affect the capitalisation of middle-level enterprises (e.g., access to start-up capital, credit and loans)? Is the women's capital adequate for investment in family well-being and reinvestment in business growth?*

Even though business growth does not follow automatically, class status does influence access to capital. As start-up capital, one entrepreneur put together a package of funds from the government and a transnational corporation, another was given an initial boost by the government, and two received capital from a retirement or insurance package. Husbands helped three with capital, and four husbands (and in one case, a complete family) are full business partners. Several started slowly, saving and investing to build a capital base.

Land is a 'passport to bank credit' because it can be used as collateral to guarantee loans. A total of 60 per cent of the entrepreneurs can—and many do—access bank capital as needed through loans or overdrafts. That fact—a class factor—sets them apart from the market women and ROSCA member introduced earlier in this book. The conflict many micro entrepreneurs have between family and business investment of their profits is lessened or removed; these entrepreneurs can do both.

> *3. Is middle- or upper-class status a prerequisite to reaching this middle level of entrepreneurship, and if so, what policies and actions might allow others the possibility of joining the 'missing middle' group of small- and medium-scale enterprises?*

There are exceptions to the rule, but post-secondary education, previous salaried employment and collateral for credit characterise this group of small- and medium-scale entrepreneurs. While further, quantitative research is essential to verify the validity of this sample, there is little doubt that two new policies in Uganda: Universal primary education and the Land Bill of 1998—pending clarification, full promulgation and analysis—are steps in the right direction. Secondary and further post-secondary education programmes will be necessary to boost women's opportunities, as will widespread dissemination of information about, and careful monitoring of implementation and likely amendment of, the Land Bill. Wage employment is less possible in today's Uganda, but some of its merits might be had through apprenticeship programmes and more open access to start-up capital.

These issues are discussed more fully in the final chapter of this book. Meanwhile, there follows a more detailed summary of the entrepreneurs' class status, access to resources, achievements and advice.

Parentage: the start of generational change

Recall that the father of Vicky Muwanga, the matatu driver, never said, 'Victoria cannot do this because she is a girl,' and that she and her brothers and sisters took turns working in the kitchen and shopping on the bicycle. Her upbringing was more egalitarian than most, but equal opportunity for education among siblings regardless of sex is common in all the families of respondents, indicating the possibility of a correlation between that fact and the status of parents, especially fathers. Asked about their parents' positions in their communities, respondents invariably spoke of their fathers, who were teachers, principals, chiefs, clergymen, administrators and medical assistants. It was her father's position, Vicky says, that kept the neighbours from going beyond taunts when a daughter braved riding to town on the family bike. Only three women said their parents were peasants.

Fathers were very important in the lives of several respondents: Vicky, Lilian and Victoria speak of them with great fondness and respect; Mary, Olivia and Joyce got a head start in business with land inherited from their fathers that they used as collateral. Mothers are important too: Mary speaks of her mother's achievements despite little education, and Joyce learned her professional skills from her mother. Today, as mothers have more education and income, their importance to the next generation is increased.

Education and early employment

Three of the respondents are Makerere University graduates. They are among the 87 per cent who had post-secondary education or training in fields such as nursing, administration, secretarial and teacher training. A striking number of them got working experience and accumulated capital in secretarial jobs—seventy-three per cent of those who worked for wages! One woman, trained in administration, took a secretarial course because 'secretaries have opportunities'. East African societies of the 1970s and 1980s offered women the 'traditional'—in western terms—wage employment: To be a professional was to become a teacher, a nurse or a secretary. Secretarial jobs no doubt intrigued many women, not only because they had been a 'men-only' field but also because they offered entry to government and business employment rather than the extension of female-care responsibilities that teaching and nursing represent.

Overseas experience

Another defining characteristic of this group is their residence outside Uganda—almost exclusively in other African countries and predominantly in Kenya—for study or employment before they became entrepreneurs. Most departed during the tumultuous Amin and Obote years, seeking education, or simply safety, and were exposed to new ideas and lifestyles as they sought ways to survive. Recall Joy Kwesiga's comment in Chapter 1, that the years of exile experienced by many Ugandans to forced them find ways to survive in new environments, and they returned home with an 'investment spirit'. Several went to Nairobi as secretarial trainees at prestigious colleges.

Start-up capital

Although the group tend to be married (67 per cent), with a few widowed or separated, the number who obtained start-up capital from their husbands or other family members persists in being low despite comments that husbands are 'supportive'. It is the women's own savings that launched them in business in 57 per cent of cases, while in 20 per cent husbands were among the sources of start-up capital. They saved little by little, or used a pension package or just started making clothes with customers' materials to create their initial investment capital. That self-reliance in building a capital base ought to have earned for more of them chances to borrow from formal financial institutions, had banks been more alert at the time to the existence and potential of women's economic activity.

Robinah's is a special case, worth repeating. She persuaded both government and a multinational corporation to invest in her idea, and her life partner is also her business partner. Mary, Theresa and Sarah also have husbands as business partners, and Sarah's lends his accounting skills as needed.

Land as collateral for credit

Land ownership is a key element of business survival and expansion because it makes access to capital possible. 'It is hard to get loans because our banks demand things like property—houses and land—as collateral. The land has to be urban rather than rural, where it is less valuable,' an entrepreneur explains. Although women are Uganda's main land users (see Chapter 4), they own only 7 per cent of the land. Mary Ssonko says succinctly, 'Lack of land ownership contributes to women's poverty and that of the community' (*The Monitor*, 30 June 1998).

There are few alternatives to bank credit or overdrafts for middle-level entrepreneurs in search of capital. One respondent considered turning to ROSCAs for the US$1,000 to $2,000 that would be appropriate to her business but found that the amounts they can lend are too small. The same is most often true of the newly multiplying MFIs studied in Chapter 3, with loans averaging $220 per person (USAID/PRESTO *Training Needs Assessment* 1997). As to bank loans, the property they demand as collateral is usually urban. Overall, the subject of credit to micro-, small- and medium-size enterprises is a subject needing government policy.[3]

As landowners, most of the businesswomen in this chapter have relatively easy access to bank capital or overdrafts, which they often prefer for short-term needs. Some inherited property from fathers or husbands and thus could offer the collateral demanded to secure loans; others invested in land over time. The Land Act of 1998, once clarified, could make most married women co-owners with their husbands of the family homestead and subsistence land; its effectiveness remains to be seen, as discussed in the final chapter of this study.

Competition from new enterprises and grandmother's trunk: 'previously enjoyed' clothing

Competition is a recognised fact of business life, but its impact was felt only after a decade or so by the pioneering businesswomen of the 1970s and 1980s who dominated their entrepreneurial fields for the first few years. Victoria's flowers and Sarah's butchery find competition increasing as Kampala grows, and it intensified with the economic liberalisation policies that arrived with the IMF, World Bank and other lenders. Uganda was soon awash with cheap second-hand clothing that has challenged local manufacturers who must pay taxes which in turn make their items comparatively expensive. 'Imported second-hand clothes are some kind of abstract competitor,' Solaire Fashions' owner says, referring also to prevailing economic conditions that lead to the desire for cheap, ready-made clothing. An Owino market dealer (see Chapter 2) argues the opposite, that imported used clothing is good for people 'who cannot afford new clothes, and without the second-hand ones some would go naked'.

The effects in Uganda are similar to the impacts of trade liberalisation on other African countries. In Ghana in the late 1980s, 'The only few commodities whose sales were booming were the cheap substitutes for the newly poor, notably imported second-hand clothes' (Clark 1994: 407). In Zambia, the imported clothes were found to be 'very pretty, durable and cheap', and they drove local tailors out of the market (Snyder 1995).

Faced with this market crisis, a UWEAL caucus of garment industry members is exploring export markets for their products. Visits to several countries—India, Taiwan, Thailand—found production costs low because most of the raw materials are local, which is not the case in Uganda. European and American markets are also under consideration although UWEAL members are aware of the stiff competition, the need for a lot of capital and the importance of large quantities to meet market demands.

Meanwhile, Joyce is finding a market niche. She decided 'to get out of the box', as she puts it, and started manufacturing workwear and curtains for individual homes and institutions. Ida's Mona Enterprises weaves kikoi—a local fabric used for clothing, spreads and throws.

Professional association

Nearly three quarters of the respondents—seventy-three per cent—sought to promote women in business, themselves included, through UWEAL, UWFT, MWODET and other business-oriented organisations. It is indisputable that the majority found women-specific organisations more useful than the mixed gender groups they also joined, such as UMA and Uganda National Chamber of Commerce and Industry. Some businesswomen share their success with other, less well-endowed micro entrepreneurs. Ida Wanendeya is active in UWFT, AFWE, UMA, UAUW and NAWOU.

Nine of the entrepreneurs interviewed are among UWEAL's 200 members; one is secretary and another vice-chair. UWEAL's members include interior decorators, tailors, farmers, butchers and sellers of spare parts for cars. The organisation was created in 1987 by a group of entrepreneurs who agreed that despite women's active presence in the economy, 'the country's education system, the private sector and the business environment were not exactly conducive to women's entrepreneurial development' (UWEAL n.d.). Their vision was 'to see the Uganda women economically empowered [and] integrated into the mainstream of economic development of the country; [and] through advocacy and lobbying to influence public policies that affect them for the betterment of the family, society and Uganda at large' (Ibid. n.d.). UWEAL opened new headquarters on Lumumba Street in June 1998, having secured a loan to purchase and renovate an old building that is big enough to have rental space to repay the loan.

UWEAL's leadership in influencing government policy toward micro- and small-scale enterprise by protesting proposed preshipment charges is evidence of the group's strength and its concern for the broader society. Joyce Rwakasisi of Solaire Fashions explained that the 1997–98 national budget proposed requirements that would impose a fine on all imports valued at over US$2,000. UWEAL members joined UMA in protesting the proposed policy, seeing it as hurtful to petty traders while of no benefit to government (*The New Vision*, 26 June 1997). Their objection was based on the high taxes and complex bureaucracy that would be involved in paying them. Further, most women are only 'small-timers' who cannot afford the preshipment fees. UWEAL members and other businesswomen, including those on the crowded Luwum, William and Ben Kiwanuka Streets, joined in fighting the legislation. They petitioned parliament, then went on strike. 'Shops were closed for about a week, the entire economy was paralysed, nothing was going. Eventually government had second thoughts about it. The preshipment threshold was raised to US$10,000 so that a woman who imports a few metres of cloth or a few kilos of merchandise to sell is not strangled in the process. Then everything went back to normal,' a respondent says.

As it turns out, their victory is a partial one. In his 1998–99 budget speech, the Minister of Finance, Planning and Economic Development, speaking of East Africa cooperation, said Uganda had agreed with Kenya and Tanzania 'to adopt a common threshold of US$5,000 for preshipment inspection purposes' and that it was already in effect (Ssendaula 12 June 1998).

Giving back to the community

Businesswomen go beyond supporting their families, expanding their businesses and promoting entrepreneurship: They invest time and money in their communities. Robinah and her international investor joined forces a second time to reinvest in the communities they serve. The Rorash–Heinemann Education Fund donated US$37,000 to primary and secondary schools in 2 districts of the country. The fund also provides 1-day teacher upgrading seminars, with the help of retired teachers. 'When one thinks of [Robinah], two words come to mind: confidence and self-esteem,' says *The New Vision* (28 April 1998).

Mary gives thanks to her community by giving time to their activities. Recently elected chairperson of MWODET, she also founded two other organisations for women's economic advancement in her village. Pauline's voluntary work with the Faith Outreach group in Ntinda encourages them to enter non-traditional activities, such as collecting waste paper and using it to make small envelopes for doctors (see Chapter 3). She and others realise that entrepreneurs need business skills, so they have training modules adaptable to individual situations. Victoria Sebageleka spends weekends in her late husband's village working with women's groups.

Advice to aspiring businesswomen

One of the main objectives of this book is to hear the voices of experienced women entrepreneurs and pass their advice on to young women who aspire to create private-sector businesses. Some of that advice follows.

Getting started

The first thing that Pauline Ofong tells a young person is, 'Do what you are good at. Do what you are interested in, and because of that interest you will make a success of it.' But she adds quickly that the young must get business skills. Joyce Rwakasisi speaks about commitment: 'They must believe in themselves, in what they are doing. They have to have a genuine interest, not just want to go in business to make money.' One reason the girls who work for her leave before they master tailoring skills is that they want quick money, Olive Kitui adds. Mary Nsubuga urges them to start small, knowing that it is not easy to get a lot of capital to begin with. Cothilda Busulwa agrees: 'A new businessperson does not just get money.'

Aspiring entrepreneurs are advised first of all to study the business that interests them. 'You need to have the market so do a feasibility study—a simple one. Listen to the lady on Sanyo TV who teaches how you can have a dream, develop it and not give it up. If it is impossible, try another. And go to seminars,' Olive says. Mary Nsubuga adds, seek advice on business—on the risks and the taxes, rent and other expenditures—in order to have a business plan before starting. Theresa Kayondo gives an example from her own business: 'If you want to open a hotel, how many hotels are in the area, what are their standards, what will your maintenance costs be?'

Ida Wanendeya stresses knowing the basics of the particular business. 'You must know what you are doing even better than your workers know it because if they find out that they are better than you, I am sure you will be cheated.' An example comes from her own textile business: 'Know that it takes 30 minutes to do this so that the workers can't sit there for two hours, and you lose the time you are paying for.' Angela, who jumped into the computer business without being computer literate herself, advises young women to read widely and get expert information if they want to do business. 'Sometimes the learning process is a bit expensive,' she says.

Sarah Kibuuka has clear priorities: first, quality control; second, ensuring financial strength through keeping good records and staying on good terms with banks; third, having a strong and selective focus on business, resisting temptation to get involved in other areas; fourth, keeping suppliers happy.

Mary Nsubuga also urges new entrepreneurs to keep financial records. 'If it were not for record-keeping in my business, bankers would not give me money. Even if you have very little capital, you can record that today I sold or I began with capital of Ush 30,000. Record-keeping is essential for business progress.' Olivia adds that you must economise, 'otherwise you end up eating all the profits. Most of us do not pay salary to ourselves. If you have a profit of 200,000 shillings, and you buy a dress for 100,000 shillings, you spoil your business. To handle this kind of problem you can borrow from your business and faithfully pay it back.' You have to be very honest, and have very good public relations, Joyce adds.

Ida believes there are men as well as women who do business without knowing what they are actually doing. 'They may not do it right, but because they are men perhaps it does not filter through that quickly. If a woman does it wrong, it is magnified, and if a man does it wrong, it is covered up,' she says, urging women to get technical and business-management training. Joyce praises the value not only of technical training but of the broad-based education she received at Makerere. Her university education gave her confidence and knowledge. 'I may not have done garment manufacturing at the university, but I do not regret the fact that I went there.' She encourages young people not to think that all they need is English before venturing into business: 'You need more education than that to be able to handle the business world.'

Strength through community and organisation

Lilian advises new businesswomen, 'First, join business associations'—both women's and mixed associations—to be encouraged by other owners and get training too. 'When you meet with women alone you are freer to say what you want, but because men are more advanced in business we learn from them.' Mary Nsubuga speaks of UWFT as a source of ideas and training, stressing that its organisations cut across class lines. Girls who drop out of school and some married women who have spare time can join small groups in their villages to get training and access to capital through ROSCAs; church and Muslim organisations all have them. Saving among themselves helps women build start-up capital. If a woman wants to make a tablecloth for sale, she can get Ush 30,000 to start. If she is hard-working and wants to do business, she can get advice from her peers.

Bucking some customs

Victoria emphasises a point made by the progressive farmers in Chapter 4: the importance of valuing women's non-monetary production. 'When you ask women, "What do you do?" they say, "Oh, I don't do anything. I don't work." Yet they produce children, look after them, look after the husband, look after the home and cook. Imagine how much they pay a house helper who comes just a few hours, and you are there from the day you marry up until the day you die. So quantify. Also, make sure you are doing things that are visible. If you have money, buy a piece of land and have the title in your name. Don't just contribute perishables for the family table.'

Pauline goes further to challenge women to move out of traditional modes: 'In Ugandan society, women have always fended for themselves and for their families. It is they who feed, clothe—they do all the work. Every woman additionally does something to support or supplement family cash income—rears chickens or tailors or bakes. Those home-based activities eventually become businesses.' Now, she adds, it is time for women to move out of the traditional modes and try new fields.

As she explains, Vicky was trained at her father's knee to expect criticism and jokes about her conduct when it was gender-stereotyped as male. As an adult she handles taunts with grace and good humour: When teased she teases back with a big smile. She hears people say of her, 'Well, I thought she was a bit educated and polished,' as if it is a shame to drive a taxi. 'Driving it does not make me a man or half a woman. I am a mother. How I carry myself is really what matters.' She extends her father's advice to other widows: 'There is no reason why other widows cannot drive vehicles,' she says. "You have to be very patient, very hard-working, know what you are doing and put in a bit of your own money.'

Separating business from household money

Ida deplores the tendency of some entrepreneurs to mingle business money with household money. 'Accounting is important,' she says, adding 'If your bankers realise that you know what you are doing, you can be sure they will support you. But if they think that you are just one of those who want an income-generating activity, they may look at you favourably, but if you need credit, they will have their doubts.' Joyce emphasises the same point: 'If you go into business, your business income should be totally separate from your domestic money.'

Victoria Sebageleka speaks even more strongly:

> Where we go wrong is the tendency to mix business with family. When a rural woman gets money, the first thing she will do is please her husband, her children—the profit gets swallowed there. That is where businesses fail; we do not treat profit as profit. We treat profit as our money so we do not inject it back into business. We should separate business and family as men do. Very few men let their wives know how much profit their company gets. But when a husband says, 'Today I do not have money to take you out for a holiday', a wife will say that she made some profit, so she takes the whole family on holiday using company profit. We really have to learn from men to separate family from business.

Pauline believes that women entrepreneurs are honest but face problems: 'You can't let your child go hungry or stay out of school if you have business income. Relatives come and the man will not bother, but the woman takes money from her business.'

Do women and men do business differently?

Some men do business in such a way that they prosper very quickly, in Mary Nsubuga's experience. But sometimes women fear risks, they fear taking loans. An entrepreneur adds, 'I think some women—especially those married—are oppressed by men; single women do better in business than married women because they are more free. If they want, they can close the shop at eleven. I remember when I was just beginning business my husband, who was a civil servant, wanted a little money for this or that. Husbands sometimes make such demands on businesswomen that they do not prosper. They cannot move ahead. Nonetheless, women can do a lot if they make the effort.'

Victoria also believes that there are distinct differences between women and men in the way they do business. Women are very good creditors; they repay loans. 'For men, a debt is a matter of course. When I have a debt I do not sleep, but when a man has a debt he considers it a normal thing.'

Marriage, family and entrepreneurial success

The advice of the group of respondents in this chapter is of special interest since almost all are or were married—sixty-seven per cent are still married, three are widows and just one is single—a distinct change from the groups in earlier chapters. Spouses are co-owners of 5 of the enterprises—several of them actively assisting in the business. And those who mentioned inheritance of their businesses selected daughters rather than sons—in this they differ profoundly from the farmers.

Florence speaks of the marital relationships of working women. It is true that men think a woman with money is hard to control, she says. Staying together with her husband for many years has helped them to understand each other. There is not much problem now in how she spends her money; when there is no food she automatically buys. Only when she is financially down does she say, 'I think you should step in.'

'Keep your husband informed; get him involved so that from the beginning he knows what you are doing,' says Lilian, adding another piece of advice: 'Plan properly to have time for your home and for the children so that your husband doesn't feel that they are neglected.' Other respondents say that family discussion and an agreed division of responsibility between spouses can ward off the too common eventuality that men stop paying for the household or for school fees when a woman earns money. When a woman is successful in business, the husband will join her and support her, Pauline says. But if she is not doing well, he will tell her that she is wasting time. 'It is important to do well, interest your husband in your work, and let him support you.'

Pauline also believes in involving the children: 'Let them know what you are doing, come and see your work, and participate. Because of the problems young people face in finding wage employment today, your children can begin thinking of something other than white-collar jobs. Even those of my children who are not very entrepreneurial do my books and records.' Among the entrepreneurs interviewed, Mary, Olivia, Victoria, Joyce, Pauline and Olive all had their children working with them, most often on school holidays.

Financial autonomy in marriage?

'Since this is an African society I feel that every woman should be financially independent,' Victoria the florist says. She is adamant: 'Every woman should have full control of her own money and not be over-dependent. If you sweat for your money, have it on your own account. You should know that one day either you or your husband dies, but family life must continue. My little boy misses his father because they were buddies, but for food, clothing, home care he still gets what he needs from me.'

Recapitulation

Women who went into exile during the terrible Amin years either went to prestigious schools or simply had to survive with their families, and some had a very hard time, Dean Joy Kwesiga says. 'They either found paid employment or found something to sell, and they returned home with an investment spirit as well as a popcorn or dry cleaning machine.'

Today many of those women own small- to medium-size businesses—in food and lodging, clothing and textiles, wholesale and retail, and non-traditional fields such as bus driving and book publishing. They are in what is called the 'missing middle' level of entrepreneurship, because so few occupy it.

This study shows beyond doubt that education and land ownership are critical productive assets for these businesswomen. Some 82 per cent of the respondents enjoyed post-secondary education. At least 9 of the 15 entrepreneurs (60 per cent) are landowners. Three of them inherited land from their fathers—a somewhat surprising fact in a country where 'culturally it is the men/boys who inherit land and other property' (UWONET 1998). More than half of the landowners used that asset as collateral for bank loans, to expand their businesses.

They are also unique for their time by having had paid employment for many years—eighty-seven per cent—and by their marital status—sixty-seven per cent are married and 20 per cent widowed, in comparison with previous groups that have more separated and single women. They had an intergenerational push by parents who were themselves well educated for their time and were community leaders.

Yet most started their businesses slowly, saving and creating a capital base. They were in some ways fortunate—competition was scarce in the 1970s and 1980s—but they also had to endure civil strife and lived under the constant threat of looting by soldiers.

Today they face internal and external competition. Internally there are ever more retrenched, educated Ugandans and foreigners entering the private sector. Externally there is the competition created by slashed import tariffs on competitive manufactures, such as textiles and clothing under the government's trade liberalisation programmes. And in addition, they often feel the pinch of a society that is short on cash.

These entrepreneurs band together to protect their interests and promote women's empowerment through professional associations such as UWEAL, which had grown to some 200 members by 1997. Several also reach out to assist their less well-endowed sisters through associations like UWFT, MWODET and community-based organisations.

They know that business needs patience and an eye to an often-shifting market. They know too that their husbands' support can be critical, not only to the family but to their business. Unlike the progressive farmers, several of them hope to turn over their businesses to daughters one day.

In summary, like the progressive farmers in Chapter 4, the small- and middle-level businesswomen enjoy a different lifestyle. Yet at present their numbers are limited by factors that make them an elite group having opportunities to seize today. 'The support we have from the current government has thrown a challenge into our hands. Do we just let it pass?' Ida asks, adding, 'People are looking at the private sector as the area where they can get a livelihood, and government is encouraging that as the way to create more jobs. Yes, women are creating wealth; we are broadening the area where one can find employment and where one can make a contribution to development, too.'

[1] The matatu owner and the owner of Computech Systems are exceptions to some of the characteristics of small enterprises but are included here because of their profit and growth orientation.

[2] Kianda is still there but has changed its role to a senior secondary school.

[3] The government sells much of the power generated in Uganda to neighbouring countries (for prices higher than can be fetched in Uganda); Uganda consequently does not have enough power to go around, so power is alternately shut off in various areas for a few hours every morning or evening on a schedule referred to as 'load-shedding' or 'power-shedding'. Even when power is on, it is not necessarily very strong: Brown-outs (not to mention surges) are daily occurrences.

[4] At this writing, the Bank of Uganda is drafting a policy for MFIs.

Table 5.1. Independent entrepreneurs: the missing middle class

Name	Victoria Muwanga	Angela Bazirake	Robinah Kafeeke	Florence Munduru
Age	44	50ish	41	46
Education	some nursing school; secretarial school	BS; Diploma in Education	senior secondary; Kenya Inst. of Admin.; secretarial; BA Human. (Zimb.)	medical degree, Makerere University
Marital status	widowed	married	life partner	married
Children	4	—	2	5
Previous employment	served on Produce Marketing Board; restaurant, food business; farmed	taught; worked at Central Bank	High Court; World Bank; merchant bank; Oxford Univ. Press (Nairobi); Heinemann-UK	worked in a government hospital
Business	minibus owner–driver	Computech Systems	Rorash Press; Rorash–Heinemann Educational Fund	government doctor w/ a private clinic
Employees	1	3	many	5
Source of start-up capital	inheritance from husband	retirement package	government grant and private-sector investment	personal savings; husband
Source of loans/credit	—	commercial banks	multinational business	none
Spousal reaction	N/A	supportive	partner in business	supportive
Land owner?	—	no	—	joint owner
How income invested	school fees; vehicle	business; family expenses	school fees; business; educational fund	family
% woman pays of household expenses	100%	less than 50%	—	as needed
Major problems	not enough time	under-capitalisation; moving merchandise	—	time-allocation
Member-ships	—	—	—	—
Advice	Put profit back into the business	Read widely and get expert information	—	Continue your education

Table 5.1. Independent entrepreneurs: the missing middle class (cont'd)

Name	Sarah Kibuuka	Lilian Kahenano	Pauline Ofong
Age	mid-40s	late 40s	50s
Education	Makerere University, major in economics	Cambridge School Certificate; secretarial school	Makerere University, social science degree
Marital status	married	married	separated
Children	3	1 + 2 relatives'	5
Previous employment	worked for the Red Cross	employed as secretary to governor of Central Bank	worked in government; real estate; taught in Nigeria; partnered in supermarket; owned a clothing shop
Business	co-owns a butchery	owns a supermarket	owns a restaurant; makes candles
Employees	4	5	5
Source of start-up capital	used joint property as collateral	used then-partner's land title for collateral	brother and sister
Source of loans/credit	East Africa Development Bank; DANIDA	bank	—
Spousal reaction	partner in business	supportive	N/A
Land owner?	Yes	yes	yes
How income invested	family; business	family; land	family
% woman pays of household expenses	—	—	100%
Major problems	competition; finance	others' honesty; record-keeping; high rent	lack of capital
Memberships	—	UWEAL	UWEAL
Advice	Control quality; do market research; have good records and relations with banks	Join business associations; keep husband informed and involved	Get business skills; do what you are good at; involve the children

Table 5.1. Independent entrepreneurs: the missing middle class (cont'd)

Name	Theresa Kayondo	Mary Nsubuga	Olivia Mwebeiha	Victoria Sebageleka
Age	40s	48	50s	50ish
Education	teacher-training college	secretarial training	Kianda Business College, Nairobi	Kianda Business College, Nairobi
Marital status	married	married	widowed	widowed
Children	8	6	5	6
Previous employment	taught	worked as secretary; importer/ wholesaler of textiles, clothing, shoes, jewellery	worked as secretary; importer of clothes and shoes	worked as high-level secretary; elected to NRC and Constituent Assembly
Business	owns hotel and printing press	sells food and sundries from 2 shops	owns flower and craft gift shop	owns flower shop; sells vanilla, milk & produce
Employees	4	5	5	2 part-time; family
Source of start-up captl.	savings	bank	inheritance	household allowance
Source of loans/credit	—	husband	banks	bank
Spousal reaction	partner in business	co-owner of business	N/A	N/A
Land owner?	yes	yes	yes	yes
How income invested	children	car; built 2 houses; household	family	family; business
% woman pays of household expenses	—	50%	100%	100%
Major problems	growing competition	shop rent; taxes; competition	taxes	rent; taxes; competition
Memberships	ROSCA; plans to join UWFT; FINCA	MWODET; 2 other local groups	UWEAL	Uganda Florist Association; UWEAL
Advice	Be patient, hard-working; know what you are doing; use your own money	Start small, get advice and have a business plan; keep good financial records	Economise, or you'll eat up all your profits	Buy land in your own name

Table 5.1. Independent entrepreneurs: the missing middle class (cont'd)

Name	Joyce Rwakasisi	Cothilda Busulwa	Olive Kitui	Ida Wanendeya
Age	40s	50s	40	50s
Education	B.A., Makerere Univ; secretarial course; teaching diploma	studied nursing; secretarial course in UK	Evelyne College, Kenya	university
Marital status	separated	married	married	married
Children	3	10	7	—
Previous employment	started from home	taught nursing; worked as government secretary	employed w/ Uganda Garment Industries Ltd; managed companies in Mbale	sold wine & spirits; worked w/ Uganda Peoples' Congress; Makerere Univ. Council
Business	makes women's clothes, workwear, curtains	makes women's clothes and sells in own shop	makes women's clothes, sells from her 2 shops	makes and sells various textile products
Employees	3 + part-time	4	3	5 + part-time
Source of start-up capital	self	savings	savings	own savings and family
Source of loans/credit	bank	bank	husband	considering bank loan
Spousal reaction	—	co-owner	cooperative	supportive
Land owner?	yes	yes	yes	yes
How income invested	family; business	family; business	school fees; business; built a house, poultry shelter	—
% woman pays of household expenses	100%	—	less than 50%	—
Major problems	imported clothes; other manufacturers, capital shortage	imports; taxes; unemployed customers; electricity failures; credit	high rent	—
Memberships	UWEAL; UAUW	UWEAL; UMA	Kampala Women Tailors' Assoc.; Women's Council II/ K'la Central; ROSCA	UWFT; UMA; UWEAL; many others
Advice	Separate bus. and domestic income; be honest; have good public relations	Be serious, determined; work hard; get tax advice; have business plan, market strategies	Study the business that interests you; listen and learn	Know the basics of your business; know accounting; get technical, mgmt. training

6 Small to Large Enterprise

Evelyn Biribonwa began a bakery

Daisy Roy owns and runs Das–Air Ltd and several other companies

Fang Min owns four restaurants

World-prize entrepreneur Tereza Mbire owns a garment industry and Habitat Interiors and co-founded UWFT and UWEAL (She is pictured with her son)

Alice Wacha owns Peacock Fashions and another shops (shown with a family worker)

Edith Nakuya sells imported women's wear, rents out ten shops and owns a private school

Maria Theresa Makayi makes bread in a five-metre-long oven at her MTM Catering and bakery

Hamida Hudani and Shamin Kassam co-own the Tinga Tinga Boutique Shamin and Dressing Room

Mirjam Black partners with Delia Almeida in Delmira Travel and Tours, Ltd

Chapter 6

Small to Large Enterprise: Questions of Capital

It's a very competitive world out there.
Daisy Roy, owner, Das–Air Ltd

> When I started, I did not think I would make it ... because I started with almost nothing. Honestly, to tell the truth ... I had only 25,000 shillings in my account.... I tried this and that, here and there, but life was difficult because I had no salary.... I thank God that I have a lot of determination to go through with things.

Hesitant but willing to take a risk, Maria Theresa Makayi moved from salaried employment to the unknown—self-employment. Today she is one of Kampala's most successful businesswomen. Her story is told in this chapter, which introduces small- to large-scale enterprises.[1]

These successful businesswomen share many of the same class characteristics in terms of parentage, education, overseas experience and ownership of land found among those in the previous chapter. But new characteristics appear as the scale of operations becomes larger. The focus of this chapter is capital—its accumulation and investment. Needless to say, if indicators other than number of employees are used, such as property ownership and number of outlets, some of the entrepreneurs of earlier chapters would be brought forward to this one: Margaret Ssajjabi of Kalerwe market with her extensive property; Teddy Birungi of Wandegeya who has three shops; Robinah Kafeeke the publisher; Mary Nsubuga of Nateete with two shops and other property; Lilian Kahenano of downtown Kampala who is preparing to start a second supermarket; and Sarah Kibuuka who has a butchery.

To emphasise the special characteristics of the capitalisation of this group of 13 small- to large-scale entrepreneurs who average 13 years in their particular business (3 additional women are managing directors of businesses they do not own), the entrepreneurs are organised in 5 illustrative groups:

- those who start their businesses while holding salaried positions;
- those who begin their working lives as full-time entrepreneurs and build their businesses gradually;
- those who accumulate capital through salaried employment, then leave to start a business;
- large-scale entrepreneurs who diversify their investments beyond their primary business; and
- those who designed and created enterprises, then became the managing directors rather than owners.

These entrepreneurs have a more intense concentration on business and greater economic empowerment. Women's overriding concern for home and family continues, but this group finds it easier than the earlier ones to meet family obligations and still retain a surplus to reinvest in the business. Here again further research is called for to test some of the conclusions tentatively reached.

Four questions are asked at the end of the chapter before the entrepreneurs' advice to aspiring businesswomen is summarised:

1. *How is start-up capital accessed by the small- to large-scale entrepreneurs, and what is the significance of its size to the future prosperity of the business?*

2. *How is working capital increased, and what obstacles stand in the way of accessing capital?*

3. *How do these entrepreneurs resolve the dilemma other businesswomen face, namely: the choice between investing their profits in family well-being and reinvesting in business?*

4. *Is there a correlation between involvement of family members in the enterprise and business growth?*

Working for wages, with a business on the side

As indicated in the preceding chapter, a major means of accumulating capital is to hold a paid job while building up a private business during evenings and weekends until the personal enterprise becomes very demanding and is a more lucrative source of income than the job. Maria Theresa Makayi, Jolly Rwanguha, Alice Karugaba and Alice Wacha started that way.

I have had three bank loans and paid them off on time.

Maria Theresa Makayi, MTM Catering

Maria Theresa Makayi (50ish): nurse's training; married with eight children; owns and runs MTM Catering and bakery

In Luzira district at the edge of Kampala, Nakawa town is a fast-growing suburb on Port Bell Road. A roadside commercial building with a long, protective veranda is under construction. It will house a supermarket, a bakery outlet and a small restaurant. Down some steps in the back and across a courtyard is a shelter over a very deep brick oven five or more metres long. The fragrance of baking bread emanates from dozens of browning loaves and rolls. The owner of all this is Maria Theresa Makayi, who is best known for the long-established business conducted from her home: MTM Catering.

Maria Theresa trained as a nurse then switched to a position in a bank for 11 years in order to be home at night with her children. As her 8 youngsters grew and made demands, she decided to try independent business to earn more money. In 1980 she began catering services at Uganda Breweries and later added organisations including Uganda Blanket, the National Textiles Board, the Uganda Development Bank and UNICEF. She also does mobile catering for special occasions such as weddings and graduations, specialising in African food. The prepared food is put in a pickup truck together with plates, cutlery, food warmers and table linens, taken to the site and served. About 4 months ago she started the bakery 'to see if it [would] work', and 'it is doing well', she says.

Reflecting on those early years, Maria Theresa says:

> When I started, I did not think I would make it. Thank God I have managed—because I started with almost nothing. Honestly, to tell the truth, when I left the Bank of Uganda I had only 25,000 shillings in my account. Then I said, 'Lord, what do I do?' I tried this and that, here and there, but life was difficult because I had no salary. I began cooking at home, but if people did not come to eat the food I prepared, I had to think of where to get money to buy food for the next day. In business one has got to be very patient and determined. With determination things can go well. For me, I thank God that I have a lot of determination to go through with things.

When Maria Theresa started, the family lived in a brewery-owned house because of her husband's work. Even though they own a house in their village, she thought they should have one near the town as well, but the money was not there. Her husband advised her not to buy a city council plot because the city would reclaim it if it was not developed in two years. 'But we decided to try it anyway, in 1984,' she says.

She bought the plot and began buying bricks and sand to build. She says:

> I started construction. I saw our house coming up to the windows. When it came to putting on the roof tiles, not iron sheets, I was a bit stuck because it was difficult to get tiles at that time [1986–89]. Still, I knew I would make it. The roof went on, and about then the breweries decided to retire six senior staff, including my husband (who was a production manager), so we lost our company house. I proposed that we move into our unfinished house. My husband couldn't believe it, but I said, 'Let's try because the windows and doors are there.' The children were very happy and very encouraging. There was no plaster, but we moved and then finished it room by room. Even now, it is not fully completed.

To date Maria Theresa has had 3 loans that she has paid off on time. The first was with a commercial bank—Ush 4 million. About 6 years ago she borrowed again to purchase a generator so that when the power goes off they can still work throughout the night.

> My bank manager was very pleased when I repaid that loan, so I decided to borrow again, and I recently took another loan, now in progress. I decided against taking a loan for construction because I didn't think that would be wise. Any loan I get from the bank is just to uplift my business, like replacing old equipment—freezers, cookers.
>
> I have run my catering business from home all these years, so I have no rent to pay. Rent is prohibitive so I said let me build a building right here in my trading-centre area. I own the building. I do not have any partners. I decided to rent the largest room to someone for a supermarket because I cannot manage everything alone. But I shall have a small restaurant behind the supermarket so that people who don't work at the places where I cater can get my food regularly. My oven for the new bakery, made locally, is here in back of the new building. Perhaps after a time we will purchase machines from abroad.

When her husband was retired, he could not find another job. But they still had children in school, so Maria Theresa had to support them through secondary school and university. 'I have sent them abroad, built our house and put up this building. I have 4 cars and about 30 employees, most of whom cater, cook and serve the food at the Breweries; there are another 8 workers in the bakery and a few here in the new building,' she explains.

Born in Masaka, Maria Theresa was one of ten children—five brothers and four sisters. She studied nursing at Nsambya, then psychiatric nursing at Butabika. All her siblings also had the chance to go to school. One brother completed engineering studies in Germany, a sister is a teacher and three others are in small businesses. Her uncle wanted to sponsor her to go to UK for a course, but by that time she had a large family and thought it would be unwise to leave the children with just her husband, so the uncle sent her books instead—about catering. 'At the time it was not easy to get essential commodities; one had to line up for milk, for sugar, everything,' she says.

Maria Theresa's eight children, six of them daughters, are still at school. The first son, who is in the US studying business administration, recently told his mother by phone that he would return soon to take over 'because you are growing old and you are tired'. Another son is doing a master's degree in pharmacy in Texas, and a daughter who completed university at Makerere studies business management in the UK will return soon; she is very interested in catering. 'Whenever she needs pocket money, she works in restaurants and they really like her,' her mother says proudly. A daughter who stays at home is studying accounting; two are at Makerere and the last one is at Namagunga in the sixth year of secondary school. Maria says, 'It is the boys who are most interested in my business.'

For Maria Theresa, 'There are different kinds of jobs. There are businesses that are really tough and you know they need men. But I don't think there is much of a difference. If you are a very good person, gender doesn't come into it. Some women even manage better than men.' However, she has seen men behave badly when their wives are in business and is happy that her husband is very cooperative. 'If I go off for a week to work, he has no complaint at all. I would advise women in business to try and talk it over with their husbands. Tell them what they are going to do. I think the most important part of it is being really faithful and doing business to help the family. I do not see why husbands should not support such businesswomen.'

Not unlike her peers, Maria Theresa finds that most women spend more of their own income than men do for family support. 'I have experienced that myself. When I started working, my husband was also working, but in fact I was actually giving more than he did. Yet there are some men who object to their wives working. I think that we have to sit as businesswomen and see how we can resolve this dilemma.'

Maria Theresa is helping to form an association of women entrepreneurs in Nakawa. She belongs to Ladies Circle International, which visits other countries, including the UK, to meet businesswomen. She gives her time to humanitarian causes as a director at the Pope Paul Memorial Community

Centre, a member of the task force of Kateyamba–Nalukolongo for disabled people, and a director of St James Primary School.

It's been possible to build a house, educate six children and acquire property.
Jolly Rwanguha, People's Footwear

Jolly Rwanguha (39): university education; married with six children; owns shoe factory

Jolly Rwanguha started making shoes at home to supplement the income she had as agriculture officer in charge of a cotton project in Jinja district. She cobbled after work and on weekends, assisted by her husband Benon, the district labour officer. Starting with one leather sewing machine and a few hand tools purchased from her savings, she made four pairs of shoes a day. In 1989 she decided that shoemaking rather than civil service was her calling and retired from her agriculture job. That is how People's Footwear was born.

Jolly's husband still helps design men's shoes, belts and other products, and she employs ten workers, who clearly know that she is the skilled expert in the group. To top off her expertise she recently earned a certificate in shoemaking. But despite improving her business, Jolly, like other clothing manufacturers, faces competition from imported second-hand shoes. 'Given the cost of raw materials, it is hard to compete with second-hand shoes which dominate the market,' she says (*The New Vision*, 5 May 1998).

'The "old boys" from my Makerere University class think I am crazy to be a shoemaker, given my academic background,' she says. But the step into private-sector entrepreneurship has made an enormous difference in their family life—made it possible to build a permanent house, educate six children and acquire property.

Salary alone can't make ends meet.
Alice Karugaba, Nina Interiors, Ltd

Alice Karugaba (50ish): trained in the U.S. as a secretary; separated with 4 children plus her brothers' 18; owns two furniture and soft-goods stores

Alice Karugaba, the driving force and mater familia of Nina Interiors, Ltd, tells how she started the business from her own kitchen:

> I was a secretary for government's Ministry of Foreign Affairs, then the medical school, then the East African Development Bank. During the very difficult times of General Idi Amin, our salaries couldn't make ends meet, and I had a growing family. So I started what they were calling magendo [informal trade] in those days, that is, buying

> sweets and selling them, making a little profit to add to my salary. Later I baked buns and that was more rewarding. When I started baking I sold to little coffee houses, but I knew that if I had my own shop, I would get even the last profit because I would sell to the last consumer. So I started looking for a shop. I got a small place in Kisura, but I lived in Nakasero so it took me a long time to commute. I had to run the shop after office hours. At 5 p.m. I would pick [up] my children, take them home, give them tea, run through their homework then rush to the shop. Kisura was hard.
>
> I knelt down and asked God to give me a shop in Wandegeya and he gave it to me—a very big one that belonged to a Haji who owned most of the buildings there and had given this particular shop to his daughter from whom I rented it. I started with 36,000 shillings, so I used only the middle shelves in the supermarket. I had special prices for Makerere University students. Every day, business became better and better, but it was so demanding! The children were still quite young and I was getting home after 10 p.m. I needed to have more time with them. I prayed to get a job where I did not have to work so late.'

There was a vacant shop on Mackinnon Road, in Uganda House, so Alice approached the owner. She wanted to continue with the supermarket, but he asked, 'Why don't you do furniture?' She replied, 'Because I do not know anything about it.' He said he would give her the furniture to sell, and she would get a percentage of any sales. He owned the most outstanding furniture factory in Kampala—McCrae's (U) Ltd Furniture Makers and Antique Restorers. She started that new business line, but the furniture moved slowly because people could purchase directly from the factory. So she brought in fabrics and made curtains to complement the furniture, and so became an interior decorator. Alice's daughter Nina recalls, 'At the time, there were no interior decorators in Kampala so we moved to provide materials that were not on the local market.'

In 1988 Alice retired from her secretarial job because she was making a little more in business than in the office, and she needed more time for business. 'When I began to devote full time to that shop, I felt a bit insecure because I could sell only the owner's furniture,' she says. 'So I found a shop of my own, then wrote to the furniture makers saying that they could have their shop back. But they declined, and I had two shops!' That is when daughter Nina entered and Nina Ltd became Nina Interiors Ltd.

Nina Interiors is truly a family business. Its five directors are all family members and many of its ten permanent staff are selected from the extended family. Daughter Nina (actually Joanina), the eldest, who assisted her mother in her early days of baking, runs one shop and Alice the other, assisted by daughter Juliana. Her son is the company lawyer. 'My children really care; they are supportive and they control our money,' she says. Alice is separated from her husband, so all decisions are hers. 'I was doing business when I was married, and I do not think that our marriage broke because I was earning money and was sustaining the home. I think the marriage just broke.'

The two retail outlets of Nina Interiors sell furniture, soft goods such as curtains and upholstery fabrics, carpets, bed sheets and other household linen and related products. A small tailoring unit with 10 industrial machines and one domestic sewing machine makes curtains, upholstery and other furnishings. Apart from its 10 permanent employees, there are another 15 on subcontract to do overflow work.

Alice considers herself very lucky about getting bank credit. The manager of Barclay's Bank came to her shop years ago to ask why his order was delayed. When she explained that her problem was capital, he took her to the bank to open an account. She got an overdraft of Ush 5 million and was allowed to surpass that amount if it became really necessary. 'We used some land titles we had as collateral. From 5 million I went to 15, then to 30. Now I have 50 million and my overdraft lasts for a year, when I renew it. Of course the bank monitors us.'

The biggest problem Nina Interiors has is rent. 'The rent is too high: It is US$3,400 a month and must be paid quarterly. There is no way to solve this problem except to have a building of our own. I have gone everywhere for funding but am told one can't get a loan to put up a commercial building.'

The second problem Alice cites is the work ethic: motivating workers to do what is needed in the time available. 'They may not all be as dedicated as you are, so it's a bit complicated to supervise the factory and get everything done. There are other problems of course. Competition is there. A problem resolved is finding inexpensive sources of supply.' Like Cothilda, the clothing manufacturer in Chapter 5, in the past Alice had problems with soldiers whose looting 'did not give us the confidence to do much'. Even today there can be robberies, but things are much better now. 'We are not so scared. We have an alarm system. If you meet us at gunpoint, we press a button and guards come,' she says. At the time of the interview, Alice was also concerned, as were other entrepreneurs, that VAT—soon to be instituted—could cause confusion and cut into profits.

Alice considers herself fortunate to have friends to turn to when she has business problems. 'I share a lot with one particular friend. I can tell her to find a cheaper source or she can tell me of such a source. If I run short of stock, I buy from her on credit.' She belongs to UWEAL, whose members are another source of support. She was also a member of the Chamber of Commerce and Industry, but found, as other women did, that it was not very active.

Alice was born in Kabale, where her father was a ssaza (county) chief who died young, when she was in second year of primary school. The Kigezi government took over the children and paid their school fees until Alice was in her third year at Gayaza High School. Her older sister, who worked at Radio Uganda, paid for her last two years, after which she took a secretarial course in the USA. 'I lost 2 brothers, one of whom left 13 children, the other 5,' Alice says. 'I have supported them, paying school fees for 5. My own children have all graduated, but I still look after those orphans with food and clothing.'

> Our responsibilities would be eased if I could manage to put up a commercial building, however small, so that we are on our own and no longer pay rent. I have a small plot in the suburbs but need an investor. The savings could be ploughed back into the business. For example, we could make other household items like bedspreads and build the furniture frames ourselves. It would be easier to deal with the heightening competition. While our future is bright, there is room for improvement.

Alice's daughter Joanina Karugaba—the Nina of Nina Interiors Ltd.—manages the smaller retail shop that is filled with enormous bolts of cloth—embroidered satins, damasks, silks, cottons and artificial fabrics. Nina finished her degree in sociology at Makerere University in 1993 and started working at the store while looking for another job. Like her two sisters—one a graduate in political science and the other in hotel management—and her lawyer brother, she was involved in her mother's enterprises from an early age and speaks with knowledge and pride about the evolution of their business.

Nina prioritises problems of the business a bit differently from her mother:

> Our biggest problem is controlling credit because interior furnishings cost a lot of money. Customers ask you to start the work and want to pay in instalments. That is how you get a number of debtors and lose your working capital. We have learned to trust some steady customers and ask others for a post-dated cheque. We give them the opportunity to call us before we cash the cheque so that neither party is embarrassed.

Nina also cites as a problem high rents and the challenge of ensuring that profit margins are wide enough to cover them. 'If they aren't covered, we run the risk of having someone with the same business move into these premises and then we would never work again because customers would simply walk in here and never ask for us or where we had moved.' Nina Interiors imports supplies from Europe but is looking around Africa. South Africa has goods but is not yet experienced with the export market. 'Things you order take forever to come. If you order from Europe, you do not need even to fly there because they put the goods on a ship and send them,' Nina explains.

No longer a monopoly as many similar businesses crop up, Nina Interiors faces competition calmly, by drawing on Alice's experience or consulting suppliers and competitors to determine which new markets to venture into, in order to provide a wide choice for customers. Nina speaks enthusiastically about her work, 'Our customers are diverse: offices, NGOs, government and residential. Some can pay only in instalments, while others pay all at once.'

Nina thinks that it should not be as hard as it seems to be for women to get bank loans. She observes:

> Most do not have collateral, and that is their biggest problem when they want to take a loan to start up a business. But if you have a business already going, you can form a relationship with a bank and they will give you a small loan that you can use to multiply your funds, and you go on like that. That is how we started: We would trade, pay back the loan and get bigger and bigger loans. So one should always start her business before asking for a loan.

Nina Interiors has a number of projects on the drawing boards, but they need to get enough new capital for them, because taking the money out of existing business would cripple it. Nina is hopeful: 'Uganda is developing every day and people are beginning to appreciate good homes,' she says. 'I think we have a very bright future.'

God made me a builder.

Alice Wacha, Peacock Fashions

Alice Wacha (60): trained as a teacher and in embroidery; married with seven children, and helps relatives; owns Peacock Fashions and another shop

'God made me a builder,' says Alice Wacha, owner of Peacock Fashions. When she was still teaching she built herself a house. When she married, she built another house in a trading centre in Lira for her mother. She built a 15-room lodge and 3 houses in Kampala, then bought a fourth in Ntinda. 'I like building,' she says. 'If you find the right builder, it's very easy.'

Alice's main enterprise is Peacock Fashions, located on Bombo Road in Kampala, where brilliant print and striped dresses, dashikis (flowing garments) and T-shirts fill the 4 long racks, shelves and ceiling hangers. Upstairs and at the back of the ground floor is a small factory where Alice's son Abdu Musa and his wife Lucy Abdu work with 15 employees whom she has taught to sew and sell. Alice's husband Olwal who retired from government service often stops by with a greeting and some help if it is needed.

How did she get started? Alice explains:

> I started this business a long time ago—in 1956—when I was 20 years old and still teaching. I started making dresses at home using a hand machine called [an] Uza. I had been very interested in needlework during my teaching, and I taught it to girls even after I married. I stopped teaching because my husband was in government, a permanent secretary, then district commissioner. At first I stayed at home, then joined Radio Uganda, then worked for the Bank of Uganda as an examiner. But when Amin came in, we ran to Kenya in exile. I trained there in embroidery to teach my workers later. The training in Kenya gave me skills that attract good customers.

When the family returned from exile in 1979, she applied to government for a shop and got one, but when the Asian owner also returned she bought one of her own, where she has been for nearly two years. She and her husband also have a big wholesale shop in Lira.

The proposed VAT was of great concern; she feared she would have to raise the price of a shirt from Ush 25,000 to 27,000, 'which is a lot of money', says Alice.

Alice was born in Kitgum in 1936. One of her brothers got a master's degree in law, a second earned a degree in commerce and a third in education. But bad luck came and all of them died, leaving their wives and children. 'I help those children. I also have my family of eight children, one of whom died, but they are grown. I am still with my husband,' she says. 'We no longer have young ones. We are old and only look after ourselves.'

The reasons for her success?

> It's true that you have to look after your children and do business at the same time, so it is not easy. But one can take a 5-year-old child to a nursery and put bigger children in boarding schools. I manage because my husband is a man who is not interested in ladies' money. So whatever I get I use for business only, but I do have to prepare food for him. If you are a man and your wife is working very hard, you have to give her a chance, he says. He knows that I work for the family, that the houses I have built help to meet our family needs, with rents of Ush 400,000 a month initially. That is how I approach marriage and that is why I work very hard. And in addition, I like my work!

Maria Theresa, Jolly, Nina and Alice all saved initial capital while working for wages. More than that, they also invested it in an after-working-hours enterprise that tested and expanded their entrepreneurial skills and would in time demand their full attention. Two of them bought land immediately. In other words, they used their salaries to create wealth that could both meet family needs and create private-sector businesses of their own.

Starting small and growing with confidence

Sarah Namusisi, Edith Nakuya, Gera Harriet Mosha and Evelyn Biribonwa started their working lives as entrepreneurs and gradually built strong businesses. Sarah opened her first restaurant behind Nakasero market, now owns 2 restaurants and repaid her bank loan long before it was due. Edith began by selling cement and auto parts, took a wage job while still pursuing her private business, then returned to full-time entrepreneurship. Gera has 3 restaurants and turned what was to have been her family home into a hostel. Evelyn went straight from university to baking, producing 2,000 loaves of bread a day.

I shall repay my loan in three months, not six.
Sarah Namusisi, restaurateur

Sarah Namusisi (36) four years secondary school; separated with three children; owns two restaurants

Sarah Namusisi, a gentle, hospitable and efficient restaurant owner, explains how she built up her business over the years. 'I started preparing for my restaurant business in 1994 when I worked with my elder sister, then decided to go on my own with a small restaurant behind Nakasero market.' She was chased away from there a year later because others were jealous of her many regular customers—even many Bazungu (Caucasians), who said they were first attracted by my tablecloths, she says. So she returned home for two months, then found another location, but after two years the owner evicted her, throwing all her possessions out on the street.

Sarah then started a restaurant on William Street in Kampala and, just 7 weeks before responding to this study, opened a new restaurant. To get to it, you leave the road above Nakasero market, pass through a courtyard and climb a flight of stairs. Just inside the entrance is the customers' water urn for hand-washing, complete with soap and freshly boiled water (a wise practice since cholera came to Kampala following El Niño's drenching rains). Blue-and-white-chequered tablecloths grace the 6 tables—four in one dining room, two in the other. The restaurant can seat only 17, but there is a fast turnover at lunchtime—three or 4 sittings within 2 hours. Young professionals—mostly men—crowd in to have an inexpensive, generous plate of Ugandan food: matoke, rice, peas, squash, fish and cooked whole sweet banana.

Her start-up capital was a Ush 1 million loan from a church-sponsored bank, with 6 months to repay. Sarah expects to repay in 3 months. She decided to borrow from the bank because it helps many people like herself: makes it easy to get a loan, repay and get another one. 'They do not mind when you bring small amounts of cash savings to deposit,' she says. A ROSCA she had joined earlier didn't work for her. 'We each put in 300,000 shillings a month, but you can find yourself eating your money. It disappears.'

Her other restaurant, on William Street, is managed by her youngest sister, who will take over some day when she can no longer work, Sarah says. There are 5 workers at the Nakasero restaurant and 8 on William Street. In addition, she has a large take-away business: About 500 plates a day go from Nakasero to neighbouring businesses like Jada Lottery and Wina Classic. Working hours are breakfast time to 4 p.m.; she does not keep either place open in the evening.

Sarah has a powerful motivation to succeed:

> I started business when my marriage failed because of my husband's behaviour. When I separated, I had 3 young children to support. The oldest one, Betty Nabirye, now age 10, is in school in my village, Kigoloba. The second one, Isima Sebuguzi, is 8 and the last, Nasali, is 5. The little ones are with me in Kawempe where I own a house, and they go to primary school there. I also have my brother's son in the village to care for; he is in first-year primary. The father was killed in the war, so I help the mother, too. Because my Kawempe house has 'boys' quarters', I can rent it from time to time. I also have a plot, and want to buy more land.

Born in 1962 in Luwero district, Sarah had three brothers and five sisters—all of whom went to school. She went to Bubulo High School in Mbale, but stopped after four years because of the war.

Why do women work so hard to make their businesses succeed, and why are they such good credit risks? 'Women are the ones who look after children. We have to see to it that our business goes well,' says Sarah, 'so women work harder than men. I work ten hours every day, except Sunday when I go to church. Men are often interested in finding women.' Her dream is to see London and America.

I started business the Uganda way, with no capital.

Edith Nakuya, retailer

Edith Nakuya (40ish): three years secondary school; separated with four children; sells imported women's wear, rents out ten shops, owns a private school

Edith Nakuya started as an entrepreneur, added paid work at a bank, then launched herself again into full-time entrepreneurship on a larger scale and with diverse investments. She tells her story:

> I became a businesswoman some 20 years ago, in Idi Amin's era, when I was about 20 years old. My husband went into exile, and I had nothing to feed my children—three girls and a boy—or to pay their school fees. I started business the Uganda way, with no capital. At that time, the country needed cement for building, so one would go and ask the bosses to sell some, then go to the headquarters next door to pay and find out where to get the cement. Once you had the allocation chit, you could sell the cement for a bit more than you paid. You might make 20 dollars, 30 dollars. Because I knew some people who would do the allocation, I started accumulating money.

She then developed the idea of trade with Kenya, so she went to the Bank of Uganda, where it was reputedly hard to get foreign (Kenyan) money. 'I knew some people so I could do that,' she says. 'A friend took me to Nairobi, where I bought gents' trousers, ladies' and children's clothing to sell in Kampala. I abandoned that business and switched to spare parts for cars, like Fiats. I would go in the morning by air and come back in the evening.'

Edith had problems in those times—her goods were looted almost every time government changed. Unfortunately, when her husband returned after a five-year separation, their marriage came apart. She continued her businesses to support her children, then started selling imported women's dresses and shoes about a year ago. Having seen a friend open a shop at the front of her house, she did the same in central Kampala where she now employs three salespersons.

> At first I was the sole importer of head-scarves in Uganda, but when the Asians came back they brought less costly scarves from India so my scarf business collapsed. I could not compete because my scarves were of better quality and demanded higher prices, and of course people like more reasonable prices. I then imported goods from Italy like shoes, sandals, clothes. Now I go to Hong Kong and Bangkok. That's where I got the goods for this shop and a small branch shop in town that I sublet. Sometimes I do wholesale, but direct selling is better because you get quick money. My customers are mostly local people.

Because she likes investing, Edith built a house and then a commercial building with ten shops in her home area of Ibanda in Mbarara district. The shops are occupied, but she has not yet completed the hostel; she is saving money to finish it. Her investments are diversified: 'I also own a school in Ibanda where my sister teaches. When I went home for Christmas, ... I had about a million shillings with me because the banks had closed at the time I left Kampala, [so] I went to the village, hired some architects and surveyors and started building. Now I have both a nursery and 2 grades of primary school, with about 150 children in all. There are 6 teachers.'

Why did Edith become an entrepreneur? Born in a family of 21 children of her father and his 2 wives, she finished primary education (then 8 years) and passed very well, so got a certificate to go on to secondary school. But her father would not take her to the school where she had been admitted—he thought she had enough education. When Nyakatukura School opened in her area, her mother secured a place there, but after 3 years, there was not enough money to pay school fees so she dropped out. Some of her brothers and sisters went to school, but not many reached secondary, she said. She applied for courses like nurse's training in Lira and Mulago, then abandoned that idea and went to stay with a sister. Soon married with children, she got a job as a machine operator at UCB and worked there for 10 years while doing business on the side.

Personal experience convinced her that her three daughters must finish school. One is a designer, another just married and the third is learning languages in Sweden. Her son is in secondary school. Apart from her own children, she also looks after the family of her brother who died in an accident.

Capital is of great importance to Edith.

> I have had difficulties getting capital, but I have managed, slowly. Why do we have such difficulty getting capital? Number one is that bank managers tend to favour men—who know each other's language, so to speak. Most women do not have support or collateral like land titles, so the bankers ask us for extra money. Some time back when I wanted to borrow 5 million shillings to boost my business, I was told that I would have to give 30 per cent for each million, to be paid on a monthly basis even before the goods I was buying arrived in the country. Before you finish with bankers, you may even offer to give them a car.

What other possibilities exist to get capital? Edith heard of ROSCAs but found them too small scale—Ush 200,000 would not help her. She needs about Ush 20 million to finish her hotel in Mbarara. 'If I got it, I would go and sit there for a month and supervise everyone so that no single cement bag is stolen, no nail is lost,' she says.

The soft loans given by government, called entandikwa, are another source of capital. Says Edith:

> The people who return this money are women, and that is a compliment to women. But there are also women who are weak and being overpowered. When the man knows that you receive entandikwa money, he may force you to surrender it. You give him the money or you lose the marriage. He wants to use that money to drink, or maybe to get another woman. The children are sick, but he wants to marry a

> second wife. But a determined woman finds a way to do business. Women are now progressing as entrepreneurs. In the middle class, it is women who have money these days.
>
> Will women go for bigger businesses? If we are encouraged. We do not waste money, but we use it quite differently from men. If I have a million shillings to spend, I will buy for myself and my family. But the man will spend to show that he has money, for example for a girlfriend. A man doesn't even mind spending money which is not his, which is from a loan. It is really a problem.

She is fully aware that women, too, can be troublesome. 'The problems women face are sometimes of their own doing,' she explains, speaking of leaders who create groups for their own personal benefit—trips to Sweden or UK, or getting milling machines. That selfishness among leaders can destroy trust, she believes—a situation the leaders of the MWODET group in Mpigi have determined to avoid (see Chapter 3).

> In this world things tend to become tougher and tougher. When that happens it is the women who worry, who stay at home and see the children crying of hunger. That is what inspires women to work hard. This is Africa, where there is polygamy. For 213 days your husband is away, so you are forced to do some marketing in order to pay school fees for your children. He cannot even afford to take care of himself, but here he has 6 children, there he has 4. When you complain, he does not want you to leave. He does not take care of the school fees for the children, yet at the same time he wants to keep you here on his land. You dig for him. That is the problem we women face.

'The future of my business is not bad. My daughters would take over if something happened to me. They are capable and determined,' Edith says.

Do not think you can get a million-shilling start-up loan.
Gera Harriet Mosha, restaurateur and guest-house owner

Gera Harriet Mosha (50s): studied nursing and dressmaking in the UK; widowed with six children; owns three restaurants and a guest house

After 20 years of self-support, Gera Harriet Mosha now owns 3 restaurants and a guest house. She used her own savings plus the insurance money received when her husband died as the initial capital to start business as a designer, the first step in her career. Neither her husband's family nor her own helped her with the children.

Bon Appetit Fried Chicken House on Jinja Road has four tables for four customers each plus an outdoor table with an umbrella. On the counter of the restaurant a large glass cabinet displays meat pies, samosas and other home-made delicacies. Behind the service counter are stoves and food-preparation tables; a tall glass cooler holds soda and beer.

'I am happy in the restaurant business because everybody needs to eat,' says Gera. She takes overdrafts from a bank rather than loans and repays within a month. That is how she started new branches of Bon Appetit. She now has a total of 25 employees at the 3 restaurants.

In the mornings she stays at home in Muyenga because her G8 Rest-House is next door; she helps out when there is a lot of business. It was her own house. Her husband died when she was building it. 'Most of the guests just want bed and breakfast, but when business is especially busy I go and help.' Hosting a party there costs Ush 300,000 for the place; food and drink are extra. The guest rooms range from Ush 25,000 to 60,000 a night, but rates are reduced if the guest stays a longer time. 'One guest stayed a year,' she says, adding, if there's an overflow, 'My sister also owns a guest house nearby.'

Gera has a special concern about workers:

> Many people do not want to pay their workers, but employees must have money at least at the end of every month because they have responsibilities. They have homes. They have problems.

She urges employers to get to know their workers.

> Some do not want to work, but they want money. Some just work when the boss is around. It is best to listen to them. Do not cut their salaries and do not be too free to dismiss them. Some of my workers have stayed for five years, some ten. A young woman who started out as my housegirl is now my cook at the guest house. If you change workers, you have to teach once again, and you can get worse people, too.

Gera thinks that women can work better than men because women 'listen to the people.' Nonetheless she prefers men as her own workers. Male workers are easier to manage, to understand, she says.

Gera Harriet Mosha, looking younger than her years, lost her Tanzanian husband 20 years ago. She tells her personal story:

> I was born as one of 12 children in a village in Masaka where my father was a chief. I have 2 younger brothers—the one who works in the East African Development Bank is a lawyer, as is my youngest brother, who works at Makerere University. In 1962 I went to England on a British scholarship to study nursing as my sister had done.

> It was easy to get a visa during colonial times, when we carried British passports—not like now.

Finding nursing uninteresting, she switched to dressmaking for one year, started working and met her late husband, who had a post-graduate scholarship in England.

All of Gera's 6 children are college graduates. The first one studied botany at Makerere, then went to Canada for her degree in biochemistry and remained there. The second, a pharmacist, is married in America. The third works in a bank, the fourth did postgraduate studies in England, and the fifth is on scholarship for postgraduate studies at Harvard in the USA. The last one also studied in the U.S. Gera's 28-year-old son helps her even though he has his own pest-control business. He is the one she expects will take over the business; he is unmarried and stays with her at her house. 'He is a very strict boy, like a father. He wakes up early, leaves home at a quarter to seven and comes to check up on my business and discuss with the workers,' she says.

> Work is very important. Your children will respect you for it. People love you if you do not cheat them. Women, wake up! Work! There no longer are men who will work for us, and you will be happy if you own the home that you sleep in. I am happy: I eat well, sleep well, have enough. I have everything.

Business can be very hard going.

Evelyn Biribonwa, bakery owner

Evelyn Biribonwa (mid 40s): studied economics and German at Makerere University; married with three children; owned a bakery (later sold)

Evanna Bakery owner Evelyn Biribonwa muses:

> This is a very hard business. The competition is high and dealing in perishables is difficult. The market is small because there are substitutes for bread, and people here think bread is a luxury. They have other things to eat. Sometimes I wonder why I am a baker. But at times you have little to do, as was my case after university. So you start up something, and then don't want to get out of it. You want to keep trying.

She articulates the need for technical knowledge and management skills, speaks about the size of start-up capital and its lasting impact on one's business, about customers' debts and the demands a family makes on income.

Evelyn bakes 2,000 loaves of bread plus pastries at a building she owns, not far from the retail shop she rents that is located at a busy intersection on Gaba

Road, with bus stops nearby and parking spaces in front. The business employs 15 at the bakery and 20 salespersons. The bakers are mostly men—because of the heat and because women will not work at night—and the bread must be ready by 6 in the morning. Loaves are delivered to neighbouring towns by car. The Evanna Bakery retail shop is attractive. Most of its baked goods are enclosed in glass cases and some are in small bundles. Just to the side of the shop a door leads to Evelyn's small office.

Evelyn did not always live in Kampala. 'I grew up in Hoima, [in the] western region of Uganda, in a big family of 14, of which she is thirteenth. Her childhood was full of care because there were big sisters and brothers and elders. 'Everyone in my family went to school; everybody is able to look after him or herself,' she says.

She started school in Hoima, then went to Nakawa for secretarial training and worked as a secretary before marrying. Despite having three children, with support from her husband she graduated from Makerere University in 1987 with a degree in economics and German.

Evelyn's explanation of her entry into business sheds light on why she sold her bakery not long after our interview:

> I think I got into business by accident. It is not something I chose to do. When I finished university I started looking for a job, but it was difficult. Meanwhile my husband had bought these machines, thinking that he would run a bakery himself. He is a public servant and found it hard to do two jobs. So he said to me, 'Why don't you start baking bread?' That's how I started.

She began business with her sister, who soon decided it was taking too long to generate any money, so, while remaining a legal partner, she left and became an importer. They found premises and in a very small way started producing bread. At first Evelyn had neither the machines nor the know-how for her business. She didn't know how to bake bread or to run a business, and it had never occurred to her that she needed those things. 'I just said, "Well, people are doing business so why not?" Somehow through trial and error I have gotten by and acquired some skills.'

There were difficult lessons to learn.

> I can assure you it has been very, very hard going, because if you don't know how to bake, you depend on the workers. If you don't have somebody who can bake today, then you will not bake. You will not even supervise because you cannot tell somebody what to do when you don't know, and don't even know how to run a business. But slowly I started attending a few courses and have picked up a bit. This was my first business and I am still in it.

Evelyn gained confidence by getting others' ideas when she joined UWEAL.

> I didn't seek credit until well into the business. I didn't get a loan at the beginning—I never even thought about it. I just started with the little money I had, and my husband added a little money. Only later did I realise that if you do not have enough capital, you do not grow, and the little you have gets swallowed up. I kept limping along until a good friend said, 'Why don't you get a loan from the bank?' I thought it would be hard, but fortunately I had collateral and all they wanted was an evaluation of the property. That was expensive, but I managed to do it with the help of my husband, and I got an overdraft that I stayed with for about three years.
>
> I learned that you begin by developing a relationship with your bankers and then convince them to give you a loan. My loan was 3 million shillings at first, then 5 million. Then I stopped because the interest was too high. But more than that, I was having production problems and lower sales. So I said, 'Let me get rid of the overdraft for the time being and limp on without problems.' Right now I can sleep better, but it doesn't mean that I am doing better!

Entrepreneurship is full of challenges. Problems arise with electric power, with taxes and with customers' debts. Evelyn believes entrepreneurs are overtaxed. Another problem she faces is that people fail to pay and over time, debts accumulate. 'I think I must go for a course in debt management. Debts just wipe you out. I do not know how many I have written off,' Evelyn says. However, she finds that business becomes a bit easier with experience and as the size of your family's dependent group grows smaller. She had lots of children from extended family to support—two went to university and are working. Her eldest daughter—actually a step-daughter—is doing her masters degree, and her own eldest is going into a second year at Makerere University, while two are in secondary school. She hopes that her children will take over some day. 'The girls have done courses in business and probably would want to take over. But right now I have no thought about that,' Evelyn says. She sold her bakery less than two years later.

Sarah, Edith and Gera honed their business skills and accumulated capital before launching their small-scale businesses. Sarah and Gera had strategic infusions of capital at the transition period: a bank loan and an insurance grant. Evelyn's case is different: she relied on her husband's and her savings and equipment her husband had earlier purchased; by her own accounting her capital was insufficient to allow growth of the bakery without eating up her capital. Unlike Sarah the butcher in Chapter 5, who learned together with her relatively few employees, Evelyn soon had 35 workers—some of them more skilled bakers than she was. That situation implies a heavy personal management load combined with the challenges of productivity and marketing and dependants to support. A difficult combination.

Motivation to succeed in business was intense for Sarah and Edith—both separated from their husbands—and Gera, widowed with children to support.

Building start-up capital from paycheques

The third group of small- to medium-scale entrepreneurs saved enough through paid employment or had enough financial credibility to make a break and start full-time with new businesses of their own. Among these are two partnerships: Delmira Travel and Tours, owned by a Ugandan and a Dutch citizen, and Boutique Shamin (also known as Tinga Tinga) owned by two sisters. In this group also is the much-respected Tereza Mbire, who is celebrated as the first Ugandan businesswoman (rather than trader) of the 1970s and who co-founded both UWFT and UWEAL. Nina Joyce Muyanda also started in wage employment—she has become a venture capitalist with a major interest in eco-tourism.

There are three directors of my companies: my two sons and myself.
Tereza Mbire, co-founder, UWEAL and UWFT

Tereza Mbire (60s): widowed with six children; co-founder of UWFT and UWEAL; owns a garment industry and Habitat Interiors

Tereza Mbire's first enterprise was a floral shop; she then ventured into tailoring and later had a bakery called Home Pride. Reaching retirement age, she wanted a peaceful, enjoyable, treasured business—she calls it Habitat Interiors—that combined easily with her tailoring experience.

In the early 1970s, Tereza was executive housekeeper, then trainer, for the Apollo Hotel, now called the Sheraton. After the expulsion of the Asians in 1972, when many women started petty trade businesses to provide for their families after the death or exile of their husbands, she decided to venture into something bigger. She transformed her love of flowers into a business. 'I felt I could take it as a challenge in a male-dominated environment, and I must say I managed very well,' she told *Success Magazine* (no. 1, 1998).

Since her home area, Kabale, has a climate similar to that of Nakuru and North Kinangop in Kenya where flowers are grown, Tereza borrowed a bit of money from her husband, visited Kenya, bought seedlings and started her enterprise. Faced with foreign-exchange restrictions, as Edith was, she had to negotiate her way through her government's bureaucracy for permission to import from Kenya. She was successful and was the only florist in Uganda for about a decade.

Frustrated by threats of eviction, Tereza left the flower business in 1985 to embark on another project—a garment industry—manufacturing children's and women's wear, draperies, bedsheets, tablecloths and such. The wholesale market for garments was good—she supplied many retailers. 'We had less competition, and people mistook ours to be garments imported from Europe,' she recalls. As was common, her plant was looted time and again by soldiers; in 1979 all of her 100 sewing machines were taken. So she started to produce bread. Later, she was able to buy back 15 machines from the looters and get a bank loan to import more.

Tereza sold off the bakery but still owns the garment factory as well as her newer, related venture, Habitat Interiors. She currently employs about 30 people in the two enterprises. Like Joyce, Cothilda and Olive in Chapter 5, she feels the impact of trade liberalisation pushing Uganda into the global economy through SAPs. The demand for locally made garments declined as imported second-hand clothing flooded the market. As she explains, 'With the increase in the amount of used clothes imported in the country, we had to reduce the size of the staff in the garment business' (*Success* 1998).

There are three directors of her companies: Tereza and two of her children—her sons. A widow, Tereza explains that her husband, who was employed by the Coffee Marketing Board, encouraged her but never interfered in her running of the business. Her entrepreneurial experience led her to sharing with her fellow women as a co-founder of UWFT and UWEAL (see Chapter 5).

We pay the workers first.

Hamida Hudani and Shamin Kassam, Tinga Tinga store owners

Hamida Hudani and Shamin Kassam (both in their 40s): married with one child each; co-own the Tinga Tinga Boutique Shamin and Dressing Room

Boutique Shamin—also known as Tinga Tinga ('shake, shake')—and the Dressing Room are a combined shop known by its huge 'Tinga Tinga' flag waving outside 12 Buganda Road. Inside are quality T-shirts with tourist-attracting designs of animals, flowers and catchy sayings like hakuna matata ('no problem'). There are also sporty safari clothes and high-fashion wear, as well as three rooms with saris and other Asian clothing.

Owners Hamida Hudani and Shamin Kassam are sisters who grew up in Kampala in a family of five girls. They finished secondary school at the Aga

Khan School, then continued their education in England. Their father had a factory in Kampala until 1972 but lost everything during the Amin regime. The whole family moved to Canada to start their lives over again. Shamin had a surgery in Canada until a cousin suggested she go into the clothing business, for Shamin had always loved clothes. Eventually, she and Hamida opened three boutiques as a 'hobby' preferable to staying at home. But even in Canada they found that 'one has to work very hard to make a cent'.

They returned to Uganda in 1991 and started business in Kampala in 1995. Two of their sisters also returned to Africa. One works in tourism in Mombasa, Kenya, another owns a fish factory in Tanzania, and the third stayed in Canada, where she assists with her husband's business.

Hamida and Shamin began their new business with a franchise from Tinga Tinga of Kenya. Realising that teens and young women need more than casual wear, the sisters expanded by stocking office and evening clothes.

The sisters say:

> Good customer relations are essential to success in a retail shop; you can't just sit and watch customers. Here we get to know our customers, and they really love it. They are happy when we give them a first chance to choose new merchandise; it makes them feel special. Sometimes we help them select styles, especially for dressing up. A lot of people are not sure of themselves so you can help them dress in what suits them, what colours look best on them. We have learned a lot over time about advising our customers.

The partners had both bank and personal start-up capital to purchase the land, the building and initial stock, and were able to repay. They prefer loans to overdrafts because the former are long-term, and they need new inventory as they expand the shop. Tinga Tinga has six local and two expatriate staff in addition to security staff, and each partner spends a half-day at the shop. They pay the workers first and if there's a bad month, draw little or no money themselves. Like Gera, they are convinced that staff must come first. 'If we decide to expand, it will be to open upcountry or on the other side of Kampala but not at this location—unless we decide to have a coffee shop here. We are thinking along those lines.

Problems? One must of course watch for shoplifting. Having been in business in two countries, Hamida and Shamin find Uganda more difficult than Canada for persons who import because there is more bureaucracy and higher customs duties—it almost seems they are paying more than the value of the goods being imported.

> Usually people say that there is so much stress in the western world, but for businesspersons there is more stress here. Women entrepre-

> neurs have special problems. For example, inspectors come from the city council in groups of six or more men to check licenses. They tend to frighten both staff and customers in a country that had such disruption within recent memory. Men find it easier to deal with groups of men in this kind of situation, and businesswomen think that the inspectors are easier on male entrepreneurs.

Shamin has one daughter with her and Hamida has a son in school in Canada. Their husbands support their families, although the sisters contribute when needs arise. They reinvest their profits in their business in order to help it grow. The sisters are members of the Ugandan Asian Women's Association, which raises money for street children and other charities and for the Aga Khan community. They are also members of their mosque committee.

It is good to have theory and diplomas, but working experience is quite different.
Mirjam Black, co-owner Delmira Travel and Tours Ltd

Delia Almeida (37) and Mirjam Black (30s): educated in UK and Holland; both single; partners in Delmira Travel and Tours, Ltd

The Thomas Cook representative in Uganda is Delmira Travel and Tours Ltd, owned by Ugandan Delia Almeida, whose business partner is Mirjam Black of the Netherlands. Before starting their venture, Delia worked with Sabena Airlines in Kampala and Mirjam was in East Africa with the Office of the UNHCR, and afterwards founded her own advisory service in Nairobi.

Delmira is located in a large and charming house near Ruth Towers and the United Nations offices, a bit away from the city centre. It offers a variety of safari packages: to the Mountains of the Moon, Murchison Falls, the source of the River Nile and national parks. It invites eco-tourists to track mountain gorillas in the Bwindi Impenetrable Forest or to visit an unspoiled land with a climate averaging 26° centigrade all year round. Delmira is a member of the International Air Transport Association (IATA).

Delia's family has no business background. Her parents came to Uganda from Goa; her father was a civil servant who managed to buy land and a house. Her brother is a dentist, and her late sister was a music teacher; another sister also teaches. Delia studied in England, then was a fashion designer for three years. She says:

> I am the only one of my family here. My siblings went to Canada and the States, but to me this is home. I love Uganda. It is very difficult to uproot yourself and go to another country and start all over. Here I know the system, I know everybody so I have my identity. I have a boyfriend, and I go out and socialise. At 37, I am not married. I own

> the business and have about 20 employees. It takes a lot of time so I have no other business.

After 12 years as a sales manager at Sabena Airlines, Delia was joined by Mirjam to start their own agency in 1989. Mirjam put in the initial capital, and they picked up very quickly, partly because Delia's Sabena customers followed her.

Mirjam explains:

> When we started Delmira Travel and Tours about eight years ago, I had my own legal and marketing consultancy firm. Delia and I planned that she would run the business, and I would stay in the background because I already had an established office. Then Delmira grew so big in a few months that it became necessary for me to be more involved, and as a result I did less work in the other business. I took some courses to know ticketing and other aspects of tourism.

Mirjam came to East Africa as a legal adviser seconded by the Dutch government to the UNHCR in Nairobi for three years, at a time when the asylum seekers were Ugandans running from the Obote regime. After her tour of duty, she decided to stay and start a consultancy business in Kenya. She says that some Ugandans returning from Sweden said, 'Well, Mirjam, when we take over Kampala you must come with us.' She went three days after the take-over on 29 January 1986.

The partners find that doing business in Uganda demands financial backing. And success with a travel agency depends on who you know in the community, Ugandan and expatriate alike, and it takes a lot of money to make those connections. Also, much depends on corporate planning. They say people have told them, 'We visited several agencies and we find you more professional.'

Delmira is officially recognised as an IATA travel agency by virtue of banking US$50,000 as a guarantee. There are running expenses: Tour operations need expensive 4-wheel-drive vehicles and smart-looking offices. On top of those substantial investments, the partners add, there is marketing to do abroad. Sometimes business expands, leaving administration lagging behind, and that is a risk to your financial investment because when you provide air tickets, ninety-one per cent of the price goes back to the airlines. So if people are not paying well, you incur a lot of debts. 'Starting capital goes well beyond US$100,000,' they say.

Mirjam observes that dealings with bureaucracies can take a lot of time. She adds:

> No matter how much you favour the government or an organisation, you cannot run your business when they owe you 150,000 dollars. We have cases where, even after three and a half years, the full amount has not been paid—we almost went bankrupt! You must be very careful if you issue tickets before payment, even when you trust someone. Business is very tough indeed. We have invested quite a lot of money over the years, but it is gradually building up.

Delia adds: You have to work very hard. You do not put up a business and leave it and think it is going to run. You have to be a step ahead. If you are not careful, the business can just collapse.' Echoing Edith, she says, 'I sometimes think women do business the hard way, without enough capital. So they either borrow or start without. But at the end they are more successful than men.'

Delmira's biggest competitor eight years ago is still its biggest competitor, so there is room for others in the travel and tourism business. Says Mirjam:

> When we started business, it was difficult to promote a country just recovering from the insecurity, lawlessness and destruction of a civil war. Promoting a country like this as a place for a holiday takes a lot of time—it takes years to rebuild up its reputation. Uganda is known first for Idi Amin and second for AIDS. You have to convince people that Amin is no longer here and then convince them that AIDS is not contagious. One has to take a lot of time with the media and other promotion campaigns.

Delmira's future success is in large part beyond the control of its owners. External factors, such as political instability in the Great Lakes region, caused a reduction in tourism in late 1996 and 1997. 'Marketing will not pay off when people abroad are influenced by a negative media image, even when it is not a true one.' Mirjam explains. 'When they see the situation in Rwanda or Eastern Zaire every day on CNN and BBC, people think the war is spilling over into Uganda. In reality we had little insecurity. With the exception of the time when the Rwenzori Mountains were closed, we were always able to take visitors to see gorillas and all of the national parks. But those brief stories on TV make people fear to come here. It is very, very difficult to persuade them that the country is safe.' Mirjam continues:

> Uganda can thrive because it is a most beautiful country in terms of every conceivable eco-system: swamps, rivers, lakes, mountains, impenetrable forests, savannah, desert. There are many possibilities for specialised tourism [such as] mountaineering, seeing primates, birding for people who love nature and who do not mind rough roads. Uganda has not been spoiled by human hands. You don't have to be in a little

matatu (minibus) and follow one little lion, waiting your turn to take pictures.

Looking back, it is wonderful to be in Uganda and to have come at a time when there were many business opportunities. There was a vacuum to be filled. There are still a lot of opportunities, especially in manufacturing, if you have enough capital. When Delia and I got together we gradually expanded. We set ourselves goals to survive through thick and thin—we had to work! But it is an exciting business to be in. Promoting Uganda's tourism is nice. Despite the problems we have, tourism is going to thrive.

I travelled to a number of countries worldwide.

Nina Joyce Muyanda, beach resort and travel agency owner

Nina Joyce Muyanda (40+): diploma in tours and travel; married with five children; created Ssese Palm Beach Resort and East–West Travel Ltd

Uganda's 'best businesswoman of 1996' was Nina Joyce Muyanda, creator of Ssese Palm Beach Resort on Buggala, the largest of the 84 Ssese Islands of Lake Victoria.

Nina trained as an airline hostess for three years with TWA in the United States and served East African Airlines in Nairobi for over five years. During that time she saw the world, including many beautiful islands. She then took additional training as a secretary and worked at the World Bank in Nairobi, returning to Uganda with her savings in 1987.

Born in Soroti, the first of 19 children of her father, a retired teacher, Nina attended Nakivubo Asian School and Gayaza Catholic School. In 1974, Nina married Professor Muyanda Mutebi of Makerere University, who, she says, 'has played a very big role' in her business. They have 5 children, the eldest at Makerere.

After her travels, Nina's entrepreneurship began with 3 years of ranching, farming and rabbit-rearing in Mawogola. She took a diploma in tours and travel in 1994 and, having seen her husband's home islands—the Ssese, was struck with the idea of opening a beach resort (*The New Vision* 23 April 1998). In May 1997 she leased 20 scrubby acres and used more than Ush 15 million of her own savings clearing it. Within a year she had built workers' quarters, a kitchen, six cottages, a dining hall, a storeroom and put up 20 camping tents—all this with 7 permanent and 30 casual labourers.

'It has been very rough constructing that beach,' she says. 'But it is a lovely destination for persons wanting a peaceful holiday in the midst of natural wonders. Visitors can relax at the edge of the lake, take boat rides and go fishing or bird-watching. There are many animals to see: monkeys, hippos, antelopes and exotic birds.' Plans for the second phase of construction include a conference hall, games and tennis courts, swimming pool and a piggery project.

Nina has diversified her investments and tried to ensure occupancy at Ssese Palm Beach Resort by opening jointly with her husband a tour company called East–West Travel Limited that specialises in eco-tourism; it is located on Bombo Road in Kampala.

Tereza, Hamida and Shamin, Delia and Mirjam, and Nina Joyce are unique: Three are partnerships—two with other family members, and Nina Interiors has family members as directors. All have previous entrepreneurial experience: Tereza's capacity to move from one business to another helped her survive the looting and shortages during the years of civil strife. The exiled partners of Tinga Tinga became entrepreneurs while in Canada where they got a head start in business experience. The Delmira team combination of accumulated capital (Mirjam) and customers brought from earlier employment (Delia) strengthened the partnership. Nina Joyce travelled extensively with East African Airways before starting her tourism.

Making it with large-scale, diversified investments

Fang Min—a Chinese citizen—is among a small group of women from other countries who came to Uganda as small- and medium-scale entrepreneurs; she employs 100 persons in her restaurants. Daisy Roy employs 150 persons in her primary enterprise, an air cargo business, and owns other businesses too. Both are large-scale entrepreneurs and venture capitalists who concentrate first on a single enterprise until it is successful, then look for further investments.

If you make a loss today,
you solve the problem and continue.
Fang Min, restaurateur

Fang Min (42): secondary school in China; divorced with one child; owns four restaurants

Fang Min, owner of Fang Fang Restaurant, arguably Kampala's finest, began her business life working for someone else, then became an entrepreneur and built up her capital base slowly, reinvesting as she went along. She is 42 years old and has been in Uganda 9 years, since her first visit as a tourist when she decided to return as an entrepreneur. Fang Fang is her second Chinese restaurant. The first, a small one called China Great Wall, is on Kampala Road opposite the Commercial Bank. She opened Fang Fang above Greenland Bank in 1994. 'At first only Wazungu (Caucasians) and Asians came to eat,' she says, 'but after a year or two, African Ugandans began to come. Kampala is going forward, changing in nice way.'

The decor at Fang Fang is striking: deep red draperies and carpets, dark wood chairs upholstered with floral patterns embroidered in ecru and white, a pale wood carved mural of peacocks and geese across the whole entry wall. Posts are mirrored to reflect that ambience. On entering one is greeted personally by the proprietor, Fang Min, whose name means 'strong flower'.

Fang Min grew up in China, in Beijing, as the fourth of five children, finished high school and worked for the government for six years. She met Ugandan students who pushed her, saying, 'Uganda welcomes nice people,' so she visited in 1989 and liked it so much that she returned as an entrepreneur in 1991. Her sister, a banker, is her accountant and cashier; her brother manages a third restaurant, in Jinja, near the petrol station on Jinja road.

Fang Min arrived in Kampala speaking no English. She confesses:

> It was hard. When I first came, people gave me a lot of trouble because of that. I cried sometimes, but my heart pushed me to keep trying. I learned from books, slowly, as I worked. Sometimes I wanted to leave—I almost closed the restaurant—but I wanted to succeed so I persisted. When I had problems I would just wait for tomorrow, when things could be better. If you like your business, you just give—openheartedly. If you make a loss today, you try to solve the problem and continue.

She trained the first of her 100 workers herself. Now old waiters train new waiters. She has a Ugandan manager, and Ugandan and Chinese staff (about 500 Chinese live in Uganda). 'Business in Kampala can grow very fast,' Fang Min says. 'You can initiate new businesses, and people are interested in them. I may open in other Ugandan cities in future.'

When she first came she never borrowed any money from the bank, she says,

> because it is not easy if you are not known and because interest is too high. I brought money with me from China. Now I reinvest my profit in business. For example, I came in 1991 and opened the Great Wall, then when I had enough money I opened Fang Fang in 1994. In 1995 I opened the Jinja branch and in 1997 the bar and restaurant. Money helps me to give people jobs and keeps my 16-year-old daughter in boarding school in Canada. I try to help workers whose families are in need. I feel very happy when I can do that.

In the beginning Fang had one business partner, largely because she could not speak English. But after one year she found that money was not being accounted for so she remains alone. She rented, then bought, Fang Fang. Exceptionally dedicated, she works from 10 in the morning to 11 or 12 every night, even on Sunday, seven days of the week. No holiday, no Christmas, no New Year. 'I get tired,' she admits, 'but I just close my eyes and forget and get to work again.'

Three years ago Fang and her husband divorced, agreeing that it would be better for him to have a wife who would take care of him and a family. She does not intend to remarry. 'It is not very easy to take care of both family and business. The family needs you, and the business needs you, and which is first'? she asks. 'I have my daughter here. She cried in the beginning,' Fang says. 'But after two years she grew up. Now I have 100 staff and a daughter. I can handle it.'

You cannot give up as some women do after they have been rejected by one bank.
Daisy Roy, owner, Das–Air Ltd

Daisy Roy (50): University of London; married with three children; owns and runs several companies, including Das–Air Ltd

Daisy Roy is managing director of an air cargo company, Das–Air Ltd. She says:

> It is a family business I started that is now owned by my husband and myself. My husband, an airline pilot, flies the planes and I do the ground work. For example, yesterday the plane came in at 9 in the evening at Entebbe Airport, and I had to attend to it. We finished about midnight, drove back the 34 kilometres to Kampala, and this morning I had to get up at 5 to prepare for tomorrow's flight.

A small- to medium-size business compared to other airlines, Das–Air is large-scale in Ugandan terms, with 6 planes and 150 employees. It is a Ugandan company—both Daisy and her husband are Ugandan—so Daisy stays in Kampala even though their flights normally originate in the United Kingdom. 'We are contracted to fly all over the world and cover Africa very extensively, with regular flights to Accra, Lagos and Port Harcourt in West Africa. We go south to Lusaka, Johannesburg, Harare and Nairobi, and also to Dubai,' she explains.

Daisy was born in a small district in the Bunyoro kingdom of western Uganda. She is very proud of her father, John William Nyakatura, who wrote a book about the Ugandan kingdoms in 1971. After schooling at Hoima, she went to Fort Portal, then joined East African Airways as a stewardess. There she met and married Joe Roy, a cadet in the airlines. After a few years she was grounded because she was pregnant. She stayed at home with her four babies. Unfortunately, one, John Conrad, died. Now there are Bonnie Wendy, Joe Clyde and Jeffrey Charles. Daisy talks about those years:

> We were in Nairobi until 1976, when the East African Community had problems because of Idi Amin, who couldn't see eye to eye with the Presidents of Kenya and Tanzania, and the airline collapsed. We then went to Nigeria, where my husband found a job with an airline. While he was flying I decided in 1980 to take the children to England where they could continue the type of education they had begun in Kenya; West African education was different. When I put the children in boarding schools in the UK, I started doing small business—petty trading. I traded in textiles, dresses and other garments. I made purchases in New York to sell in Nigeria, went to Kenya to buy batiks. As I got a little capital I even started going to the Far East and Europe to buy lace, particularly for East Africa, where they would pay good money for it.

She admits that her schedule was 'quite taxing'.

The children were all at school, doing very well, so Daisy enrolled at the University of London, and after graduate studies in business and accountancy started her own air cargo business in 1983. She employed three pilots at first, when her husband was still working in Nigeria. She explains:

> The beginnings were really humble and hard work because I had to do everything: equip the aircraft, negotiate contracts, pay landing fees. I did all of it myself. After six months, I employed another person but went a whole year before hiring others. Finally my husband left his job in Nigeria and joined me in London to become our chief pilot and route-training captain—everything—because he was qualified for all of that.

Why don't women get capital to start a business? Daisy looks to her own experience:

> Women can fail to get start-up capital because their projects are not well presented. You must plan, get a professional to do a feasibility study and then take it to the bank and defend it. To defend it you must believe in what you are doing. If you do, some bankers will be sympathetic. You cannot give up as some women do after they have been rejected by one bank. I am very persistent. I will go to each bank until someone hears my voice. You must be persistent. Go and knock at the doors of those banks.

> If a woman has a good plan and believes in what she is doing, her opportunities should be equal with men. But if you are a married woman, you had better talk over the idea of starting up a business with your husband. Otherwise you cause problems. The two spouses must sit down, discuss and agree. If your husband opposes your idea, then bring another idea. But if you go ahead and do it regardless of his view, you can cause a rift. If you are going to use your home as collateral, he must sign for that.

In Daisy's view, an entrepreneur must always start with very little and build on it. If you go immediately to the bank to take out a loan to start a project, you can be charged a very high rate of interest, as she discovered when starting the airline.

> We started up on very small capital, using our house as collateral. When we set up in Uganda, we got into other ventures: ranching and growing flowers, horticulture, representing a Japanese vehicle company, providing ground transportation, hauling petroleum products from Kenya to Uganda then crossing to Zaire with them.

From many years of experience, Daisy points out a formidable obstacle to Ugandan, and especially women's, entrepreneurship:

> The interest rates at Ugandan banks are very high and hard for beginners. The worst is the horticultural: non-traditional cash crops that the government has been urging us to grow. The lenders charge 14 per cent a year for dollars. That is very high because even in the USA the Federal Reserve Bank doesn't do that. When you start a business the interest can choke you up. And if your business wasn't well thought out by experts, you will have even more problems.

Kikoi-maker Ida Wanendeya spoke of Kampala bank interest rates to borrow shillings as ranging 20 to 25 per cent, which she considered very high (see Chapter 5); MFIs often charge 30 to 40 per cent interest (see Chapter 3).

A global business such as Das-Air needs a fast information system, and they have it.

> We are computerised. Of course no one organisation has everything we need, but the Internet is good. For example, when we are dealing with the aircraft, I can access their status very quickly by calling McDonnell Douglas because we have two DC10s. I belong to [such executive organisations as] the Institute of Directors and am an associate member of the Business Executives in the UK.

For Daisy and Das-Air, the biggest problem is competition.

> You must accept your opponents, know their strengths so that you can counter them. If you go into business blindly, you will never survive. It is a very, very competitive world out there. Take the examples of aviation and agriculture, which I am conversant with. In aviation you must have a very good maintenance organisation backing you up every time you break down, so that you do not delay, you do not disappoint your clients. In the agriculture sector, you have got to bring fertilisers, and your marketing companies must be able to move your products quickly.

There are now five ventures under Daisy's umbrella; the airline, ground transportation and ranching are the biggest. There are also the horticulture and warehousing at the airport, which she does for government. Daisy's Deli is Daisy's hobby.

> When I came back to Uganda to live for good, I found that small things which ladies need every day were lacking. We decided to put up that little shop just to cater for those things. We ran into problems by stocking local supplies, which are available everywhere, so now I concentrate on the expatriate community, which wants things that are not locally available.

'The future is bright, especially in Uganda,' Daisy believes, 'if we can continue the trend we have now, with no destabilising factors. If the North and West of the country are settled, if they stop the petty fighting, the future is bright.'

Fang Min and Daisy share personality traits: Both are exceptionally persistent in reaching their goals. Like most of the small-scale entrepreneurs met in this chapter, they also involve family: Daisy's husband is co-owner of Das-Air and Fang Min relies on her brother and sister to manage her money and another restaurant. Both started small and face competition squarely; one method they use to defeat it is sheer hard work.

Designer, creator and managing director

Three entrepreneurs are not the owners of their enterprises. Like Robinah the publisher, they attracted large-scale investment through their creative ideas. Unlike her, they are managing directors who carry responsibility for those enterprises. Maria Kiwanuka is general manager of a radio station—Radio One. Edith Byanyima is managing director of TNT Express Worldwide in Uganda. Joan Mubiru is headmistress of a community-owned school.

I designed the place, then became the executive.
Maria Kiwanuka, general manager, Radio One

Maria Kiwanuka (30s): Makerere University, post-graduate studies in UK; designed and manages a radio station

Radio One, found just behind Greenland Towers where Fang Fang is located, has a 'New-Age look' (*The Sunday Monitor* 25 Jan. 1998). Its reception area is uncluttered, with a light-coloured wood desk against a background of cream stucco walls that are bare except for a clock whose face reads 90 FM Radio One. The casual dress of the young staff could be found anywhere in the world. General Manager Maria Kiwanuka is young too, in her 30s. In 1998, she was named Entrepreneur of the Year for, as the citation said, having 'stormed into the congested airwaves with her Radio One, attracted some of the best radio journalists, and introduced programmes like Spectrum that gained instant popularity.' Maria says:

> I am the only woman in Uganda who is general manager of a radio station. I am Kampala-born and bred and did all my schooling through Makerere University here, then did post-graduate studies in London and was with the World Bank in Washington for nine years. I also worked at a radio station in the USA. My father is an engineer, and my mother a teacher. All of my siblings are educated.

On her return from Washington, Maria was a consultant to the World Bank in Kampala for five years, then joined Radio One at the feasibility study stage. 'I designed the place, then became the executive,' she explains. The station is owned jointly by indigenous Ugandans and international investors. Radio One started broadcasting in September 1997 as a 24-hour station that targets people who are 30 years old and older by offering popular music, both African and western.

> I am responsible to see that the product gets on the air and the station remains a viable entity. That means managing a combination of human resources, finances, equipment and clients, including advertisers. I oversee the production, set guidelines for the directors and for the products. I have to anticipate how much money we will need, double that and then present it to our board of directors. We have about 30 full-time employees—fifty per cent of them women. We get them young and train them in the way we like. Those young people and I are growing together.

As an executive I must be ready to face any problem. I must plan ahead and never say 'because I am a woman'. There is a myth that people do not expect to find a woman in management, but I must say that I have not encountered that. I must think carefully about what I want to do and why, and how to do it better if somebody else is doing it. There are loads of problems: gender, racial and age discrimination, and not having attended the right college.

'It is very difficult to give advice when you are still in a learning process yourself. But one thing I can say is that it is a tough world. One has to learn what one's abilities are, one's assets, and use them within a given framework.'

I did a feasibility study, got a job immediately and never looked back.
Edith Byanyima, managing director, TNT Express Worldwide

Edith Byanyima (40+): law degree; single with one child; managing director of TNT Express Worldwide in Uganda

Like Maria Kiwanuka, Edith Byanyima set a goal, did a feasibility study and was hired immediately to introduce the business she envisioned. Edith tells her story:

> In 1986 I returned to Uganda from England where I was working, but the Law Development Centre was full and I would have had to wait a year or two. In addition, the legal profession had eroded over the Amin/Obote years of injustice—morale was very low. When I returned to England, the 9 o'clock TV news announced a postal strike, and Margaret Thatcher's government called in private companies to do the Royal Mail. One of the companies that won the tender was TNT Express Worldwide. I had not heard of it in Uganda so I looked for the managing director and asked, 'Why are you not in Uganda?' He said they actually were in Uganda, but offices were in Kenya. I said, 'Why don't you have an office in Uganda?' and he said, 'Are you interested in that?' I replied, 'Yes, I am interested. I want to go back and see whether there is an opportunity.' So I did a research here over about six months in 1988, sent the manager my report and went back to see him. I got a job immediately to represent TNT in Uganda, so I never looked back. I never returned to my legal profession. I have no regrets. I have been working hard since 1989 to build this courier company. It is doing very well.

Edith Byanyima, who grew up three miles from Mbarara, the major city south-west of Kampala, was the eldest of seven children, all educated as were their parents. She is single, with a child whose father died when he was one and a half years old. She also has a big extended family, so there are seven people living in her house.

The offices of TNT Express are at the spacious International Conference Centre, a copper-trimmed structure set in gardens and greenery in central

Kampala. It was completed in the era of Idi Amin and is in constant use by groups large and small. TNT Express Worldwide is a computer-equipped office with a spirit of efficiency and public service that are immediately obvious to a visitor.

Edith considers herself fortunate because at the start her mother advanced her some money which she did not have to repay directly, so she repaid indirectly. Since then she has had overdrafts from banks from time to time to help with working capital. Twenty employees and several vehicles, including motorcycles, comprise the operation. At times, members of her family work with her before taking up other jobs. Radio, telephone and fax communications are supplemented by the Internet, where Central TNT Computer Systems has a web site so that Edith can trace every shipment that leaves and comes into Uganda.

TNT faces stiff competition.

> My competitor is an expatriate, and most courier business here comes from expatriates. So I have to compete with an expatriate for their business. But I am doing very well. A lot of people are looking for good service so we concentrate on offering that. If we can get through your door, we will do a very good job.

She plans to expand in Uganda in the next five years; like the post office, TNT would be represented throughout the country. A grant from the Private Sector Foundation (PSF) allowed her to study the possibilities of expansion, and she is looking for capital to begin.

On the subject of entrepreneurship, her views are firm:

> A lot of women are coming up in business in Uganda because business is one of the best options that we have. A young woman interested in doing business must first have a very good idea; second, she must make a good business plan; and third, be ready for long hours and for foregoing a salary and things that we take for granted, like social life. Business can be very demanding. As for me, I have no regrets. I am doing what I wanted to do.

A UWEAL member and a co-founder of the newly formed Uganda Services Export Association, Edith has honed her business philosophy: 'To me, business is part of life, so the way I live with people is the way I also do business. If I live in a community, business must be taken in that context; it is business in that particular community.'

To do all this one has to programme herself.
Joan Mubiru, headmistress

Joan Mubiru (40): teacher training; married; headmistress of community-owned school

Like Maria Kiwanuka and Edith Byanyima, Joan Mubiru produced an idea that others supported, then became its manager. Joan is headmistress of Our Lady of Fatima, a private women's school that is owned by women of the Catholic Church who sat down in 1990 and, with Joan's advice, decided they needed it. She tells the story:

> Women picked a school as a project because they wanted something that would support them financially; in other words they wanted to stop begging from their husbands. So they invested in the small nursery school. They had an advantage in that among them were teachers, such as their group chairperson Mrs Kayondo. Their start-up capital came from fund-raising. They sold their old shoes and clothes (a jumble sale). The money collected was used to renovate an abandoned house to use as a nursery school.
>
> For the first three years the school remained a nursery attached to the church. The women approached me in 1993 because I am a trained secondary school teacher. So I suddenly had 2 jobs—I would teach in the secondary school and run the primary school at the same time. But the work and responsibility were too much, so I chose to concentrate on the women's school. When I started full-time with them, nothing much had been done. They had only a skeleton, up to primary 3, with 160 students. There was a primary school in another place called Kigo that was not performing well and was dissolved, so we invited the children to come here. Once the school was doing well, the parish priest provided the church land on which the present school is built. Now we have over 400 students.

Joan says the school prospectus is given to each parent so that they know the teachers' qualifications, and she contacts parents of primary six and seven students to show them all the books that were purchased for their children. Joan says:

> I have a competent staff. Right now I have 20 teachers, and only one is a man. Others left—they may have felt out of place because of the large female population. In addition, when I looked at their performance I did not see their work. I have a system of checking all the teachers' performance—I check prep books, look at their work plans.
>
> It has not been easy; to do all this one has to program herself. Every beginning of term I have a planning week to review each teacher's workplan. I retain a copy of each one. Every Monday every teacher has to produce prep books and every Tuesday I look at the home-

> work books. In our school we offer medical services; we have a school doctor. We have a guide for the children at the road crossing.

The daughter of a secretary and a social worker, Joan was the only girl among 8 children. 'I was lucky,' she says, 'that my father was aware of developing both sexes—all children in the same way. I remember how when I was in primary 2 we would compete and whoever won got a chicken. My father would even favour the girl by giving me more books.' Her parents made her a signatory to their 300 acres of land. Now she is married with one child. 'My husband found me working and in that circumstance you stay working. Some men only promise to care for you, but he is still supportive,' she says.

Joan is secretary to the local Women's Council and a member of the YWCA, which lends money to women starting with Ush 50,000 and also teaches them how to budget, invest and spend. She helps to sensitise women to appreciate the fact that the money given them is a loan for business and not for school fees or for the husband. 'Women do not "eat money", but they have a weakness,' Joan says. 'When the child is sick, she uses loan money instead of making profit with it. In addition, the nature of women's businesses is such that they have not yet identified those that make money.'

'Many women in the countryside are badly off,' she says. 'You think women are emancipated but many are very poor. In and around Kampala the greatest percentage of women drop out of school by primary seven. This implies that the situation is even worse in rural areas.'

The two managers, Maria and Edith, and the headmistress, Joan, each turned creative ideas into actions. Their vision and determination attracted others to assist the realisation of their goals. They are not owners, but still entrepreneurs.

Profile and conclusions

'If you do not have enough capital, your business does not grow and the little you have gets swallowed up,' Evelyn says. Approaches to accumulating sufficient capital to move beyond the micro-enterprise sector into small-, medium- and large-scale business are the subject of this chapter. Characteristics of this group are first compared with those of the group in the preceding chapter, who were distinguished largely by their class status, in an effort to identify factors that influence the scale of enterprise. Then the questions about capital, investment and business growth that were posed at the start of this chapter are answered and advice to aspiring entrepreneurs is summarised.

A socio-economic profile

In terms of class this group resembles the micro entrepreneurs of Chapter 5 in many ways. Their fathers' status was high in their birthplaces, the vast majority were educated beyond secondary school, they had lived overseas—mainly within Africa—and had access to factors of production. But each of these indicators shows a higher level, and most are significantly higher. Additional distinctions between the two groups that are worth exploring through research include the position of the entrepreneurs as sole support of families—suggesting that sole support is a motivating factor—and the extent to which relatives are partners, directors or workers—suggesting the importance of trust. Details of findings in these and other areas follow.

Parentage, education and overseas experience

The status of parents is influential with this group as with those of the preceding chapter, but the entrepreneurs' own education is higher on average. Daisy is particularly proud of her father for having written a book about the Bunyoro kingdom of Uganda as early as 1971. Others identify their fathers as civil servants, chiefs and teachers (one owned a factory). As to education, although 87 per cent of business owners in the previous chapter and 81 per cent of this group have post-secondary education in the professions or at university, this group stands out because 44 per cent have university degrees, compared with only 20 per cent of the previous business owners. Yet the importance of higher education must be compared with high motivation, for neither Sarah Namusisi nor Edith Nakuya finished high school, and Fang Min, employer of 100 workers, has no education beyond secondary school; it may be significant that all 3 are sole heads of household. Curiously, there are few former secretaries in this new group—only 2 as compared with 73 per cent of the earlier group—a fact that deserves consideration and analysis.

Although 75 per cent of the respondents, compared with 67 per cent of the earlier group, had overseas learning experiences shows little difference, it is significant that six of this group took specialised courses before becoming entrepreneurs. Hamida and Shamin of the new group had three boutiques in Canada before returning to open Tinga Tinga Uganda. Two of the largest scale entrepreneurs had literally seen the world as airline hostesses and drew on that experience to establish their businesses: Daisy created Das-Air while living in the UK after residing in Nairobi and Lagos during Uganda's years of terror, and Nina travelled extensively with East African Airways before constructing her Ssese Island Resort and establishing a tour company. Of importance too is the fact that both of those women sought further education in their business fields: Daisy did a post-graduate degree in business and accountancy in London and Nina got a diploma in tours and travel. Alice Wacha learned to embroider dashikis in Nairobi during exile, Jolly got a certificate in shoemaking after graduating university and Mirjam took courses in tourism in the early years of creating Delmira Tours and Travel. Tereza prepared for her first wage employment with a hotel management course in Israel before turning to private business.

Providing for a household

A unique feature of the entrepreneurs in Chapter 5 is the number who carry sole responsibility for providing for a household: Sixty-five per cent are single (3), widowed (2), divorced or separated (4), or have husbands who are retired and apparently dependent (2). That is in stark contrast with the group of Chapter 6, sixty-seven per cent of whom are married. Is there a correlation between being single and being successful in business? Recall that although married herself, Mary Nsubuga thinks that there is: She said that some married women 'fear so much'—they fear to keep their shops open lest their husbands and in-laws see them as errant, and they fear that husbands will come and demand their money. The reverse side of that coin is that when a woman who is already overwhelmingly committed to the well-being of her children and other family is the sole provider, she is even more determined to succeed in business.

Organisations: technical are best

Another difference from the previous group is their membership in organisations. Maria Theresa, Jolly, Hamida and Shamin are among the few in this group of entrepreneurs who are known to be active in both business and charitable organisations. Several others belong to UWEAL or specialised business organisations, but this group on the whole joins fewer organisations than those of previous chapters. One explanation for this difference is that family members who are so closely involved in the businesses in this chapter provide the support that other entrepreneurs find in associations; another is that this group has more time-consuming responsibilities due to the scale of their operations, thus having less time for participation in organisations.

With that socio-economic profile in mind, the questions posed at the start of this chapter are considered:

> *1. How is start-up capital accessed by the small- to large-scale entrepreneurs, and what is the significance of its size to the future prosperity of the business?*

The critical role of capital as a production factor is found in Evelyn's words of hindsight: 'Only later did I realise that if you do not have enough capital, you do not grow and the little you have gets swallowed up.' Aware of that reality, most entrepreneurs accumulate as much start-up capital as they can, but they do it in different ways. The financial autonomy of this group is revealed by the fact that 73 per cent of them started their business using their own savings. That figure contrasts strongly with the 57 per cent figure among those in Chapter 5. Of note too is that just 2 of this group had some help with start-up capital from their husbands (one was a loan rather than a grant), while 20 per cent of the earlier group did so.

Initial capital

Most entrepreneurs started in a small way and built their businesses slowly, then obtained credit in-kind or got a substantial infusion of capital at a critical point. When she left work at the Bank of Uganda, Maria Theresa had just Ush 25,000 in her bank account to start her catering business. 'All that I managed to do I originally did without cash,' she explains. Because her honesty became well known, she was able to get goods on credit, just as Teddy does at Wandegeya and Edith does when purchasing air tickets. Jolly bought a few hand tools and a leather sewing machine for making shoes while she was still an agriculture officer, and Alice Wacha continued teaching while starting her clothing business. Combining her secretarial salary with a bit of magendo, Alice Karugaba had just Ush 36,000 to open her first shop, so used a few shelves and let others use the rest.

'I started the Ugandan way—no capital,' says Edith Nakuya, who is by far the least conventional accumulator of capital. She made $20 or $30 each time she sold construction cement, then switched to buying spare parts for Fiat automobiles in Nairobi to sell in Kampala after a one-day round trip. She drew on old contacts from her days of working at UCB to get foreign exchange to make her purchases. Edith was highly motivated: Her husband was in exile, and her 4 children were hungry and in need of school fees.

Mirjam's savings and Delia's former customers formed the capital needed to start up Delmira Travel and Tours. The partners estimate well over US$100,000 is required to start a tour agency today. Nina Joyce had adequate savings from her work with East African Airways, the World Bank in Nairobi and ranching to get construction of her Ssese Palm Beach Resort underway. Daisy, another large-scale entrepreneur, had savings from the petty and then international trading she did at the start, then used her house in UK as collateral for an initial 'very, very small' loan to start up Das-Air. She was a one-person business for the first 6 months and had only one helper through that first year. Fang Min was stymied—as a foreigner and because she found loan interest high—so she depended on her own capital brought from China to start her first, small restaurant.

Husbands were even less important sources of capital to this group than to those of Chapter 5. Tereza borrowed 'a little bit' from her husband to purchase the seedlings and other supplies for her horticulture business; Evelyn started with a little money she had, and her husband 'brought in some little money'. Sarah was able to get a million shillings loan from a bank to complement her small savings and open her first full-scale restaurant. Hamida and Shamin used both bank and personal loans to launch Tinga Tinga.

Accessing working capital

2. How is working capital increased, and what obstacles stand in the way of accessing capital?

In the search for alternative ways to access capital, Sarah tried a ROSCA and put in Ush 300,000 a month. But, she says, 'You can find yourself eating your money; it disappears,' and opted out of the group, moving back to the bank where, she found, they do not mind receiving small amounts of cash for deposit. Edith Nakuya says that if she found a group that saves big amounts, she would join in order to get money to complete her hotel in Ibanda, although she is wary of some groups whose leaders manage to be the biggest beneficiaries. Recall that Joyce found the amounts that ROSCAs can give just too small to have an impact on her business, that needed about $2,000 so she too turned to bank credit.

For many well-established entrepreneurs who are able to access capital from the formal banking system, an overdraft is preferable to a loan. Alice at Nina Interiors spoke of her customer who took her to Barclay's Bank and, once she had opened an account, she got an overdraft—first Ush 5 million, then 15, then 30, and up to 50 million. Nonetheless, she has not yet found a source of credit for construction of a new building. Gera finds an overdraft better than taking a loan for 6 months that is difficult to repay. Maria Theresa prefers a loan, and to date has had 3 of them—all paid off on time. She will not take a loan for construction but only to uplift her business, for example by replacing old equipment.

Saving on overhead costs is a form of accessing capital: Maria Theresa has run her catering business from her home, thus avoiding rent. She has gone a step further with her philosophy that rent is prohibitive and built her own building, part of which she will lease as a supermarket. Alice seeks to do that: put up a building for her business, even if it is out of the city centre, in order to save the high rental costs in Kampala. Her daughter has no qualms about the proposed move, 'If you have quality goods and services,' she says, 'people will always drive out and look for you.' Wholesaler Mary (Chapter 5) found no difficulty with her move from Kampala to Nateete to save on rent either, and opened two shops there.

Threats to the integrity of working capital come from allowing customers to purchase on credit and from ever-increasing competition. Daughter Nina of Nina Interiors sees credit control as the biggest threat to their working capital. Credit is often requested because they sell expensive products so that few customers have ready cash to pay immediately. Her mother believes that she could put up a new building if all debts were paid. 'Debts can wipe you out,' in Evelyn's view. For travel agencies such as Delmira, Mirjam says, 'You have to be very careful if you issue tickets before payment, even when you trust someone.'

Alert to the capricious market, Edith Nakuya conserves her initial capital through her readiness to switch her specialisation when competition appears to pose insurmountable problems. In one case she ceased carrying expensive Italian scarves and in another stopped manufacturing safari suits. Evelyn found the competition very high in the bakery business, where she has the added burden of dealing with perishables. Daisy speaks simply and wisely of competition: 'You must accept your opponents, know their strengths so that you can counter them. If you go into business blindly, you will never survive. It's a very competitive world out there.'

Why do women fail to get start-up capital? Daisy is blunt: 'Interest rates at Ugandan banks would kill you before you start any ventures. They are very high and hard for beginners.' The local bank borrowing rate for shillings can go as high as 25 per cent, and that does not include associated costs such as payment for paperwork, travel to the bank, and the time demanded to consider and close a loan, all of which are prohibitive. A 14 per cent rate is charged for borrowing dollars—arguably high by international standards but lower than local shilling costs.

Daisy and Nina believe that there is also an underlying failure of technical presentation: Women do not present their projects with the proper feasibility studies or defend their proposals vigorously enough. 'You cannot give up as some women do after they have been rejected by one bank.... Go and knock at the doors of those banks,' Daisy urges. Nina thinks that it should not be so hard for women to get bank credit. The underlying problem for most women is that they do not have collateral. That being said, she believes that having a going business is key—a small loan can be obtained and repaid, then a larger one and so forth. She concludes, 'One should always start her business before asking for a loan.'

That approach seems to have benefited Edith, who 'has managed slowly'. She believes that the problem is deeper than the issue of collateral, that bank managers tend to favour men and to ask women to pay extra money and some perks. 'Before you finish you even offer to give them a car,' she says. It is no surprise that of Bank of Uganda loans made available with World Bank capital, women accessed only two per cent of the available credit one year and one per cent a few years later! (See Chapter 7.)

But for many entrepreneurs, getting loans that are sufficient is very difficult indeed. Few women have collateral—as compared with men—to access the amount of money required to purchase goods or expand facilities to the extent needed to move from micro to small business, or small to medium. 'The little you have gets swallowed up' if the amount of capital is insufficient, and one limps along, as Evelyn says. Delia summarises: 'I sometimes think women do business the hard way, without enough capital. So they either borrow or start without. In the end,' she says, 'they are more successful than men.'

In Uganda, 'there are still a lot of opportunities, especially in manufacturing, if you have enough capital,' Mirjam insists.

One can only imagine the capital growth, creation of employment and distribution of income that would be possible were more women entrepreneurs able to take advantage of their excellent repayment records and expand from small- to large-scale enterprise.

The reinvestment dilemma

> 3. *How do these entrepreneurs resolve the dilemma other businesswomen face, namely: the choice between investing their profits in family well-being and reinvesting in business?*

Nearly 70 per cent of these small- and large-scale entrepreneurs are the main providers for their households. As Maria Theresa says, even when a spouse is present most women spend more of their own money than men do for family support. Our research confirms that observation: Many married women entrepreneurs with husbands present and employed provide more than half of the family income. It is widely acknowledged that women invest their earnings in family, especially in their children who are the country's future. But facts about the amount of income provided by each spouse are regrettably hidden in household surveys that speak of 'household income'. They are among the missing facts—the insufficient information (Stiglitz 1995)—that skew the results of surveys and distort national planning (see Chapters 4 and 7).

Capital accumulation by the businesswomen in this chapter is sufficient both to provide family needs—especially those of children—and to expand or diversify their business investments, for example:

> I had to manage to take [the children] to secondary and university. I have sent them abroad, bought a plot, built our house, and put up this [commercial] building. *Maria Theresa Makayi*

> The step into private-sector entrepreneurship made an enormous difference in family life, made it possible to build a permanent house, educate six children and acquire property. *Jolly Rwanguha*

> I have had to support the children of my 2 brothers who died—eighteen children in all—paying school fees for 5 of them, in addition to my own 4 children. *Alice Karugaba*

> The houses I have built help to meet our family needs with rents of 400,000 shillings a month initially. *Alice Wacha*

> I had three young children to support. They are all in school. I also have my brother's son to care for; I help the mother too. Women are the ones who look after children so we have to see to it that our business goes well. *Sarah Namusisi*

> I had to see that my three girls finished school. I am also looking after the family of my late brother. *Edith Nakuya*

> No family member—neither my late husband's nor my own—helped me with the six children. *Gera Harriet Mosha*

> Business becomes a bit easier as the size of your family's dependent group grows smaller. *Evelyn Biribonwa*

> Money helps me to give people jobs and keeps my 16-year-old daughter in boarding school in Canada. I also help workers whose families are in need. *Fang Min*

The pattern is consistent with that of all the women in this study: After investing in the children and household, invest in the business. Fewer businesswomen of this group inherited land, but most purchase it and invest in their businesses, including premises, then turn to diverse investments, all of which create employment opportunities in Uganda. Some examples:

> I put up a building, which houses a bakery and restaurant, with space to rent to a supermarket. I employ more than 40 workers. *Maria Theresa Makayi*

> I have a small plot in the suburbs to put up a commercial building. We employ 10 full-time and 15 others. *Alice Karugaba*

In addition to my shop here, my husband and I have a big wholesale shop that we employ people to manage in Lira. I built a 15-room lodge and 3 houses in Kampala, then bought a fourth in Ntinda. God made me a builder. We employ more than 20 people. *Alice Wacha*

I have another restaurant like this one on William Street. I employ 13 workers and have a take-away of 500 plates a day. Besides my house I own a plot and want to buy more land. *Sarah Namusisi*

I managed to build a house in my home area. Then I built a commercial building with 10 shops. I also own a school for 150 children. I employ about 10 people. *Edith Nakuya*

I used the overdraft to start new branches of my restaurant. I now have 3 restaurants plus a guest house. I employ 27 people. *Gera Harriet Mosha*

I bake down the road at a place that I own. The business employs about 15 at the bakery and 20 salespersons. *Evelyn Biribonwa*

We reinvest our profits in the business in order to make it grow. If we decide to expand, it will be to open on the other side of Kampala or in the country—unless we decide to build a coffee shop here. *Hamida Hudani and Shamin Kassam*

I started with a ranch in Mawogola and became a farmer. At Ssese Palm Beach Resort we have 7 permanent and 40 casual workers doing the construction. My husband and I jointly opened a tour company called East–West Travel Limited. *Nina Joyce Muyanda*

There are now five ventures under my umbrella: the airline, ground transport, ranching, horticulture and warehousing. Daisy's Deli is a hobby. *Daisy Roy*

Business in Kampala can grow very fast—I now employ 100 workers. You can initiate new businesses, and people are interested in them. I may open in other Ugandan cities in future. *Fang Min*

The important role relatives play

4. Is there a correlation between involvement of family members in the enterprise and business growth?

For the first time in this study, relatives play markedly important roles in the enterprises. This characteristic may be the most significant of any of this group, and it is surely a contributing factor to growth from micro- or small- to medium- or large-scale business. Recall that in earlier chapters businesswomen would say that their children 'are too young to be involved' with their businesses.

The larger scale businesses of this chapter rely on family involvement, not as a source of capital but rather as co-owners, trusted advisers and reliable workers: Sixty-three per cent of this group hire relatives in key positions, and five of the entrepreneurs have relatives as partners or directors. Hamida and Shamin are sisters who both own and manage jointly. Nina Interiors is indeed a family business: All five directors are family members, one daughter is a store manager, another daughter assists her mother, and many of the ten permanent staff are relatives. Tereza Mbire's two sons are directors of her businesses. Both Das–Air and the East–West Travel Ltd are jointly owned with husbands. Sarah has her sister managing one of her restaurants. Evelyn and her sister started business as partners and remain so legally even though the sister opened her own importing enterprise. Fang started with a partner but dropped the arrangement after a year when money was not well accounted for; now her sister, a banker, is her accountant and her brother manages one of her restaurants. Gera's son has his own business but checks on her business and its workers early each morning. Alice Wacha's son and daughter-in-law work with her at Peacock Fashions. Maria Theresa's eight children, six of them daughters, help her a lot, and her first son will soon work full time with her. Jolly's husband helps her design men's shoes and other products. The conclusion is clear: family members make essential contributions to the success of these medium- and large-scale businesses.

A final note: national policies and international influences

There is little question that many entrepreneurs benefit from education in finance and credit. However, the availability of capital and its cost depend upon national policies rather than the entrepreneur's ability and willingness to repay a loan. This study and innumerable others demonstrate that women are good credit risks. The question then is how to bring the costs of borrowing to a reasonable level.

SAPs affect this group as they do others. UWEAL members fought together with others and won a battle to raise the threshold of tariffs on imports from US$2,000 to $10,000—only to see it lowered to $5,000 for the whole of East Africa a year later. The second-hand clothes issue rises again also: 'With the increase in the amount of used clothes imported in the country, demand for our garments declined,' says Tereza. Shoemaker Jolly also feels the pinch: 'Given the cost of raw materials, it is hard to compete with second-hand shoes, which dominate the market,' she says.

There are also factors that are beyond the control of government. 'No matter how much we spend on marketing, the effort will not pay off when people abroad are influenced by a negative media image of Uganda, even when it is not a true one,' says travel manager Mirjam. Several of the respondents qualify their confidence in the future: 'The future is bright in Uganda if we can continue the trend we have now, with no destabilising factors,' and 'If the North and West are settled, if they stop the petty fighting, the future is bright.'

Advice to aspiring entrepreneurs

With an average of 13 years in private enterprise behind them, these businesswomen have a good deal of advice for young women who want to enter the private sector as entrepreneurs.

Selecting your business

The exceptionally successful Daisy Roy, who entered a field in which she had some years of experience, has clear advice for a young woman who wants to go into business:

> First of all, I would ask her what business she wants to run. Seeing me and thinking I am successful cannot be the criteria for somebody else to start a business. I must first ask her, 'Do you believe in what you are going to do? Are you dedicated to it?' Once she says yes, I tell her to go for it. You must believe in what you are doing and you must like it. First of all, enjoy it. Forget about the money aspects. Put in the hard work and in time you will be remunerated.

Nina of Nina Interiors adds to that advice the dimensions of market research and a readiness to sacrifice:

> I would advise a young woman first of all to look at the kind of business she wants to enter and the kind of demand that is on the market. One shouldn't look at somebody and say: 'Oh, she must make a lot of money so let me enter that business.' Study the business very well, know that rain or shine, you will have a demand for your goods. Secondly, be prepared to work very hard and to sacrifice anything—time or money.

Evelyn passes on her own harsh experience with her bakery:

> First of all, if you choose a line, do a lot of research on that line. If you are going to bake bread, learn to bake. Can you tell whether it is only half-baked? Do not start when you know nothing. Learn skills first. That is very important. Lack of skills caused me a lot of hardship at first.

Mirjam, Hamida and Fang Min all independently advise an aspiring entrepreneur to get appropriate work experience before going on her own. Here is Mirjam: 'Before starting a business it is wise to get experience working in a similar enterprise. That way you can learn from mistakes other people have already made. If you are new, coming from university, you are still green—we are all green at that point.' Hamida and Shamin also strongly believe that young women just coming out of university should work for at least a short time in order to learn the pros and cons of going into business. That should open one's eyes: 'A young woman going into business must not go in blindly, but look carefully into the prospects. Cash flows should be anticipated and monitored because businesses go up and down and one can go bankrupt or have to close, or at the least run the business inefficiently.'

'Someone who wants to go into business should first work for someone else,' Fang Min also states. 'Then begin very slowly and small on your own. Go step by step. If you are young, you must give up a lot of your freedom. Twice I have had young women to manage the dining room, but they want free time, and that is not easy.'

The primacy of capital

'The most difficult thing is capital. You have to have capital,' is Alice Wacha's advice to young women who might wish to go into business. Recall that Alice started her business at home when she was still teaching school and that she accumulated enough money to buy houses before becoming an independent entrepreneur. In Evelyn's experience, accessing capital is not easy: 'I have known people who are members of the Women's Finance Trust (UWFT) for some years. They have done the cash flow, everything, and what they need are small loans. Very little money is needed for mushroom growing, for example, but they fail to get it.' Gera also has strong views on accessing start-up capital:

> Do not think that you can get a million-shilling start-up loan for a business. Even if you have 500,000 shillings, you can start small, small. I started this restaurant with a very small table here and a small teapot, making tea—good tea. Do not think that you are going to get money every day. Just get it little by little.

Getting money to finance the requirements for a loan, such as the evaluation of the property that one wants to use as collateral or writing a business plan are other obstacles to getting the needed capital. Evelyn explains, 'It was very expensive to value my property, but I was lucky and managed to do it. Cash flow systems also cost money if you cannot do them yourself. All those things have to be paid when you want to start a business.'

Because Maria Theresa has found ways to access capital in-kind rather than in cash, she believes that women should not be discouraged by people who say that in order to start a business you need a lot of money. She says:

> Sometimes it is true you need a lot of capital, but what is most important is that you need a lot of determination. You have got to be honest. Honesty is very, very important, because to tell you the truth, all that I have managed to do I originally did without cash. I have been getting things on credit. I have managed to build quite a big house, with four rooms, a guest wing, sitting room, dining, big kitchen, servants' quarter. I have done it with hire purchase. But then I make sure I repay. So before you enter any business, carry honesty on your head or your back. Otherwise you cannot have cash every day. I have no problem getting food wherever I go. Because I am known, I can get it on credit. I know the breweries will pay me and then I can pay my own debts. If a young person who wants to start a business is not honest, I doubt that she can make it.

Entrepreneurial skills

Evelyn firmly believes that young women should acquire business skills before they start business: 'We take things for granted, thinking we can run a business without knowing how to start, how to do costing, bookkeeping.' Edith elaborates, 'When you are in business you need to know accounting, marketing, business administration. You must identify what the people want, your customers. After that you must know how much they would pay, or prefer to pay. When you go abroad you must have about five things in your mind. You have to calculate capital needed, taxes, profit, consumer preferences, import duty.' Another management skill is essential to some businesses these days, as Mirjam insists: 'For young persons going into the tourism business, without computer knowledge you will not get anywhere in this world.'

Besides the business management skills, there are technical ones that are specific to each business. For Sarah:

> If you want to go into the restaurant business, you must first know how to cook. Warm relations with customers are also critical. Business becomes easy later when you have many customers and you make profit every day. Now I don't have enough tables for all the people who come, but that was not the case when I started.

Attitudes

What personal characteristics should someone going into business have? 'First of all, be faithful,' Edith advises.

> If someone gives you money, make sure you are in touch with him or her. Tell him or her the progress, then pay the money back. If you meet any problem, tell him. Then there can be trust. For example my travel agents have learned to trust me so that I can go to them on Wednesday and say that I want to go overseas on Saturday and will pay for the ticket next week when I return.

That same faithfulness Gera calls honesty: 'It is very, very important to be honest with everyone—customers and workers. If you do not have money, tell them so. Sometimes I do not have money at the end of the month so I go to a friend and borrow. This means that first of all you must work hard.' Alice of Nina Interiors seconds that: 'I would encourage a young woman to go into business if she has the stamina, because one must work very hard. If you are very careful, work hard and are honest, you can get there,' she says. For Tereza, hard work demands a lot of time and determination. 'The family must come first and then business second, but one has to put in as much time as possible in order to be successful,' she says.

Alice Wacha is firm: 'Start one thing and follow it up. Get one line and stand firm on it. If you try many lines at a time it will be very difficult,' she says. Hamida is of the same mind: 'Some women rush into a business like crafts and soon go into another completely different kind of business like secretarial because they have not planned well, not put enough thought into it,' she says. Edith qualifies those views, lest they become too extreme: 'You also have to be flexible in business and not stick with something that is no longer profitable.'

Fang Min believes that business is not very difficult for women. 'But you must take care, and not think, "I am a lady. I am weak",' she says, echoing Margaret of Kalerwe market and Maria of Radio One. 'Think in your heart, "I am half lady, half man", then you will do well. I hope that young women will make Uganda very rich!' she says.

Education and class consciousness

'When they graduate, most of our girls want to start from the top. I would advise them to start climbing from the bottom,' says Tereza, adding, 'Uganda is blessed with fertile land so we do not need a million shillings to start with. When I started, I grew the flowers myself. I never imported. I went back to my home county and started growing flowers on a small scale, and from my profits I was able to buy sewing machines.'

'Even if you have university degrees, you can still do business. There is nothing wrong with that,' says Maria Theresa. Tereza adds some special advice for university women: 'When our women complete university education, they always look for white-collar jobs. They should try to start business in a small way. The other day I read in the newspaper about a boy who completed Makerere University and started selling newspapers. That impressed me so much. He is now the manager who has other people selling the papers. Our young ladies should not be ashamed of starting small like that in any type of business they can go into.'

Mirjam has noticed that people think that if they have done a course, for example in tourism, they can get into business. 'They should not forget that when they have their theory and their diplomas, that is good, but then a working experience is quite different in every aspect! So experience is very important,' she believes, affirming the idea of working in another business before starting your own as Hamida and Fang had also urged.

Encountering challenges and facing mistakes

Mistakes and problems to surmount are many. The respondents cited just a few. For example, Sarah says, 'The first problem can come just when you are well settled, and the city council people arrive to evict you from your place. A second problem is high prices; for example you get losses when costs of raw foods are too high for the prices you can charge for meals. And sometimes the things you need are scarce.'

In agreement with many other women entrepreneurs, Evelyn finds that knowing other businesswomen is a very helpful way to avoid or face difficulties. 'Join associations, talk to people because you get ideas; you stop feeling that the problem you have is huge and unusual. Membership in UWEAL costs 20,000 shillings and the annual subscription is 50,000. That is a lot, but it is worth it,' in her judgement.

Mirjam cites an example of the kind of situation one experiences: 'One of our costly mistakes was when an employee embezzled US$70,000. Because you have to trust employees, such mistakes are difficult to avoid. Even before that embezzlement we had started employing women. Now we deliberately avoid employing men, as you can see here in the office. I think that women are more hard-working and much more committed because they often have to bring up the children alone when husbands have other women or other children to care for. Women are very concerned about bringing up the children, paying school fees and making sure there is food on the table. I think that is why women are less inclined toward fraud and embezzlement: They know that the working relationship they have entered is not short-term. They build for a long-term future.

'In Europe it is different,' Mirjam continues, 'Employers are hesitant to employ women because they get pregnant and take maternity leave. If the children are sick, they must take time off, or they can't go on missions abroad. Women here have young relatives or house-girls looking after their children, and that makes a difference, I think. That is why women here are a lot more committed and a lot more serious about work. Men have pressure to get money quickly, but women work for the long-term future of their children.'

Mixing marriage and business

Is it hard to be in business as well as married? For Edith, there is no single answer to that question.

> There are some men who are understanding, who do not mind their wives being in business. Others believe that if a woman gets money, she will abandon the marriage. It is not true. No woman does not want to get married. But many men want to be the sole earner. They want someone who will sit and wait even if there is no food or she does not have enough money to buy a pair of shoes.

Even though 65 per cent of the entrepreneurs of this chapter are sole household heads, several of them are strongly committed to marriage. Nina of Nina Interiors asks herself, 'Will marriage affect my business life? I don't think so. My sister is married, and she still puts in time at work, even at times more than I do. She is happy. I have not noticed any conflicts arising because of her work.'

Daisy says,

> When you have a joint bank account, whoever survives the other operates it and provides for the children. There is no law that says a man dies first; the woman could go first and leave him with the children. I have been married 30 years and that view comes from my experience. But it is up to you how you run your family, how you arrange your affairs. If you think the man is not worth opening a joint account, just move along and open your own account. I married in church, my husband and I are united, we are one. So we pull together. It does not matter who provides because when he buys me a perfume, he does not question, 'Why should I take Daisy a perfume?' He brings it out of love. When you have love you do everything together. If it is love, you do not separate. It is not necessary.

Like Tereza, Daisy places primary emphasis on the family:

> Young people—those married and unmarried mothers—once they start up business and want to start families should never, never let their businesses be priority. They should have their families first. It is important to the family fabric. Once you have the family sorted out, you can do your business. But if you give priority to business, your

> family will suffer. You must fix food for the children, take them to school, collect them from school, check their homework—all that has to be done by the mother. The men can help as well if so inclined, but in Uganda you may not expect him to help in those ways. If you are educated and are a woman, it is your responsibility to make sure you are driving, you are sitting in the driver's seat and off you go!

A word to widows

Like other widows, Gera has plenty of advice for her kind:

> I appeal to other widows not to be self-indulgent but to work wisely and care for their children. Be trustworthy and do not rush into marriage because it can be a downfall for widows. Young boys take their money while pretending to love them. I have seen many of my friends who inherited money left with nothing. Their children cannot even go to school. I do not mean that one should stop loving someone, but just do not forget your children. Always put your children first, and don't use their property for a friend. If you are trustworthy and truthful, your children will like you,' she says, adding, 'Nowadays it is difficult to get into business—very difficult. But you can sell clusters of matoke, shine shoes or wash cars to get money every day. The point for widows is to know how to use the money.'

Being part of Uganda's development

Mirjam encourages people to get into their own business because it is so satisfying. 'Of course it is most satisfying when you are successful, as is true in the whole of life. I worked 18 hours a day for the United Nations and was paid the same as if I worked 8 hours. If you put all that effort and energy into your own private business, you know that returns will also come. You can be proud of what you managed to achieve. And in a country like Uganda we still have positive views of development; we are going up, not down. It is nice to be part of that economic growth rather than the economic decline you find in so many countries.'

Edith leaves us with a lesson: 'In this world things tend to become tougher and tougher. When that happens it is the women who worry, who stay at home and see the children crying of hunger. That is what inspires women to work harder.'

Recapitulation

'The interest on a bank loan can choke you,' large-scale entrepreneur Daisy Roy says, identifying one of the reasons why large-scale businesses run by women are relatively few. Most (73 per cent) of the small- and large-scale entrepreneurs in this chapter—those having independent premises and employing 6 to 150 persons—used their own savings from wage employment as start-up capital. Their businesses range from restaurants to interior decorating to international air freight in the formal economy. While their socio-economic profiles resemble those of other small-scale business owners in Chapter 5, more of them have university education (44 per cent) and more are single, widowed, separated or otherwise responsible for the whole household income (65 per cent), a situation that is a clear source of their motivation to succeed in business.

Few of this group inherited land (27 per cent), but it is important to record that many of them purchased it early in their careers, thus giving themselves family housing, income property and potential collateral for credit from the formal banking system. They often prefer overdrafts to loans, however, in part because the short-term duration of overdrafts is appealing but also because conditions attached to loans are complex, costly, strict and not infrequently gendered. They are aware of the importance of capital injections, else 'the little you have gets swallowed up if the amount of capital is insufficient'. Saving on overhead costs, such as rent, by working from home and getting raw materials on credit are among the alternative ways of accumulating capital without being choked by high interest rates. Having collateral and trust from bankers, they are less needful of the clout that groups provide, so are less inclined to join organisations.

The pattern of investment of their income is consistent with those found among businesswomen of earlier chapters in this book: Household—especially children, including adopted ones—comes first, then reinvestment in or diversification of business. The latter is impressive: construction of commercial buildings and houses to rent, opening branches of the central enterprise and simply expanding the scale of a single business. These are smart, determined and hard-working women.

The size of their profits resolves the dilemma most women entrepreneurs face—whether to put profits in a child's education or in expansion of business—and its predictable resolution in favour of family. Their profit is large enough for both purposes, so they can create jobs for others.

In addition to their higher levels of education, this group stands out through another unique characteristic: For the first time in this study, relatives play essential roles in the enterprises. They are not hangers-on, but partners, directors and workers, and they are trusted, so that the entrepreneur herself is free to concentrate on broad issues and tasks.

These entrepreneurs raise several policy issues, the most important being the high cost of capital, already noted, and the burdens that accompany economic restructuring with its trade liberalisation and debt load. Long-standing government debts to overseas lenders strangle the development efforts of poor countries; cancelling them would allow a government to create its own policy framework for development, especially to improve education and health services so that more potential entrepreneurs would be prepared for their business lives. Even while the campaign continues for debt forgiveness, tackling the issues of access to capital and expanding education and training opportunities are imperatives.

[1] As in previous chapters, categories are based on the criteria used in Uganda—the number of employees: Small ranges from 6 to 50, medium from 51 to 100, large above 100.

Table 6.1. Entrepreneurs in small- to large-scale enterprise

Name	Maria Theresa Makayi	Jolly Rwanguha	Alice Karugaba	Alice Wacha
Age	50ish	39	50ish	60
Education	nurse's training	Makerere Univ.; shoemaking certificate	secretarial course in USA	teacher training; embroidery training
Marital status	married	married	separated	married
Children	8	6	4 + her brothers' 18	7
Previous employment	nursing; worked in a bank	agricultural officer; shoemaking	secretary; ran own bakery shop	taught; worked with Radio Uganda; bank examiner
Business	MTM Catering; bakery	People's Footwear	Nina Interiors (2 furniture / soft goods stores)	Peacock Fashions; another shop
Employees	40	10	10, incl. family, + 15 on subcontract	15 + son, daughter-in-law, husband
Source of start-up capital	personal savings	personal savings	Ush 36,000 savings	savings
Source of loans/credit	commercial bank	—	Ush 50 million from Barclay's Bank	—
Spousal reaction	cooperative / retired	partner	N/A	helpful / retired
Land owner?	yes	yes	yes	yes
How income invested	education; building a house and business centre; vehicles	education; building a house; property; business	brothers' orphaned children; business	brothers' kids; business, building rental houses, lodge
% woman pays of household expenses	most	—	100%	minimal
Major problems	husband forced to retire	imported second-hand shoes	rent; worker motivation; controlling credit; competition	VAT might require her to raise prices
Memberships	Ladies Circle International; others	—	UWEAL; Chamber of Commerce	—
Advice	Be honest and determined	—	Do market research; be prepared to sacrifice	Have capital; start one thing and follow it up

Table 6.1. Entrepreneurs in small- to large-scale enterprise (continued)

Name	Sarah Namusisi	Edith Nakuya	Gera Harriet Mosha	Evelyn Biribonwa
Age	36	40ish	50ish	45ish
Education	3 yrs secondary school	3 yrs secondary school	studied nursing, then dress-making, in UK	Makerere Univ.: economics and German
Marital status	separated	separated	widowed	married
Children	3	4	6	3
Previous employment	ran restaurant with sister	operated machines; sold cement, auto parts, clothing	made dresses	worked as a secretary
Business	owns 2 restaurants w/ large take-away business	sells imported women's wear in 2 shops; rents out 10 shops; owns a private school	owns 3 restaurants and a guest house	owns a bakery (later sold)
Employees	13	3, + 6 in her school	25	35
Source of start-up capital	savings	savings	personal savings and husband's life insurance	her own and husband's savings
Source of loans/credit	Ush 1 million from church-sponsored bank	—	bank overdrafts	bank loans and overdrafts
Spousal reaction	N/A	N/A	N/A	supportive
Land owner?	yes	yes	yes	yes
How income invested	school fees; household; brother's family; business	bought school; business; household; school fees; brother's family	household; children's education; businesses	extended family; school fees
% woman pays of household expenses	100%	100%	100%	—
Major problems	—	acquiring capital	—	taxes; debt management; under-capitalisation
Memberships	—	—	—	UWEAL
Advice	—	Pay workers promptly; be trustworthy	Access capital little by little; be honest	Research; learn business skills; join associations

Table 6.1. Entrepreneurs in small- to large-scale enterprise (continued)

Name	Tereza Mbire	Hamida Hudani (H), Shamin Kassam (S)	Delia Almeida (D), Mirjam Black (M)	Nina Joyce Muyanda	Fang Min
Age	post-retired	both 40s	both mid-30s	40+	42
Education	hotel management course in Israel	post-secondary school	D studied in UK, M in Holland; also tourism	diploma in tours and travel	finished high school
Marital status	widowed	both married	both single	married	divorced
Children	6	1 each	—	5	1
Previous employment	hotel housekeeper, trainer; florist; baker	S had a surgery	D: Sabena Airlines; M: UNHCR; consulting firm	air hostess; secretary; rancher; farmer; rabbit-rearer	worked for Chinese government
Business	garment industry; Habitat Interiors	Tinga Tinga Boutique; S: Dressing Room	Delmira Travel and Tours, Ltd	Ssese Palm Beach Resort; East-West Travel Ltd	owns 4 restaurants
Employees	30	8, security staff	20	7 + 30 temps	100
Source of start-up cap.	borrowed from husband	personal savings	Mirjam's savings	personal savings	personal savings
Source of loans/credit	bank	bank	bank	—	none
Spousal reaction	was encouraging	supportive	N/A	tour company partner	N/A
Land owner?	—	yes	—	yes	yes
How income invested	in businesses (kids grown)	in business	in business	in business	in business; education
% woman pays of household expenses	100%	small amount	100%	—	100%
Major problems	imported second-hand clothes	shoplifting; high import duties	late payment; political instability	—	no English at first; no time off
Memberships	UWFT; UWEAL	Ugandan Asian Women's Association	Int'l. Air Transport Association (IATA)	—	—
Advice	Family first, then business; give it as much time as possible	Have work experience; anticipate and monitor cash flows	Get experience in similar business; learn computer skills	—	First work for others; begin slowly and small; give up free time

Table 6.1. Entrepreneurs in small- to large-scale enterprise (continued)

Name	Daisy Roy	Maria Kiwanuka	Edith Byanyima	Joan Mubiru
Age	50	30s	40+	40
Education	University of London: business, accountancy	Makerere University; post-grad in UK	law degree	teacher's training
Marital status	married	—	single	married
Children	3	—	1	1
Previous employment	air hostess; trader in textiles and clothing	worked for World Bank; US radio station	lawyer	secondary school teacher; ran hair salon
Business	Das-Air Ltd air cargo; ranching; horticulture; warehouse; etc.	General Manager, Radio One	represents TNT Express Worldwide in Uganda	headmistress of a private women's school
Employees	150	30 (half women)	20 + family	20
Source of start-up capital	personal savings	—	mother	—
Source of loans/credit	bank, using house as collateral	—	bank overdrafts, grant	—
Spousal reaction	partner in business	—	N/A	supportive
Land owner?	yes	—	—	yes
How income invested	business (children grown)	—	business; extended family	—
% woman pays of household expenses	—	—	100%	—
Major problems	competition	—	expatriate competition	—
Memberships	Institute of Directors; Business Executives (UK)	—	UWEAL; Uganda Services Export Association	Women's Council; YWCA
Advice	Start with little and build on it; believe in what you do, enjoy it	Assess your abilities and assets and use them	Have a good idea; have a good business plan and skills; work hard	—

Chapter 7

Economic Justice: Theoretical and Practical Issues

To fail to pay attention to women's economic activities is both morally indefensible and economically absurd.

Bradford Morse, former administrator, UNDP

Women's economic activity—as farmers, merchants and entrepreneurs—has the potential to reverse the growth of poverty. Farm and businesswomen create wealth where there was none; it is not just redistributed. They promote growth by investing their wealth, whatever its size, in the health and education of their children, the new generation, empowering them for the future Uganda. They promote growth when their capital is sufficient to reinvest in their businesses or other ventures, increase their production and employ more people. By boosting women's entrepreneurship with positive policies and actions—transferring resources from other areas as necessary—Uganda can counter poverty while giving the world a new and unique non-western model for grassroots, participatory development, triggering a process of economic democracy.

For those reasons, economic empowerment is the second major challenge chosen by Ugandan women leaders, now that the instruments of their political empowerment are in place in the 1995 constitution. This book contributes to that goal with the businesswomen's own voices supplying information that has been missing until now but is key to Uganda's development.

This final chapter is not a complete summary of the book; the reader seeking a summary may review the profiles and recapitulations that close each preceding chapter. This chapter is divided into two main sections: theoretical and practical issues. Although not exhaustive, it is intended to be thought provoking. It sets out the research findings in the form of a strategy for economic justice and growth.

Theoretical issues: a philosophy of development

A central, philosophical issue facing developing countries is the meaning of the word 'development'. A choice is usually made between the allegedly competing values of economic growth, expressed as GDP, and human well-being—between efficiency and equity. The meaning that a government or a multilateral organisation selects is profoundly important because it forms the basis for other decisions, such as allocating resources in the national budget. Thus it influences whether a child is educated, a pregnant mother is cared for, a business gets a loan, a farmer receives extension services. The prevailing tendency is to equate economic growth with development, with the result that a country's GDP is used to measure development, as is the practice of the World Bank and the IMF. A dilemma created by that choice is found in countries undergoing economic restructuring—a world-class GDP growth can conceal a disturbing persistence of poverty.

Nobel Prize winner in economics Amartya Sen brings human development and economic growth together: 'The choice between economic growth and social opportunity is a "false dilemma",' he says. 'Growth must be "high and participatory" ' (*The Economist,* Jan. 1999: 37). This study has considered economic growth as an essential means and human well-being as the final goal of development. Each chapter calls the attention of the reader to women's consistent commitment to those means and that end: Women work to succeed in business so that their own and their adopted children will be healthy and educated. They are determined to eliminate poverty in a generation.

After a nation defines its development goals, it needs a correct and complete description of the national economy—the sources and uses of its wealth—in order to make policies and allocate resources to bring the philosophy into everyday life. When the information in hand about a country's economy is not sufficient, decisions on policies and resource allocation may increase rather than decrease poverty (Stiglitz 1995). Using incomplete information can be compared with trying to make bread rise using flour and water but no yeast: The bread falls flat. A glaring example of such absence of information that severely limits a nation's capacity for growth and poverty elimination is the subject of this book, namely: the extent of women's activity in the informal and formal economy and the use they make of the income earned there.

Despite all their economic activity that is vividly portrayed in this study, the substantial cash and in-kind contributions of women to the national and the household economy remain inadequately recognised in such key documents as the national budget. The potential women offer to increase incomes and expand employment opportunities is thus forfeited: Two thirds of Ugandan women are identified simply as 'unpaid family workers' (Ministry of Gender and Community Development 1998).

Can economic growth and human well-being be maximised without awareness that it is women farmers who produce most of the country's food, more than half of its traditional farm exports and an impressive 80 per cent of its non-traditional agriculture exports (NTAEs)? Without the women who own more than half of the informal sector businesses? Without the women farmers and entrepreneurs who provide half or more of family incomes? The absurdity is obvious: The invisibility of women as economic actors permits gender disparities to continue to hold down economic growth and human development.

Once women's contributions are seen and acknowledged, they must be acted upon. A starting point for action is *The Integrated Household Survey* and its annual updates. It treats the household as if it were a single person, glossing over the question of who brings in the household income as well as who has power over its use. 'What isn't counted doesn't count', the saying goes. Opportunities are missed because when women control income and resources in a household, 'the pattern of consumption tends to be more child-focused and oriented toward meeting the basic needs of the household'; in addition, households headed by women have higher school enrolment and completion rates than those headed by men.[1]

The point is to disaggregate data by gender so that women's and men's shares of the total household budget become visible—a point that the Council for the Economic Empowerment of Women in Africa (CEEWA) is pressing in Kampala. For example, it is women, not an anonymous 'household', that produce Uganda's food for consumption and export. 'If I sold all the food I produce, I would be very rich,' Deborah Nyanzi at Mpigi told us in Chapter 3. A woman farmer's cash income can be added to the market value of the food she produces and puts on the family table—the total value is what 'disaggregation by gender' reveals (see Chapter 4). That figure would increase substantially yet again if women's reproductive activities such as childcare, fuel and water provision, and other 'household tasks' were given market values.

When research instruments are sharpened to capture the missing information on sources of household income, and joined together with information on households headed by women, a foundation can be laid for recognising women's involvement in the national economy (Bantebya and Snyder 1996) Government can then take steps to provide an enabling environment for the private sector—'the key driving force in promoting rapid economic growth (Ssendaula 1998), and foster grassroots development in informal micro and small enterprises and small-scale farms, where four of every five Ugandan find their livelihoods. Within that sector, corrective actions can assure gender balance in areas where gender disparities are widening, such as access to productive resources (capital and technology), information, and education and employment opportunities (UNDP 1997: 4).

The economic justice and growth model that follows finds its origins in this study and is in line with economist Amartya Sen's recognition of the systematically inferior position of women despite their 'economic agency' and his call for 'high and participatory' growth. It also agrees with Joseph E. Stiglitz's view that the equity and efficiency of a nation's economy are inseparable and that a more equal distribution of wealth is advantageous to a country (Sen 1990: 149; Stiglitz 1995: 265). And it is in line with Uganda's *National Gender Policy* (Ministry of Gender and Community Development 1997) and the *Nairobi Forward Looking Strategies for the Advancement of Women* and the *Platform for Action* of the United Nations World Conferences in Nairobi, 1985, and Beijing, 1995 (UN 1985, 1995b).[2]

Ugandan women's priorities, as the businesswomen in this book lived and expressed them, reflect the African women's paradigm for sustainable development, with its five main features (Snyder 1999):

- People are the primary subjects of sustainable development, not profits;
- economic growth is essential for human well-being; to succeed it must tackle poverty at the grassroots by involving both female and male farmers and entrepreneurs;
- education and health care are prerequisites for the expansion of productivity;
- access to land, credit, technology and information are basic components that enable women to increase their farm and business output and add to the national wealth; and
- gender-based data for planning and resource allocation, and gender-inclusive organisations and governments, are all critical to the future of development.

The government of Uganda has begun to take a strong human development stance. The Minister of Finance, Planning and Economic Development stated in his 1998 budget speech that 'Reducing poverty must remain the overall and highest objective for public expenditure and action'. The means is 'a policy mix which promotes rapid growth and provides active assistance to enable the poor to raise their incomes' (Ssendaula 1998). The women's development model offers strategies having that policy mix: Peoples' well-being is its goal and economic growth its means.

Practical issues: towards a new development model

Based on the experience and advice of the respondents to this study, other studies and knowledgeable people we interviewed (see Appendix 1), strategies for an economic justice and growth model in the productive sectors begin to emerge. Education, land ownership—or guaranteed land use—and access to capital are the three most important variables influencing women's agribusiness and other entrepreneurship. For those at the lower and middle levels of income, membership in organisations is an additional key to learning, personal support and access to resources. For all entrepreneurs, men and women alike (although they are affected in different ways), government policies, laws and actions enhance or stifle productive possibilities; and in an era of globalisation, the force of international financial institutions, bilateral donors and multinational corporations is an additional, invisible power. The strategies are discussed under four headings: personal empowerment, factors of production, institutions, and national and local policies.

Personal empowerment

The path from candlelight-market women studied in Chapter 2 to large-scale businesswomen in Chapter 6 is a path of ascending education and ascending income. The candlelight women are illiterate or have just a little education, most of the market women have some secondary schooling, while 82 per cent of the middle-level entrepreneurs have post-secondary and 40 per cent of the large-scale entrepreneurs are university graduates. The farmers' levels of productivity and income increase with education also. Because they know that education offers unique advantages, businesswomen, from those working in the burning sun to the affluent, see to it that their children make a generational leap by getting more education than the parents have. Betty Nakiganda at Kasubi market says, 'I have been able to educate my children. That is an even better achievement than building a home'.

Universal primary education (UPE), introduced in 1997, enrols four children from every family—at least two of them must be girls—in primary school, and has increased primary enrolment by nearly half, thanks to a long-term soft loan from the World Bank (Ssendaula 1998). But the system is not yet evaluated, and even poor parents must still purchase uniforms, books and other necessities and pay secondary school fees in full, although government is looking into purchasing primary school books and improving secondary facilities. At the university level, although much is privatised, government still offers scholarships and gives women a 1.5 percentage point boost for entry—a boost that succeeded in raising the number of women graduates from Makerere University to one third of all graduates in 1998.

Concentration on primary schooling is essential to having a literate nation, and girls are winning prizes now: Fifteen girls were among the top 20 students in the 1997 primary leaving examination; the 4 top students were girls. Of late, individual girls and girls' schools top the lists of examination results right through to fourth and sixth years of secondary school. Despite such laudable achievements, the few who excel are 'not satisfying when the majority are breaking their backs in rural areas' (*The Monitor* 24 Jan. 1998). Girls drop out of school faster than boys do: Nation-wide, by the seventh year of primary school, only 38 per 100 students are girls and by the fifth and sixth years of secondary school, only 20 per cent.

A major bottleneck exists for girls at the secondary level, and the importance of removing it is underlined by this research: Nearly all of the Kampala market stall owners in Chapter 2 have some secondary education. The scholarship programme Action for Development (ACFODE) organised using the Makerere University women studies' slogan, 'Empower Africa: Keep girls in school', is a start. Much more is needed. The international financial institutions and bilateral donors' stress on primary education should extend to secondary and higher education for girls, of necessity in a more limited way, until a 50/50 gender ratio is reached.[3]

Technical training supplements education. Participants in the Mpigi Women's Development Trust (MWODET) already profit from Uganda Women's Finance Trust (UWFT) courses, and the Ntinda Faith Outreach group is training with the Private Sector Development Programme (PSDP). Most MFIs offer training and/or extension services in business management, bookkeeping, marketing and skills relevant to the individual enterprises as conditions for taking out loans. Educational services are important too, to help women tackle problems such as reliable and timely information on marketing opportunities. CEEWA is facing that need by setting up Women's Information Resource and Electronic Services (WIRES) specifically to support businesswomen and develop their electronic skills. The medium- and large-scale enterprise owners in this study invest in management and skill training for themselves. The senior family farmers cherish the technical training and extension services they have accessed through their farmers' organisations prior to receiving credit to improve their farms.

People empower themselves through education and also through responding to incentives—of which the vast majority of female farmers have few. Women do most of the work, but men sell the crops and pocket the income.

Discouraged by the lack of access to their labour product, women farmers can fail to respond to incentives to increase production, such as higher prices or markets for crops. They are also known to resist intensifying their economic efforts because they are overwhelmed with responsibility for the well-being of their husbands and other family. When husbands lay claim on a wife's produce, her inventory or her cash, they have sole control over all family earnings and may acquire a new wife rather than enhance the welfare and education of the first family and reinvest in the farm. Wamage's story in Chapter 4 is but one tragic example of that disincentive in rural areas where 95 per cent of the poorest Ugandans live and where the incidence of poverty among women is very high (UNDP 1997). The nation is the loser.

Education is essential for both women and men. Catherine Ddamulira spoke in Chapter 3 of friends whose husbands do not allow them to start businesses even from home for fear that economically empowered wives will lack respect for men. The progressive farmers and some other women farmers who control their income contradict that fear; one even barters her produce as school fees. They adopt sustainable agricultural methods that pay off in increased produce per acre so that everyone, including husband and adopted children, benefits. Once husbands realise the rewards of women's economic activities, many become supportive, whether the enterprise is catering, farming or retailing fabrics (Snyder 1995). Other men should hear their voices.

Factors of production

Beyond personal empowerment, farmers and entrepreneurs must have access to the factors of production—land, labour and capital. Here too, as in education, 'male privilege often overrides the development agenda.'

Land

Land ownership or permanent use of it is the second of the four critical variables affecting women's level of business. Market and credit-group women (Chapters 2 and 3) invest in small plots and build houses on them as a form of social security for the family. Well over half of the small-scale entrepreneurs (Chapter 5) own land that is appropriately located to be used as collateral for bank loans to expand their businesses. Four fifths of the larger-scale businesswomen (Chapter 6) now own sizeable pieces of land. The farmers own, co-own with spouses or have other firm rights to use of land. Victoria Namusisi and her sisters (Chapter 4) each received plots from their father when she was six years old; she farms hers today.[4]

Two issues associated with land arise from this study. The first is one of absence—the 'missing middle', small-scale entrepreneurs. Generally, they are land owners (Chapter 5), and it is their land that is most frequently used as collateral for bank loans. One must conclude that not owning land is a major impediment to the growth of small-scale enterprises. The second issue arises from the observation that rural women in several areas of Uganda are not yet ready to will land to their daughters, who by custom move to their husbands' locations when they marry. But the daughters cannot inherit land in their new situations, either: 'In essence, women belong nowhere, which makes it difficult for them to access land,' Aramanzan Madanda observes in Chapter 4. This is an issue for women themselves to resolve, perhaps with reference to other African societies where women have land and home security in their natal area despite marital status (Dwyer and Bruce 1988: 159).

Newly adopted legislation—the contentious Land Act of 1998—concerns tenure, ownership and land management and could make most Ugandan women landowners or, more accurately, co-owners with their husbands of land where the matrimonial home is located and that on which they depend for sustenance. However, at this writing it remains uncertain whether that provision is included and whether the names of both spouses are to appear on certificates of customary ownership and freehold titles acquired on former public land.[5]

A provision that was pushed by proponents of large-scale agriculture and 'agricultural modernisation' is a matter of concern to advocates for the poor and for women. It allows the sale of customary land as a commodity and arouses fears of landlessness among the poor who opt to sell and have no other firm source of livelihood. Finally, as pointed out by the Ugandan Women's Network (UWONET), the bill fails to set criteria for service on land committees —the bodies that resolve land issues at parish (county) levels. The Uganda Land Alliance had proposed a 50/50 representation of men and women on all committees, boards and commissions created by the bill (1997: 10).

It remains to be seen how the bill will be interpreted and implemented and whether, for example, women will find it possible to put up their shared title deeds as collateral for loans to enhance their own or family-owned enterprises. Much will depend on a widespread educational programme and on gender balance in the membership of the land committees. The overwhelming evidence of this study underscores the necessity of land ownership for businesswomen. 'Lack of land ownership contributes to women's poverty and that of the community,' Mary Ssonko says succinctly in Chapter 5.

Labour

Labour is the third critical variable affecting women's enterprises. Most of the labour women access is their own. Few market women, savings-group members or farmers hire labour, although many say that their children help out during school holidays and farmers say their husbands and children help (although little of the latter shows on the division-of-labour charts in Chapter 4). Hilda Tadria speaks of the 'missing men' in agriculture and the urgency of enhancing their participation in productive and reproductive activities (1999). Most rural women's labour shortages are more severe than those of their husbands. And for those who wish to get cash income working on another's farm, there are gender-based price distortions: Ibanda women receive Ush 500 to 600 a day while men earn Ush 700 for similar work.

Technological inputs and improved tools that enhance labour output and reduce time and energy burdens are a subject of importance to the senior farmers and an indicator of women's progress. Only Anna Ndoshore among the progressive farmers speaks of using a shovel and a bicycle. When asked about adopting new technologies, the others respond, 'I have not yet tried any new tools' or 'I have not used modern equipment' (Chapter 4). History teaches us the importance of technology and the power gained by societies that possess it. The Danish economist Esther Boserup, praised for her 1970 book *Woman's Role in Economic Development* and an earlier book, *Conditions of Agricultural Growth*, speaks of technology as the most influential factor in the history of human societies—and of women, who don't have much of it in rural Uganda. The large-scale, urban-based entrepreneurs such as Daisy Roy and Edith Byanyima are acutely aware of the importance of technology for feasibility studies, business plans and fast, computerised information (see Chapter 6).

Capital

Capital is the fourth critical variable influencing women's entrepreneurship, according to the findings of this study. The dilemma for most businesswomen is identified by Daisy Kayizzi of Kasubi market: 'If you have little capital you get little profit, but if you have much capital you get big profits.' It is the size of their capital that narrows the passage of businesswomen from micro- to small-scale business. The most common, and often the only, way for market women and farmers to access capital is the ROSCA—the rotating savings and credit association—that is 'spreading like fire' across the country. Admittedly, some have had bad experiences with ROSCAs—members failing to pay and leaders grabbing the benefits—but many groups are working well and beginning to be stepping stones to bigger business for members. As with MWODET in Mpigi (Chapter 3), their systems are improving: Members can access money in their own bank accounts at any time, and 'leaders last' is the motto for borrowing. Small ROSCAs federate under MWODET, thus enabling members to access training programmes and be eligible for credit from external organisations.

The demand for micro-finance products and services that is being addressed by formal banking institutions, non-bank MFIs and government ministries far outstrips the current supply despite many promising initiatives. There is hope for increasing indigenous savings against which loans can be made. 'We are very poor but we can learn how to save money,' Deborah Nyanzi told her group; they soon had Ush 1 million.[6] The Post Bank Uganda that was incorporated in 1998 as a public financial institution having a network of 129 branches throughout the country is a promising resource. Post Bank operates as a savings and credit institution to 'offer basic financial services while paying better interest rates to attract deposits from small earners' (*The East African* 20–27 July 1998). As little as Ush 10,000 is needed to open an account. The bank is said to target retail businesses, farmers and women.

'Men get loans from fellow men, through banks or privately, but not many women have money to lend,' Margaret Ssajjabi at Kalerwe summed up. In this study, only landowners were found to have easy access to the formal banking system, and some of them still find the costs of credit—nominal interest rates of 20 to 25 per cent plus several related costs such as fees and commissions—daunting if not prohibitive. The surge of MFIs—some 60 operating in Uganda today—brings micro credit to many entrepreneurs, but it still leaves behind thousands of women. The MFIs seldom lend to farmers, that vast group for whom chronic undercapitalisation is a plague. 'I want to expand but I can't', and, 'I have an acute need for capital', say even the progressive farmers, who are far more privileged than most. 'Women are locked out of the whole capital accumulation process,' Madanda says of women farmers in Chapter 4.

The new crop of MFIs such as the Foundation for International Community Assistance (FINCA) and older ones such as UWFT show promise as they mature and respond to internal and external evaluations. Together with PSDP they offer entrepreneurship and skills training for micro and small entrepreneurs as prospective savers and borrowers. The well-known weaknesses of MFIs include institutional cultures that are more socially than financially directed, greater stress on the efficiency of the MFI than on that of the businesses supported, over-dependence on donor funds, which can discourage indigenous savings, and less than stellar records of loan retrieval. The Bank of Uganda is devising regulations for MFIs, the Minister stated (Ssendaula 1998).[7] The idea advanced by Sylvia Musoke of Jinja might also assist the solution of some of the problems of capital: She proposed that rural women who have idle capital invest in their fellow women—a venture-capital scheme such as the one created in Zimbabwe.

Credit is not widely available or easily obtained by women who need more than the now highly popular MFIs give. Businesses needing capital input beyond US$1,000 are not well catered for, as Joyce Rwakasisi explains in Chapter 6: 'When you want to expand you must bring in a new market and new equipment and the money is never readily available. It is very, very difficult.' From that perspective, the comment of one bank loan officer is indicative: 'You women come to borrow 4 million shillings,' he said, 'but now we can lend you 100 million. Would you please ask for more?'[8] Therein lies a likely reason for the 'missing middle' class of entrepreneurs and the related inability of micro entrepreneurs to expand the scale of their businesses: There is small money and large money to borrow, but seldom medium-scale money.

A recent research proposal focuses on access by women, who dominate the small- and medium-enterprise sector, to World Bank loans managed by the Bank of Uganda (Kiiza et al. 1997). The authors cite a survey of Bank of Uganda-managed schemes showing that in 1992 women borrowed only two per cent of total funds disbursed and in 1995 the figure dropped to one per cent.[9] The proposal concludes that while World Bank-funded programmes are intended to increase institutional credit for on-lending to the private sector, they have not benefited the operations of small and medium enterprises. Yet those very enterprises produce four fifths of the country's manufactured goods, contribute 20 per cent of GDP and provide the principal source of employment. The authors add that, compared to men, women entrepreneurs have less start-up capital or equity; they hardly ever own land and their enterprises are often located near their rural homes—so 'their chance of benefiting from the World Bank funded programmes is dismal' (Kiiza et al. 1997).

In a comparison of interest rates, there is a startling inverse ratio between the entrepreneurs' size and their credit costs. The poorest are pinched: MFIs charge 30 to 40 per cent nominal interest to micro entrepreneurs, banks charge 20 to 25 per cent nominal interest to small-scale entrepreneurs, and the cost of borrowing US dollars in Kampala is 14 per cent. While one must acknowledge the difficulties in administering small credit, those facts indicate that the vicious cycle is yet to be broken: Low business investment because of the high cost of borrowing hinders entrepreneurial growth, which keeps profits low so that the businesswoman cannot both invest in family well-being and reinvest in or diversify her business. Yet the availability of capital to micro- and small-scale entrepreneurs is central to economic justice and growth.

Institutions

This study demonstrates that businesswomen gain a great deal from women's and mixed groups. They have created innumerable community and national organisations in the civil society—many of them for economic survival and/or solidarity purposes. A striking feature is their inclusive, non-sectarian nature—their mix of religions and ethnic groups—essential characteristics for a nation like Uganda with its history of civil unrest.

The women's group in the countryside or village may combine several survival strategies such as the Ibanda groups do: They sell their labour on the labour exchange, create crafts, engage in petty trade and organise ROSCAs. Those in towns form ROSCAs or groups, such as the ones in Wandegeya and Kasubi markets that are affiliated with UWFT. Women band together as farmers—often with husbands as well—not least to access training and credit or grants such as MWODET and Africa-2000 affiliates offer. Many of the nation-wide women's NGOs—most of them formed since the NRA government took power in 1986—are impressive for their economic activities coupled with education and other support. UWFT, UWEAL, CEEWA, the YWCA and ACFODE are among them. Supermarket owner Lilian Kahenano advises in Chapter 5, 'Join business associations to be encouraged by other business owners and get training too.' A new grassroots economic justice and growth model can find some of its roots in these voluntary groups.

Institutions such as labour and produce markets are distinctly less favourable to women than to men, as the studies of Ibanda and Kabarole report. Women are paid less, even when their work is similar to that of men. They are bound by household responsibilities to sell in local markets while men can travel further to increase their profits. In addition, men control transport, as Table 4.14 on access to and control of resources and benefits shows. Market liberalisation is a mixed blessing: Some women profit from NTAEs such as vanilla while others find insuperable competition from low-cost imports. The Private Sector Development/MSE Policy Unit within the Ministry of Finance and Economic Planning proposes removal of the market constraints caused by poor communication through public works such as roads and telephones and marketing systems. It envisions micro and small enterprises (MSEs) benefiting both from improved communications and from contracts established to assist in their creation. It also encourages market surveys to identify new opportunities for products and promote exports—actions that should benefit all MSEs, although it will be necessary to monitor businesswomen's benefits from them (Republic of Uganda 1999).

National and local policies

Government as well as the private sector must be involved in promoting the 850,000 micro- and small-scale enterprises that employ 2.6 million Ugandans and together with agriculture comprise the informal sector (Impact Associates 1995). Recognising those overwhelming facts, the Minister of Finance and Economic Planning in his budget speech of June 1998 urged parliament as a matter of urgency to put 'the right legal and policy frameworks in place regarding access to land and credit, support to micro and small scale enterprises...' (Ssendaula 1998). The *Draft Policy Paper on Micro and Small Enterprise Development* of 1999 meets that request and includes strategic policy recommendations and an agenda of action (Republic of Uganda 1999).

In-depth interviews with nearly 100 people for this book reinforced the need for national and city governments to review their legal and policy positions. The Ugandan farmers and businesswomen cited heavy bureaucratic blockages, burdensome taxes (nearly a third of profits go to income taxes and a cumulative 17 per cent of the price of manufactured goods goes to VAT—value added tax), and urban entrepreneurs have had to contend with 120 bylaws and their amendments. A positive and supportive environment is absolutely essential to eliminate unfair constraints on all enterprises, with attention to what Sen calls 'the systemic disparities in the freedoms men and women enjoy' (1992: 122). The MSE *Policy Paper* finds women 'severely disadvantaged' in access to financial services, education, training, and knowledge of their legal rights. In addition, it points to 'social attitudes and practices' that inhibit their activities (Republic of Uganda 1999).

Detailed technical proposals concerning legal and policy constraints on the MSE sector are available in two recent documents from USAID/PRESTO and PSDP.[10] However, gender issues are poorly presented in those documents. For example, in the latter women are grouped with the young and the disabled, hinting that women are still thought of as minors and suggesting that the authors are uninformed about women's extensive participation in the national economy. The documents should therefore be read in tandem with 'Gender aware country economic reports: Working paper number 2, Uganda' (Elson and Evers 1997), which defines the links between gender equality and the achievement of sustainable economic growth within a macro, meso and micro framework of the economy of Uganda. When completed by FOWODE, the 'Uganda women's budget' will be similarly useful. Nevertheless, those who understand the specific issues related to women entrepreneurs must continually participate in national economic decision-making.

There is a global dimension of MSE policies. As is well known, governments heavily indebted to, and seeking credit from, multi- and bilateral organisations are under enormous pressure to adopt stringent economic adjustment measures. Uganda has not been immune to such conditions but has become one of the fortunate few countries to have partial relief of multilateral debt.[11] The 'Highly Indebted Poor Country (HIPC) initiative' has released $40 million that was to be paid against the overseas debt annually for five years. The money is placed in a new 'poverty action fund' in Kampala; priorities are maintenance of rural roads, agriculture extension, safe rural water supplies and primary health care.

This new anti-poverty fund, if monitored for gender concerns, could have an impact on the gender gap that Sen describes as 'systemic disparities in freedom enjoyed by men and women'. While due in part to tradition and colonial influence, in the view of many observers that gap has been severely exacerbated by the punishing programmes of economic reform that governments must agree on with IMF, World Bank and bilateral donors as a condition for obtaining new credit. Structural adjustment programmes (SAPs) have failed to foster a strong future labour force in a country where nearly half of the people are poor. As seen in this study, SAPs include cost-sharing of health and education services—responsibilities that devolve upon already overburdened women.

Uganda is beginning to rebuild its education and health systems after years of neglect, but economic disparities that have differential gender impacts still continue. The economic liberalisation programmes of SAPs tend to channel resources to big business—often foreign-owned—to the neglect and disadvantage of micro and small enterprise on which poor men and women depend for their livelihoods and which, as we have seen, are the largest future employers—expected to provide 60 to 70 per cent of new jobs in Africa. An economic justice and growth model calls for reconsideration of policies that primarily favour big business, toward building a grassroots economic democracy.

The poverty these programmes prolong afflicts women and children most adversely, as innumerable studies have shown (see Chapters 1 and 4). Women's workloads are 'grossly increased' (Kyamureku 1997) when production of NTAEs is encouraged, because they are the producers of such food exports as maize and beans. Mary Mugyenyi spoke for many: 'Women subsist at the margin of the poverty line and any further impoverishing policy package, however noble in its long-term objective, is unacceptable' (Mugyenyi 1992). What is astonishing is how women farmers and entrepreneurs survive, thrive, educate their children and even reinvest in their businesses. One can only imagine the transformation of Uganda's economy that could come about through them were the strategies that they propose—summarised in this chapter—fully implemented.

Refrain: a gigantic job ahead

At a time in the world's history when socialist models have failed and capitalist models are found wanting, the opportunity exists to create a model of economic growth that tackles poverty at the grassroots level. The economic-justice-and-growth model is based on the evidence in this study that whether a farmer, a market trader or owner of a supermarket, an entrepreneur makes an inter-generational investment first—in the education and well-being of her children. She then purchases a plot of land, puts a house on it that she can rent or live in and, capital permitting, expands her business. In other words, the economic growth she creates is the means of a better life for her and her family, and so for Uganda.

But opportunities are still severely limited for women and often for men too. Rose Kiggundu, coordinator of CEEWA, says, 'Women find it harder to enter and stay in the MSE sector because a big number of them [are] driven out by trade liberalisation, inadequate skills, low capacity utilisation, lack of access to capital and reproductive responsibilities.'[12] The vicious circle is that low business investment hinders growth, which in turn keeps profits too low to increase business investment. As a result, most market traders remain at a near-subsistence level, with micro credit at times tiding them over periods of slumps in sales or helping them to expand their business slightly once their primary family commitments are met. Senior family farmers—the women—are undercapitalised as well, and even small- and medium-size businesswomen encounter difficulties because borrowing is so expensive, and in addition, banks prefer to lend to large-scale businesses.

'Confining women traders to low-profit enterprises for the most part, whose profits must overwhelmingly be devoted to family subsistence needs, is not a smart economic strategy for development,' Claire Robertson writes (1995: 117). As regards Uganda, the women entrepreneurs introduced in this study and thousands of others are an economic and social force that the nation cannot afford to overlook as it seeks a balanced development of the economy and of its people.

'To fail to pay attention to women's economic activities is both morally unacceptable and economically absurd', former UNDP head Bradford Morse told thousands of participants at the Nairobi Women's Conference in 1985. With positive policies and actions towards the micro- and small-enterprise sector and the women who form its majority—transferring resources from less vital areas as necessary—Uganda can counter poverty while giving the world a unique grassroots, non-western, participatory development model—an economic justice and growth model.

But let no one judge that it will be easy to convince policy makers and others of this potential transformation of the economy. Custom will work against it because many men, and some women too, are not yet aware of the benefits to themselves, their families and their country that come with women's earning potential. Male privilege still overrides the development agenda. Democratising the economy and creating economic justice through women will take a huge educational effort by women leaders and voluntary organisations, the political will of national leaders, and steps as bold as those already taken in the political arena through the 1995 constitution.

[1] World Bank, 1999, *Gender, Growth and Poverty Reduction in sub-Saharan Africa*, Washington, DC. It is increasingly recognised that the prevailing system does not capture the 'co-operative conflict' (Sen, Amartya K. 1990) and 'intra-household bargaining' (Agarwal, Bina 1990) which take place. See also United Nations, 1995, *The World's Women, 1995*; and UN, 1993, *Methods of Measuring Women's Economic Activity*.

[2] The UNDP has in its annual global *Human Development Reports* since 1990 sought to complement the IMF measure with a human development index (HDI) that is comprised of life expectancy, educational attainment and adjusted income. The *Uganda Human Development Report, 1997* cites 'the satisfaction of the basic needs of all as not only the end but also a critical means of development', Kampala: UNDP.

[3] One opportunity for an individual donor to promote gender awareness may be found in the Department of Women and Gender Studies at Makerere University, which needs a new classroom and office building.

[4] Gordon, April A., 1996, in *Transforming Capitalism and Patriarchy: Gender and Development in Africa*: 167, criticises the motives behind Kenyan entrepreneurs' buying land: '[R]ather than investing profits back into their businesses, Kenyan entrepreneurs have a "sentimental value for land" often of little economic value, and a "fascination with rural homes" even when they are no longer residing there. Such practices are expensive and wasteful, and they retard economic development.' As is obvious in this study, the lower-income women who would otherwise have no secure habitat purchase a plot and build a house as social security for themselves and their families. The better-off purchase commercially valuable land that can be used as collateral or built on for rental purposes. Both uses are legitimate and wise in the view of this author.

[5] *The New Vision*, 1 July 1998: 23. Debate on the Land Act sparked the creation of an NGO coalition called the Uganda Land Alliance and was the object of many pressure groups, including women's organisations and women parliamentarians. There was an avalanche of comment on the subject of consulting wives and children on matters of land. 'The land and family home cannot be a man's personal thing,' and, 'Any man who wants to be free to do with the property on which he lives as he wishes can stay single and not get married and have children,' proclaimed *The Monitor* newspaper on 17 June 1998. Parliamentarian Miria Matembe says she has seen women suffering in her district: 'After 30 years, if a cruel husband chases her, she belongs nowhere.'

[6] Here national practices enter: Uganda has one of the lowest domestic savings ratios (savings as a percentage of GDP) in Africa, a fact likely to be related to the years of

civil unrest. The ratio for 1993–94 was 2.2 percent; Africa's average was 17.7 per cent (see Private Sector Development Programme, n.d., *Towards a National Strategy*, UGA/95/002).

[7] A study in Uganda considers micro-finance to be less than US$1,000; among 62 MFIs the typical loan averaged $220 per person while hovering at $100; government Entandikwa and PAP loans averaged $248 per borrower (USAID/PRESTO, 1997, *Training Needs Assessment*).

[8] Interview, 1998, Joy Kwesiga and Snyder.

[9] This is a disturbing but not surprising figure when compared with the United States, where '[d]espite the fact that women started businesses at twice the rate of men (in 1997), they received just 2 percent of the institutional venture capital money...' (*The New York Times,* 26 July 1998).

The Kiiza et al. study cited above finds several reasons why small and medium enterprises (SMEs) do not benefit from the World Bank resources: interest rates on borrowing are as high as 22 to 26 per cent per annum, and there are additional costs to the borrower such as valuation fees, commitment fee, processing fee and transport costs to and from the bank. A further obstacle is the equity requirements set by some lenders—contributions as high as 25 per cent of project costs. The researchers summarise the impact of those conditions: 'The policies and procedures resulted in World Bank funded programs mainly benefiting large enterprises based in Kampala and leaving out most of the SMEs in the urban and rural areas.' The large entrepreneurs can offer the collateral that often amounts to more than 100 per cent of the loan amount.

[10] USAID/PRESTO Development Project, July 1997, *Legal, Policy and Regulatory Constraints which Impede Private Sector Growth*, Kampala: USAID/PRESTO; and *Uganda National Strategy and Programme of Action for Private Sector Development*, 1997, Kampala: PSDP.

[11] The Uganda Debt Network (an NGO coalition) has joined the Jubilee 2000 International Campaign in calling for total cancellation of external debt for sub-Saharan Africa, arguing that existing debts 'will only be repaid by sacrificing the health and education of poor people', since the debt service calls for more than the combined budgets for education and health, according to Zai Gariyo, coordinator of the Uganda Debt Network, quoted in *The Daily Nation,* 24 March 1998.

[12] Personal communication with the author (1999).

Interviewees

NOTE: Where known and important, dates of interviews and initials of interviewers are indicated in brackets. For the full names of interviewers, see the Acknowledgements on page x.

Chapter 2: Market Traders

Kasubi market [10 Jan. 1998; R.N.]

- Esther Nankumi: serves as secretary of the Kasubi Market Women's Forum
- Margaret Namuga (46): three years secondary school; widowed with five children; sells vegetables
- Teddy Nakasumba (34): one year secondary school; married with six children; sells vegetables
- Betty Nakiganda (48): widowed with eight children; sells cassava
- Madina Nampijja: one year secondary school; married with four children; sells potatoes
- Daisy Kayizzi (38): single mother with five children; sells matoke and Irish potatoes

Wandegeya market [except as indicated, 10 Jan. 1998; R.N. & M.S.]

- Teddy Birungi (36): two years secondary school; married with five children; wholesales beer, soda and whiskey
- Margaret Ssewanyana (45): three years secondary school, married with three children (plus relatives); serves as chairperson of the Obumu Women's Group; sells fruit and vegetables
- Jane Namayanja (36): five years secondary school; widowed with three children; serves as treasurer of the Obumu Women's Group; owns two shops selling beverages and sundries
- Frida Obua (40+): one year secondary school; married with eight children; sells vegetables [1 Feb. 1998; M.S.]
- Miriam Nakalyana (45): learned reading and accounting from a neighbour; separated and supporting 4 children and 13 other relatives; sells matoke [24 April 1996; R.N.]

Kalerwe market [24 April 1996; R.N. & M.S.]

- Margaret Ssajjabi (52): two years secondary school; separated with 6 children and brothers' 19 children; owns land with 27 market spaces and a parking yard and sells water

Kaveda market [19 Jan. 1998; N.B.T.]

- Sergeant Alice Mugabekazi (Rtd) (32): completed secondary school and army service; serves as chairperson of the On Sena Women Veterans Association
- Oliver Ntale (Mrs): accountant, studied business; deals in produce
- John Calami: executive secretary to the National Chamber of Commerce, Kampala district

Nakivubo market [23 Jan. 1998; R.N.]

- Monica Bateganya: six years of school; married with four children; sells curtains

Owino market [19 Jan. 1998; N.B.T.]

- Godfrey Nkaya Kayongo: serves as chairman of Owino market
- Margaret Nalwoga: two years secondary school; single mother with several children; sells second-hand clothes
- Jacent Nakayemba: four years secondary school; married with children; sells vegetables and clothes
- Deborah Kyalusi: four years secondary school then worked in government; sells dry produce

Wholesaler [Sept. 1996; R.N.]

- Christina Nasuna (45): six years primary school; separated with eight children (plus her brother's); wholesales and retails matoke, dried fish, Irish potatoes and cowpeas

Slum Aid Project [23, 27 Jan. 1998; M. Snyder]

- Rose Gawaya: serves as coordinator for the Slum Aid Project

Chapter 3: Informal Savings Groups

Mpigi/MWODET [17 Jan. 1998; R.K. & M.S.]

- Rosern Segujja: co-founder, serves as coordinator, of MWODET
- Sophia Nababi Nalongo: married with five children; co-founder of MWODET; grows and sells mushrooms and other vegetables
- Catherine Ddamulira: four years secondary school; married with three children; practices midwifery in her own clinic
- Deborah Nyanzi: married with four children at home plus five other dependants; farms and sells milk
- Justine Lwanga–Budo: married; sells vegetables

Ntinda Faith Outreach [21 Jan. 1998; M.S.]

- Pauline Ofong: entrepreneur, mentor
- Ruth Twesigye: widowed with four children; raises and sells poultry and rabbits
- Jane Wanyama: four years secondary school; widowed with eight children; deals in waste paper

Jinja [25 May 1996; R.N. & M.S.]

- Goreth: four years secondary school and some computer courses; married; in a partnership selling second-hand shoes
- Shaban (Mr): married; in a partnership selling second-hand shoes
- Sylvia Musoke: four years secondary school; separated with one daughter; owns a second-hand clothes shop
- Irene Kalikwani: high school certificate and secretarial school; married with two children; printer
- Sekabira Nakakoza: seven years primary school; married with six children plus her brother's four; beautician

Chapter 4: Women Farmers and Traders

Iganga district [March 1998; N.T.B.]

- Zahara Kasolo (34): one year secondary school; married with a household of 14, including her 8 children; grows vegetables and rears cattle
- Zulaika Mutumba (35): secondary school; married with a household of 14, including her 3 children; grows and sells rabbits, bananas, beans, coffee
- Jalilah Galiwango (35): two years secondary school; married with a household of 10, including her 6 children; grows and sells vegetables, bananas

Kampala/Entebbe Area

- Joyce Bwagu (33): seven years primary school; married with nine children; sells surplus milk and produce [19 Jan. 1998; N.T.B.]
- Regina Nalongo Kabanda (47): six years primary school; married with eight children; grows and sells vanilla, beans, heifers and pigs [19 Jan. 1998; N.T.B. & M.S.]
- Hajat Nabakooza Kalema (45): six years primary school; married with a household of 13 (10 children); farms and sells rabbits, milk, coffee and surplus food [19 March 1998; N.T.B.]

- Agnes Kityo: owns cattle and a paraffin station; organised the Twezimbe Women's Group, which runs a maize grinding mill [13 Jan. 1998; M.S.]
- Aisa Nalongo (56): four years primary school; widowed with eight children; army veteran; certified midwife/traditional-birth attendant; sells surplus food crops [19 Jan. 1998; N.T.B.]
- Victoria Nalongo Namusisi (32): diplomas in journalism and business management; divorced and supporting 18 children (3 hers); raises and sells poultry, bananas and vegetables [14 April 1998; N.T.B.]
- Rebecca Njulungi: four years high school: single and supporting 12 children (none hers); sells bananas and vegetables [20 March 1998; N.T.B.]

Kabale district

- Anna Ndoshore (38): four years secondary school and teacher-training college; married with three children; school teacher, general store owner, sells milk and vegetables she produces [11 April 1998; J.K.]
- Christina Night Bekunda (30): seven years primary school; married with five children; sells milk and sorghum–honey beverages she makes, trains in appropriate technology [12 April 1998; J.K.]
- Paskazia Zalibugire: completed junior secondary school; married with eight children; grows and sells trees and vegetables [11 April 1998; J.K.]
- Efurazia Bamuturaki (40): completed primary school; married with nine children; grows and sells vegetables, milk, forestry products and prepared food [4 April 1998; J.K.]

Chapter 5: Independent Entrepreneurs

Non-traditional enterprises

- Victoria Muwanga (44): secretarial school; widow with four children; matatu owner–driver [5 July 1998; P.M.]
- Angela Bazirake (50ish): B.S. and diploma in education; married; founded Computech Systems [7 July 1996; M.S.]
- Robinah Kafeeke (41): B.A. in humanities, Kenya Institute of Administration; life partner with two children; established a publishing house [*The New Vision*, 28 April 1998; Keturah Kamugasa]
- Florence Munduru (46): medical degree, Makerere University; married with five children; opened a private clinic [16 April 1997; R.N.]

Food and lodging businesses

- Sarah Kibuuka (mid 40s): economics major, Makerere University; married with three children; manages and co-owns a butchery [6 Aug. 1996; M.S.]
- Lilian Kahenano (late 40s): Cambridge School Certificate, secretarial school; married with one child; owns a supermarket [16 May 1996; M.S.]
- Pauline Ofong (50s): studied social science at Makerere University; separated with five children; owned a restaurant (later sold), makes candles [13 Jan. 1998; M.S.]
- Theresa Kayondo (40s): teacher-training college; married with eight children; owns a hotel and runs a printing press [1997; R.N.]

Shops: wholesale and retail

- Mary Nsubuga (48): secretarial school; married with six children; owns two shops that sell sundries and food [13 Jan. 1998; M.S.]
- Olivia Mwebeiha (50s): Kianda Business College; widowed with five children; owns a gift shop [Dec. 1996; R.N.]
- Victoria Sebageleka (50ish): Kianda Business College; widowed with six children; owns a flower shop, also sells vanilla, milk and produce [8, 24 Jan. 1998; M.S.]

Textiles and clothing

- Joyce Rwakasisi (40s): B.A., Makerere University, secretarial course, teaching diploma; separated with three children; makes women's clothes, workwear, curtains [3 Feb. 1998; M.S.]
- Cothilda Busulwa (50s): studied nursing, secretarial course; married with ten children; makes women's clothes, sells in own shop [31 Jan. 1998; M.S.]
- Olive Kitui (40): Evelyne College, Kenya; married with seven children; makes women's clothes and sells them in two shops [11 Dec. 1996; R.N.]
- Ida Wanendeya (50s): married; co-founder of UWFT, makes and sells various textile products [10 Jan. 1998; M.S.]

Chapter 6: Small to Large Enterprise: Questions of Capital

Working for wages, with a side business

- Maria Theresa Makayi (50ish): nurse's training; married with eight children; owns and runs MTM Catering and bakery [13 Jan. 1998; M.S.]
- Jolly Rwanguha (39): university education; married with six children; owns shoe factory [*The New Vision*, 5 May 1998; author unknown]
- Alice Karugaba (50ish): trained in the U.S. as a secretary; separated with 4 children plus her brothers' 18; owns two furniture and soft-goods stores [July 1996; R.N. & M.S.]
- Joanina Karugaba: degree in sociology, Makerere University; manages a retail store for her mother, Alice (above)
- Alice Wacha (60): trained as a teacher and in embroidery; married with seven children, and helps relatives; owns Peacock Fashions and another shop

Started small and growing

- Sarah Namusisi (36) four years secondary school; separated with three children; owns two restaurants [22 Jan. 1998; M.S.]
- Edith Nakuya (40ish): three years secondary school; separated with four children; sells imported women's wear, rents out ten shops, owns a private school [4 May 1996; R.N. & M.S.]
- Gera Harriet Mosha (50s): studied nursing and dressmaking in the UK; widowed with six children; owns three restaurants and a guest house [23 Jan. 1998; R.N. & M.S.]
- Evelyn Biribonwa (mid 40s): studied economics and German at Makerere University; married with three children; owned a bakery (later sold) [6 Aug. 1996; M.S. & R.N.]

Building start-up capital from paycheques

- Tereza Mbire (60s): widowed with six children; co-founder of UWFT and UWEAL; owns a garment industry and Habitat Interiors [28 Jan. 1998; M.S.]
- Hamida Hudani and Shamin Kassam (both in their 40s): married with one child each; co-own the Tinga Tinga Boutique Shamin and Dressing Room [23 Jan. 1998; M.S.]
- Delia Almeida (37) and Mirjam Black (30s): educated in UK and Holland; both single; partners in Delmira Travel and Tours, Ltd [28 Jan. 1998; M.S.]

- Nina Joyce Muyanda (40+): diploma in tours and travel; married with five children; created Ssese Palm Beach Resort and East–West Travel Ltd [*The New Vision*, 23 April 1998; author unknown]

Large-scale, diversified investments

- Fang Min (42): secondary school in China; divorced with one child; owns four restaurants [1 Feb. 1998; M.S.]
- Daisy Roy (50): University of London; married with three children; owns and runs several companies, including Das–Air Ltd [31 Jan. 1998; M.S.]

Entrepreneurs but not owners

- Maria Kiwanuka (30s): Makerere University, post-graduate studies in UK; designed and manages a radio station [30 Jan. 1998; M.S.]
- Edith Byanyima (40+): law degree; single with one child; managing director of TNT Express Worldwide in Uganda [23 Jan. 1998; M.S.]
- Joan Mubiru (40): teacher training; married; headmistress of community-owned school [April 1997; R.N.]

Additional entrepreneurs

- Mrs Kabanda: owner of Executive Secretarial Services [13 Dec. 1996; R.N.]
- Jonathan Kyebanako Kolanga: miller [23 Jan. 1998; M.S.]

Technical advisors

- The Hon. Winnie Byanyima, M.P., Mbarara [20 Jan. 1998; M.S.]
- Joy Kwesiga, dean of the Faculty of Social Sciences, Makerere University [3 Feb. 1998; M.S.]

Council for the Economic Empowerment of Women in Uganda (CEEWA)

- Rose Kiggundu, advisor [9 Jan. 1998; M.S.]
- Rosern Segujja, coordinator [9 Jan. 1998; M.S.]
- Alice Nankya
- Agnes Yawe

Economic Policy Research Centre (EPRC)

- Fred Opio, executive director
- Marios Obwona

*Department of Women (*after 1998 *and Gender) Studies, Makerere University*

- Joy Kwesiga, head
- Josephine Ahikire, lecturer
- Grace Bantebya, senior lecturer
- Esther Kapampara, M.A. 1996
- Mary Mugyenyi, lecturer
- Nite Baza Tanzam, lecturer

Ministry of Planning: Micro and Small Enterprises Unit (MSEPU)

- Francis Luwanga
- Wiebe Van Rij

Private Enterprise Support, Training and Organisational Development Project (PRESTO)

- Sarah Kitakule, senior advisor, Policy and Regulatory Reform
- Rose Kiggundu, coordinator of CEEWA; advisor to MWODET

Private Sector Development Programme (PSPD)

- Prof. Ephraim Kamuntu, national coordinator
- Mary Amajo, head, Small Enterprise Unit

Private Sector Foundation (PSF)

- Sam Rutega, executive director

Twezimbe Women's Group, Wakiso village

- Hadija Kagwa
- Agnes Kityo
- Anet Nattambo

Uganda Veterans Assistance Board

- Anthony Uzzi, financial controller
- Samuel Mweru, public relations officer

Uganda Women's Finance Trust (UWFT)

- Lydia Rugasira, deputy manager
- Sarah Nsimbe, loan officer

United Nations Development Programme (UNDP)

- Aeneas Chuma, deputy resident representative

Young Women's Christian Association (YWCA)

- Joyce Mungherera, president

Glossary

BAFUMBO ASSOCIATION. the Catholic equivalent to the Mother's Union of the Church of Uganda

BAZUNGU. plural of Mazungu (see below)

BIKA OGUZE. literally, 'save and borrow': meaning the more you save, the more credit you will get; a ROSCA or unity group

BODA BODA. bicycle or motorbike (transport for hire)

BUSUTI, OR GOMESI. a national dress made of six yards of fabric, with butterfly sleeves and a wide sash

'CANDLELIGHT MARKETS'. (usually) unlicensed evening roadside markets

CHAI. tea; also slang for a bribe

DASHIKI. a flowing garment

DECIMAL (OF LAND). about one-tenth acre, or one-eighth of a hectare

DODO. amaranths: a green vegetable indigenous to Uganda

EL NIÑO. unusually warm oceanic conditions recurring every few years in the tropical Pacific, accompanied by abnormally high rainfall and resulting in adverse effects on agriculture

ENTANDIKWA; ENTANDIKWA. literally, 'a beginning,' or start-up capital; a government scheme providing start-up capital

ENTREPRENEUR. 'a person who is creative and highly motivated to identify a business opportunity and take the risk to successfully implement the venture by pulling together the necessary resources' (McCormack and Pedersen 1996 quoting Seierup)

ESHOGI. a green vegetable indigenous to Uganda

ESHWIGA OR ENSUGA. a green vegetable indigenous to Uganda

FANYA JUU AND FANYA CHINI. literally, 'do it up' and 'do it down': using trenches to prevent soil erosion

'FOOTLOOSE TRADERS'. mobile merchants

GOMESI. see busuti, above

GWOSSUSA EMWANYI (GROUP). literally, 'more than coffee'; roasted coffee beans are given to guests before the meal: the message is that women should not be ignored

HAJI/HAJAT. a Muslim man/woman who has made the pilgrimage to Mecca

HAKUNA MATATA. 'no problem' in Kiswahili

JUA KALI. 'the burning sun' in Kiswahili; also an expression for the peoples' economy, or second economy, or informal economy, so named because its 'offices', 'shops' and 'workshops' are in the open air

KABAKA. the Buganda king

KARUBANDA BAKYALA TUTUNGUKE (GROUP). literally, 'self-elevation of Karubanda women'

KASHEMEIRE. 'the fine one'

KEMBABAZI. 'of grace'

KIKOI. a multi-purpose cloth with striped edges

KITIKYAMWOGO (WOMEN'S GROUP). a single cassava stem-cutting which, when thrown away, will re-enforce itself and grow anew: refers to small amounts saved and lent; meant to suggest that women have been ignored but they will soon produce foods

KUNKUMURA. literally, 'shake and see'; second-hand clothes

KUSHUKIRANA (GROUP). literally, 'refilling one another's basket'

KWEZIKA. a burial association

LWIGULE IDHA NIWE TWEGAITE (LINT) (FARMER'S GROUP). literally, 'it is open; come join'

MAGENDO. informal or illegal trade

MANDAZI. hole-less donuts

MATATU. 'minibus' (public transport) in Kiswahili, named for the three coins it originally cost for a ride

MATOKE. cooking bananas; plantain

MAZUNGU (FROM KISWAHILI WAZUNGU). Caucasian/ European

MERRY-GO-ROUND. a ROSCA or unity group

MIVUMBA. second-hand (clothes)

MUTUNDWE TWEGAME WOMEN'S GROUP. –

MUYAYE. a delinquent, unreliable or uncouth child

MUYUMBU BAKYALA TWEHEYO KUKOLA (GROUP). literally, 'Muyumbu women, let's work harder'

MWAGA MWAGA. literally, 'pour and pour': increasing stock slowly from profits; also collective (packed) transportation for group goods for sale

NAKATI. a green vegetable indigenous to Uganda

NAGGALABI WOMEN'S GROUP. –

NALONGO. a mother of twins

NDIZI. small, apple-bananas

NYARWEHINDURE. a plant used for treating malaria

NYEZIKYE ASSOCIATION . a collaborative burial group

OBUMU. literally, 'unity'; refers to a ROSCA or unity group

OMUTANGO OR OMWETANGO. a plant used for treating various ailments

ON SENA WOMEN VETERANS ASSOCIATION. –

PAIDHA FARMER'S GROUP. –

PANGA. a large curved-blade knife; machete

PAWPAW. papaya

POSHO. ground maize-flour or maize meal

RUKOMBE TUKYENGANE AGRICULTURAL GROUP. literally, 'Rukombe group, trust one another'

SAMBUSA OR SAMOSA. a triangular pastry filled with vegetables or meat

SSAZA. 'county': in Buganda, a ssaza chief represented the kabaka and was very powerful

TAKATAKA. literally, trash; odds and ends

TINGA TINGA. literally, 'shake, shake'

TWEGOMBE WOMEN'S DEVELOPMENT ASSOCIATION. literally, 'let's enjoy/ imitate others'

TWEKOLERE WOMEN'S GROUP. literally, 'let us help ourselves'

TWEZIMBE WOMEN'S GROUP. literally, 'let's build'

TYONINYIRA MUKANGE; (TM) . literally, 'step not in mine'; refers to (generally unlicensed) roadside markets

UNITY GROUP; UNITY REVOLVING FUND. a ROSCA or obumu

WARAGI. banana gin

ZERO-GRAZING. feeding animals in a small space (to maintain grass cover)

Bibliography

Note: For the full names of organisations denoted by acronyms, see pages xvi–xviii.

Abidi, Syed A. H. (ed.). 1990. Uganda Women in Development. Kampala: Foundation for African Development.

Action for Development (ACFODE). 1995. *Visible at Last: Non-governmental Organisations' Contribution to Women's Recognition in Uganda*. Kampala: ACFODE.

Adagala, Kavetsa. 1986. 'Self employment: Women in the peri-urban setting: Petty traders in Nairobi: Conditions, constraints and strategies for survival. Paper prepared for the National Workshop on Policy and Planning in Kenya's Informal Sector', 5–6 June, Nairobi.

African Training and Research Centre for Women. 1984. *Marketing in Ghana: An Analysis of Operational and Environmental Conditions.* Addis Ababa: United Nations ECA.

Agarwal, Bina. 1990. *Structures of Patriarchy: The State, the Community and the Household.*

Agitta, Elizabeth. 1990. *African Traders in the Informal Sector in Lira.* Kampala.

Ahikire, Josephine. 1994. *Gender and History Reconsidered: A Quest into How to Recapture Women's History in Uganda.* The Hague: Institute of Social Studies.

Arise: A Women's Development Magazine no. 20 (Kampala). Jan.–March 1997. Published by ACFODE.

Aslanbeigui, Nahid, Steven Pressman and Gale Summerfield. 1994. *Women in the Age of Economic Transformation*. London: Routledge.

Aspen Institute. 1996. *Incubating New Enterprises.* Washington, D.C.: Aspen Institute.

Bafokuzara, Angela. 1997. 'Economic survival strategies adopted by rural poor women: A case of Ibanda sub-district'. Master's thesis, Department of Women Studies, Makerere University.

Baker, J. and P. Pedersen (eds.). 1992. *The Rural–Urban Interface in Africa*. Copenhagen: Scandinavian Institute of African Studies.

Bakkar, Isabella (ed.). 1994. *The Strategic Silence: Gender and Economic Policy.* London: Zed Books.

Bantebya, Grace. 1992. 'The role of women in petty commodity production and commerce: A case study of rural peasant women'. *Eastern Africa Social Science Research Review* 8, no. 2 (June): 1–19.

——— and Jessica Ogden. 1996. 'Six Women'. In Sandra Wallman. *Kampala Women Getting By.*

——— and Margaret Snyder. 1996. 'Productivity and poverty in the multi-breadwinner and the single parent household: A system and strategy for planners'. Kampala: Department of Women Studies, Makerere University. (Unpublished.)

Barnes, Teri and Everjoyce Win. 1992. *To Live a Better Life: An Oral History of Women in the City of Harare, 1930–1970.* Harare: Baobab Books.

Barugahara, Daisy. 1996. 'An assessment of the agricultural home economics programme: A case study of Mpigi district'. Master's thesis, Department of Women Studies, Makerere University.

Beneria, Lourdes and Shelley Feldman. 1992. *Unequal Burden: Economic Crises, Persistent Poverty and Women's Work.* Boulder: Westview Press.

Berman, Bruce and Colin Leys. 1994. *African Capitalists in African Development.* Boulder: Lynne Rienner Publishers.

Bernstein, H. 1990. 'Agricultural modernisation and the era of structural adjustment: Observations from sub-Saharan Africa'. *Journal of Peasant Studies* 18, no. 1 (Oct.): 3–35.

Bibangambah, Jossy R. 1992. 'Macro-level constraints and the growth of the informal sector in Uganda'. In J. Baker and P. Pedersen (eds.). *The Rural–Urban Interface in Africa.*

———. 1996. *Marketing of Smallholder Crops in Uganda.* Kampala: Fountain Publishers.

Bohannan, Paul and George Dalton (eds.). 1962. *Markets in Africa*. Evanston, Ill.: Northwestern University Press.

Boneparth, Ellen and Emily Stoper (eds.). 1998. *Women, Power and Policy: Toward the Year 2000.* Elmsford, New York: Pergamon Press.

Boserup, Esther. 1970. *Woman's Role in Economic Development*. New York: St. Martin's Press.

Bromley, R. and C. Gerry (eds.). 1979. *Casual Work and Poverty in Third World Cities.* New York: J. Wiley and Sons.

Bryceson, Deborah Fahy (ed.). 1995. *Women Wielding the Hoe: Lessons from Rural Africa for Feminist Theory and Development Practice.* Oxford: Berg Publishers.

Budlender, Debbie (ed.). 1996. *The Women's Budget, 1996.* Capetown: Institute for Democracy in South Africa. (Published annually.)

Byanyima, W. Karagawa. 1992. 'Women in political struggle in Uganda'. In Jill M. Bystydzienski (ed.). *Women Transforming Politics.*

Bystydzienski, Jill M. (ed.). 1992. *Women Transforming Politics: Worldwide Strategies for Empowerment.* Bloomington: Indiana University Press.

Camillus, J. S. 1993. 'Feeding urban masses? Towards an understanding of the dynamics of urban agriculture and land use change in Dar es Salaam, Tanzania'. Ph.D. diss., Clark University.

Canadian Journal of African Studies 6, no. 2. 1972. Special issue on women and development.

Carr, Marilyn. 1994. *Blacksmith, Baker, Roofing-sheet Maker*. London: IT Publishers.

——— et al. (eds.). 1996. *Speaking Out: Women's Economic Empowerment in South Asia.* London: IT Publishers.

Charlton, Sue Ellen M., Jana Everett and Kathleen Staudt (eds.). 1989. *Women, the State and Development*. Albany: State University of New York Press.

Charmes, Jacques. 1992. 'La contribution du secteur informel a l'emploi et au produit nationale en mauritanie, 1977–1992'. ('The formal sector's contribution to employment and GNP in Mauritania, 1977–1992'.) Noukchatt, Mauritania: Ministry of Planning.

———. 1997. 'Progress in measurement of the informal sector: Employment and share of GDP'. *Proceedings of the Expert Meeting in Household Satellite Accounts*. New York: United Nations Statistical Division.

Chebair, Eliana Restrepo and Rebecca Reichmann. May 1995. *Balancing the Double Day: Women as Managers of Microenterprises*. New York: Acción International.

Clark, Gracia. 1994. *Onions Are My Husband: Survival and Accumulation by West African Market Women*. Chicago: Chicago University Press.

Council for Economic Empowerment of Women in Africa (CEEWA), Uganda Chapter. 1996. *Report of a Workshop on Gender and Mainstream Economic Development, 27–29 April*. Kampala: CEEWA.

———. Sept. 1997. 'Women's visions for economic justice in Uganda'. Kampala: CEEWA.

———. [1997?]. Brochure. Kampala: CEEWA.

Crehan, Kate. 1997. *The Fractured Community: Landscapes of Power and Gender in Rural Zambia*. Berkeley: University of California Press.

The Crusader (Kampala). 1 March 1996.

———. 3 March 1996.

The Daily Nation (Nairobi). 24 March 1998.

Daniels, Lisa. 1998. 'The role of small enterprises in the household and national economy in Kenya: A significant contribution or a last resort?' *World Development* 26, no. 12 (Dec.): 55–65.

Davison, J. 1988. *Agriculture, Women and Land: The African Experience*. Boulder: Westview Press.

——— and the Women of Mutira, 1989. *Voices from Mutira*. Boulder: Lynne Rienner Publishers.

Department of Social Work and Social Administration, Makerere University. March 1992. 'Business management among market women: Constraints and prospects: A final report'. Kampala: Makerere University.

Department of Women Studies, Faculty of Social Sciences, Makerere University. Aug. 1997. 'Semesterisation of master's programme in gender studies'. Kampala: Makerere University.

———. Jan. 1998. 'Bachelor of arts (social sciences), gender and development studies'. Kampala: Makerere University.

DeSoto, Hernando. 1989. *The Other Path*. New York: Harper and Row.

Dignard, Louise and Jose Havet (eds.). 1995. *Women in Micro and Small Scale Enterprise Development*. Boulder: Westview Press.

Doro, Marion E. (ed.). Jan. 1998. 'Gender development index: Comparative: Five African states'. Kampala. (Unpublished.)

Dwyer, Daisy and Judith Bruce. 1988. *A Home Divided: Women and Income in the Third World.* Stanford: Stanford University Press.

The East African (Nairobi). 20–27 July 1998.

Economic Commission for Africa (ECA). 1977. *The New International Economic Order: What Roles for Women?* Addis Ababa: ECA/African Training and Research Centre for Women.

———. 1992. *Measures for the Stimulation, Development and Promotion of Indigenous Entrepreneurial Capability in Africa.* Addis Ababa: ECA.

———. 1997. *Report on the Economic and Social Situation in Africa 1997.* Addis Ababa: ECA.

———. 1998. 'Theme I: Developing African economies: The role of women. Working paper for an international conference, 28 April–1 May. Addis Ababa: ECA.

——— and Common Market for Eastern and Southern Africa (COMESA). 1998. *Report of the Sub-regional, High-level Policy Seminar on Gender Equity, Social and Economic Empowerment of Women.* Lusaka: ECA.

Economic Policy Research Centre (EPRC). 1996. 'Credit accessibility to the rural poor in Uganda'. *EPRC Bulletin* (Kampala, April).

———. 1996. 'Nature and determinants of domestic savings in Uganda'. *EPRC Bulletin* (Kampala, Sept.).

———. 1997. 'Investment, aid and growth in Uganda'. *EPRC Bulletin* (Sept.). Kampala: EPRC.

———. n.d. *EPRC Research Reports.* Kampala: EPRC.

Elkan, Walter. 1988. 'Entrepreneurs and entrepreneurship in Africa'. *Finance and Development* 25, no. 20: 41–2.

Elson, Diane (ed.). 1995. *Male Bias in the Development Process.* Manchester, UK: Manchester University Press.

——— and Barbara Evers. 1997. 'Gender aware country economic reports: Working paper number 2, Uganda'. Manchester, UK: Genecon Unit, Graduate School of Social Science, University of Manchester.

———. 1998. *Accounting for Gender in National Budgets.* New York: UNIFEM. (Unpublished.)

Faculty of Commerce, Makerere University. 1996. *Papers and Proceedings of the Fifth Quarterly Seminar on Coping with Taxes: VAT and Tax Policy*, 22–23 Aug. Kampala: Makerere University.

———. 1997. *Papers and Proceedings of the Eighth Quarterly Seminar: Gender and Management*, 3–4 July. Kampala: Makerere University.

——— and Uganda Debt Network. 1996. *Papers and Proceedings of the Seminar on Securing Debt Relief for Uganda*, 13 Dec. Kampala: Makerere University.

Feldman, Shelley. 1991. 'Still invisible: Women in the informal sector'. In Rita S. Gallin and Anne Ferguson (eds.). *The Women and International Development Annual, Volume 2.*

Folbre, Nancy. 1988. 'The black four of hearts: Toward a new paradigm of household economics'. In Daisy Dwyer and Judith Bruce (eds.). *A Home Divided: Women and Income in the Third World.*

Fontana, Marzia, Susan Joekes and Rachel Masika. 1998. *Global Trade Expansion and Liberalisation: Gender Issues and Impacts.* UK: Department of International Development.

Forum for Women in Democracy (FOWODE). n.d. Brochure. Kampala: FOWODE.

Foundation for International Community Assistance (FINCA). n.d. 'FINCA village banking'. Washington, D.C.: FINCA.

Gaidzanwa, R. B. 1993. 'Women entrepreneurs, donor promotion and domestic policies'. In A. H. J. Helmsing and Th. Kolstee (eds.). *Small Enterprises and Changing Policies.*

Gallin, Rita S. and Anne Ferguson (eds.). 1991. *The Women and International Development Annual, Volume 2.* Boulder: Westview Press.

Geiger, Susan. 1997. *TANU Women: Gender and Culture in the Making of Tanganyikan Nationalism, 1955–1965.* Oxford: Oxford University Press.

'Gender and governance'. 1997. Special issue of *Deniva News* (Kampala) 5, nos. 3–4 (July–Dec.).

'The gendered politics of land'. 1995. Special issue of *Safere: Southern African Feminist Review* (Harare) 1, no 1.

'Gender training for development practice in Africa'. 1998. Seminar, 25 May–19 June. Kampala: Department of Women Studies, Makerere University.

Ghai, D. (ed.). 1991. *The IMF and the South: The Social Impact of Crisis and Adjustment.* London: Zed Books.

Gibbon, Peter. 1992. 'The World Bank and African poverty, 1973–1991'. *Journal of Modern African Studies* 30, no. 2: 193–230.

Gordon, April A. 1996. *Transforming Capitalism and Patriarchy: Gender and Development in Africa.* Boulder: Lynne Rienner Publishing.

Green, R. H. 1981. 'Magendo political economy of Uganda: Pathology, parallel system or dominant submode of production?' Discussion paper #164. Sussex, UK: Institute of Development Studies.

Grosh, Barbara and Gloria Somolekae. 1996. 'Mighty oaks from little acorns: Can microenterprise serve as the seedbed of industrialisation?' *World Development* 24: 1879–90.

Guwatudde, Christine et al. Sept. 1994. *Women's Informal Credit Groups: An Exploratory Study of Some Experiences in Kampala.* Kampala: Ministry of Women in Development, Culture and Youth.

Helmsing, A. H. J. and Th. Kolstee (eds.). 1993. *Small Enterprises and Changing Policies: Structural Adjustment, Financial Policy and Assistance Programmes in Africa.* London: IT Publications.

Hesse, Mary Chinnery. 1989. *Engineering Adjustment for the 1990s.* Report of a Commonwealth Expert Group on Women and Structural Adjustment. London: Commonwealth Secretariat.

Hilhorst, Thea and Harry Oppengorth. 1992. *Financing Women's Enterprise.* New York: UNIFEM.

Hill, A. and E. King. 1995. 'Women's education and economic well being'. *Feminist Economics* 1, no. 2: 21–46.

Hill, Polly. 1963. 'Markets in Africa'. *Journal of Modern African Studies* 1: 441–53.

Himmelstrand, Ulf et al. (eds.). 1994. *African Perspectives on Development.* Kampala: Fountain Publishers.

Hodgson, Dorothy and Cheryl McCurdy (eds.). *Women and the Reconfiguration of Gender in Africa*. New Brunswick, New Jersey: Rutgers University Press, forthcoming.

Horn, Nancy E. 1994. *Cultivating Customers: Market Women in Harare, Zimbabwe.* Boulder: Lynne Rienner Publishers.

House–Midamba, Bessie and Felix K. Ekechi. 1995. *African Market Women and Economic Power: The Roles of Women in African Economic Development*. Westport, Conn.: Greenwood Press.

Impact Associates. July 1995. *Micro and Small Scale Enterprises in Uganda: A Report of the National Baseline Survey 1995*. Kampala: USAID.

Impact Business Bureau. July 1997. *Legal, Policy and Regulatory Constraints which Impede Private Sector Growth*. Kampala: USAID/PRESTO.

International Development Research Centre (IDRC). 1987. *Economic Adjustment of and Long-term Development in Uganda.* Report. Ottawa: IDRC.

International Federation of Women Lawyers (FIDA). n.d. 'FIDA Uganda: The Uganda Association of Women Lawyers'. Kampala: FIDA.

International Labour Organisation (ILO). 1972. *Employment, Incomes and Equality: A Strategy for Increasing Productive Employment in Kenya*. Geneva: ILO.

———. 1985. *Informal Sector in Africa*. Addis Ababa: ILO/JASPA.

———. 1993. *African Employment Report*. Addis Ababa: ILO/JASPA.

Juma, Calestous, Cleophas Torori and C. Kirima. 1993. *The Adaptive Economy: Economic Crisis and Technological Innovation.* Nairobi: Africa Centre for Technologies Press.

Kakande, Margaret and John Mackinnon. Revised March 1996. *An Annotated Inventory of Policies and Initiatives Relevant to Poverty Reduction in Uganda*. Kampala: EPRC.

Kalipeni, Ezekiel (ed.). 1994. *Population Growth and Environmental Degradation in Southern Africa.* Boulder: Lynne Rienner Publishers.

Kamugasa, Keturah. 1998. *The New Vision* (Kampala, 28 April).

Kapampara, Esther. 1996. 'Gender differences that affect women's participation in the marketing of maize and beans: The case of Kabarole district'. Master's thesis, Department of Women Studies, Makerere University.

Kasfir, Nelson. 1984. 'Magendo and class formation in Uganda'. *Journal of Commonwealth and Comparative Politics* 21, no. 3: 84–103.

Kasule, Margaret. Nov. 1997. 'Female entrepreneurship in Uganda: A case study of nursery school owners in Kampala City'. Kampala: Department of Women Studies, Makerere University

Keller, Bonnie. 1996. *Uganda Country Gender Profile*. Stockholm: SIDA.

Khan, Haider. 1997. *African Debt and Sustainable Development: Policies for Partnership with Africa*. New York: Phelps–Stokes Fund.

Kiggundu, Rose and Chris Malwadde. Jan. 1998. *Assessment Report on the Village Banking Program of Uganda Cooperative Alliance at Kyotamanya Savings and Credit Society*. Masindi: USAID/PRESTO.

Kigozi, James. 1995. ' "Uganda women cut out of SAPs gain", says research report'. *The East African* (Nairobi, 6–12 March).

Kiiza, Enid, Agnes Kamya and Joanita Babumba. 1997. 'A study proposal for improving World Bank lending policies and processes from a gender perspective'. Kampala: CEEWA. (Unpublished.)

Kiiza, Julius. 1997. 'Liberalisation policies and university education in Uganda'. *Makerere Political Science Review* (Kampala) 1, no. 1: 70–87.

King, Kenneth. 1996. *Jua Kali Kenya: Change and Development in an Informal Economy, 1970–96*. London: James Currey; Nairobi: EAEP; Athens: Ohio University.

Kwesiga, Joy. 1994. *Technical Cooperation and Women's Lives: Integrating Gender into Development Policy*. Geneva: UNRISD.

———. 1997. 'Women in Uganda'. *Uganda 1997/98: Yearly Review* (Kampala): 144–50.

———. 2000. *An African Woman's Trek to Higher Education: Inequalities, Barriers and Determinants*. Kampala: Fountain Publishers, forthcoming.

Kyamureku, Peace T. 1997. 'Uganda: Hope amidst obstacles'. *Issue: A Journal of Opinion* 25, no. 2: 20–3.

Kyeyune, Geoffrey Steven. 1996. *Street Children: Why Are They Out?* Kampala: Fountain Publishers.

Little, Kenneth. 1973. *African Women in Towns*. London: Cambridge University Press.

Lugala, Joe L. P. 1997. 'Development, change and poverty in the informal sector during the era of SAPs in Tanzania. *Canadian Journal of African Studies* 31, no. 3: 424–51.

Macharia, Kinuthia. 1997. *Social and Political Dynamics of the Informal Economy in African Cities*. New York: Oxford University Press.

MacKenzie, Fiona. 1990. 'Gender and land rights in Murang'a district, Kenya'. *Journal of Peasant Studies* 17, no. 4: 609–43.

Madanda, Aramanzan. 1997. 'A gender assessment of factors that affect household food security in Bungokho county—Mbale district'. Master's thesis, Department of Women Studies, Makerere University.

Mama, Amina. 1996. *Women's Studies and Studies of Women in Africa During the 1990s.* Dakar: CODESRIA; London: ABC.

Mamdani, Mahmood. 1991. 'Uganda: Contradictions in the IMF programme and perspective'. In D. Ghai. *The IMF and the South.*

———. 1994. 'A critical analysis of the IMF programme in Uganda'. In Ulf Himmelstrand et al. (eds.). *African Perspectives on Development.*

Manyire, Henry. 1992. 'Business management among market women: Constraints and prospects'. Kampala: Department of Social Work and Social Administration, Makerere University.

———. 1993. 'Gender constructs in economic and market efficiency'. Master's thesis, Department of Women Studies, Makerere University.

Martinussen, John. 1997. *Society, State and Market: A Guide to Competing Theories of Development.* London: Zed Books.

Maxwell, D. 1993. 'Land access and household logic: Urban farming in Kampala'. Kampala: Makerere Institute of Social Research.

——— and S. Zziwa. 1992. *Urban Farming in Africa: The Case of Kampala, Uganda.* Nairobi: African Centre for Technologies Press.

Mbaalu-Mukasa, Maureen Nakurunda. 1996. 'The factors promoting women-operated home-based enterprises (HBEs) in Kampala City'. Master's thesis, Department of Women Studies, Makerere University.

Mbire, T. 1990. 'Problems that hinder women's development in business and industry'. In Syed A. H. Abidi (ed.). *Uganda Women in Development.*

'Mbire wins global acclaim', *The New Vision* (Kampala). 8 April 1999: 23.

McCormick, Dorothy and Paul Ove Pedersen (eds.). 1996. *Small Enterprises: Flexibility and Networking in an African Context.* Nairobi: Longhorn Kenya.

Meer, Shamim (ed.). 1997. *Women, Land and Authority: Perspectives from South Africa.* UK: Oxfam.

Mensink. 1995. 'Women and finance in Uganda: Low-income women as respected business partners'. In Kibumbi Pontiano Ssonko. 'Gender options within the context of changing urban regulations'.

Mikell, Gwendolyn. 1997. *African Feminism: The Politics of Survival in sub-Saharan Africa.* Philadelphia: University of Pennsylvania Press.

Miner, Horace (ed.). 1967. *The City in Modern Africa.* London: Praeger.

Ministry of Finance and Economic Planning. June 1996. *Background to the Budget, 1996–97.* Kampala: Ministry of Finance and Economic Planning.

———. June 1996. *National Development Strategy, 1996–97 to 1998–99.* Kampala: Ministry of Finance and Economic Planning.

———, Statistics Department. July 1996. *1996: Statistical Abstract.* Kampala: Ministry of Finance and Economic Planning.

Ministry of Finance, Planning and Economic Development. 1997. *Report on a Visit to Mpigi District, 3–6 March 1997.* Kampala: Ministry of Finance and Economic Development.

Ministry of Gender and Community Development. 1997. *The National Gender Policy.* Kampala: Ministry of Gender and Community Development.

———, Directorate of Gender. 1996. *Gender Bulletin* (Kampala) 5, no. 1.

———. 1996. *Gender Bulletin* (Kampala) 6, nos. 1, 2, 3, & 4.

———. 1997. *Gender Bulletin* (Kampala) 7, no. 1.

——— and the Statistics Department, Ministry of Planning and Economic Development. 1998. *Women and Men in Uganda: Facts and Figures, 1998.* Kampala: Ministry of Gender and Community Development.

Ministry of Planning and Economic Development. May 1997. *Poverty Trends in Uganda, 1989–1995.* Kampala: Coordination of Poverty Eradication Project.

———. June 1997. *Poverty Eradication Action Plan: A National Challenge for Uganda vol. I.* Kampala: Coordination of Poverty Eradication Project.

———. July 1997. *An Annotated Inventory of Poverty-Related Research Publications in Uganda.* Kampala: Coordination of Poverty Eradication Project.

Ministry of Planning, Manpower and Employment. 1989. *Report of the National Manpower Survey.* Kampala: Ministry of Planning, Manpower and Employment.

Mlozi, Malongo R. S. 1997. 'Urban agriculture: Ethnicity, cattle raising and some environmental implications in the city of Dar es Salaam, Tanzania'. *African Studies Review* 40, no. 3 (Dec.).

The Monitor (Kampala). 24 Jan. 1998.

———. 17 June 1998.

———. 30 June 1998.

———. 11 Aug. 1998.

Moock, Joyce and Robert Rhodes. 1992. *Diversity, Farmer Knowledge and Sustainability.* Ithaca: Cornell University Press.

Moore, H. and M. Vaughan. 1994. *Cutting Down Trees: Gender, Nutrition and Agricultural Change in the Northern Province of Zambia, 1890–1990.* London: James Currey.

Mugyenyi, Mary. 1992. 'The impact of structural adjustment programmes on Ugandan rural women in the 1980s'. Kampala: Department of Women Studies, Makerere University.

Mukwaya, A. B. 1962. 'The marketing of staple foods in Kampala, Uganda'. In Paul Bohannan and George Dalton (eds.). *Markets in Africa.*

Mulinge, Munyae M. and Margaret M. Munyae. 1998. 'The persistent growth in size and importance of the informal economy in African countries: Implications for theorising the economy and labour markets'. *African Sociological Review* 2, no. 2: 20–46.

Munene, J. C. (ed.). [1996?]. *Empowerment, Poverty and Structural Adjustment in Uganda.* Kampala: Friederich Ebert Foundation.

Musiimenta, Peace. Sept. 1997. 'Urban agriculture and women's socio-economic empowerment: A case study of Kiswa and Luwafu areas in Kampala City. Kampala: Department of Women Studies, Makerere University.

Musisi, Jennifer Lubwama. Oct. 1996. 'Role conflict and its effect on the performance of female employees of Makerere University'. Master's thesis, Public Administration and Management, Makerere University.

Musisi, Nakanyike. 1995. 'Baganda women's night market activities'. In Bessie House-Midamba and Felix K. Ekechi (eds.). *African Market Women and Economic Power.*

———. 1998. 'Gender and the cultural construction of "bad women" in the development of Kampala-Kibuga, 1900–1962'. In Dorothy Hodgson and Cheryl McCurdy (eds.). *Women and the Reconfiguration of Gender in Africa.*

———. n.d. *Catalyst, Nature and Vitality of African-Canadian Feminism: A Panorama of an 'Emigré Feminist'.* Toronto: University of Toronto.

Musoke, Maria. 1993. 'Research on women in Uganda: An annotated bibliography'. Kampala: Department of Women Studies, Makerere University.

Mutibwa, Olivia, Betty Babirije-Ddungu and Maria Musoke. 1999. *Women in Uganda Since 1985: An Annotated Bibliography.* Kampala: UNICEF.

Mutibwa, Phares. 1992. *Uganda Since Independence.* Kampala: Fountain Publishers.

Mwaka, Victoria, Mary Mugyenyi and Grace Bantebya. [1994?]. 'Women in Uganda: A profile'. Kampala: Department of Women Studies, Makerere University.

Nabirye, Sylvia. 1998. 'The role played and the problems faced by women in policy formulation: A case study of women parliamentarians in Uganda'. LL.D. thesis, Faculty of Law, Makerere University.

Nabuguzi, Emmanuel. March 1994. 'Structural adjustment and the informal economy in Uganda'. CDR Working Paper. Copenhagen: Centre for Development Research.

National Co-ordination Committee for the Informal, Micro and Small Enterprise Sector (IMSENCC). 1997. *First Newsletter* (Kampala, Oct.).

Ncube, Welshman et al. 1997. *Paradigms of Exclusion: Women's Access to Resources in Zimbabwe.* Harare: Women and Law in Southern Africa Research Project.

Nelson, Nici. 1979. 'How women and men get by: The sexual division of labour in the informal sector of a Nairobi squatter settlement'. In R. Bromley and C. Gerry (eds.). *Casual Work and Poverty in Third World Cities.*

The New Vision (Kampala). 23 Nov. 1995.

———. 26 June 1997.

———. 20 Jan. 1998.

———. 5 May 1998.

———. 23 April 1998.

———. 28 April 1998.

———. 1 July 1998.

———. 13 July 1998.

The New York Times. 26 July 1998.

———. 19 Aug. 1998.

NGO Preparatory Committee, Uganda, for the Fourth World Conference on Women, Beijing, 1995, and African Regional Preparatory Conference, Dakar, Senegal, 1994. *NGO Status Report: Uganda*. Kampala: NAWOU.

Ninsen, Kwame. 1991. *The Informal Sector in Ghana's Political Economy*. Accra: Freedom Publications.

Ntarangwi, Mwenda G. 1998. 'Feminism and masculinity in an African capitalist context: The case of Kenya'. *Safere: Southern African Feminist Review* 3, no 1: 19–32.

Nyerere, Julius. 1998. 'Are universal social standards possible?' *The South Letter* (Geneva) 2–3: 14–17.

Obbo, Christine. 1980. *African Women: Their Struggle for Economic Independence*. London: Zed Books.

O'Connor, A. 1983. *The African City*. London: Hutchinson & Co.

Okema, Mike. 1995. 'Structural adjustment: Such a misunderstood strategy'. *The East African* (Nairobi, 15–19 March).

Okurut, Mary Karooro. 1997. ' "It is hard, demeaning, humiliating" — Flower Mirembe'. *Arise: A Women's Development Magazine* 20 (Kampala Jan.–March): 4–6.

Oloka-Onyango, J. and Sylvia Tamale. 1995. ' "The personal is political", or why women's rights are indeed human rights: An African perspective on international feminism'. *Human Rights Quarterly* 17, no. 4: 691–731.

Olson, Elizabeth. 1998. 'The sex sector: The economic and social bases of prostitution in southeast Asia'. *The New York Times*. (19 Aug.).

Omari, Cuthbert K. 1997. *Women in the Informal Sector*. Dar es Salaam: Dar es Salaam University Press.

Opio, Fred. July 1996. *The Impact of Structural Adjustment Programmes on Poverty and Income Distribution in Uganda*. Kampala: EPRC.

Osirim, Mary. 1994. 'Women, work and public policy: Structural adjustment and the informal sector in Zimbabwe'. In Ezekiel Kalipeni (ed.). *Population Growth and Environmental Degradation in Southern Africa*.

Otero, Mary. 1987. *Gender Issues in Small-scale Enterprises*. Washington, D.C.: USAID.

The Other Voice (Kampala). June 1998. Newsletter of the Media Women's Association.

Palmer, Ingrid. 1991. *Gender and Population in the Adjustment of African Economies: Planning for Change*. Women, Work and Development Series, no. 19. Geneva: ILO.

Parpart, Jane L. and Kathleen A. Staudt. 1989. *Women and the State in Africa.* Boulder: Lynne Rienner Publishing.

Pietila, Hilkka and Jeanne Vickers. 1990. *Making Women Matter: The Role of the United Nations.* London: Zed Books.

Powell, John. 1995. *The Survival of the Fitter.* London: IT Publishers.

Private Sector Development Programme (PSDP). Jan. 1997. *Uganda National Strategy and Programme of Action for Private Sector Development.* Kampala: PSDP.

———. Sept. 1997. *Support to Poverty Eradication through Private Sector Development.* Kampala: PSDP.

———. October 1997. *Assistance to Poverty Eradication Through Private Sector Development: Strategy for a Dynamic Microfinancing Programme in Uganda.* Kampala: PSDP.

———. n.d. *Towards a National Strategy for the Informal, Micro and Small Scale Sector: An Assessment Report.* Project UGA/95/002. Kampala: PSDP.

Private Sector Foundation (PSF). n.d. *List of Members.* Kampala: PSF.

———. n.d. *The Uganda Private Sector Competitiveness Project: A Brief Profile.* Kampala: PSF.

Rasheed, Sadib and David Luke (eds.). 1995. *Development Management in Africa: Toward Dynamism, Empowerment and Entrepreneurship.* Boulder: Westview Press.

Republic of Uganda. 1995. *Republic of Uganda Constitution.* Kampala: Republic of Uganda.

———. Jan. 1999. *Draft Policy Paper on Micro and Small Enterprise Development.* Kampala: Private Sector Development/Micro and Small Enterprise Policy Unit, Ministry of Finance, Planning and Economic Development.

——— and the Organisation of African Unity (OAU). 1996. *The Empowerment of Women through Functional Literacy and the Education of the Girl-child: Report of the African Conference,* 8–13 Sept. Kampala: Republic of Uganda and OAU.

Robertson, Claire C. 1984. *Sharing the Same Bowl: A Socioeconomic History of Women and Class in Accra, Ghana.* Bloomington: Indiana University Press.

———. 1995. 'Comparative advantage: Women in trade in Accra, Ghana, and Nairobi, Kenya'. In Bessie House-Midamba and Felix K. Ekechi. *African Market Women and Economic Power.*

———. 1997. *Trouble Showed the Way: Women, Men and Trade in the Nairobi Area, 1890–1990.* Bloomington: Indiana University Press.

——— and Iris Berger. 1986. *Women and Class in Africa.* New York: Holmes and Meier.

Rodrik, Dani. 1997. *Has Globalization Gone Too Far?* Washington, D.C.: Institute for International Economics.

Sachs, Carolyn. 1996. *Gendered Fields: Rural Women, Agriculture and Environment.* Boulder: Westview Press.

Scott, Catherine V. 1995. *Gender and Development: Rethinking Modernization and Dependency Theory.* Boulder: Lynne Rienner Publishing.

Sejjaaka, Samuel. 1996. 'The role of developing country governments in business after privatisation: The case for Uganda'. *Makerere Business Journal* (Kampala) 1, no. 2: 126–37.

Semboja, Joseph and Ole Therkildsen. 1995. *Service Provision Under Stress in East Africa.* Kampala: Fountain Publishers.

Sen, Amartya K. 1990. 'Gender and co-operative conflicts'. In Irene Tinker (ed.). *Persistent Inequalities: Women and World Development.*

———. 1992. *Inequality Re-examined.* Cambridge: Harvard University Press.

Seruwagi-Malunga, Jane. 1998. 'Struggle for survival: Women in the informal sector in Kampala City, Uganda, 1972–1988'. Kampala: unfinished study for the National Commission on Science and Technology.

Sheldon, Kathleen (ed.). 1996. *Courtyards, Markets, City Streets: Urban Women in Africa.* Boulder: Westview Press.

Sklair, Leslie. 1991. *Sociology of the Global System: Social Change in Global Perspective.* London: Harvester Wheatsheaf.

Slum Aid Project. March–Dec. 1996. *Annual Report.* Kampala.

Smith, Joan and Immanuel Wallerstein. 1992. *Creating and Transforming Households: The Constraints of the World Economy.* Cambridge, UK: The University Press.

Snyder, Margaret. 1994. 'Science and the woman farmer: Some profound contradictions'. *African Crop Science Conference Proceedings* (Kampala) 1: 423–9.

———. 1995. *Transforming Development: Women, Poverty and Politics.* London: IT Publishers.

———. 1999. *American Partnership with the New Africa: Questions of Power, Gender and Justice.* New York: Phelps–Stokes Fund.

——— and Mary Tadesse. 1995. *African Women and Development: A History.* London: Zed Books.

Southall, Aiden. 1967. 'Kampala–Mengo'. In Horace Miner (ed.). *The City in Modern Africa.*

Sparr, Pamela (ed.). 1994. *Mortgaging Women's Lives: Feminist Critiques of Structural Adjustment.* London: Zed Books.

Spring, Anita and Barbara E. McDade (eds.). 1998. *African Entrepreneurship: Theory and Reality.* Gainesville: University Press of Florida.

Ssendaula, Gerald. 12 June 1998. *The 1998–99 Budget Speech.* Kampala. Ministry of Finance.

Ssonko, Kibumbi Pontiano. Nov. 1997. 'Gender options within the context of changing urban regulations: The case of Kampala City 1995–96 informal sector evictees'. Master's thesis, Department of Women Studies, Makerere University.

Stamp, Patricia. 1989. *Technology, Gender and Power in Africa.* Ottawa: IDRC.

Stiglitz, Joseph. 1995. *Whither Socialism.* Cambridge: MIT Press.

Success Magazine no. 1. 1998. Interview with Tereza Mbire.

The Sunday Monitor (Kampala). 25 Jan. 1998.

The Sunday Vision (Kampala). 13 Nov. 1997.

'Support of poverty eradication through private sector development'. 1997. *Entrepreneurial Development* (Kampala, Sept.).

Swedish International Development Authority (SIDA). 1995. *Women and Men in East, Central and Southern Africa: Facts and Figures.* Nairobi: Central Bureau of Statistics.

Tadria, Hilda M.K. 1987. 'Changes and continuities in the position of women in Uganda'. In Paul Wiebe and Cole Dodge (eds.). *Beyond Crisis: Development Issues in Uganda.*

———. 1999. 'Addressing poverty alleviation and development through empowerment of women'. Paper presented at the African Development Bank. Addis Ababa: ECA.

Tamale, Sylvia. 1998. *When Hens Begin to Crow: Gender and Parliamentary Politics in Uganda.* Boulder: Westview Press; Kampala: Fountain Publishers.

Tibikoma, Annet. 1994. 'Impact of culture on informal credit systems: A study of women in Busoga'. *Informal and Institutional Credit in Uganda.* Kampala. Cited in Ministry of Women in Development, Culture and Youth. *Women's Informal Credit Groups.*

Tinker, Irene (ed.). 1990. *Persistent Inequalities: Women and World Development.* New York: Oxford University Press.

Tomesen, Leon and Janis Sabotta. June 1997. 'Training needs assessment and baseline survey'. *Volume 1: Main Report.* Kampala: USAID/PRESTO.

Tripp, Aili Mari. 1994. 'Gender, political participation and the transformation of associational life in Uganda and Tanzania'. *African Studies Review* 31, no. 1: 107–31

———. 1997. *Changing the Rules: The Politics of Liberty and the Urban Informal Economy in Tanzania.* Berkeley: University of California.

———. 1999. *Women and Politics in Uganda.* Madison: University of Wisconsin Press; London: James Currey; Kampala: Fountain Publishers.

Uchitelle, Louis. 1998. 'The economics of intervention: A prominent but impolitic theorist questions the worship of free markets'. *The New York Times.* (31 May).

Uganda Manufacturers Association (UMA). June 1997. Brochure. Kampala: UMA.

Uganda Revenue Authority (URA). n.d. *Compiled VAT Leaflets: Taxpayers Guide, Second Edition.* Kampala: URA.

Uganda Women Entrepreneurs Association Ltd (UWEAL). n.d. *The Way Forward: Women's Economic Empowerment.* Kampala: UWEAL

Uganda Women's Finance Trust Ltd (UWFT). n.d. Brochure. Kampala: UWFT.

Uganda Women's Network (UWONET). 1995. *Women and Structural Adjustment: A Case Study of Arua District.* Kampala: UWONET.

———. April 1998. *Proposed Amendments on the Land Bill, 1998.* Kampala: UWONET.

———. n.d. *We Demand a Just Domestic Law Now.* Kampala: UWONET.

——— and Friedrich Ebert Stiftung. Oct. 1997. *Women and Land Rights in Uganda: A Documentation of Women's Views and Suggestions on Land Issues in Uganda and the Proposed Land Bill*. Kampala: UWONET.

———, ——— and the Electoral Commission. 1997–98. *Vote in the Local Council Elections: Understanding the Local Government Act and Local Council Elections in Uganda*. Kampala: UWONET.

Uganda: Yearly Review, 1997–1998. 1997. Kampala: Uganda Now.

United Nations. 1985. *The Nairobi Forward Looking Strategies for the Advancement of Women*. New York: United Nations.

———. 1990. *The World's Women, 1990*. New York: United Nations.

———. 1993. *Methods of Measuring Women's Economic Activity*. New York: United Nations.

———. 1994. *Women in a Changing Global Economy*. New York: United Nations.

———. 1995. *The World's Women, 1995*. New York: United Nations.

———. 1995b. *Platform for Action of the United Nations Fourth World Conference on Women*. New York: United Nations.

———. 10 Aug. 1998. *Role of Microcredit in the Eradication of Poverty: Report of the Secretary-General, A/53/223*. New York: United Nations.

United Nations Children's Fund (UNICEF). 1989. *Children and Women in Uganda: A Situation Analysis*. Kampala: United Nations.

United Nations Development Fund for Women (UNIFEM). 1998. *UNIFEM's Economic Empowerment Programme: A Discussion Paper*. New York: United Nations.

———. 17–18 Oct. 1997. 'State of statistical knowledge and understanding, and current surveys or studies to be undertaken in Africa'. *Women in Informal Employment: Globalising and Organising*. New York: UNIFEM/WIEGO.

United Nations Development Programme (UNDP). 1997. *Uganda: Human Development Report, 1997*. Kampala: UNDP..

———. 1998. *Uganda: Human Development Report, 1998*. Kampala: UNDP.

———. 1998. *Human Development Report, 1998*. New York: Oxford University Press.

United Nations Office of the Special Coordinator for Africa and the Least Developed Countries, April 1996. *Informal Sector Development in Africa: Locating Africa's Informal Sector*. New York: United Nations.

United States Agency for International Development (USAID)/Private Enterprise Support, Training and Organizational (PRESTO) Development Project. June 1997. *Training Needs Assessment and Baseline Survey, 1997*. Kampala: USAID/PRESTO.

———. July 1997. *Legal, Policy and Regulatory Constraints Which Impede Private Sector Growth*. Kampala: USAID/PRESTO.

———. October 1997. *Doing Business in Uganda: A Practical Guide*. Kampala: USAID/PRESTO.

Urdaneta-Ferrain, Lourdes. n.d. *Contribution of Women Working in the Informal Sector.* New York: UNIFEM.

'Uses and misuses of Amartya Sen'. 1999. *The Economist* (9 Jan.).

Vision 2025: A Participatory Process for Formulating a Long-term Vision for Uganda. Oct. 1997. Kampala: Vision 2025.

The Voices (Kampala). 1997. Newsletter of FOWODE.

Wabwere, Arnest. 1996. 'Small scale manufacturing enterprises in Uganda: Politics and problems'. In Dorothy McCormick and Paul Ove Pedersen (eds.). *Small Enterprises: Flexibility and Networking in an African Context.*

Wallman, Sandra. 1996. *Kampala Women Getting By: Wellbeing in the Time of AIDS.* Kampala: Fountain Publishers.

Waring, Marilyn. 1988. *If Women Counted: A New Feminist Economics.* New York: Harper & Row.

Watkins, Kevin. 1995. *The Oxfam Poverty Report.* Oxford: Oxfam.

Webster, Leila and Peter Fidler (eds.). 1996. *The Informal Sector and Microfinance Institutions in West Africa.* Washington, D.C.: World Bank.

Wiebe, Paul and Cole Dodge (eds.). 1987. Beyond Crisis: Development Issues in Uganda. Kampala: Makerere Institute of Social Research.

Womens Bureau. 1993. *Employment and Earnings in the Formal and Informal Sectors: A Gender Analysis.* Nairobi: Ministry of Culture and Social Services.

The World Bank. 1977. *World Development Report, 1977.* New York: Oxford University Press.

———. 1993. *Uganda Growing Out of Poverty.* Washington, D.C.: World Bank.

———. 1994. *Adjustment in Africa: Reforms, Results and the Road Ahead.* Washington, D.C.: World Bank.

———. 1994. *Enhancing Women's Participation in Economic Development.* Washington, D.C.: World Bank.

———. 1999. *Gender, Growth and Poverty Reduction in sub-Saharan Africa.* Washington, D.C.: World Bank.

——— and the Ministry of Gender and Community Development. June 1995. *Report of Study on Legal Constraints to the Economic Empowerment of Women.* Kampala: Ministry of Gender and Community Development.

YWCA of Uganda. 1997. *Women's Economic Empowerment.* Kampala: YWCA.

Zake, Justin. 1996. 'Value added tax (VAT) in Uganda: Planning and implementation implications'. *Makerere Business Journal* (Kampala) 1, no. 2: 98–114.

Index

NOTE: Bold is used to denote entrepreneurs, who are listed by first name. Italics are used to denote journals, books and other document titles.

A

J

K

L

N

R

T

U

V

W